Mysticism and the Mystical Experience examines both the variety and universality of mysticism, both currently and historically. It considers how various authors have defined mysticism and raises questions about acceptable definitions. It also considers the nature of the mystical experience, its prerequisites and results, and takes up the arguments of proponents for and against the claim of a single universal mysticism in contrast to a multiplicity of mysticisms.

Proceeding to the Western perspective, the book then explores the thought of the Greek philosopher Plotinus, whose mystical philosophy, according to writer Ruth Majercik, "represents the final flower of the Greek philosophical tradition." Donald H. Bishop, the editor of the volume, then examines the thoughts of three medieval Christian mystics, St. Francis of Assisi, Meister Eckhart, and Thomas à Kempis. Quaker mysticism, as a unique form of Christian thought, is then explored by Warren Steinkraus. Jewish mysticism, with a special emphasis on mystical texts, is the subject of contributor Eliott Wolfson. Paula Allen, herself a native American, takes up the subject of American Indian mysticism, while Sandra A. Wawrytko examines the peculiar characteristics of the "feminine" mode of mysticism.

Turning to non-Western philosophies, Kuang-Ming Wu examines Chinese mysticism, elaborating on the differences between Confucian and Taoist thought. Leslie Kawamura then demonstrates how, from a Buddhist point of view, mys-

(Continued on back flap)

Mysticism
and
the Mystical Experience

Mysticism
and
the Mystical Experience

East and West

Edited by
Donald H. Bishop

SUP

Selinsgrove: Susquehanna University Press
London and Toronto: Associated University Presses

Associated University Presses
440 Forsgate Drive
Cranbury, NJ 08512

Associated University Presses
25 Sicilian Avenue
London WC1A 2QH, England

Associated University Presses
P.O. Box 338, Port Credit
Mississauga, Ontario
Canada L5G 4L8

The paper used in this publication meets the requirements of the American National Standard for Permanence of Paper for Printed Library Materials Z39.48-1984.

Library of Congress Cataloging-in-Publication Data

Mysticism and the mystical experience : East and West / edited by Donald H. Bishop.
   p. cm.
   Includes index.
   ISBN 0-945636-73-3 (alk. paper)
   1. Mysticism—Comparative studies. 2. Spiritual life—Comparative studies. 3. Psychology, Religious. I. Bishop, Donald H.
BL625.M894 1995
291.4'22—dc20
                                    94-35278
                                       CIP

PRINTED IN THE UNITED STATES OF AMERICA

Contents

Preface

THE object of this volume is to provide the reader with a sympathetic understanding of mysticism as it is found in many parts of the world. Advances in communications in the twentieth century have enabled us to recognize more readily that mysticism is a universal phenomenon, and it is much easier now to learn about mysticism as it appears in traditions other than our own.

When mysticism is studied on such a large scale, certain questions inevitably arise. How are mystics alike and how do they differ? What characterizes the mystical experience? How do mystical experiences compare? What is it that the mystic experiences? Do mystics everywhere experience the same entity or reality? How do mystics describe their experience? To what extent and in what ways are mystical experiences preconditioned?

As to similarities and differences between mystics, which are greater and more important? Is there a single universal mysticism, or are there only particular mysticisms and mystics? What leads a person to become a mystic? How are mystics' claims to be tested? Is there a single test appropriate for all mystical traditions? What contributions have mystics made? How do mystics relate to their societies and their institutions? What is the mystic's attitude toward nature?

The first chapter deals both with recent debates over mysticism and how it has been defined and evaluated by such twentieth-century authors as James, Stace, Inge, Happold, Otto, Iqbal, Scharfstein, Suzuki, Zaehner, Parrinder, Conze, Brown, and Margaret Smith. Subsequent chapters are concerned with particular mystics or mystical traditions. It should be noted that authors were given free rein to discuss their topic as they saw fit. They were not asked to write from a particular perspective or point of view. To do so, the editor felt, would be to force mysticism into a predetermined pattern which, as far as he is concerned, would be a violation of the very nature of mysticism itself.

Because diacritical markings deal with pronunciation and are

7

not essential therefore for an understanding of mysticism itself, they have been omitted and terms have been italicized instead in several chapters (Chinese, Buddhist, Hindu, and Islamic mysticism).

As this volume demonstrates, mysticism is universal. Since, given the contemporary scene, each of us is a citizen not only of a single country but of the whole world, we need to understand, not only our own particular tradition, but the tradition of others as well. This text is intended to meet that need; for, as the title indicates, it deals with mysticism east and west and, we might add, north and south as well. Contributing to the breadth of this volume are chapters on mysticism in African religion and among Native Americans and the feminine mode of mysticism. The editor believes they add to the book's uniqueness, appeal, and usefulness.

If we ask why we seek to know or what the purpose of knowing is, two answers which may be given are that we know in order to understand and we know in order to appreciate. It is hoped that this volume on mysticism will serve both the end of understanding and of appreciation.

Mysticism
and
the Mystical Experience

1

Introduction

DONALD H. BISHOP

Wʜᴇɴ we begin with the question of the nature of mysticism or the mystical experience, we see that writers, in answering, find certain categories useful. Walter Stace delineates "two main distinguishable types of mystical experience": the extrovertive and introvertive. The first "look[s] outward and through the physical senses into the external world and finds the One there," while the introvertive mystic "turns inward and finds the One at the bottom of the self." The second type, Stace believes, is more common or is "the major strand in the history of mysticism"; the extrovertive way is a minor one.[1] Dean Inge's characterizations of two schools of mystics echoes Stace's. One school, Inge writes, "distrusts and rejects the affirmations of ordinary consciousness" and turns to a deeper one; the other "welcomes the visible as a partial manifestation of the spiritual" or finds the One, in part at least, in the external world.[2]

The two types Stace and Inge refer to might be characterized by others as nature and theistic mysticism. The nature or pantheistic mystic's experience is limited to, aroused by, and finds its fulfillment in nature, experienced, of course, quite differently than a scientist does. The theistic mystic goes beyond nature to a transcendent Being that is realized in the mystical experience. What is the nature of this Being? Here again we find a major difference between mystics: Christian mystics generally tend to conceive of it as personal, Hindu mystics of the Upaninshadic-Vedantist tradition as impersonal or nonpersonal. Chinese mysticism, whether Buddhist or non-Buddhist, is also, according to many writers including this one, of the second type and according to many writers including this one, Suzuki is also of the second type. Suzuki asserts emphatically, for instance, that

11

the personal/nonpersonal distinction is the basic one between Eastern and Western mysticism.[3]

R. C. Zaehner, when using the nature and theistic distinction, points out that, while in both cases the mystic is seeking a unity, in the case of the nature mystic it is union with "some principle or other" and with the latter it is "union with God." He makes a further distinction between the monistic and theistic mystic, Sankara and Vedanta, as an example of the first and Christian mystics the second. A major difference between the two is that the monistic mystic emphasizes merging into God or the Absolute, and the theist stresses communion with God. In the mystical experience the Vedantist experiences a complete loss of selfhood, a total extinction of the self in Brahman; the Christian mystic retains a sense of individuality while united with God.

A further way of characterizing monistic and theistic mystics would be to divide them into nondualist and dualist types. In the second a distinction between the subject, man, and the object, God, remains. In the first, all multiplicities and dualities are transcended. Stace believes the first to be "the more perfect type of mysticism" and finds amusing "the horror conventional orthodoxies of the West" have of pantheistic monism.[4] Geoffrey Parrinder puts the types mentioned thus far into three categories: theistic mysticism in which the mystic "seeks union with God but not identity"; monistic mysticism wherein "identity with a universal principle, which may be called divine, though that would imply a difference from the human" is sought; and nonreligious mysticism in which the mystic "seeks union with something, or everything, rather like monism."[5]

Another interesting way of distinguishing between mystics is found in F. C. Happold's book where the mystical experience is divided into two types: the mysticism of "love and union" and the mysticism of "knowledge and understanding."[6] Although dissimilar, they are not exclusive of *each other*, in part because they spring from two different urges found in everyone. The first is the urge "to escape from a sense of separation, from the loneliness of selfhood, towards a closer participation and reunion with Nature or God, which will bring peace and rest to the soul." The second is the urge to "find the secret of the universe, to grasp it not in parts but in its wholeness." As examples of the first, Happold quotes St. Augustine in the Christian and Abu Yazid in the Muslim tradition. Nicholas of Cusa in the Christian tradition is taken as an example of the second, and, for Hinduism, Samkara might be used.

Rudolf Otto also makes an interesting twofold division of mysticism. One type he calls the mysticism of introspection of the "inward way," the other the mysticism of unifying vision of the "way of unity." The first involves a "withdrawal from all outward things, retreat into the ground of one's own soul" and "knowledge of a secret depth and of the possibility of turning in upon one's self." The chief characteristic of the second is "the emphasis on unity and the struggle against all diversity."[7] Otto believes the two types are found in both East and West and that they are often intermingled in the same person, as in the case of Plotinus.

Happold distinguishes three types of mysticism—nature, soul, and God mysticism. The first is characterized by "a sense of the immanence of the One or God or soul in Nature," as found in Wordsworth's poetry. In soul mysticism, as in Upaninshadic Hinduism for example, "the idea of the existence of God is, in any expressible form, absent . . . the soul is in itself regarded as numinous and hidden . . . the uncreated soul or spirit strives to enter not into communion with Nature or with God but into a state of complete isolation from everything that is other than itself." And the basic idea found in God mysticism is "that of the return of the spirit to its immortal and infinite ground, which is God."[8]

Happold discusses two types of God mysticism, one in which, as indicated earlier, the self is absorbed into God or the essence of God, and in the other, which is more characteristic of the West, the soul or self is "deified so that it becomes God, yet without losing its identity." He points out that mysticism, defined as "a particular and distinct sort of spirituality," may be examined from three viewpoints as a type of experience, a way of knowledge, and a state of consciousness, and his book is concerned with doing just that.[9]

What are some characteristics of the mystics' experience? The widely quoted William James indicates four: ineffability, noetic quality, transiency, and passivity. A mystical experience is ineffable in that it cannot be fully described. It "defies expression," and "no adequate report of its contents can be given in words." Although incommunicable, it is, nevertheless, authoritative or indubitable to the mystic. He gains "insights into the depths of truth unplumbed by the discursive intellect." The mystical experience does not last for long.

James says that "except in rare instances, half an hour, or at most an hour or two seems to be the limit." The mystic experiences a sense of passivity in that he "feels as if his own will were in abeyance and indeed sometimes as if he were grasped and held by a superior power."[10]

Happold agrees with James that mystical experiences are ineffable in that they can no more be fully described than can be the feeling of being in love. They are noetic in that they result in insights "which carry with them a tremendous sense of authority." They rarely last for any length of time; there is "invariably a speedy return to normality." Their passivity is reflected in their carrying with them "a feeling of something given." Happold adds three more characteristics. The mystic experiences "a consciousness of the Oneness of everything," also, "a sense of timelessness," of going beyond or not being bound by time and, finally, the conviction that "the familiar phenomenal ego is not the real I."[11]

Mohammad Iqbal, who helped to stimulate a revival of Islam in India in the nineteenth and twentieth centuries, was also interested in mysticism, and he noted four characteristics of the mystical experience. One was the "immediacy of the experience." In such immediacy the mystic knows God just as a person in an empirical experience knows an object. Second is the "unanalyzable wholeness" of the experience. The mystic experiences the totality or "the total passage" of reality, or he sees it as a "single unanalyzable unity in which the ordinary distinction of subject and object does not exist." A third characteristic is that it is a "moment of intimate association with a unique Other Self, transcending, encompassing, and momentarily suppressing the private personality of the subject of the experience." Fourth is the incommunicability of the experience due to its being "essentially a matter of inarticulate feeling, untouched by the discursive intellect."[12] He adds that it does not rule out, however, a cognitive element in mysticism.

The Japanese Buddhist, D. T. Suzuki, was also interested in mysticism; one of his books was entitled *Mysticism: Christian and Buddhist*. He finds the Buddhist's Satori experience with its eight characteristics to be comparable in several ways to the Westerner's mystical experience. One characteristic is irrationality in the sense that what one learns through Satori are not conclusions reached by reasoning. Another is intuitive insight or seeing directly into the nature of reality and recognizing its universality as well as particularity. A third characteristic of

Satori is its authoritativeness. Suzuki says that "the knowledge realized by Satori is final . . . no logical argument can refute it . . . and it is sufficient unto itself." Affirmation or "an affirmative attitude toward all things that exist" is another characteristic, as is a sense of the Beyond. Suzuki also notes that the most memorable aspect of Satori is its impersonal tone or lack of a personal reference or imagery that is characteristic of most Western mysticism. The seventh characteristic of Satori is the feeling of exaltation that is a result of the "breaking up of the restrictions imposed on one as an individual being," and the eighth is momentariness. As a Zen Buddhist, Suzuki means by this that "Satori comes upon one abruptly and is a momentary experience."[13]

Mysticism is often described using the imagery of a path as in Sufi-mysticism. It may be a path of ascent, the going from lower to higher levels. Or it may be thought of as a path into the interior, a journey inward. In the West, mysticism is most often described as a path or way consisting of the three steps or stages of preparation, illumination, and union, each being a preparation for the next. Dionysius, for example, wrote that, "Threefold is the way to God. The first is the way of purification, in which the mind is inclined to learn true wisdom. The second is the way of illumination, in which the mind by contemplation is kindled to the burning of love. The third is the way of union, in which the mind by understanding, reason and spirit, is led up by God alone."[14]

Purgation involves ridding oneself of such obstacles as self-will, pride, and self-centeredness which keep one from realizing the final goal. In mystics' writings we find such phrases associated with the first stage as "self-stripping," "dying to the self," "self surrender," "death of the self," and the "giving up of the self." In the *Imitation*, Kempis writes that "it is always necessary to resist the sensual appetites and by steady opposition subdue its power." A "total resignation of the will" is required. One must "die to the riches and honors, the cares and pleasures of this fallen world" and "learn to obey" and "learn to humble oneself."[15]

The purgation theme is found in Ruysbroeck's *Kingdom of God*, a large portion of which is spent on dealing with the seven gifts of fear of the Lord, devotion, knowledge, fortitude, counsel, understanding, wisdom, and what is required to gain each. St. John of the Cross sums up the purgative process in a series of paradoxes such as, "In order to arrive at having pleasure in everything, desire to have pleasure in nothing. . . . In order to arrive at knowing everything, desire to know nothing." And Eckhart, in one of his sermons, declared that "the agents of the soul . . . can be made sensitive and holy only through purification and renunciation."[16] Christian mystics associate the purgation stage with such scriptural passages as "Blessed are the pure in heart, for they shall see God"; "Narrow is the way which leadeth into life, and few there be that find it"; "Not everyone that saith unto me Lord, Lord, shall enter into the kingdom of heaven"; "If any man will come after me, let him deny himself and take up his cross and follow me"; and "He that finds his life shall lose it." In them the emphasis on the difficulty and need for surrender, denial, or giving up as a prerequisite for the next stage is obvious.

Eastern religions stress the same prerequisites. R. C. Zaehner of Oxford University asserts, for example, that "in every discipline that calls itself mystical, the first step must be the taming, or rather the destruction, of the sense of individuality."[17] In the Hindu tradition the Yogin is one who "having purified his soul of all dross . . . realizes it as immortal." He "renounces all things in order to find his own soul." We read in the Upanishads that "the Effulgent Self is to be realized within the lotus of the heart by continence, by steadfastness in truth, by meditation, and by superconscious vision. Their impurities washed away, the seers realize him," and "by the purified mind alone Brahmin is perceived." Similarly in the Muslim tradition, Sufism, Zaehner says, "means giving up the world, self-discipline, separating oneself from all created things, denial of self and turning to God."[18] In its doctrine of nonattachment the *Bhagavad Gita* is very definite about the need for giving up clinging to worldly things and desires. Buddhism's emphasis on the need for self-conquest is found in Buddha's words: "If someone conquer in battle a thousand times a thousand men, and if another conquers himself, he is the greatest of conquerors." In a more philosophical vein, one of Buddha's disciples is purported to have said, "He who has reached enlightenment has utterly destroyed the fetters of becoming."[19] The path or way metaphor is found in Buddhism, too. The aspirant for Buddhahood, for example, must vow to practice the "ten perfections," the first of which is renunciation.[20] In the Chinese tradition the mystic Chuang Tzu associates emptying with purgation in his famous statement: "Do not be the possessor of fame. Do not be the storehouse of schemes. Do not take over the function of things. Do not be the master of knowledge in order to manipulate things. Personally realize the infinite to the highest degree and travel in the realm of which there is no sign. Exercise fully what you have received from nature without any subjective viewpoint. In one word, be absolutely vacuous."[21]

It seems then that, whether in Eastern or Western mysticism, a major prerequisite for the mystical experience is the purging or purifying of the self through the eradicating of evils in the mind, the renouncing of worldly things, and through giving up self-will, self-assertion, and the sense of separate selfhood.

Illumination is the second state or step of the path. It naturally follows purgation. For when the mind becomes emptied of falsehoods and misconceptions, it can then be filled with or illuminated by truth. Illumination is associated with freeing also, for the mind and the self must be freed from passions, ill will, and negative attitudes such as jealousy and pride, if one is to become kind, compassionate, and humble.

Being illumined is achieved by the Buddhist through the discipline of meditation. In Zen Buddhism the mind, interestingly, is compared to a mirror. It must be wiped clean through meditation if it is to faithfully reflect reality. Christian mystics often use the term contemplation for this second stage. In Books I, IV, and V for example, Richard of Saint Victor describes in great detail six kinds of contemplation. The imagery of light and darkness is often found in mystical writings as well. When darkness and ignorance is dispelled, the mind becomes alight with the truth of reality. The Sufi mystic expresses this beautifully, "I looked upon my Lord with the eye of certainty, after that he had turned me away from all that was not he, and had illumined me with his light, and showed me marvels from his secret being and he showed me his He-ness."[22]

In the Indian tradition illumination is associated with darshana or direct insight. We read in the Upanishads, for example, "When through discrimination the heart has become pure, in meditation the Impersonal Self is revealed." Interestingly in both Hinduism and Buddhism the stage of illumination is even associated with changed bodily characteristics. Conze notes that "according to the common Indian tradition, a kind of fiery energy radiates from the bodies of great men, and the habit of meditation increases it."[23] Thus the body of Ramakrishna, a nineteenth-century Hindu mystic, is said to have taken on a new hue when he was in a state of ecstasy or rapture, and statues of the Buddha often have a halo either around the shoulders or the whole body to illustrate the association of illumination, transformation, and emanation.

Because more will be said later about the third stage of union, we can be brief here. In this stage the final goal has been reached of the union of the self with that Being or Principle that is beyond, other than, or greater than oneself. Again, the nature of this relationship is a major question: Is it a matter of the self becoming one with God yet retaining self-identity? Ruysbroeck writes of the mystic in the third stage seeking "to obtain his likeness and vehemently to be united to him in eternal fruition." St. John called this "God by participation." Or does the mystic lose all sense of separate selfhood in the uniting with God, just as, to use a favorite Hindu analogy, the river loses its identity when it has flowed into the sea and become absorbed by it? The Sufi mystic quoted previously evidently believes this: "And through his He-ness I looked on mine I-ness, and it vanished away, my light in his light."[24] According to Parrinder, Dionysius took the same view in his assertion that the mystic is "wholly absorbed in him who is beyond all."[25] This is put in another way by Richard of St. Victor, "The third degree of love is when the mind of man is ravished into the abyss of divine light, so that the soul, having forgotten all outward things, is altogether unaware of itself, and passes out completely into its God."[26] And Plotinus points in the same direction when he writes, "For he was then one with Him, and retained no differences, either in relation to himself or to others." Are there the only two possibilities of either union with, or absorption into, the Deity? Are there other quite plausible ones? We shall discuss this further later.

In the third stage of union the mystic also feels a deeper sense of unity or oneness with other persons and, in the case of nature mystics, with all of nature and her life forms as well. The Buddhist sutra says "that there is no self which I am not and no self which is not I." The Isa Upanishad declares, "The wise man beholds all beings in the Self, and the Self in all beings; for that reason he does not hate anyone."[27] Whether the "beings" referred to are only human beings is doubtful, as the Hindu emphasis on the harmony of man and nature is a preeminent one. Certainly the reference is to the union of man and all forms of life in Wordsworth's lines, "I felt the sentiment of Being spread O'er all that moves and all that seemeth still. . . . Communing in this sort through earth and heaven with every form of creature, as it looked towards the Uncreated with a countenance of Adoration, with an eye of love." And St. Francis, of course, is a mystic who exemplified "a joyous love of God and all of God's creatures."

Not only is there in this stage a sense of the unity of self with nature and others but a feeling of unity within the self as well. The mystic no longer feels torn between antinomies, contradictions, opposing aspirations, and conflicting ambitions. Doubts have been resolved. The external world no longer distracts one. A sense of integration, completeness, or wholeness is experienced. Dualities have been transcended, as the Mundaka Upanishad indicates: "The subtle Self within the living and breathing body is realized in that pure consciousness wherein is no duality." The Taoist might say that this wholeness and nonduality is the result of having "returned to the root" of one's existence, or of having been reunited with the ground of one's being, the Tao and, having done so, finding repose and tranquillity. Bernard of Clairvaux speaks of "re-acquiring the dignity of that primal honor" and thus not being "dismayed by adversity nor dissolute in prosperity."[28] And Eckhart reiterates this theme when he says that if one is to "experience this noble birth" one must "go back to the starting point, the core from which you came."

In this third stage, then, the mystic has become an integrated personality. He or she has transcended the little self, or put off the old self, as St. Paul said, to become a greater self. He has experienced a "transcending of time and space in which an infinite mode of existence is actually experienced."[29] He has been purified; St. Bernard, for example, declared that after God had "penetrated to the depths of my being," there occurred "the sudden departure of vices and carnal affections."[30] He has become humble. Humility or "submissive and humble obedience" was the third of the six fruits of grace Ruysbroeck listed, and in the Upanishads we read, "Seeing Him present in all, the wise man is humble and puts not himself forward."

Tranquillity and serenity are often indicated as characteristics accompanying the unitive state. Plotinus wrote of the mystic, "Caught up in an ecstasy, tranquil and God-possessed, he enjoyed an imperturbable calm (Enneade VI, 9.)" The Upanishads repeatedly make the same point, "Having known the Self, the sages are tranquil of mind, free from passion" (Mundaka Upanishad) and, "From Brahma down to the clump of grass, I verily am all; one who knows this for certain becomes free from conflict, pure, peaceful" (Svetasvatara Upanishad).

Joy, rapture, or ecstasy characterizes the unitive state also.

Kempis speaks of "the exquisite delight derived from the privilege of pure contemplation" (*Imitation*, 184) and St. Francis of "a rapture and uplifting of the mind intoxicated in the contemplation of the unspeakable savour of the Divine sweetness, and a happy, peaceful and sweet delight of the soul, that is rapt and uplifted in great marvel" (M. Smith, An Introduction to the History of Mysticism, 9). In Sufism, joy is carried by some to almost a state of intoxication as represented by the figure of the whirling dervish. In a more somber mode, Ziuad B. al-Arabi writes that "Ecstasy in this world comes not from revelation, but consists in the vision of the heart and realization of the truth and gaining assurance, and he who has attained to it beholds with the joy of certainty and with a devotion free of self-interest."[31] And in the Upanishads we read again that "the sages are filled with joy" once having known the Self.

In metaphysical terms the mystic in the unitive state is in harmony with the essence of the universe, has returned to his essence, or lives in terms of his essence or essential self. Again, this is emphasized universally by mystics. Plotinus writes "shut up in his proper essence, he inclined not to either side, he turned not even to himself; he was in a state of perfect stability; he had become stability itself."[32] Ruysbroeck associated the third fruit of grace with, in addition to humility, "the patient gentleness to be not other than one's own proper essence."[33] Eckhart says in one of his sermons that "contemplating the creature, God gives it being, and contemplating God, the creature receives its being. The soul has an intelligent, knowing essence and therefore, wherever God is, there is the soul, and wherever the soul is, there is God."[34] Eckhart's statement reminds one of Uddalaika's well-known admonition in the Chandogya Upanishad to his son, "Now that which is the subtle essence—in it all that exists has itself. That is the true. That is the Self. That thou art, Svetaketa."[35]

One might be tempted to conclude from the above that there is a "universal mysticism" or that the nature of mystical experience at its highest reach is the same everywhere. There are eminent people who hold such a view. Aldous Huxley wrote and spoke of a "Perennial Philosophy" which had four fundamental doctrines at its core. He claimed that the philosophy "and its ethical corollaries constitute a Highest Common Factor present in all the major religions of the world" and that it "has always and everywhere been the metaphysical system of the prophets, saints and sages."[36] A British colleague and noted Orientalist,

E. G. Browne, had written earlier, "There is hardly any soil, be it ever so barren, where mysticism will not strike root; hardly any creed, however formal, round which it will not twine itself. It is, indeed, the eternal cry of the human soul for rest; the insatiable longing of a being wherein infinite ideals are fettered and cramped by a miserable actuality; and so long as man is less than an angel and more than a beast, this cry will not for a moment fail to make itself heard."[37]

Other more recent scholars have likewise emphasized a "universal mysticism." Margaret Smith writes that mysticism "represents a spiritual tendency which is universal, for we find it in all religions worthy of the name and in all true faiths, and it is often the most vital element in such faiths." She claimed that mysticism postulates four articles of faith which are the same everywhere and that, while the three stages of the mystic way "vary somewhat in the different religions of East and West in which mysticism has taken root," the threefold division that has been accepted in the West will "to a large extent cover the stages of the way as set forth in the religious systems of the East."[38]

In his discussion of mysticism, the Jewish author Scharfstein speaks of eleven sets of "interlocking characteristics," which he calls "quintessences," found in mysticism everywhere.[39] Stace writes that, although there are differences, there are a number of "fundamental common characteristics of mysticism." He adds the interesting observation that "mysticism naturally, though not necessarily, becomes intimately associated with whatever is the religion of the culture in which it appears . . . however . . . it does not favor any particular religion."[40]

Stace is not an unequivocal supporter of mystical universalism, however. In one of his books he writes about the "great divide" between East and West. Hinduism and Buddhism as Eastern religions have different views of God than do the three Western religions of Judaism, Christianity, and Islam, and thus the nature of the mystical union is viewed differently, for example. Inge also suggests what he believes is a "very important difference between European and Asiatic mysticism." That difference, oversimplified, is the conceiving in the first instance of God as personal and, in the case of the Asiatic, God as impersonal.[41] Cheney explains the difference by writing that "the Christian founders substituted, in the place of the abstract One a sympathetic God-Father" and "the Christian mystic, while losing nothing of the sublimity of the abstract union with the

Absolute as known to Eastern sages, is likely to substitute a contemplation of the heart for intellectual meditation."[42]

Probably the most outspoken opponent of the "universal mysticism" position is R. C. Zaehner of Oxford. His book, *Mysticism Sacred and Profane,* was an investigation into the "truth of the assertion that mysticism is an unvarying phenomenon observable throughout the entire world and at all ages, and that it may and does make its appearance in all and any religious system." He proposed to "distinguish between what seems to be radically different types of mystical experience," and he concluded at the end of his book that "what goes by the name of mysticism, so far from being an identical expression of the selfsame Universal Spirit, falls into three distinct categories"[43] which he called nature, monistic, and theistic mysticism. His book was written at a time when the field of comparative religion was becoming quite popular, and he was critical of many scholars in the field "who would have us believe that all religions are equally true and that proselytizing of any sort is therefore wrong" (198).

The question of whether or not there is a "universal mysticism" is like the question regarding the nature of the mystic's relationship with God, in that both are widely debated and have vigorous proponents on each side. The question of universality will be taken up later and further alternatives will be considered. We may go on to note that there does seem to be quite some agreement among mystics and students of mysticism on what mysticism is not and what led mystics to turn to the mystic path in the first place. Inge speaks for many when he writes, "I cannot accept any definition which identifies mysticism with excited or hysterical emotionalism, with sublimated eroticism, with visions and revelations, with supernatural (dualistically opposed to natural) activities nor, on the philosophical side, with irrationalism."[44] Stace, in discussing what mysticism is not, declares that "there is nothing misty, foggy, vague or sloppy about mysticism." Nor is it a sort of "mystery mongering" and "visions and voices are not mystical phenomena, though it seems to be the case that the sort of persons who are mystics may often be the sort of persons who see visions and hear voices."[45]

Zaehner's statement is similar to Stace's in that the mystical experience "has nothing to do with visions, auditions, locutions, telepathy, telekinesis, or any other praeternatural phenomena which may be experienced by saint and sinner alike and which are usually connected with an hysterical temperament. It is true that some advanced mystics have been subject to these disturbances, but they have no essential connection with the mystic experience itself, the essence of which is union. Praeternatural phenomena that may or may not accompany it are subsidiary, accidental, parasites."[46] In regard to immoralities sometimes impugned to mystics, Tantras, for example, Wainwright writes that "for the most part, mysticism has not consisted of such colorful and shocking exceptions to moral norms."[47] As to the contemporary use of drugs and mystical experience, a basic question is whether the experience induced by drugs is a genuine mystical experience, even if it seems quite similar to the nondrug induced one. Parrinder puts the point well when he writes, "There is a natural reaction among religious people to suggestions that drugs or occult practices can provide experiences comparable with those of the great mystics. But comparability is not the same as identity."[48]

The charge that mystics are passive and escapists is met by persons such as Inge in his statement that mysticism is not "merely a way of escape from the worries of this unintelligible world."[49] No less a mystic than Meister Eckhart may be quoted in this regard. In one of his sermons he said that "no person in this life may reach the point at which he can be excused from outward service. Even if he is given to a life of contemplation, still he cannot refrain from going out and taking an active part in life . . . those who are given to the life of contemplation and avoid activities deceive themselves and are on the wrong track. I say that the contemplative person should indeed avoid even the thought of deeds to be done during the period of his contemplation but afterwards he should get busy . . . for active life is to be a respite from contemplation."[50] Mysticism, then, is not escapism. It may be a momentary, but not a permanent, retreat from the world in order that one may better deal with the world. And in regard to what Inge, Stace, and Zaehner claim mysticism is not, we may note that they do qualify their assertions somewhat so that there is room for those who accept visions, for example, as valid for the mystical experience.[51]

As was noted earlier, there seems to be quite a bit of agreement also on what led mystics to turn to the mystic path in the first place. On the personal level mystics like St. Francis finally realized the emptiness of a dissolute, negligent, indulgent life. Many experienced an extreme sense of wrong. Bernard felt his soul to be "hardened with sins, the prisoner of vices and ensnared by carnal pleasure" and declared that "Eve lives in our flesh and the serpent makes use of the concupiscence which she has passed on to us, to set snares for us by his continual temptation."[52] Mystics often experienced firsthand the tyranny of self-will and the insidiousness of pride and vanity. These are what St. John of the Cross called the second or spiritual part of the soul that must be purified even as the sensual part has been purified. Mystics experienced more intensely than others a sense of separation from both God and other persons. For example, like St. Bernard, who spoke of his soul as "torn between hope and despair," they keenly felt inner contradictions and tensions.

Often the conditions of earthly existence started the mystic on the path. The Buddha's quest for enlightenment began when he was taken out of the palace, and, seeing for the first time human suffering in four forms, he was lead to realize the impermanence and the universality of suffering of all things. Boehme pictured an earthliness "in which good and evil stand in strife" and human life as having "lost the tempermentum, or eternal rest, by its own desire made itself dark, painful, gruff, hard and rough."[53] And Brother Lawrence, told of "the sins of the wicked in this world, found nothing to wonder at; on the contrary he marveled that there were not many more transgressions, considering all the corruptions into which desire can lead a man."[54]

Mystics often anguished about the society in which they lived. A common picture is that of the Hindu seer who has withdrawn from society in despair. Cheney describes the seventeenth century in Europe as "preeminently the century of Christian wars, of a continent finally and bloodily divided, of the Mother Church broken and henceforth powerless alone to affect the Western world for peace or war." Yet there were those who experienced "the mystic attainment to God, the ascetic self-discipline, the consecration of all action to holy service."[55] Among them were the Quakers who, "establishing a religion in which contemplation and inner illumination are dominant," staunchly opposed the slave system, indentured labor, and alcoholism.

Many, of course, were the mystics who despaired of the church, some simply leaving it, others remaining in and attempting to purify it. We see this in the church of the medieval period described thus by one author: "its spiritual power had waned; its hierarchy was honeycombed with corruption; its oracles were dumb. The great church that had conquered the Empire . . . was sinking into a temporal corporation for dispensing wealth and patronage and power."[56] Catherine of Siena was one of those who felt the "corruptions of the Church and the evils of the times." Her own unhappy marriage was, as well, a force that turned her to mysticism. In our own time Thomas Merton is an example of how world conditions change or determine the direction a person's life takes. He declared that "the materialistic society, the so-called culture that has evolved under the tender mercies of capitalism, has produced what seems to be the ultimate limit of this worldliness. And nowhere, except perhaps in the analogous society of pagan Rome, has there ever been such a flowering of cheap and petty and disgusting lusts and vanities as in the world of capitalism, where there is no evil that is not fostered and encouraged for the sake of making money."[57] He, of course, dedicated his life to the changing of that society.

Following the trend in religious studies generally, twentieth-century discussions of mysticism have focused extensively on the mystical consciousness and experience.[58] Debates centered around the determinants, nature, form, authenticity, validity, verifiability, and content of the mystical experience, and the language the mystic employs to describe his or her experience. Sparking them recently was a collection of essays edited by Steven Katz published in 1978 entitled *Mysticism and Philosophical Analysis*.[59] Its aim was to disabuse scholars "of the preconceived notion that all mystical experience is the same or similar."[60] Katz's major thesis in his chapter entitled "Language, Epistemology, and Mysticism" is that there are no "pure (i.e., unmediated) experiences,"[61] that the nature of a mystic's experience is determined, or even "over-determined"[62] by his or her cultural or "socioreligious milieu," and that, since this varies with each mystic, the only acceptable conclusion is a mystical contextualism, relativism, and pluralism.

This view clashed with those of twentieth-century scholars, early and late, such as, among others, James, Underhill, Pratt, Margaret Smith, Arberry, William Johnston, Stace, Schuon, Eliade, Otto, Scharfstein, and finally, Huston Smith and Seyyed Nasr, who, to one extent or another, held to the general view that there are some attributes characteristic of mystics or mystical experience everywhere, that there is a "common core," or, as Stace put it, that there are "universal common characteristics of mysticism in all cultures, ages, religions, and civilizations of the world."[63]

Katz's position, elaborated by such followers as Hicks, Penner, Gimello, Streng, and Gill, was the "received view" in the 1970s. It was discussed and challenged, however, by a number of scholars including P. C. Almond, A. N. Perovich, W. Proudfoot, and R. Forman, editor of a set of essays published in 1990 entitled *The Problem of Pure Consciousness.*[64] Forman argued for the reality and validity of what he called a "Pure Consciousness Event" being at the heart of the mystical experience.[65] At its peak, the experience is one in which all prior antecedents are transcended or forgotten; that is, the nature of the experience is not conditioned or determined by the mystic's particular religious tradition, cultural orientation, or conceptual schemata.

To understand and evaluate Katz's position, it would be helpful to see the context out of which it arises. It has several components, among them being the logical positivism of the early 1920s with its antimetaphysical bent; A. J. Ayer and the Language Analysis School which asserted that the only meaningful statement is one which has an empirical referrent;[66] the increasing dominance of empiricism, science, and the scientific method and outlook; a materialistic metaphysics and epistemology that holds that only material reality exists and we know it only through the senses; a perceptualistic psychology and a behavioristic view of man as a biological, stimulus-response organism conditioned by his immediate environment; and a relativism that has come to dominate sociological, anthropological, cultural, and humanistic studies.[67] Given such a context, it is obvious that Katz and his followers arrive at the "constructivist" position they do.[68]

In evaluating the positions of the "constructivists" and "nonconstructivists," one might begin by indicating questions they are dealing with. Among them would be the following: What types or kinds of mysticism are there? What stimulates the mystical experience, or what leads persons to turn to mysticism? What are its prerequisites, or what is required if one is to have a mystical experience? Is the experience more cognitive or emotive? Does the intellectual or feeling element predominant? What happens regarding individuality or selfhood during the mystical experience? What can we say about similarities and differences in mysticism and the mystical experience? How is a mystical experience to be verified, or how can we distinguish between a true and false mysticism or mystical experience? And, of course, as already noted, what is and what determines the nature of a mystic's experience, as well as the language he or she employs in describing it?

Answers to the first three questions have already been noted. Obviously we find different kinds of mysticism or variations or differences in mystical experiences, at least when viewed externally or phenomenally. But does this rule out the possibility of what might be called "internal" similarities? As to animation, the turning to mysticism may be stimulated by either or both internal factors or external conditions. Of the prerequisites, self-purification in its broadest sense seems to be the major one.

As to whether the experience is cognitive or emotive, one might note that it need not be a matter of one or the other. It can and often is both, the degree of one or the other varying with each mystic or experience. On the other hand, it can be and, apparently is, in some cases, a transcending of both the intellectual and feeling elements. One wonders also if the Hindu view that, generally, one's religion or faith differs depending on the type of individual, may be true of the religious mystic as well.[69] Finally, if the mystical experience is primarily a noncognitive one, can it be fully or accurately understood and validly judged using cognitive or rational criteria?

As noted already, there are those who hold that in a genuine mystical experience all sense of individuality is lost, the individual is completely absorbed in the Other, the river analogy used by the Hindu being a very convincing one for this view. The other position is that there is a retaining of a sense of individuality to one degree or another, and it is a matter of a union of the self and Self and not a submerging of the self into the Self. It is interesting that the proponents of the first view are found primarily in Eastern cultures, which are more group than individualistically oriented, and in religious traditions such as Hinduism, and especially Buddhism, in which the notion of an absolute, independent, autonomous, separate self or selfhood is minimal or absent. On the other hand, the second position characterizes Western or mid-Eastern religions such as Judaism, Christianity, and Islam, which are grounded in a metaphysical dualism and the concept of a substantial self.

We may ask whether a "true" mysticism requires one or the other. Is it not too much to make such a demand? Indeed, theoretically at least, why could not a mystical experience incorporate both, the first level or stage of it involving a consciousness of separateness, culminating in a second stage in which it is lost? This does seem to happen, and in any case, does it really matter? Why not let each mystic meaningfully experience the Other in his or her own way? More important, perhaps, is what results from the experience.

It is interesting to note also that, if one is an epistemological and metaphysical dualist, the union alternative becomes the reasonable or logical one. This is because, for a dualist, the knower is always separated from the known or the subject from the object. On the other hand, while it makes no sense to the dualist, the nondualist finds no contradiction, a paradox perhaps in insisting on the possibility that knower and known can become one, that the subject-object distinction can be bridged as the subject becomes one with the object, and in taking a metaphysical view which sees reality as one or in terms of oneness and plurality. Dualities are apparent while reality in essence is one, or reality is one and takes on a plurality of appearances.[70]

Differences and similarities have been and continue to be disputed by the perennialist or universalist and the relativist or nominalist.[71] The first emphasizes ways in which mystical experiences vary, the second ways in which they are alike. The following comments and questions may be germane to the problem. There seems to be a natural tendency on the part of some to see and emphasize differences and by others to stress similarities. Each brings his own proclivity to an analysis of mystical experience. If one is to point out and stress differences, ought not one, in the interest of fairness, admit similarities as well? If one concentrates on the phenomena, the externals of the mystical experience, one will inevitably or obviously see differences. But again, is one not bound to go beyond the external and visible to the internal and invisible that may be characterized by similarities or communalities?

Further, if one is a metaphysical and epistemological dualist, is not one more apt to see, stress, and magnify differences? If one holds to a monistic or a monistic plus pluralistic metaphysics and correlate epistemology on the other hand, does not the opposite hold? If differences are of the categories of the relative and means and similarities of the categories of the absolute and ends, then can we not validly conclude that mystical experiences, even though different externally or in the form they take, are similar in the ends sought and gained such as a meaningful experience with God, the One, or the Absolute, and a change in the nature and resultant actions of the experiencer? Why then quibble over the means when the end or ends are what is most important? In addition, what may be true for different mystics and mysticisms may be true for different religions, namely, that each is but a different or particular means to an identical end or ends.

As to verification, the problem with using the criterion or test of verifiability or the claim that a mystical experience is either true or false is that it runs headlong into the mystic's claim of the ineffability or noetic quality of his experience. What is to be done? What alternatives face us? One is to argue, as Proudfoot does, that terms like "ineffable and paradoxical are not imprecise and vague," but are indeed "quite precise."[72] Another is to claim, epistemologically, that a mystical experience is not like a sensory experience, and it is invalid, therefore, to evaluate the former in terms of the criteria used for latter or to force a mystical into the same mold as a sensory experience.

A third alternative is to insist that it is not a matter of verifiability or being true or false but of meaningfulness and the effect the experience has on the life of the experiencer. The mystic knows that he had a mystical experience and that it was meaningful to him or her. And we are able to see and measure the effect it had on him. If a person claims to have had a genuine mystical experience, after which he becomes drunk and drives an automobile down the wrong side of the street killing the occupants of an oncoming vehicle, we would rightly have serious doubts about the validity of his experience. If the experiencer asserts that the only good people are the people of his clan, tribe, race, or country or that the adherents of his religion only will be saved, then, again, we can rightfully doubt.

Regarding the question of the nature of mystical experiences and their determinants, two points may be made. One is that we need to differentiate between the experiencer, the experience or kind of experience, and what is experienced. Admittedly there is variation because of background, prior conditioning, and other factors in the case of the first two. Is it not true, however, that what is experienced is the same (no matter how described)? The second is to note that the question, in part at least, goes back to the issue of the nature of man. Katz takes this up only briefly, claiming that "the mystical experience must be mediated by the kind of beings we are."[73] He does not indicate what kind this is, but based on what was described earlier as the origins of his views, one can conclude that it is the conditionalist one. The individual has no free will, the capacity of free choice, or the ability to transcend conditional influences, whether personal, mental, environmental, cultural, religious, or social.

One might observe, at this point, that most people, evidently, do find it difficult or almost impossible to break the bonds of conditional influences. Not all do, however, and mystics may be included in that minority, who should not then be viewed or judged as is the majority. One is reminded of Huston Smith's distinction between the exotic and esoteric, the esoteric minority consisting of "men and women who realize that they have their roots in the Absolute."[74] This is another way of saying that they, the minority, have gone beyond the conditional influences of the relative while the esoteric majority have not. Dupré also accepts a distinction between the majority and minority. McGinn writes that for Dupré "mystics are those special individuals who have immediate access to the deepest core of the self, where the laws of ordinary consciousness are suspended and the soul comes to have direct knowledge of its self-transcendence and transcendence of the world."[75]

It is obvious that language is relative or that the words people use to describe the same object or experience varies. However, it is important, is it not, to get beyond such superficial relativity and recognize that different words may refer to the same entity or reality. What is experienced is the same, although different mystics use different words to describe it.[76]

What can we expect or what should we demand of language? Can we demand too much? One is reminded of the Buddhist's example of the finger pointing at the moon.[77] Once the moon is seen, leave the finger behind. Language is like the finger. It points us to that which is beyond it, and, once the beyond is experienced, leave the pointer—language—behind. In this sense language, like the finger, is but a means or of the category of the relative pointing toward that which is of the category of the absolute.

It is quite common for mystics to admit that they find words inadequate for a full or satisfactory description of their experience, a confession their critics often focus on. However, does it follow that, because an experience cannot be fully described, it is not a valid, true, or meaningful one? Not necessarily. All it implies is the inadequacy of words, as far as a mystical experience is concerned, at least. The same may not be true of a sensory experience. By their very nature a mystical and sensory experience differs, and their language must also. The language used by an empiricist may be capable of fully describing the empiricist's experience with the physical object. Not so for the mystic. Proudfoot makes this point when he writes:

> The subject's identification of his experience as mystical entails the belief that it cannot be exhaustively explained in naturalistic terms ... any experience whose object can be captured in a descriptive phrase or that can be explained in naturalistic terms is, ipso facto, not a mystical experience ... the mystic's identification of his experience requires a commitment to a certain kind of explanation or, what comes to the same thing, the exclusion of a particular kind of explanation. He must identify his experience under a certain description, and that description must preclude naturalistic explanation. The assumption that the experience cannot be exhaustively accounted for in naturalistic terms is included in the criteria for identifying an experience as mystical.[78]

What Proudfoot is asserting is, again, that one cannot expect the language a mystic uses to describe his experience to be the same as the language an empiricist or scientist uses to describe his, because they are two different types of experiences or realities and one cannot demand the same of the language of both.

In closing, what shall we say about the debate between the constructivist and nonconstructivist and the future of studies in mysticism and comparative mysticism? Regarding the former, we may note that constructivism has rendered a valuable service in insisting that mysticism be studied in context, that beginning with a priori assumptions may be a questionable method, that selectivity in gathering evidence for one's preconceived views is invalid, that greater exactness in dealing with the literature of mysticism is necessary, and that differences not be overlooked or minimized.[79] As to the future of studies in mysticism, Katz indicates two things that need to be undertaken, both of which, however, are but further explications of the constructivist position.[80] What really is needed is to get beyond both contextual and noncontextualism, as noted, for example, by Forman in his statement that there is a need for a more "complex theory of mystical experience than that suggested by either Katz or the essentialists."[81]

Similarly Perovich suggests that a "qualified" contextualism be worked out "based on the thesis that some (not all) beliefs shape experience."[82] Perovich is also concerned about another timely subject, that is, science and mysticism. Ewert Cousin believes that we need to study mysticism empathetically as well as objectively.[83] And much more needs to be done in the epistemology of mysticism, if McGinn's recent contention is true that "the stand-off between empiricism and transempirical epistemology is as strong now as it was at the beginning of the century."[84] He is troubled, too, by the lack of cooperation between those who investigate mysticism from a psychological perspective and a historical and theoretical one.

In a quite different vein, one might suggest that mystical studies follow the lead of philosophy, which is no longer dominated by the analytical and language analysis movement, but has moved in the direction of "applied philosophy" that is concerned with what philosophy or philosophers have to say about the state of the world in which we live.[85] In the case of mystical studies, for example, this would include an investigation of how mysticism can help to soften or minimize the dogmatism of institutionalized religion that has led in single religious traditions to the persecution by the orthodox of the mystic and to conflict between religions whose proponents claim theirs as the only true religion or means of salvation.[86] Further, if a pluralism of mystical types and experiences can be agreed on, how can mysticism stimulate a similar pluralism that makes room for unity in diversity among the religious traditions of the world? And surely, if a mystical experience brings beneficial results to the experiencer such as a sense of peace and serenity, and positive attitudes and relationships with his fellow human beings, why would not mysticism, if applied to society or the world as a whole have similar good consequences? We need, then, studies in how mysticism and mystics can contribute to the bringing about of a less pugnacious, competitive, and belligerent and a more peaceful, congenial, integrated world, one in which people are more caring, empathetic, unselfish, and loving. Let us not forget, too, that worthy of speculation is the question of why there are so few mystics or what there is about the contemporary world that makes for such a paucity of mysticism today.

Notes

1. Walter Stace, *The Teachings of the Mystics* (New York: New American Library, 1960), 15.

2. William Inge, *Mysticism in Religion* (Chicago: University of Chicago Press, 1948), 26.

3. R. C. Zaehner, *Mysticism, Sacred and Profane* (New York: Galaxy Books, 1961), 32.

4. Stace, *Teachings*, 202.

5. Geoffrey Parrinder, *Mysticism in the World's Religions* (London: Sheldon Press, 1976), 15.

6. F. C. Happold, *Mysticism, A Study and an Anthology* (Baltimore: Penguin Books, 1963), 40.

7. Rudolf Otto, *Mysticism East and West* (New York: Meridian Books, 1957), 62.

8. Happold, *Mysticism*, 43–44.

9. Ibid., 34.

10. William James, *Varieties of Religious Experience* (London: Longmans, Green and Co., 1902), 380. In regard to the ineffability of the mystical experience, it is instructive to note what the Zen Buddhist says about the limitations to the use of words: "They build up a false world in which other people are reduced to stereotypes; even if description is accurate, it isn't adequate because words dilute the intensity of immediate experience even when they do not distort it; the highest mode of experience transcends the reach of words entirely."

11. Happold, *Mysticism*, 48.

12. Mohammad Iqbal, *The Reconstruction of Religious Thought* (Lahore: J. Iqbal Publisher, 1954), 18–26.

13. D. T. Suzuki, *Mysticism: Christian and Buddhist* (New York: Harper and Brothers, 1957), 61.

14. Evelyn Underhill, *The Essential of Mysticism* (London: J. M. Dent and Sons, 1920), 11. The three stages are described by Bernard of Clairvaux in terms of the three kisses, that is, the kiss of the Lord's feet, hands, and mouth. Another symbolism, that of the spiritual ladder by which one climbs up the "mountain without summit," is used by Ruysbroeck. It has three steps: the active life, the inward life, and the contemplative life.

15. Thomas à Kempis, *The Imitation of Christ*, trans. John Payne (New York: Robert Collins, 1851), 188.

16. Happold, *Mysticism*, 361.

17. Zaehner, *Mysticism, Sacred and Profane*, 191.

18. R. C. Zaehner, *Hindu and Muslim Mysticism* (New York: Schocken Books, 1969), 6.

19. Sidney Spencer, *Mysticism in World Religion* (Baltimore: Penguin Books, 1963), 70. That the disciple's quote says "fetters of becoming" indicates a singular characteristic of the original Buddhism, namely its an-atman or "no self" doctrine. Buddha took the nonsubstantialist view that there is no eternal existing self in the form of a soul. Thus, if there is no self to be renounced, how can we talk about self-renunciation in Buddhism?

20. Bhikkhu Khantipalo, *What Is Buddhism* (Bangkok: Social Science Association Press of Thailand, 1965), 113–14.

21. Wing-Tsit Chan, *A Source Book in Chinese Philosophy* (Princeton: Princeton University Press, 1963), 207.

22. Zaehner, *Hindu and Muslim Mysticism*, 198.

23. Edward Conze, *Buddhism: Its Essence and Development* (New York: Harper & Row, 1959), 38.

24. Zaehner, *Hindu and Muslim Mysticism*, 198.

25. Parrinder, *World's Religions*, 10.

26. Spencer, *Mysticism in World Religion*, 228.

27. Swami Nikhilananda, ed., *The Upanishads* (New York: Harper Torchbooks, n.d.), 90.

28. Kilian Walsh, trans., *The Works of Bernard of Clairvaux*, vol. 3 (Kalamazoo, Mich.: Cistercian Publications, 1976), 8.

29. Zaehner, *Mysticism, Sacred and Profane*, 50.

30. Ben-Ami Scharfstein, *Mystical Experience* (Baltimore: Penguin Books, 1974), 5.

31. Stace, *Teachings*, 204. One must be careful as to how the phenomenon of the dance in Sufism is to be viewed or interpreted.

32. Georgia Harkness, *Mysticism, Its Meaning and Message* (Nashville, Tenn.: Abingdon Press, 1973), 68.

33. Jan Ruysbroeck, *The Kingdom of the Lovers of God* (New York: E. Hutton and Co., 1919), 210.

34. Raymond Blakney, trans., *Meister Eckhart* (New York: Harper Torchbooks, 1941), 214.

35. Nikhilananda, *The Upanishads*, 69.

36. Swami Prabhavananda, trans., *The Bhagavad-Gita* (New York: New American Library, 1972), 21–22.

37. Margaret Smith, *An Introduction to Mysticism* (New York: Oxford University Press, 1977), 2.

38. Ibid.

39. Scharfstein, *Mystical Experience*, 142–45.

40. Stace, *Teachings*, 25.

41. Inge, *Mysticism in Religion*, 153.

42. Sheldon Cheney, *Men Who Have Walked with God* (New York: Alfred A. Knopf, 1945), 143.

43. Zaehner, *Mysticism, Sacred and Profane*, 198.

44. Inge, *Mysticism in Religion*, 154.

45. Stace, *Teachings*, 10.

46. Zaehner, *Mysticism, Sacred and Profane*, 32.

47. William I. Wainwright, *Philosophy of Religion* (Belmont, Calif.: Wadsworth Publishing Company, 1988), 176.

48. Parrinder, *World's Religions*, 183.

49. Inge, *Mysticism in Religion*, 9.

50. Blakney, *Meister Eckhart*, 238. In the 1958 volume, *Christian Mysticism*, Inge wrote that "a very short study will be sufficient to dispel some of the prejudice still hovering round the name of mysticism, e.g., that its professors are unpractical dreamers, and that this type of religion is antagonistic to the English mind. As a matter of fact, all the great mystics have been energetic and influential, and their business capacity is specially noted in a curiously large number of cases" xvii.

51. In regard to his point, see William Inge, *Christian Mysticism* (New York: Meridian Books, 1956), 14–19.

52. Kilian Walsh, trans., *Works of Bernard of Clairvaux*, Vol. 2 (Shannon, Ireland: Irish University Press, 1971), xii.

53. Jacob Boehme, *The Way to Christ*, trans. J. J. Stoudt (London: John M. Watkins, 1953), 173–74.

54. Cheney, *Men Who Have Walked*, 294.

55. Ibid., 286. The Indian author Sisirbuma Ghose puts the matter thus: "the mystic's sense of life and adventure of mind strain upward beyond all present maps. The world of the senses, of material facts and goals of life is never enough for his. In all this he feels the sense of something missing."

56. Rufus Jones, *Studies in Mystical Religion* (London: Macmillan and Co., 1923), 299.

57. Thomas McDonnell, ed., *A Thomas Merton Reader* (New York: Harcourt, Brace and World Inc., 1962), 42.

58. Early examples of that trend in religious studies are James's *Varieties of Religious Experience* (London: Longmans, Green and Co., 1902) and Pratt's *The Religious Consciousness* (New York: Macmillan, 1920). Proudfoot claims that the trend begins earlier with Schleiermacher's *On Religion* (1799) and *The Christian Faith* (1822). Wayne Proudfoot, *Religious Experience* (Berkeley, Los Angeles, and London: University of California Press, 1985), XIII.

59. Steven T. Katz, ed., *Mysticism and Philosophical Analysis* (New York: Oxford University Press, 1978).

60. Ibid., 65.

61. Ibid. "There are no pure (i.e., unmediated) experiences. Neither mystical experience nor more ordinary forms of experience give any indication, or any grounds for believing that they are unmediated . . . the notion of unmediated experience seems, if not self-contradictory, at best empty" (26).

62. Ibid., 46.

63. W. T. Stace, *Mysticism and Philosophy* (New York and London: Macmillan, 1960), 132. Huxley's "perennial philosophy" was quite influential in supporting this view. Aldous Huxley, *The Perennial Philosophy* (New York: Harper, 1945).

64. K. C. Forman, ed., *The Problem of Pure Consciousness* (New York: Oxford University Press, 1990). He uses the characterization "received view" on pages 3 and 8. See also his critique of constructivism in a penetrating article in the October 1989 issue of *Philosophy: East and West*, entitled "Paramantha and Modern Constructivists on Mysticism: Epistemological Monomorphism versus Duomorphism" (398–418).

65. Forman, ed., *Problem*, 8.

66. Ayer's attitude toward the mystic was that "if a mystic admits that the object of his vision is something which cannot be described, then he must also admit that he is bound to talk nonsense when he describes it." A. J. Ayer, *Language, Truth and Logic* (New York: Dover, 1952), 118.

67. According to Philip Almond in his chapter in Forman's book, the underlying cause for perennialism coming into disfavor was "the broad paradigm shift in the humanities and social sciences toward constructivism," the view that "all experiences . . . are in significant ways formed, shaped, and constructed by the terms, categories, beliefs, and linguistic backgrounds which the subject brings to them," a view that became so common it took on the status of a "self-evident truism." Forman, ed., *Problem*, 4.

68. Constructivism is the term Forman uses in his book when discussing Katz's views. He delineates three types: complete, incomplete, and catalytic constructivism (13–14).

69. The three ways or paths are Bhakti, Karma, and Jnana marga.

70. For my own discussion of Buddhist and Western views of the Self, see "Buddhist and Western Views of the Self," *The Eastern Buddhist, Journal of the Eastern Buddhist Society* 2, no. 2 (Kyoto, Japan: Otani University, 1969): 111–23.

71. Nominalism is a term used on page 324 by McGinn to describe Katz's position. His book contains a very extensive and helpful summary of twentieth-century studies in theological, philosophical, comparativist, and

psychological approaches to mysticism. Bernard McGinn, *The Foundations of Mysticism* (New York: Crossroad, 1992), 266–343. His use of the term leads one to wonder if the present controversy between constructivists and nonconstructivists is but an example of the centuries-long conflict between nominalists and realists.

72. Proudfoot, *Religious Experience*, 125.

73. Katz, *Philosophical Analysis*, 66.

74. Page XV of Huston Smith's Introduction to the 1975 revised edition published by Harper & Row of Frithjof Schuon's *The Transcendent Unity of Religions*.

75. McGinn, *Foundations of Mysticism*, 324. Louis Dupré's very stimulating discussion of mysticism and the self is found on pages 92–104 of his book, *Transcendent Selfhood* (New York: Seabury, 1976). McGinn makes an interesting observation in his article The God Beyond God in the 1981 *Journal of Religion*, 3: "Eckhart's distinction between the trinitarian God and the hidden unity of the Godhead might be interpreted as a breakthrough beyond Christian trinitarianism to a form of mystical unitarianism." Also dealt with is the "Birth of the Son in the Soul."

76. Forman uses two examples to illustrate this: "As Friedrich Frege pointed out, like the North Star and the Pole Star, two terms with different senses can have the same referent . . . Were a Hindu guru and a Buddhist roshi to simultaneously hear someone report an experience, it would make sense that the guru might say, 'That's an experience of samadhi,' whereas the roshi might say, 'Oh, you've experienced shunyata'" (18).

77. The finger example reminds one of the Muslim Rumi's. He wrote: "The lamps are different, but the light is the same; it comes from beyond. If thou keep looking at the lamp, thou art lost; for thence arises the appearance of number and plurality. Fix thy gaze upon the Light, and thou art delivered from the dualism inherent in the finite body." Quoted by Stace, *Teachings*, 215.

78. Proudfoot, *Religious Experience*, 144, 148, 137.

79. See Forman, *Problem*, 4.

80. "Two things have to continue to be done: (1) further, careful, expert, study of specific mystical traditions has to be undertaken to uncover what their characteristics are and especially how they relate to the larger theological milieu out of which they emerge; and (2) further fundamental epistemological research into the conditions of mystical experience has to be undertaken in order to lay bare the skeleton of such experience insofar as this is possible." Katz, *Philosophical Analysis*, 66. Katz's continuing interest in mystical language is reflected in the volume he edited and contributed to entitled *Mysticism and Language*, published by Oxford University press in 1992. See also chapter 3 on "The Nature of Language" in Frank Tobin, *Meister Eckhart: Thought and Language* (Philadelphia: University of Pennsylvania Press, 1986).

81. Forman, *Problem*, 218.

82. McGinn, *Foundations of Mysticism*, 325. Regarding Perovich's concern for science and mysticism, see his article, "Mysticism and the Philosophy of Science," *Journal of Religion* (January 1985): 63–82.

83. McGinn, *Foundations of Mysticism*, 325.

84. Ibid., 343. We might add also the need for dialogue between the scientist and mystic and the sociologist and anthropologist and mystics or investigators in the respective fields. Three such are (1) R. Jones, *Science and Mysticism* (Lewisburg, Pa.: Bucknell University Press, 1986); (2) J. Pandian, *Culture, Reli-*

gion and the Sacred Self (Englewood Cliffs, N.J.: Prentice Hall, 1991); and (3) C. Batson and W. L. Ventis, *The Religious Experience, A Social-Psychological Perspective* (New York: Oxford University Press, 1982).

85. Note, for example, the diversity of courses offered by philosophy departments such as Philosophy and the Environment, Business Ethics, Philosophy and War and Peace, Philosophy and Contemporary Social Problems, etc.

86. See H. Smith's remarks on p. xv of Schuon's *The Transcendent Unity of Religions.*

2

Plotinus and Greek Mysticism

RUTH MAJERCIK

The mystical philosophy of Plotinus represents the final flower of the Greek philosophical tradition. Although modern scholars identify this development as Neoplatonism, Plotinus regarded himself simply as a Platonist, that is, one who expounds and interprets the doctrines of Plato. In particular, Plotinus was drawn to the religious aspects of Plato's teachings, especially Plato's doctrines concerning the immortality and ascent of the soul, the suprasensible world of intelligible Forms, the One, the Good. In this regard, it has often been noted that Plotinus, although living during one of the most turbulent periods of the Roman empire, virtually ignores the political and social teachings of Plato. For Plotinus, the Good was not to be found in the vicissitudes of the world but in withdrawal from society, in contemplation, and in the solitary perfection of the soul.

This emphasis on contemplation and mystical insight is a central feature of Plotinus's philosophy. For Plotinus, it is not enough merely to know about the One, it is necessary to experience the One at the apex of the soul's ascent. It has sometimes been argued that this mystical strain in Plotinus's teaching must have been borrowed from the East, especially India, as mysticism is not properly a part of the Greek rationalist tradition.[1] Although this view still has its adherents, Plotinus's thinking, as a whole, can be best regarded as a logical outgrowth of various tendencies within the Greek philosophical tradition itself.[2] A brief survey of these tendencies will underscore this point.

The Platonic Tradition in Greek Philosophy

The Platonic tradition in Greek philosophy is characterized by a strong religious strain, beginning with Plato himself.[3]

Plato's thinking is based on a dualistic understanding of the universe: this world, the sensible material world, is only a dim reflection of the true world, the transcendent world of intelligible Forms or Ideas which exists outside and beyond this world. In Plato's writings, the words for Form *(eidos)* and Idea *(idea)* are used synonymously and convey the notion of "pattern," "type," or "kind." As such, the Forms constitute the archetypal models or patterns—the ideal types—on which all specific things in this world depend and in which all things participate. Plato, however, is vague and imprecise when he attempts to explain the exact relation between the Forms and sensible objects. Although he often uses the expression "participation" to describe this relation, he never then elaborates on what this term means. Instead, he often resorts to myth to "explain the unexplainable." This he does in the *Timaeus*, where the creation of the universe is described as the handiwork of a mythic Demiurge or Craftsman. The Demiurge, explains Plato, creates because he is good, and being good, desires that all things be as much like him as possible. To this end, he takes all the preexisting material "stuff" in the universe and shapes and forms it on the model of the Ideas as a good act. In this account, the world of Forms is not something that is initially "thought" by the Demiurge (as a human craftsman might first "think" or conceive a project), but the Forms are simply there as a kind of eternal blueprint for the Demiurge to use in his capacity as creator.

Now among the Forms, the Good is represented as the Supreme Reality, the Form from which all the other Forms derive their being and existence. It is described by Plato as the "source of truth and reason," "the most blessed part of being," "the universal author of all things right and beautiful."[4] It is toward the Good, says Plato, that all created beings intuitively aspire. We all desire, at some level (consciously or not) to "know" the Good. Although this kind of language has obvious religious overtones, the Good is neither a personal God nor a creator. (This is true of the Demiurge as well, whose function as "creator" actually reflects the operation of the principle of reason in the world.) Nonetheless, the Good does function for Plato as an absolute principle of existence and thus has true ontological status. Plato also speaks of the One as an ultimate principle, a concept borrowed from Pythagorean speculation and which Plato equates, in some sense, with the Good. Toward the end of his life, Plato was apparently drawn to the possibility of conceptualizing the Forms as Ideal numbers, a process that would be carried out in more detail by his immediate successors. A third principle is Beauty, the ultimate Form of all beautiful things. In the *Symposium,* the priestess, Diotima, describes the ascent to Beauty as a kind of spiritual discipline. Under the impulse of Eros, elevated here to the status of a cosmic force, one first contemplates beautiful objects, then moves on to moral beauty, then to the beauty of knowledge, and finally contemplates Beauty itself. A similar process of ascent is described in the *Republic* but in connection with "knowing" the Good. In his famous Allegory of the Cave, Plato represents the ascent to the Good as a movement away from the shadowy world of images within the cave toward the intelligible world of sun-illumined Forms outside. This is conceived as a dialectical ascent through various mental states, from opinion *(doxa)* and belief *(pistis)* through discursive thought *(dianoia)* to pure thought or *noesis.* In this last stage, the Good itself (represented by the Sun) is directly perceived. In his *Seventh Letter,* Plato describes this ultimate state of knowing as beyond language: it happens "suddenly, like light kindled by a leaping spark." It is a kind of inner illumination or intuitive insight achieved after much labor and mental toil.

Despite statements of this kind, Plato cannot with confidence be called a mystic. What is missing from his writings is any sense of ecstatic union with the Supreme—the merging of the individual soul with the Absolute—or that kind of experience so vividly described by Plotinus. Nevertheless, Plato's religious teaching as a whole would have far-reaching effects on subsequent thinkers, although his immediate successors in the Academy moved in another direction—toward a concern with the sensible, the material, the scientific. The Old Academy associated with Speussippus and Xenocrates focused principally on mathematics and astronomy; the New Academy of Arcesilaus and Carneades was dominated by a philosophical skepticism. It is not until the first century B.C. that the Academy shifts back to Plato's philosophical dogmatism, but now with a strong eclectic element. By this time, a philosophical eclecticism had pervaded all the schools (except that of the Epicureans), although doctrinal differences, even antagonisms, continued. In the Academy, elements of Aristotelianism and Stoicism, combined with a renewed interest in Plato's spiritual doctrines, led to that development in the Platonic tradition known as Middle Platonism. A further influence on this development was the revived Pythagoreanism of the first century B.C. later known as Neopythagoreanism. The individuals associated with this movement were sometimes wandering ascetics and miracle workers like Apollonius of Tyana (fl. late first century A.D.), other times, more traditional philosophers such as Moderatus of Gades (ca. A.D. 50–100) and Nichomacus of Gerasa (ca. A.D. 50–150). At times, the distinction between Middle Platonism and Neopythagoreanism was so fluid that certain philosophers, notably Numenius of Apamea (fl. second century A.D.), were sometimes referred to by contemporaries as Pythagoreans, other times as Platonists. In any event, it is this eclectic Middle Platonism, dating from the first century B.C. to the early third century A.D., that forms the immediate background of Plotinus's thinking.

In general terms, Middle Platonism can be characterized by several important developments.[5] First of all, there is a tendency to elevate the Supreme to a position of extreme transcendence. This teaching was motivated, in part, by reflections on Aristotle's First Principle—the Unmoved Mover—conceived by Aristotle as a self-contemplating Divine Mind that is completely removed from any direct contact with the material universe. In the Middle Platonic reformulation of this doctrine, this Supreme Mind becomes identified with Plato's Good and the Neopythagorean One. A further development involved identifying the "thoughts" of this Divine Mind with Plato's Ideas, thus making the Ideas the "thoughts" of God Himself (a step not taken by Plato). As a First Principle, this Divine Mind is also understood as a self-contemplating entity: it is not actively engaged in shaping or forming matter. This task is properly that of the Second Principle, the active or "demiurgic" Mind. A Third Principle is the Platonic World Soul, the animating force of the visible universe. It is Soul which effectively bridges the gap between the divine and sensible realms. (A "lower" aspect of Soul is sometimes equated with Nature.) At the lowest level of this chain of realities is prime matter, viewed by many Middle Platonic thinkers as a principle of "darkness" or "evil" in some sense. For thinkers like Plutarch and Numenius, an "evil" world soul is also suggested, but this more radical dualism is the exception rather than the rule. Lesser entities and beings (e.g., star gods, angels, demons) also help fill up the spaces between the higher and lower worlds, a multiplying effect that becomes the most exaggerated in what John Dillon aptly terms the "Platonic underworld," or that class of quasi-philosophical, quasi-religious phenomena represented by Gnosticism, Hermeticism, and the *Chaldean Oracles*.[6] Among the Gnostics, the gulf between God and the world becomes so vast that in some systems (especially varieties of Valentinianism) creation itself becomes the evil work of an evil Demiurge who creates in defiance (or ignorance) of the High God above. This extreme anticosmic position was vehemently opposed by Plotinus, who wrote a long treatise against the Gnostics.[7] Similar attacks were made by various Christian writers, who condemned the Gnostics as heretics. Despite attacks and criticisms of this type, Gnosticism exerted a powerful appeal on many, especially during its heyday in the second century. A principal doctrine emphasized salvation for the "elect" through revelatory "gnosis" or knowledge imparted by a divine revealer figure. This "gnosis" involved awakening the "sleeping" soul to full awareness of its divine origin and destiny accompanied by instructions on how best to escape the fetters of material existence. This might include a life of ascetic denial coupled with various sacramental, ritual, and magical practices. Techniques of contemplative ascent were also practiced by certain Gnostics, culminating in an ecstatic vision of God or an experience of deification. Techniques of this type are also found in the Hermetic literature as well as the *Chaldean Oracles* and are close in many respects to the type of mystical experience found in Plotinus's writings.

A mystical strain is also apparent in the school tradition of Middle Platonism, most notably in the figure of Philo of Alexandria, the first century B.C. Hellenistic-Jewish philosopher. Philo is unique in that he attempted to combine Jewish ideas about God with Middle Platonic speculation and, in doing so, is the first philosopher we know of to describe God as "ineffable" and "unnameable" and, thus, as essentially unknowable.[8] Despite this kind of speculation, Philo remained a devout Jew, attempting to harmonize the Hebrew Bible with Greek philosophy by utilizing a thoroughgoing method of allegorical interpretation. Importantly, Philo's philosophy includes a strong mystical element. He speaks of the soul's ascent as a process of inward contemplation "in solitude and darkness" that culminates in the direct vision of the Uncreated or Divine Unity.[9] This final state is one of mystical ecstasy, which Philo likens to the experiences of the Hebrew prophets. Like the prophet possessed by the divine Spirit, so the mystic in ecstasy is filled with the light of God.[10] Because of his Jewish background, Philo is ambiguous about claiming deification or even union with God for the illumined soul, but his description of the mystic vision, in many ways, anticipates the experience of Plotinus.[11]

However, evidence of direct influence on Plotinus is weak. This is also the case with other Middle Platonists, although a number of them, including Numenius, were read in Plotinus's school. Indeed, Plotinus was even accused by his detractors of plagiarizing his philosophy from Numenius.[12] But this is exaggeration although the influence of Middle Platonic speculation in general is obvious in a good deal of Plotinus's thinking.[13] What needs to be stressed, however, is that Middle Platonism remained a "middle" or transitional phase in the history of Platonism. Plotinus built on this tradition and, in doing so, created something quite different, that development we identify as "new" or Neoplatonism.

Plotinus: Life

The factual information we have about Plotinus's life comes principally from his student, Porphyry.[14] Porphyry, however, reveals nothing about Plotinus's family, birthplace, or early life, noting that Plotinus "seemed ashamed of being in a body" and was thus reluctant to reveal information of this kind about himself.[15] From other sources, however, we learn that Plotinus was born in Lycopolis in Upper Egypt, probably around A.D. 204.[16] But this information cannot be verified. Whatever his origins, it is clear from his writings that Plotinus was thoroughly educated in Greek culture and language, although we know nothing about his formative years. Porphyry does tell us, however, that the crucial moment in Plotinus's intellectual development occurred in his late twenties when he attended the lectures of a certain Ammonius Saccas in Alexandria. So impressed was Plotinus with Ammonius's teaching that he ceased attending the lectures of other philosophers in the city and proceeded to study solely with Ammonius for the next eleven years.[17] Unfortunately, we know next to nothing about Ammonius's teaching. He may have been brought up as a Christian and then have abandoned Christianity in favor of philosophy. One of his pupils may have been Origen, the Platonizing Christian theologian of the third century A.D.[18] Beyond these bits of information, our knowledge of Ammonius's teaching and the extent to which it influenced Plotinus's thinking can only be conjectured, as primary evidence is simply lacking. Ammonius, himself, apparently wrote nothing.

In A.D. 243, Plotinus left Ammonius Saccas to join the military expedition of Gordian III against the Persians. Plotinus evidently did not enlist in the army as a regular soldier but simply accompanied the troops with the purpose of making contact with learned men in the East. But this desire was never realized. Gordian was assassinated a year later in Mesopotamia, and Plotinus was forced to make an escape.[19] Eventually he made his way to Rome where he remained almost to the end of his life, gathering about him a close circle of friends and admirers, including a number of women. It was in the home of a wealthy widow that Plotinus actually lived and taught, not only giving instruction to his pupils, but also caring for orphaned children who had been willed to his custody by prominent individuals. Porphyry gives us a charming picture of Plotinus, patiently attending to the various needs of his extended family while, at the same time, continuously engaged in contemplation.[20]

As a teacher, Plotinus's style was to engage in discussion and debate on specific problems and issues. This conversational style of teaching, on one occasion, elicited criticism from a certain Thaumasius, who had become quite annoyed at Porphyry's persistent questioning of Plotinus about the nature of the soul. Thaumasius wanted Plotinus to speak in a traditional lecture style, in the manner of a "set treatise." Plotinus responded by stating that if Porphyry's difficulties with the subject were not resolved, "what then would go into the treatise?"[21] Despite his preference for oral instruction, Plotinus was eventually persuaded by his pupils to put his thoughts into writing. It is these writings, composed over a period of fifteen years toward the end of his life, that Porphyry later edited as the *Enneads (Nines)* by arranging this material into six books of nine treatises each.

Plotinus, at one point, also came under the patronage of the Emperor Gallienus (A.D. 260–268), whom he apparently persuaded to establish a city of philosophers ("Platonopolis") in Campania. This was envisioned as a "model city" where the citizens would be governed by the principles set down in Plato's *Laws.* This dream, however, was never realized, put to an end by court politics and intrigue.[22]

Plotinus's life comes to an end in A.D. 270 following a painful illness. His condition was such that he was forced to leave Rome and retire to a friend's estate, where only his doctor was present at the time of death. To him, Plotinus is reported as saying at the moment of death: "Try to bring back the god in you to the Divine in the universe."[23]

What is important to note about Plotinus's life is that although he continued to function in society in a useful way as teacher, friend, and advisor, nevertheless his main concern was with the life of the soul and how one can disentangle himself or herself from the demands of the everyday world and live peacefully at the level of intelligible existence. Although, as mentioned above, Plotinus lived during one of the most turbulent periods of the Empire, significantly, there is no mention in his writings of the political, social, and economic turmoil that was going on all around him. Plotinus's response to this period of unrest was one of withdrawal, epitomized by his desire to establish the city of Platonopolis as a philosopher's retreat from all these worldly concerns.

Metaphysics

To fully appreciate Plotinus's mysticism, it is first necessary to have some idea of his metaphysical system. As will shortly become apparent, Plotinus's system clearly reflects the tendencies and concerns of his intellectual predecessors but with significant innovations. Plotinus's First Principle is the One, described by Plotinus with a series of negations. Nothing positive can be ascribed to it because it is beyond any term or expression that would limit it in any way.[24] Thus, for Plotinus, unlike the Middle Platonists, the One is something not only beyond Mind or Intellect but even beyond Being.[25] The most that can be said about the One is what it is not ("negative theology"), not what it is. Since the One is perfect unity or unity-in-itself, to predicate being, existence, life or other qualities to the One is to introduce an element of duality and thus to compromise its intrinsic unity.[26] The One cannot be other than one: it is one absolutely.

But with this said, Plotinus, by using the term One to describe his First Principle, is affirming something about it. However, he is quick to state that the expression One should be understood only as a negation of plurality, as meaning "not many."[27] The other term Plotinus uses in a positive sense to describe the One is Good, but this term, like One, has to be understood not in any qualitative sense but only as describing the One's function as the supreme object of desire toward which all lesser entities aspire.[28] Simply put, the One is Good for others, it is not Good itself.[29] The One as Good, then, is not to be understood in the traditional Platonic sense—it is neither Form nor Idea—but something other than or beyond such categories. It is a "Beyond-Good" as well as a "Beyond-Beauty."[30] In the final analysis, the true nature of the One can only be revealed in mystical union, it can never be known through philosophical speculation alone.[31]

From the One a Second Principle or hypostasis eternally emanates or "flows forth." This is Nous or the Divine Mind, the principle of intelligibility. This process of emanation is not only eternal (it does not occur in time), it is also automatic, in that the production of Nous occurs without any will, intent, or even movement on the part of the One.[32] It is simply the involuntary overflow of the One's perfection.[33] In this regard, Plotinus often makes an analogy with the sun: As the sun continues to generate heat and light without any diminution of its energy, so the One continuously generates Nous without in any way diminishing itself.[34] The One, then, is in no sense a personal, loving creator (Plotinus rarely calls it God);[35] rather, it is an impersonal Absolute that creates without knowledge of its creation, indeed, without even knowledge of itself, as the One transcends all distinctions of subject and object.[36] The most that can be said, then, is that the process of emanation from the One is something that must happen, and having happened, has happened in the best and only possible way.[37]

Beneath the One, then, exists Nous, the outflow of the One. However, Nous only becomes a fully constituted hypostasis when it "turns back" and contemplates the One. By "turning back," Nous achieves its own state of stability and perfection.[38] This double rhythm of procession and return is a key feature of Plotinus's system, evidently developed under Stoic influence.[39] The result is that Plotinus infuses the static, hierarchical world of Middle Platonic speculation with a dynamic aliveness—the going forth and return is a constant process that occurs eternally at every level of reality.

This procession from the One is also a movement away from simplicity and unity toward greater and greater degrees of multiplicity. This first occurs at the level of Nous which, as Divine Mind, contains the Forms or the Ideas. As such, Nous is less perfect than the One and can thus be regarded as a principle of unity-in-multiplicity.[40] In addition, the activity of Nous consists not only of contemplating the One but of intuitively apprehending itself, all at once, as Mind.[41] As such, Nous can be regarded as a self-contemplating entity akin to the First Principle of Middle Platonic speculation.

From Nous, the third and last hypostasis, emanates the World Soul. Like Nous, Soul is fully constituted only when it turns back and contemplates the principle above it. In this case, Soul turns back and contemplates Nous and is thus perfected.[42] Now the World Soul is the link between the intelligible world and the sphere of material existence. As such, the World Soul looks both upward toward Nous and downward toward the world of Nature. In doing so, it "splits" into a higher and lower part.[43] The function of the higher part or phase of Soul is to contemplate the Ideas of Nous, but unlike Nous, the World Soul does not contemplate the Ideas directly in a single moment of intuitive insight, but contemplates only reflections of these Ideas, and contemplates these reflections one by one.[44] In other words, at the level of Soul, multiplicity becomes the dominant factor. Soul, then, is a principle of unity-and-multiplicity.[45]

The higher World Soul is also that aspect of Soul which rules over and orders the universe. As such, it eternally remains above and removed from Nature.[46] In contrast, the lower phase of Soul functions like the World Soul of Plato's *Timaeus*: it is the animating force that pervades or "ensouls" all of created existence and which Plotinus identifies with Nature itself.[47] It is from this lower Soul that matter emanates. Plotinus describes this primal "stuff" as utter darkness and void: it is "absolute evil."[48] However, unlike Numenius and some of the Gnostic dualists, Plotinus does not regard primal matter as an independent, aggressive force which engulfs or "traps" a part of the Divine. Rather, he sees matter as the lowest degree of reality; it is the final outflow of the One and thus is evil only in a negative sense. It is that which is without Being, form and order.[49] Thus, although matter itself can be called absolute evil, the created or formed world is always good as it participates, however dimly, in the intelligible world of Forms above.[50]

It is from the lower World Soul that individual souls originate. Now Plotinus is not always clear as to why souls incarnate at all. At times he suggests that they do so because of an inexorable divine law;[51] at other times, it is because of a willful "boldness" *(tolma)*.[52] In either case, the higher or rational soul never descends; it always remains above in the intelligible order, united in contemplation with Nous.[53] It is the lower, irrational soul that becomes embodied, and it is this part of the soul, along with the material "vestiges" it accrues in its descent through

the heavenly spheres, that is subjected to the passions and de-
filements of material existence.[54] Thus, the goal of the wise man
is to detach himself as much as possible from the distractions
of the material world—to "cut away everything"[55] with the hope
of mystically ascending to the One. This is the proper goal and
end for humankind: a life of contemplative retreat from the
world.

Mysticism

The mystical ascent of the soul, although a difficult and arduous process, was nevertheless believed by Plotinus to be potentially possible for everyone. Because all humans have something
of the divine within their souls, one need only recognize this
fact, turn away from the distractions of the senses, and begin
preparation for the journey.[56] But with this said, Plotinus quali-
fies his remarks by noting that few persons will, in fact, attempt
this journey, since the ascent involves a lengthy period of preparation, purification, and various mental disciplines. Hence,
those most qualified or naturally disposed to the contemplative
life are philosophers, who are already trained in the life of the
mind.[57] Two other types of individuals are also likely to make
the ascent, at least to the level of Nous or the world of Forms.
These are the musician and "born lover": the musician, because
he is easily moved by beautiful sounds and harmonies and thus
has the potential of contemplating Beauty itself; the "born
lover" because he admires beautiful objects and can similarly
be trained to direct his inner eye toward the abstract reality of
Beauty in its essential nature.[58] The influence of the *Symposium*
is obvious here. But Plotinus goes beyond Plato by not only
making the vision or contemplation of the One the final goal
but actual union with the One as the desideratum. This step
was not taken by Plato, for whom "likeness to God" always
implied separation; for Plotinus, it meant surrender, union, the
merging of the soul with the One. This kind of language is based
on Plotinus's belief that the One (as well as Nous and Soul) is
both transcendent and immanent, that the ontological order
"out there" is perfectly mirrored within the soul of each person.[59] Plotinus's recognition of the psychological reality of his
metaphysical principles—that the One above is also within, as
are Nous and Soul—is a striking insight. He is the first Greek
philosopher to make this identity and, in doing so, ensures that

his metaphysical speculation is securely grounded in mystical experience.[60] Thus, the ascent upward toward the One is at the same time a turning inward, an awakening of our inner selves, a movement toward the center of the soul where the One is also to be found. This does not then mean that Plotinus was a pantheist; he did not believe that God and the world were identical, that the One was All, as did the Stoics. Rather, Plotinus believed that the One existed outside the world but at the same time was also present with the world as its ultimate source and power.[61] Hence, the ascent toward the One was both a movement outward beyond the Self as well as a movement inward toward the Self. It was also a movement away from multiplicity (characteristic of the world) toward greater and greater degrees of simplicity (characteristic of the One), repeating here in reverse the ontological procession from the One.

The beginnings of this journey first involve the practice of various virtues, specifically the "civic virtues" of prudence, courage, temperance, and justice. The practice of these virtues is a form of purification, a way of disengaging the soul from worldly things, of cleansing it from the irrational impurities of corporeal existence. Temperance, for example, means abstaining from the pleasures of the flesh; courage accustoms the soul to be unafraid of death; prudence turns the soul away from earthly pursuits and draws it upward. But this is only the beginning. The desired state of "perfect purity" can only be achieved when the individual no longer patterns his or her actions after the actions of virtuous individuals but rises to the level of the gods and patterns his or her life after the divine. In other words, it is not enough to limit the practice of temperance, for example, to just control of pleasure, but to go one step further and, to the extent possible, to live in actual "isolation" or emotional detachment from the body, i.e., as a passionless, godlike being.[62] This state of detachment or isolation is a higher virtue, but one that cannot be achieved without first mastering the lower virtue. This progression from lower to higher applies to all the virtues, and Plotinus is critical of those who are not able to take the necessary steps.[63] However, once the higher values are achieved and sustained, the soul is cleansed, like gold purged of its dross, and it now can exist at the level of pure reason, as everything "alien" or material has been "cut" or "stripped away." At this point, the individual has completely withdrawn into himself, nothing outside can affect him, and he is now able

to move upward or ascend within the realm of intelligible
being.[64]

The first step at this higher level is preparation in philosophy,
especially the art or skill of dialectic. For Plotinus, dialectic is
the most valuable part of philosophy, as it alone "knows the
truth."[65] With this training, for which the philosopher is especially prepared, the soul is able to make progress within the
realm of Ideas. But even the philosopher must first be skilled in
the lesser disciplines, especially mathematics, which first accustoms the mind to think abstractly and to have "faith" in the
incorporeal.[66] Once this is satisfactorily accomplished, then the
individual can move on to the practice of dialectic. This is apparently a lifelong process, as the ultimate goal of this arduous
discipline is the mystic vision itself.[67]

Within the intelligible order, the ascent proceeds in stages.
The lowest level is within the realm of Soul, to which the individual soul is naturally attracted because of its innate kinship.
By ascending to the World Soul, the individual soul is, in fact,
awakening the Soul of All within itself. At this level, aided by
dialectic, the intelligible Ideas are contemplated one by one in
their simplicity and purity.[68] But the soul does not remain here.
Firmly rooted in the intelligible order it now moves toward Divine Intelligence itself. Here, the Ideas are contemplated in their
unity, and the perception is one of overarching Beauty as the
true essence and being of the Ideas as a whole.[69] Indeed, the soul
not only contemplates the Beauty of Mind or Nous, it itself
becomes Beautiful. It becomes a Form, the Form of Beauty, as
well as the Form of Being. At this point, the soul recognizes and
unites with the whole intelligible order.[70]

Plotinus is also careful to distinguish here between Beauty
and the Good. Beauty, like Being, is characteristic of the intelligible order as a whole, but the Good lies beyond Beauty as
its source and principle.[71] The Good is "gentle," "friendly,"
"tender," whereas Beauty, or specifically the desire for Beauty,
is characterized by pain as well as pleasure. This desire stirs up
the passions and thus has an element of violence; the Good, on
the other hand, is always present and thus is always calmly
possessed.[72] The Good, then, is primary; Beauty, secondary, and
beyond both lies the One. Thus the ascent to Nous or Divine
Intelligence is the penultimate goal; the final step is the ascent
to the One itself.

Plotinus's description of this final stage is a bit curious. He
states that the One simply "appears" once the ascending soul

is firmly established at the summit of Nous. The soul awaits the vision "as the eye awaits the rising sun."[73] The vision cannot be forced; certainly we must be prepared for it, but this is a state of passive readiness, not one of active pursuit. It has sometimes been argued that the arrival of the One involves a kind of "grace"—that there is a turning of the One toward the waiting soul.[74] But this is not the case, as the One is always present with the soul; consequently, the "turning" is in actuality the soul's own profound awareness and recognition of that which it already possesses.[75] Stripped of all multiplicity, of everything "alien," the soul, utterly pure, utterly simple, recognizes its ontological ground. On this point, Plotinus stresses that it is not simply the soul that recognizes the One, but "that in *nous* which is not *nous*," the highest part of the soul or that which is most akin to the One.[76] It is this highest part of the soul that ultimately merges and unites with the One.

When Plotinus talks about this final stage of union, he often uses metaphors of both "sight" and "touch." He speaks of the "vision" of the One, the "light" of the Supreme, a "seeing" or contemplation with the "eyes of the soul."[77] This language still implies a separation between the seeker and his object. Plotinus, unlike Plato, is not content to rest here; what he desires is actual union, a state where the soul and the One "are no longer two, but both are one."[78] It is in this context that Plotinus often uses metaphors of "touch" and "contact." He speaks of a "going forth from the Self," a "reach toward contact," the "moment of touch."[79] This movement toward the One is also described by Plotinus as a kind of love or *eros*. In *Enneads*, VI.7.35, Plotinus actually distinguishes between two kinds of love: the first he characterizes as "Intellect knowing"; the second as "Intellect loving." The first kind of love occurs at the level of Nous, when the soul intellectively knows itself as Mind. The second kind of love occurs when the soul as unified Mind passes beyond intellection and becomes "intoxicated" or "drunk." It is in this state that the soul becomes entirely happy, entirely simple, as there is no longer any element of multiplicity or "otherness" to mar its approach to the One. But this "divine drunkenness" is not a state of frenzied ecstasy, like a moment of Bacchic madness, but one of calm intensity, more a rational than emotional ecstasy, provided we do not understand the word rational here as having intellective content.[80] It is that moment of the ascent when the soul is completely and totally itself and, as such, is completely and totally one, and thus is able to be "oned," merged, or united with that One, which is both without and deep within.[81]

Thus this final moment of ascent is one of enraptured union, and Plotinus is not loathe to use images of physical intimacy when describing this state: "It is as lover and beloved here, in a copy of that union, long to blend."[82] As such, it is a state of self-surrender and abandon, when the two are one to such a degree that subject and object, lover and beloved, can no longer be distinguished. In Plotinus's words:

> He is merged with the Supreme, sunken into it, one with it. Center coincides with center, for center of circles, even here below, are one when they unite. . . . This is why the vision baffles telling; we cannot detach the Supreme to state it . . . [it is] to be known only as one with ourselves. . . . This is the life of gods and of the godlike and blessed among men . . . a life taking no pleasure in the things of the earth, the passing of the alone to the Alone.[83]

In the final analysis, then, this mystical union at the highest level of ascent cannot be described, cannot be talked about. It is a pure experience of "undifferentiated unity,"[84] which can only be known in the experience itself and not in the telling of it. In other words, in the same way that the One itself cannot be described, we can only say what it is not, so the ascent to the One becomes an ineffable or inexpressible experience.

Finally, this ultimate state is also described by Plotinus as one of complete calm or rest. It is a "perfect stillness," a "repose," when the soul no longer looks here nor there—not even within—as "filled with God" it has become "rest" itself.[85] This then is the culmination of the mystical ascent: the soul is rapturously one with the Supreme, it is perfectly still, at rest, fully realized as divine. What needs to be stressed, however, is that this merging, blending, or union with the One is not a state of absolute identity; although the soul is "oned," it is not the One. There is still a distinction. It would be more accurate to say that the soul is "present with" the One—as the One is "present with" the world—rather than it is the One. The latter is a position Plotinus is careful to avoid.[86]

This union with the One is also a temporary state. In time it fades and must be experienced again and again. Porphyry tells us that Plotinus experienced this state four times when he was associated with him. Porphyry claims that he himself experienced it once.[87] Thus, as noted above, the ascent is a difficult and arduous undertaking; there are no shortcuts; one must proceed slowly, step by step, until everything extraneous, both physical and mental, is cut away. This is the only way. Indeed, although Nous or Mind is abandoned in the final union with the One, nevertheless it is only through Nous or Mind that the One can be found. The way to the One is always through Nous, as the path to Nous is always through Soul. And the way to Soul is always through the practice of virtue. No step can be missed or bypassed.

It is also important to note that Plotinus eschews all techniques of magic as having any positive effect on the soul's ascent.[88] Such practices are of limited value at the level of the lower or irrational soul but are completely useless in the context of the soul's return to the One. Since the highest part of the soul, the rational part, never descends into matter—it always remains above in the intelligible order—then the ascent upward is properly aided only by various mental and moral disciplines. The ascending soul has no need of ritual or material supports. This applies as well to traditional prayer and sacrifice. Such practices are of value, of course, to the average man, but are of no consequence to the philosopher. The One is not a personal God but an impersonal Absolute and is thus not affected in any way by human entreaties. This applies to Soul and Nous as well.

With this said, two clarifying points must be made. First, Plotinus, at times, does use theistic language when referring to the One, calling the One "Father" and the return to the One a "return to the Fatherland."[89] However, the name "Father" is simply a common expression used by Plato and others for the Supreme principle and thus has no special theistic significance. Similarly, when Plotinus refers to the One as "Love," he is not then limiting or qualifying the One in any sense—the One is always beyond any attempt to define it—but rather is describing the soul's relation to the One when the two are united and "seeker and sought become one."[90] If there is a quasi-personal emphasis here, as certain scholars suggest,[91] it is not because Plotinus is a "theistic" mystic (the One is never worshipped nor does it love or care for its products)[92] but that he felt compelled to use language borrowed from Plato and, perhaps, the Stoics,[93] which, in the final analysis, was inadequate for his purposes.

Second, in terms of prayer, Plotinus acknowledges the ordinary sense of petitionary appeals and verbal utterances directed toward the lower powers,[94] but he acknowledges as well a special kind of prayer directed toward the One. In Plotinus's words, this

kind of prayer is a "leaning in soul towards Him by aspiration
. . . alone toward the Alone."[95] In other words, prayer, at this
level, is nothing more or less than the soul's "leaning," "tending," or "leap" toward the One itself as the final act of the
mystic union. This kind of prayer, then, is obviously not prayer
in the usual sense of the word, but it comes closer to that "ori-
son of union" so well articulated by certain Christian mystics.[96]

Last, it needs to be repeated that Plotinian mysticism has
nothing analogous to a feeling of "grace."[97] The movement toward the One is always the work of the soul, not of the One.
Consequently, there is no sense of sin or need for redemption.
Plotinus, unlike the Christian mystics, has no "dark night of
the soul" experience, with its emphasis on a divided self and
separation from God. Plotinus's mysticism is a mysticism of
light: the One is always present with the soul as its center and
source, and, thus, there is no need for divine intervention. We
need only recognize this fact, turn away from the distractions
of the world, and begin the necessary steps to make the journey
back "home."

As for the destiny of the soul after death, Plotinus believed
in periodic cycles of rebirth, in human and animal form, as an
unavoidable divine law.[98] Apparently no one escaped this law,
including philosophers. Thus achievement of union with the
One in this life did not then guarantee a permanent release from
the cycle of birth in a future life.[99] But such a permanent release
was not a crucial issue for Plotinus. Because Plotinus argued
that the rational part of the soul never descended in the first
place, in some sense, it was already in a state of permanent
deliverance. Thus, a life of "philosophical separation" for the
embodied soul was desired more as way of avoiding punishment
in the next life (the purified soul returned to the intelligible
realm after death, not to Hades), rather than as a means of
achieving permanent escape from the wheel of rebirth. The latter was not a Plotinian concern.

Later Neoplatonism

The Later Neoplatonists,[100] beginning with Porphyry (ca A.D.
232–305), made several innovations in Plotinus's system. At the
metaphysical level, the tendency was toward a more rigid system of hierarchy and classification, with a special emphasis on
the multiplication of triads. Over time, a system developed

wherein each level of reality was considered to undergo a triadic process of "remaining," "procession," and "return." The divine world itself was now further distinguished by descending degrees of intelligible existence (identified with Being), intelligible and intellectual existence (identified with Life), and intellectual existence (identified with Mind). Innovations of this type can be attributed to Iamblichus (ca. A.D. 250–325), the leading figure in the Syrian school of Neoplatonism, and Proclus (ca. A.D. 410–85), the head of the Athenian School (formerly Plato's Academy). Iamblichus also posited a One beyond the One of Plotinus; Proclus is noted for developing a complicated series of henads or "ones" at every level of reality. These abstract entities or "ones" were then equated by Proclus with the various deities of the popular religion.

As for Plotinus's mysticism, only Porphyry, according to his own statement, is reported as having attained union with the One in the manner outlined by Plotinus. And this only once. The fact is that the later Neoplatonists all recognized the difficulties in Plotinus's strictly intellectual ascent and thus turned toward more popular forms of religiosity as a way of universalizing Plotinus's system. This move was prompted in part by the growing strength of Christianity, which not only had a sacramental system in which all Christians could participate and thus be "saved," but it also possessed a sacred book of divine revelation, the Bible. In response, the successors of Plotinus turned to the *Chaldean Oracles*, a collection of abstruse, hexameter verses purportedly "handed down" by the gods (perhaps via mediumistic trance) to a certain Julian the Chaldean and his son, Julian the Theurgist, both of whom lived during the second century A.D. (The *Oracles* were mentioned briefly above in connection with the Platonic "underworld"; see p. 100.) Porphyry is credited with discovering the *Oracles*; he wrote a commentary on them with the purpose of harmonizing their teaching with that of Neoplatonic teaching. Iamblichus and Proclus also wrote commentaries on this "divine book," but unfortunately none of this material is extant (with the exception of a few extracts from Proclus's commentary). The *Oracles* themselves exist only in fragmentary form.[101]

Of particular importance were the theurgic practices advocated in the *Oracles*.[102] The word theurgy can be translated as "divine action" or "divine work," a term generally understood to mean that the theurgist, like the magician, "works" on the gods as a way of controlling their power for his own ends. But theurgy is more than magical manipulation. First of all, theurgy involves a passive relation with the gods. Although the theurgist uses many of the techniques familiar to the magician (incantations, magical instruments, and objects, etc.), he employs these techniques only with the hope that the gods will appear; he does not actively coerce them. Second, the techniques of theurgy, unlike those of magic, are aimed primarily at sacred rather than profane ends. In other words, the magician might perform his acts as a way of affecting the weather or influencing a lover, but the theurgist acts with the intent of purifying and ultimately saving his soul. He can do this with confidence because of a belief in the "sympathetic" relation between the divine and material worlds, i.e., that higher principles, though a series of "sympathies," participate in and illumine even the lowest elements of matter. Thus, by invoking the mysterious, divine substances, or "tokens" *(Synthemata)* in stones, herbs, and other material objects, the theurgist could cause a deity to appear, either through the agency of a medium or by "calling down" the god to his or her consecrated statue. The theurgist would then commune with the deity and, by doing so, experience a form of spiritual purification. Practices of this sort were intended principally to purify the irrational soul and its quasi-material "vehicle." Although Porphyry acceded the value of theurgy at this level of the soul for the average person, he nonetheless continued to maintain that for the philosopher only the disciplined moral and intellectual ascent of Plotinus could effect union with the One. In contrast, Iamblichus and Proclus accepted the efficacy of theurgy at every level of the soul and, consequently, at every level of the divine world, even hinting that union with the One might be possible through theurgic means. But theurgy at this highest level is something quite different than the material practices aimed at purifying the lower soul. This "higher theurgy" is close, in many respects, to the Plotinian mystic union, but a union aided by immaterial theurgic supports (e.g., theurgic "faith," sacred silences, *voces mysticae)* rather than sheer intellection.

Theurgy, then, in the strict sense, is neither mysticism nor magic, but a technique of ascent that incorporates aspects of both while remaining something distinct. In any event, the incorporation of theurgy into Neoplatonic theory and practice did not then produce the universal religion hoped for by its advocates. The Neoplatonism of Plotinus's successors remained an elitist pursuit for only the highly motivated few. The fourth century emperor, Julian "the Apostate" (A.D. 361–63), is the most famous example in this regard. Nevertheless, a school tradition of Neoplatonism continued in Athens until A.D. 529, at which time the school was closed by the Christian emperor, Justinian. The Neoplatonic school in Alexandria was never officially closed but passed into Christian hands under the leadership of John Philoponus (ca. A.D. 490–570). Despite the demise of Neoplatonism as a separate and distinct pagan philosophy, many of its teachings were incorporated into Christianity. In the west, Augustine (A.D. 354–430) is the great continuator of the Neoplatonic tradition. In the East, significant figures are the "Cappadocian Fathers" Gregory of Nazianzus (ca. A.D. 330–90), Basil of Caesarea (ca. A.D. 330–79), and Gregory of Nyssa (ca. A.D. 330–95)—and the pseudonymous Dionysius the Areopagite (fl. ca. A.D. 500). "Pseudo-Dionysius" is of particular importance because his numerous mystical writings, which combined aspects of Proclan Neoplatonism with Christianity, had a profound influence on the development of medieval Christian mysticism. Beyond this period, the influence of Neoplatonism in various guises can be traced up to modern times, finding expression in theology, philosophy, literature, and psychology.[103] To appreciate this influence, one must return to Plotinus, whose *Enneads* ring with the affirmation of a life "turned to God."

Notes

1. On this view, the classical statement is that of Emile Bréhier, *The Philosophy of Plotinus* (Chicago, 1928; rpt. 1958), 106–31. More recently, cf. J. F. Staal, *Advaita and Neoplatonism* (Madras, 1961), 235–49; R. Baine Harris, ed., *Neoplatonism and Indian Thought* (Albany, 1982).

2. In refutation of Bréhier, see A. H. Armstrong, "Plotinus and India," *Classical Quarterly*, 30 (1936), 22–28; rpt. in idem, *Plotinian and Christian Studies* (London, 1979), Section I. See also the essays in *Les Sources de Plotin*, Entretiéns Hardt V (Vandoeuvres-Genève, 1967).

3. Plato's religiosity, especially his reflections on the soul, is attributed to Orphic and Pythagorean influences. See, especially the discussions in the *Phaedo, Phaedrus,* and *Republic.*

4. Plato, *Republic*, VII, 517c; 526e, in *The Collected Dialogues of Plato*, eds., Edith Hamilton and Huntington Cairns (Princeton, 1963).

5. The best current introduction to all aspects of Middle Platonism is that of John Dillon, *The Middle Platonists* (London, 1977).

6. See, Dillon, *The Middle Platonists*, 384–96, for a general discussion of the Platonic "underworld." On all aspects of Gnosticism, see Kurt Rudolph, *Gnosis*, trans. Robert McL. Wilson (New York, 1983); on Hermeticism, see A. J. Festugière, *La Revelation—d'Hermès Trismégiste*, 4 vols. (Paris, 1950–54)

and cf. the recent study of Garth Fowden, *The Egyptian Hermes* (Cambridge, 1986); on the *Chaldean Oracles,* see Hans Lewy, *Chaldean Oracles and Theurgy,* new ed. by M. Tardieu (Paris, 1978).

7. Plotinus, *Enneads,* II.9; supplemented by III.8.30; V.5.32; V.8.31.

8. See, e.g., Philo, *On Dreams* I.67 in *Philo,* Vol. 5, Loeb Classical Library, trans. F. H. Colson and G. H. Whitaker (Cambridge, MA, 1949).

9. See Philo, *On the Migration of Abraham,* chs. 187–95 in *Philo,* Vol. IV, Loeb Classical Library where Philo likens the soul's movement or "migration" away from the senses toward intelligible reality in terms of Abraham's migration from Chaldea and Haran (= land of the senses) to Ur (= realm of intelligible existence).

10. See, e.g., Philo, *Who Is the Heir?* chs. 69; 264–66 in *Philo,* Vol. IV, Loeb Classical Library.

11. On Philo's mysticism in general, see E. R. Goodenough, *By Light, Light: The Mystic Gospel of Hellenistic Judaism* (Amsterdam, 1969). See also Dillon, *The Middle Platonists,* 139–83; Henry Chadwick, "Philo and the Beginnings of Christian Thought," in *The Cambridge History of Later Greek and Early Medieval Thought,* ed. A. H. Armstrong (Cambridge, 1967), 137–57.

12. Porphyry, *Life of Plotinus,* chs. 17–18. See n. 14.

13. On the sources of Neoplatonism, see *Les Sources de Plotin,* cited in n. 2; R. T. Wallis, *Neoplatonism* (London, 1972), 16–36.

14. Porphyry's *Life of Plotinus* can be found in all modern editions and translations of Plotinus's *Enneads.* For the purpose of this essay, the translation of MacKenna-Page (London, 1962) has been used. Direct citations from the *Enneads* in this essay are taken from this translation with some minor variations.

15. Porphyry, *Life,* ch. 1.

16. See, e.g., Eunapius, *Life of the Sophists, ch. 455 in Philostratus and Eunapius: Lives of the Sophists,* Loeb Classical Library, trans. Wilmer C. Wright (Cambridge, 1968).

17. Porphyry, *Life,* ch. 3.

18. Eusebius, *Ecclesiastical History,* 6.19 (quoting Porphyry), trans. G. A. Williamson (Minneapolis, 1975). Ch. 3, states that another Origen, a pagan philosopher, was also a pupil of Ammonius Saccas.

19. Porphyry, *Life,* ch. 3.

10. Ibid., chs. 8 and 9.

21. Ibid., ch. 13.

22. Ibid., ch. 12.

23. Ibid., ch. 2.

24. Plotinus, *Enneads,* V.3.13–14; VI.8.11, 13; VI.9.6. For further discussion on the negation of the One, see A. H. Armstrong, *The Architecture of the Intelligible Universe in the Philosophy of Plotinus* (Cambridge, 1940), 14–28.

25. Plotinus, *Enneads,* V.1.10; V.5.6; VI.7.38.

26. Ibid., III.8.10–11; V.5.4,11; VI.9.2–3, 6.

27. Ibid., V.5.6.

28. Ibid., I.7.1; I.8.2; V.5.9.

29. Ibid., VI.7.24, 41; VI.9.6. For further discussion on positive terms applied to the One, see Armstrong, *Architecture,* 1–13.

30. Plotinus, *Enneads,* VI.7.32–33; VI.9.6; cf. II.9.1; V.5.6, 10, 13.

31. Ibid., VI.8.19; VI.9.4, 10–11.

32. Ibid., V.1.6; V.4.1.

33. Ibid., V.2.1.

34. Ibid., I.7.1; V.1.6–7; V.3.12.

35. See Plotinus, *Enneads*, VI.9.6, where Plotinus states that to think of the One as God is to "think meanly" as the One is "more authentically one than God." Cf. J. Katz, *Plotinus's Search for the Good* (New York, 1950), 26.

36. Plotinus, *Enneads*, V.5.12; VI.7.37–41; VI.8.16.

37. Ibid., VI.7.1; cf. VI.8–10.

38. Ibid., V.3.11; V.4.2.

39. See Armstrong, *Architecture*, 52–58, for a discussion of the Stoic influences on Plotinus's theory of emanation.

40. Plotinus, *Enneads*, V.9.6, 8; VI.6.7; VI.7.14, 17.

41. Ibid., VI.7.35.

42. Ibid., V.1.3.

43. Ibid., IV.1.1; V.1.3; V.2.1; V.3.9.

44. Ibid., III.8.5; V.1.4.

45. Ibid., IV.2.2; IV.3.8.

46. Ibid., III.9.3; IV.8.2,7–8.

47. Ibid., III.8.4; IV.4.13; V.1.2; V.2.1.

48. Ibid., I.8.3–4,8; III.4.16; III.6.11.

49. Ibid., I.8.7; II.5.5; III.6.14.

50. This point is especially emphasized in Plotinus's treatise *Against the Gnostics*, *Enneads*, II.9 passim.

51. Ibid., IV.3.13; IV.8.5.

52. Ibid., V.1.1; cf. III.9.3; IV.3. The confusion between these two positions derives from an attempt to reconcile similar views in Plato's *Phaedrus* and *Timaeus*. Cf. Plotinus, *Enneads* IV.8.5 and Wallis, *Neoplatonism*, 77–78.

53. Plotinus, *Enneads*, IV.3.12; IV.8.4,8.

54. Ibid., IV.3.15, 17, 23. For further discussion on the "material vestiges" of the soul, see J. M. Rist, *Plotinus: The Road to Reality* (Cambridge, 1977), 188–98.

55. Plotinus, *Enneads*, V.3.17.

56. Ibid., I.6.5–9.

57. Ibid., I.3.3; V.9.2.

58. Ibid., I.3.1–2.

59. Ibid., VI.5.12; VI.8.18; cf. R. Arnou, *Le Désir de Dieu dans la Philosophie de Plotin* (Paris, 1921), 162–81.

60. See Wallis, *Neoplatonism*, 4–5; cf. Arnou, *Le Désir de Dieu*, 265–71.

61. Plotinus, *Enneads*, VI.9.7–8.

62. Ibid., I.2.1–6.

63. Ibid., I.2.7; I.3.6.

64. Ibid., I.6.7–9; cf. Arnou, *Le Désir de Dieu*, 191–202; J. Trouillard, *La Purification Plotinienne* (Paris, 1955), 187–203.

65. Plotinus, *Enneads*, I.3.4–6; cf. Trouillard, *La Purification*, 163–66.

66. Plotinus, *Enneads*, I.3.3.

67. Ibid., I.3.4.

68. Ibid., I.6.9; V.1.3–4, 10–12.

69. Ibid., I.6.6,9; VI.7.31–32.

70. Ibid., VI.5.7,12.

71. Ibid., I.8.2.

72. Ibid., V.5.12.

73. Ibid., V.5.8; cf. V.3.17; V.5.3,7; VI.7.34. In Hamilton and Cairns, *Col-*

lected Dialogues. The image of the sudden appearance of the One is based on Plato, *Symposium* 210e; *Epistle* VII, 341c–d.

74. See, e.g., P. Aubin, "L'Image dans l'Oeuvre de Plotin," *Recherches de Science Religieuse,* 41 (1953), 376. J. M. Rist, "Mysticism and Transcendence in Later Neoplatonism," *Hermes* 92 (1964), 215, suggests that "some kind of superadded grace" is necessary for union with the One: . . . there is an element in the procedure that is outside the control of even the noblest philosopher."

75. Plotinus, *Enneads,* VI.9.7–8. Cf. A. H. Armstrong, "Plotinus," in *The Cambridge History,* 261; P. Henry, "The Place of Plotinus in the History of Thought," Introduction to MacKenna-Page's edition of the *Enneads* (1962), lxix. Both scholars emphasize that the idea of grace, especially in a Christian sense, is foreign to Plotinus's thinking. Cf. also Arnou, *Le Désir de Dieu,* 225–27; Trouillard, *La Purification,* 122–32.

76. Plotinus, *Enneads,* V.5.8; cf. III.8.1; V.3.14; VI.7.35; VI.9.8

77. Cf., e.g., Plotinus, *Enneads,* I.6.7–9; V.3.17; VI.9.10.

78. Ibid., VI.7.34.

79. Ibid., VI.9.7–9, 11.

80. Cf. Ibid., VI.7.22; VI.9.7; J. M. Rist, *Eros and Psyche* (Toronto, 1964), 95–103; Trouillard, *La Purification,* 154–62.

81. Plotinus, *Enneads,* VI.8.18.

82. Ibid., VI.7.34.

83. Ibid., VI.9.10–11. W. T. Stace identifies this experience as an example of "introvertive mysticism." See *Mysticism and Philosophy* (Philadelphia and New York, 1960), 104–5.

84. The expression is Stace's; see Ibid.

85. Plotinus, *Enneads,* VI.9.11.

86. Plotinus, therefore, is not a monist in the strict sense of the word. See Rist, *Plotinus: The Road to Reality,* 226–30; Armstrong, "Plotinus," 263.

87. Porphyry, *Life,* ch. 23. Plotinus undoubtedly had numerous experiences of this type; see *Enneads,* IV.8.1.

88. On magic and its effects, see Plotinus, *Enneads,* IV.4.40–44.

89. Ibid., I.6.8; cf. VI.9.9.

90. Ibid., VI.8.15.

91. See Armstrong, "Plotinus," 263; Rist, *Plotinus,* 228; Rist, *Eros and Psyche,* 72–73. Armstrong and Rist categorize Plotinus as a "theistic" mystic based on Zaehner's distinctions. See R. C. Zaehner, *Mysticism: Sacred & Profane* (New York, 1961), 153–97. But Zaehner's categories are problematic, as Ninian Smart has pointed out; see "Interpretation and Mystical Experience," *Religious Studies* 1 (1965), 74–87 and "Understanding Religious Experience" in *Mysticism and Philosophical Analysis,* Steven T. Katz, ed. (New York, 1978), 10–21. Thus, in the case of Plotinus's mysticism, terms like "monistic" and "theistic" should be used with caution, if at all.

92. Plotinus, *Enneads,* V.5.12; cf. Wallis, *Neoplatonism,* 64, 90.

93. See Armstrong, *Architecture,* 32–33, who suggests that Plotinus's "passionate devotion to the Supreme" reflects Stoic influence.

94. Plotinus, *Enneads,* IV.4.26, 30, 38, 40–41. Plotinus regards prayer in this sense as a form of "sympathetic magic."

95. Ibid., V.1.6. For further discussion of Plotinus's concept of prayer, see Rist, *Plotinus,* 199–212.

96. See E. Underhill, *Mysticism* (New York, 1972), 306–13.

97. See n. 75, 100.

98. Plotinus, *Enneads*, III.4; IV.3.8.

99. Seemingly only Porphyry, among the Neoplatonists, believed in the idea of a permanent release of the soul for the philosopher. See Porphyry, *On the Return of the Soul*, in J. Bidez, *Vie de Porphyre* (Hildesheim, 1964) 38*, 10–15. cf. Andrew Smith, *Porphyry's Place in the Neoplatonic Tradition* (The Hague, 1974), 55–78.

100. On later Neoplatonism, see A. C. Lloyd, "The Later Neoplatonists," in *The Cambridge History*, 272–325; Wallis, *Neoplatonism*, 94–159.

101. See R. Majercik, *The Chaldean Oracles: Text, Translation, Commentary* (Leiden, 1989); E. des Places, *Oracles Chaldäiques* (Paris, 1971).

102. On what follows, see esp. Hans Lewy, *Chaldean Oracles*, 177–256; 461–66; E. R. Dodds, "Theurgy and Its Relationship to Neoplatonism," *Journal of Roman Studies*, 37 (1947), 55–59; rpt. in E. R. Dodds, *The Greek and the Irrational* (Boston, 1957), 283–311; R. Majercik, *Chaldean Oracles*, 21–45; A. Smith, *Porphyry's Place*, 83 ff.

103. See Wallis, *Neoplatonism*, 160–78.

3

Three Medieval Christian Mystics

DONALD H. BISHOP

St. Francis of Assisi

Even before the close of the twelfth century, when St. Francis was born (1181/2–1226), the church had become the dominant institution in Europe. She was wealthy and powerful. She was the major intellectual force. Her dogma prevailed. Her clergy's voice was authoritative. In village and town the church spire towered above all else. Medieval mysticism may be viewed as a response to the dominance and institutionalization of Christianity. And, while each mystic reacted in his or her own particular way, they also shared much in common.

The first medieval mystic I shall deal with is Saint Francis of Assisi. He was born into the family of a well-to-do cloth merchant in Assisi, Italy. He received a minimal education from the priests of San Georgia, one of the city's churches. As a youth he lived a life of pleasure and indulgence. He worked sporadically in his father's shop and, at the age of twenty-two, had a serious illness which caused him to reflect on the direction his life was taking. Subsequently, he began to spend less time with his worldly companions and more time in solitude, spiritual reflection, and contemplation, resulting in his increased compassion and liberality toward the poor.

In 1202 Francis joined the forces of Assisi in a battle against neighboring Perugia. The latter won, and Francis was taken prisoner for a year. On his release and return to Assisi, Francis experienced a growing dissatisfaction with his life. He then went on a pilgrimage to Rome where, instead of making a small offering at the tomb of Saint Peter's, as other visitors did, he was led to throw all the contents of his purse through the grated window and then exchange his own fine clothes for those of a beggar for a day.

Shortly after his return from Rome, Francis went to the small chapel of San Damiano outside Assisi. There, kneeling before the crucifix, he experienced Christ—he was to make the work of the church his life's task. One aspect of that task became evident soon thereafter when he met a leper on the road. Although Francis was always generous to them, he was loathe to touch them. This time there was no hesitation. Jumping from his horse, he took the surprised leper in his arms, gave him the full contents of his purse, kissed him, and let him go.

A second form of service to the church was the rebuilding of decaying chapels around Assisi. The first was San Damiano. To do so he took some clothes from his father's store, sold them, and gave the money to the resident prior. A confrontation with his angry father, who had learned of it, led to Francis's severing of family ties and the undertaking of his religious pilgrimage in earnest.

The remaining details of Francis's life may be noted briefly. From 1206 to 1209 he went about restoring San Damiano and other chapels in and around Assisi, as well as soliciting support for bands of lepers in the area. His own life was one of simplicity and austerity. Still he was restless of soul. In February of 1209, a vision of the path he was to finally follow came to him as the verses of Luke were being read in the San Damiano chapel, "Then said Jesus unto him, go and sell all thou hast, and give to the poor, and thou shalt have treasure in heaven; and come and follow me" (Luke 18:22). Francis now knew his was the path of the wandering preacher and mendicant, obeying Christ's injunction to the apostles, "Take nothing for your journey, neither staves, nor scrip, neither bread, nor money" (Matthew 10:9).

In less than two months he was joined by three others. The San Maria di Porticuncula chapel became the base out of which the brothers worked. As more came, the Order of the Minores was set up. Pope Innocent III approved it, reluctantly, in 1210. He knew of Francis's insistence on taking the vow of poverty seriously, and he would rather have Francis and his brothers practicing within an official Order where he hoped the practice would not be carried to an extreme.

The next sixteen years until Francis's death saw a rapid growth of the Order. Organizational tasks were given to others, because Francis was too intent on spreading the Gospel. He be-

came widely acknowledged as a fervent preacher.[1] He was seized
by the crusading spirit, and, in 1219, he arrived in Egypt where
he preached to the bemused sultan. Disciplined solitude, prayer,
meditation, and rapture strengthened his preaching and activity.[2] His work for the lepers and the poor drew much support.
His life of self-denial was extreme, even to the point of being
detrimental to his health. The climatic mystical event of his
life came in 1224 when he so fully experienced the poverty
and suffering of Christ that the stigmata was said to have been
implanted on his own body.[3] He bore the marks of the cross
until his death two years later on October 3. In the evening of
that day, tradition says that multitudes of singing larks gathered
around his hut while he passed away.[4]

Francis's mysticism involved a joyous union with God and a
sense of oneness with his fellow men, especially among the
poor. It was partly on their behalf that he undertook the vow of
poverty, carrying it to a degree unusual among mystics. Why
did he undertake such a vow? Several answers to that question
will give us insight into his life and work as a mystic.

In the first place, it may have been a reaction to his youthful
life of indulgence and satiation that he now saw as selfish and
egoistic. He came to recognize how momentary were its pleasures and reoccurring its desires. He yearned instead for something that would transcend the fleeting and the temporal, that
which would make his life truly significant and meaningful.

Francis's vow of poverty also may be seen as a repudiation of
much of the medieval church as he experienced it. It was an
institution too often concerned with continuing its power, status, and privileges; it was a church marked by pomp and ostentation, tied down in ritual and formality, intent on increasing its
wealth. Too often it compromised the secular powers. Frequently its clergy failed to be examples of the message preached,
and the message itself was at times diluted or lukewarm.

Francis was not the only one who railed against churchly opulence. Others before him were the mystic Bernard of Clairvaux
(1091–1153), Arnold of Brescia, Peter of Bruya, and Henry of
Lausanne, to name a few. Although he carried it further than
others, all insisted on a return to ascetic living and apostolic
poverty, even as did such groups as the Cistercians at the end of
the eleventh century and the Cathari, Humiliati, and Waldness
groups later. Their efforts, however, did not deter Pope John
XXII, in 1323, to decree it a heresy to allege that Christ and his
disciples did not possess property.

Francis's vow and life of poverty was a result, in the third place, of his recognition that it is not enough simply to have compassion for the poor—one must become poor oneself. One cannot fully realize what poverty is like or how the poor feel until one has been poor. The person who practices charity may believe he or she has thereby discharged a Christian duty to the poor, but, as Francis reminded his perplexed mother, for him at least, that was not enough.[5] His compassion required that he become poor himself, and, as he gave up everything, he found his compassion to be even greater and his identification with his fellows even closer. Opulence would have achieved just the opposite effect.

Furthermore, to live by the vow of privation was both to imitate Christ and to be drawn closer to him. As with Thomas à Kempis, Francis's goal was to be like Christ in thought, word, and deed.[6] Christ lived a life of self-imposed poverty. He owned no estates, held no titles, headed no institution. He simply went about doing good, taking with him his cloak and staff only. He associated with the meek and lowly, cured the ill, succored the poor, and uplifted the downtrodden. And this, Francis insisted, is what must be done to be a true follower of Christ. To be a Christian is to follow Christ, and to do that one must deny oneself completely, give up everything even as the rich ruler was loath to do, and leave all behind as the apostles did. To imitate Christ is to heed his words to the disciples, "If any man will come after me, let him deny himself, and take up his cross, and follow me" (Matthew 16:24). To follow Christ to the fullest is to experience the suffering of Christ on the cross, and in the suffering or grieving of the poor, Francis saw the suffering of Christ.

In addition, Francis saw his poverty as symbolic of his surrendering of everything to God. All worldly things must be given up and no longer valued or yearned for. And one must surrender one's will to God, just a Christ did when he uttered the words, "Let not my will but thine be done" (Luke 22:42).

Francis found that it was in a state of poverty that he would most fully experience God or achieve union with the divine. Only after he had severed all ties with mundane things could he be bound to God. To reach the transcendent one must reject the earthly. Renunciation, he discovered, was a prerequisite for the mystical unitive experience. One must empty oneself before one can be filled with God. Francis had no reservations about the beatitude, "Blessed are the poor in spirit for they shall see

God." And he took it to mean poorness not only in spirit but in body as well. He found that the more complete one's surrender, the more fully one experienced the divine, and also the greater was the consecration that followed for doing the will of God through serving the poor and outcast.

To Francis God was both immanent and transcendent. He is not so transcendent as to be beyond man's reach. God comes down to man even as man rises up to God. God is the one before whom man humbles himself. To Francis, humbleness meant self-effacement but not self-abasement. It meant the giving up, not of self-integrity but of pride in oneself and one's accomplishments. God is a God of love, and we are to love unreservedly both God and our fellowmen. To love only the former is to fail to emulate God and carry out His will. As God's love goes out to all, so should ours.

We see a strain of pacifism in Francis in his emphasis on God's universal and unlimited love and his practice of Christ's injunction to love enemy as well as friend. To Francis the term neighbor was all inclusive. Unlike Bernard of Clairvaux, he included the heretic or the enemies of the Lord in his circle of love.[7] The wicked he would reform by good example. He absented himself from those who would make war in the name of God.

Francis's repudiation of force stemmed not from fear or cowardice but from his trust in the power and providence of God. Moreover, God's providence was a further reason for his vow of poverty. That providence was made explicit in Christ's words, "Take no thought for your life, what ye shall eat, or what ye shall drink; nor yet for your body, what ye shall put on. . . . Behold the fowls of the air. For they sow not, neither do they reap, nor gather into barns. Yet your heavenly father feedeth them. . . . Consider the lilies how they grow. They toil not. They spin not. Yet I say unto you, Solomon in all his glory was not arrayed like one of these. If then God so clothes the grass, which is today in the field and tomorrow is cast into the oven, how much more will he clothe you, O ye of little faith" (Matthew 6:25–30). Others of his time might trust in the weapons of battle, their possessions, their strength.[8] Francis would put his faith, as Christ did, in that which surpassed himself and all others, a benevolent, loving, caring, trustworthy, providential God.

Francis is unique in that he is known not just as a mystic but a nature mystic as well. In nature he saw God's immanence.[9]

Nature offered him both inspiration and consolation as well as a setting for his experiences of rapture. His compassion extended to all its life forms.[10] Tradition has it that one day he saw doves taken in a basket to a market, and he immediately bought and released them. His sympathy went out to birds, animals, and flowers, even as it did to people, for they are an integral part of God's creation.

Francis experienced God both in and through nature. He was often reminded of the Psalmist's words, "Heaven and earth are full of thy glory" (Psalm 72:19). Nature reflects the divine creative activity, the handiwork of God. All created things point beyond themselves to God. The beauty of nature is a manifestation of God's beauty; its harmony reflects God's unity; its sacredness manifests God's holiness. The harmony of man and animals is a part of a larger theme, the harmony of God, man and nature, the central theme is his Canticle of the Sun. The "Song of the Creatures," as it is sometimes called, was composed only a year before Francis's death. It was a poem praising the Lord for the various components of creation: the sun, moon, wind, water, fire and earth, whom he called brother and sister, and, in the case of the last, mother. Its final stanza, "Praise ye and bless the Lord, and give thanks unto Him and serve Him with great humility" (Okey, *Little Flowers*, 295), ends, fittingly, on a note of service and humility or poverty.

If Francis's poverty was a protest against church opulence, it was a reproof also of the society in which he lived. It was one in which most put their trust in wealth, power, and possession rather than God's providence—a time when man's attitude toward nature was not the stewardship one implied in the Canticle. Francis viewed nature as created by God for the benefit of all. There was enough in nature for everyone, if each would not seek more than he needed. But that did not happen. Instead, people acted selfishly, greedily, seeking to wrest from nature as much as they could for themselves, regardless of others. The spirit of acquisition, the drive to possess, was everywhere, as well as "the growing organization of machinery for procuring it."[11] The result was a society divided into classes, factions, and localities at odds with each other. The rich lived in disregard of the poor, and the latter had no recourse in law or popular power.

Historians characterize the thirteenth century as an "era of growing commercialism and rising capitalism." It was the beginning of the Age of Mercantilism, and Francis's father was a representative. It was a time of change from a barter to a money

economy.[12] The notion of exclusive individual ownership pre-
dominated. Increasingly men became the "instruments for the
facilitation of material profit."[13] Society was losing its communal nature, and the social fabric was becoming more and more
ruptured. Such changes brought to the surface facets of human
nature that in an earlier, simpler time might have remained
quiescent.

Francis's vow of poverty shows that he did not share in his
countrymen's concern for worldly fame and benefits. He reminded them in word and deed that the ownership of wealth,
in whatever form it took, made love of God and neighbor difficult and the rationalizing of and resorting to arms easy. Both
were contrary to Christ's example and his warning that "ye
cannot love God and mammon both" (Matthew 6:24). He saw
the drive to possess as an obstacle to human fraternity and
peace. It led, not to an identification with, but to a disdain of
others who were less fortunate. Possessed by the desire to accu-
mulate wealth, one is easily tempted to use devious means to
do so. Francis believed the majority of his fellows had not only
set the wrong goals for themselves but had acquiesced in the
wrong means of reaching them. They had disregarded the biblical injunctions that "the meek shall inherit the earth" and
"they that live by the sword shall die by it" (Matthew 26:52).

Francis would have a society based on such principles as sharing, cooperation, concern, and the common good. He recognized
that the well-being of one is tied up with the good of others.
Because self-fulfillment is a common, universal goal, we need
to help each other in achieving that goal. The end of individual
perfection cannot be accomplished in isolation; he who would
perfect himself must help others to perfection also.

Furthermore, Francis wanted a society in which people lived
by the rule of simplicity, motivated, not by acquiring, but by
doing God's will. Like Gandhi, he believed that to have more
than one needs or to keep something when someone else needs
it more is a form of theft.[14]

Francis believed godly love and the prosecution of selfish
rights and interests were exclusive or contrary to each other.
He shared with other mystics a profound belief in individual
dignity and worth, its source being God, and he would have a
society in which that dignity and sanctity was being affirmed,
not denied, by the institutions therein.

Francis was not a social reformer in the contemporary sense
of the term. He proposed no revolutionary socioeconomic mea-

sures to change existing institutions and bring about the kind of society he envisaged. Rather, he believed that a good society would be brought about through purified or redeemed individuals. He hoped to bring about changes in enough individuals, through his own example and those of his brothers in the order, that society itself would be changed eventually.

Francis's lack of enthusiasm for material things was matched by a similar attitude toward creed and doctrine. Such an attitude is consistent with a definition of religion as the realization of, and union with, God and the doing of God's will through the imitation of Christ. God is a being to be experienced in the inner self, not an object to be known through rational categories.

Francis's was a religion of the heart. It found expression, not in abstract formulations, but in feelings, attitudes, and acts of love. Francis found little value in theological hairsplitting. He did not exalt learning for the sake of learning; rather, he believed learning should increase piety, and the pursuit of truth was to be an avenue to self-purification. One should study, Francis told the Brethren, "that they might be doers of the word."[15] It might be noted that Francis accepted an ontological, rather than conceptualistic, method of knowing. Knowing is not an objective process of drawing conclusions from premises—knowing is a matter of being. Another person is known, for example, through identifying with, being empathetic toward, putting oneself in the place of, having sympathy for, or being compassionate toward that person. It means treating persons as beings, not objects, and establishing a monistic, not dualistic, relationship with them.

It is significant to note that poverty was not a burden to Francis. It did not make him sad or remorseful. Those times when he was sad were due to his sensitivity to the condition of the world. Paradoxically, poverty gave him inner serenity and paved the way for his joyful mystical experiences. The suffering and pain he experienced made his joy all the more intense, for it was a joy that transcended the physical and partook of the spiritual or the soul.

Francis was a mystic of ecstasy, his was a mysticism of ecstasy. He discovered that self-realization was not through self-assertion but self-denial, that only by giving up himself could he become an instrument of that which is greater than himself—God's love and peace. He had learned that, strangely enough, the more he emptied himself the more he found himself filled with God's strength, grace, and love. It became apparent to him that denying himself in order to serve others in Christ was genuine happiness and fulfillment. To love others was an act of joy, not of stern duty. To love others was to follow Christ and become Christlike.

Finally, poverty was the means by which Francis's noble nature was drawn out. He was a spiritual hero who sacrificed, yet he was unaware of his sacrifice. Poverty was the means by which he became a spiritual hero, one who, by the grace and love of God and the inspiration of Christ, found himself by conquering himself, not others. That was the first heroic step. The second was the giving of his transcendent or uplifted self in loving service to others. Through the mystical experience Francis transcended the world and ascended to God. Each transcending experience was followed by an act of descent or the coming back into the world, for his compassion would not permit him to remain ever aloof from the world, even as his nobility would not allow him to be of the world. For Francis, being was far more important than having. And being, for him, included, even necessitated rather than excluded, doing.

Meister Eckhart

Meister Eckhart's life overlapped the thirteenth and fourteenth centuries. He was born at Hochheim in central Germany (ca. 1260) and died in 1327. He studied for nine years in the Dominican monastery at Erfurt and later joined the order. From 1277 for several years he undertook further study in Paris, and from 1294 to 1300 he was prior of the Dominican house at Erfurt and vicar of Thuringa. During this time he wrote the *Talks of Instruction* containing advice to his Dominican charges. From 1303 to 1311 his duties included that of the province of Saxony when he wrote the most famous of his vernacular treatises, the *Book Benedictus.* The first part was titled the *Book of Divine Consolation,* the second, *On the Nobleman.* His well-known essay, *On Disinterest,* was written later.

From 1314 to 1323, Eckhart lived at Strasbourg where he became a popular preacher. His sermons, it is believed, were written down by members of his congregation and by nuns in Dominican convents where he preached. He went to the Dominican center in Cologne in 1323. Strasbourg and Cologne were both centers for Inner Light sects and Rhineland mysticism. In 1326, accusations of heresy were made against him which he staunchly denied, asserting his loyalty to the church, and he wrote a *Defense* of himself. He died in 1328 before the conclusion of the trial against him that same year—a trial at which he was declared guilty.

The number of his extant works makes a study of Eckhart as a mystic easier than in the case of Francis. Eckhart was a scholar of great erudition. In his many years of study he steeped himself in both ancient and contemporary thinkers, both inside and outside the church. He was influenced by Plotinus, the Neoplatonists, and the Pseudo-Dionysius, but he was a creator, not a mere emulator.

Eckhart, like Francis, placed much emphasis on union with God. It cannot be achieved easily, for its prerequisites are several and exhaustive. One must give up the worldly and the creaturely. "The pleasure we take in the comfort of transitory things," Eckhart says, will be "a barrier against God." Moreover, "the more subject to creatures a man is, the less he conforms to God," and "the soul that is empty of creatures is lifted up to God."[16]

The theme of emptying is continued in Eckhart's statement: "To be full of things is to be empty of God, while to be empty of things is to be full of God." Similarly, eliminating the self is necessary, for "to the extent that you eliminate self from your activities, God comes into them." One must also learn "to get away from selfishness" and to forget or be less aware of oneself. In one of his sermons he says, "If the soul is to know God, it must forget itself and lose consciousness of itself, for as long as it is self-aware and self-conscious, it will not see, or be conscious of, God."[17] Mystical union, then, requires a complete absence of self-centeredness.

In a philosophical vein, Eckhart emphasizes the transcending of time and space in order to be united with God. If the soul is to know God, it must know him above time and outside of space, for "as long as the soul dwells on time or space or any image of them it may never know God (*Sermons*, No. 6)." As we shall see later, such statements are quite consistent with Eckhart's concept of God as Absolute Being transcending the relative categories of time and space.

Eckhart also associates God with the Word and, in order to hear the Word, stillness is a prerequisite. To hear it, "all voices and sounds must die away and there must be pure quiet-perfect stillness" (*Fragments*, No. 26). Moreover, hearing the Word requires "complete self-surrender." Eckhart associates the soul and God in an interesting way when he says of the soul or man who is inhabited by the Word that is God, "The soul is thus like a byword, working together with God and finding its beatification in the same self-knowledge that exalts him. That to all time we may be bywords of God may ... the Holy Spirit help us."[18]

Eckhart says that, metaphysically, there are three things "that hinder one from hearing the eternal Word. The first is corporeality, the second, number, and the third, time." When a person has overcome them "he dwells in eternity, is alive spiritually, and remains in the unity, the desert of solitude, and there he hears the eternal Word." The emphasis on both stillness and solitude is typically mystical, and one sees a note of metaphysical monism or nondualism in other of Eckhart's statements such as "He who hears and that which is heard are identical constituents of the eternal Word," and "What the eternal Father teaches is ... that we are to be identical with him."[19]

What are the results of union with God? Eckhart notes several. Such a person will reside in a state of "highest conceivable beatitude." He will experience inner peace and the Kingdom within. "The man to whom God is ever present, and who controls and uses his mind to the highest degree—that man knows what peace is and he has the Kingdom of Heaven within him," Eckhart told his protégés. If one "really has God," then nothing disturbs him "and one is not ... hindered by the things he handles" (*Talk of Instruction*, No. 5). We are reminded of the Buddhist simile of the lotus. No matter how foul the water it grows in, the beauty of the lotus is undiminished.

That one who is united with God will both experience a sense of freedom and innocence and be motivated by love is seen by Eckhart's statement, "That is why the person who is united to God acts that way—he, too, will be innocent and free, whatever he does, and will act out of love and without asking why." Selfishness will be eliminated, and one will trust in God, not self. Eckhart says that "when you get rid of selfishness, together with things and what pertains to them, and have transferred all to God, and united with him, and abandoned all for him in complete trust and love, then whatever your lot, whatever touches you, for better or worse, none of it is yours but it is all God's to whom you have left it."[20]

Eckhart also refers to the results of transcending time and space in his statement, "Once we get beyond time and temporal things, we are free and joyous and then comes the 'fullness of time' when the Son of God is born" (*Sermons*, No. 12). Eckhart's reference here is to the state of holy rapture. By the Son he is referring, of course, to Christ. Eckhart does not stress Christ nearly as much as Francis did. For Eckhart Christ is the "source of the Holy Spirit." He is the channel through which the Holy Spirit flows into the individual who, once that has occurred, experiences a state of freedom, joy, unselfishness, and abandonment.

Although he did not emphasize the point as much as Francis, Eckhart asserted that the doing of good deeds is both a condition and result of union with God. In one of the *Talks of Instructions,* which were conversations with a group of followers, he says that "it is also a good thing for a person not to be content with entertaining the notion of virtues, such as obedience, poverty, and the like, but to exhibit their fruits in his deeds." And in another talk he said, "if a person were in such a rapturous state as St. Paul once entered, and he knew of a sick man who wanted a cup of soup, it would be far better to withdraw from the rapture for love's sake and serve him who is in need."[21] Union with God who is a God of love, results in, if it is true unity, works of love.

One of Eckhart's basic notions is that of permeation and radiation. He concludes his talk on solitude and the attainment of God as follows: "So man should shine with the divine Presence without having to work at it. He should get the essence out of things and let the things themselves alone. That requires at first attentiveness and exact impressions, as with the student and his art. So one must be permeated with divine Presence, informed with the form of the beloved God who is within him, so that he may radiate that Presence without working at it."[22]

The idea of being so filled with the divine that it radiates out of, or overflows, the self is an interesting one. It is found in the Christian tradition, of course, as reflected in Christian art in which figures of saints are garbed in shining attire or are surrounded by a halo. Its roots may be in the transfiguration experience of Jesus, but it is not exclusive to Christianity. One notes it in the "aura" of the Theosophists, through whom it is traced to the Jains of India who believed in the life-monad in each person, whose degree of luminosity is determined by the degree of purity of the monad.

Eckhart emphasized the immanence of God, not so much in nature as Francis did, but in persons. God is within each of us, and one aspect of the religious experience is the realization of that simple fact. In one sermon he said, "God is nearer to me than I am to myself" (*Sermons*, No. 6). One is reminded of the statement in the Upanishads that "Brahman is nearer to me than are the fingernails to my fingers" (Brihadaranyaka Upanishad). Eckhart disdained those not conscious of God's presence within "who must always be going out to get him from this and that, who has to seek him by special methods, as by means of some activity, person or place." Such people "have not attained God," and "not only will evil company be to them a stumbling block, but good company as well, not only the street but the church; not only bad deeds and words, but good ones as well" (*Talks of Instructions*, No. 6). Such statements must have offended some churchgoers of his day, an offense that might have been the real root of the heresy charges against Eckhart.

Eckhart admonished his listeners to "set your mind in virtue to contemplation, in which the God you bear in your heart shall be your steady object, the object from which your attention never waivers." One is reminded of Socrates' dictum "know thyself," which Eckhart supplements with "To know God, know thyself." He says that "to get at the core of God at his greatest, one must first get into the core of himself at his least, for no one can know God who has not first known himself," and "In all his work, and on every occasion, a man should make clear use of his reason and have a conscious insight into himself and his spirituality and distinguish God to the highest possible degree in everything."[23] For Eckhart, then, self-knowledge and God-knowledge are inextricably intertwined. To know one is to know the other.

Eckhart did not necessarily overlook or minimize God as transcendent as well. For if there is divine presence in man, it must have a source or origin. Since it cannot come from man himself, it must be the Deity transcendent, which Eckhart refers to in one instance as "the One itself . . . a source that had no beginning." Similarly the world as a whole has a transcendent origin. Its divinity as a created object, or emanated one as we shall see later, comes not from itself but from the Divine One. The distinction between creator and created, although not a sharp one, is seen in such affirmations of Eckhart's as "anything which has being, date, or location, does not belong to God, for he is above them all, and although he is in all creatures, yet he is more than all of them" (*Sermons*, No. 6).

Eckhart's emphasis on God being immanent in man is seen in his assertion that "there is an agent in my soul which is perfectly sensitive to God" (*Sermons*, No. 6). On the one hand this is a reminder of Francis's ontological view of knowing as being empathetic or sensitive to. But Eckhart is more intellectually oriented, as we see in numerous statements by him, if we mean intellectual in a broad sense and not in the narrow one the term rational implies today.

In one sermon Eckhart speaks of three kinds of knowledge, the first being sensual, "the eyes see things at a distance." The second, intellectual, is much higher, or sees things more closely. The third "represents the function of that aristocratic agent of the soul, which ranks so high that it communes with God, face to face, as He is." Intuition would not be a correct characterization of the third. Rather, what Eckhart seems to have in mind is the individual's capacity to know God directly, immediately, or in a transnatural, supranatural way. No intermediary is necessary, whether a person or method of knowing. This is reflected in Eckhart's statement, "We ought not to have or let ourselves be satisfied with the God we have thought of, for when the thought slips the mind, that God slips with it. What we want is rather the reality of God, exalted far above any human thought or creature."[24]

Eckhart notes that the God-man relationship is a two-way one. If there is an "intellectual return to God" on the part of man, there is a reciprocal act by God. Eckhart says that "to the man who cleaves to God, God cleaves and adds virtue. Thus what you have sought before, now seeks you; what once you pursued, now pursues you; what you once fled, now flees you." This is reminiscent of Francis Thompson's *Hound of Heaven* (*Poems* [London: Burns and Oates, 1893], 48–54). We are reminded, too, of the juxtaposition of the immanent and the transcendent and that, while they may be conceived of and verbalized as separate, they are interrelated, interdependent, or interfused. The transcendent God comes down to man even as man, in whom he is immanent, reaches up to God.

Eckhart also uses the image of light in describing the God-man relationship. He speaks of "a light in the soul that is uncreated." He says this divine light "is far too aristocratic to make common cause with the soul's agents. For all that touches creatures or can be touched by them is far from God and alien from him. As the agents of the soul touch the world and are touched by it, they lose their virginity. The divine light cannot shine in them and they can be made sensitive and holy only through purification and renunciation" (*Sermons*, No. 25).

There are three agents of the soul according to Eckhart—intuition, the soul's striving for God (*irascibilis*), and the will. When the second is achieved, that is, "when the soul comes to know the real truth by that simple agent through which one knows God," the soul is called light. Continuing the metaphor, Eckhart says, "God, too, is light and when the divine light pours into the soul, the soul is united with God, as light blends with light."[25] We see once more, in these statements of Eckhart's, the notions of illumination, permeation, and radiation, and in the last quote perhaps, even, the loss of individuality in the unitive experience.

Interesting is Eckhart's threefold characterization of the intellect into the active, passive, and potential. The active intellect, characterized by drive and energy, is manifested when the mind is at work understanding the external world of things and passive when the action at hand is undertaken by God. God, not the self, is the doer. The potential intellect incorporates both, that is, what man and God do together. The potential intellect has been actualized when what one does is done for God and through God's help.

If there are shades of Aristotle in the above, Platoism is also evident in Eckhart's same sermon when he says, "The mind has a pure, unadulterated being of its own. When it comes across truth or essence, at once it is attracted and settles down to utter its oracle" (*Sermons*, No. 3). The being Eckhart is referring to is the soul. Thus, when the soul discovers God, or God is discovered in the depths of the soul, the soul is immediately or naturally drawn to God and the doing of God's will, just as we are, as Plato notes, attracted by or drawn to Truth and the doing of it.

Eckhart also speaks of the soul as having two eyes, "one looking inwards and the other outwards. It is the inner eye of the soul that looks into essence and takes being directly from God. The soul's outward eye is directed toward creatures and perceives their external forms but when a person turns inward and knows God in terms of his own awareness of him, he is then freed from all creation and is secure in the castle of truth." Eckhart also says, "there is Truth at the core of the soul but it is covered up and hidden from the mind."[26]

In general it would seem that Eckhart suggests there are two ways of knowing and two kinds of knowledge. One is empirical knowledge of the material world gained through the senses; the second, often emphasized by mystics, is that kind of knowledge of which the soul is the instrument and is of the interior self or of the deep recesses of the soul in which dwells the essential self waiting and longing to be united with the Divine. Eckhart speaks of this longing as a thirst that, no matter the degree to which it is quenched, is never fully satisfied in this lifetime.

Eckhart associates God not only with the Word, Light, and Stillness, but Truth as well, in what, one suspects, is a Gandhian fashion. In a sermon titled "Truth is not Merchandise," he links God with truth and light, and ignorance with darkness—"Light and darkness cannot exist side by side. God is the truth and a light in himself. When he enters the temple, he drives out ignorance and darkness and reveals himself in light and truth. Then, when the truth is known, the merchants must be gone—for truth wants no merchandising."[27] In these stern words, Eckhart reminds his listeners of the necessity of constantly choosing between truth and falsehood and good and evil.

It is interesting to see the similarities between Gandhi, who had mystical tendencies, and Eckhart. Gandhi says that, after fifty years of searching, he came to the conclusion that "God is truth and truth is God." To see and choose truth is to see and choose God as well. Both emphasized, further, that truth is not only a matter of truth—seeking but truth being, or being truthful. To be truthful is to be in tune with or one with God.

In the *Fragments* and other writings, we find Eckhart holding to a primarily New Testament view of God. He refers to God as forgiving, merciful, a fulfiller, not destroyer, and especially as love. He gives "existence and life to every creature, supporting them all with his love." Just as the color of the wall depends on the wall, so "the existence of creatures depends on the love of God. Separate the color from the wall and it would cease to be; so all creation would cease to exist if separate from the love that God is" (*Fragments*, No. 32).

Eckhart also associates knowledge and love, declaring that "knowledge is better than love but the two together are better than one of them, for knowledge really contains love."[28] He says that love has to do with desires, purposes, and feelings that although commendable, may be partial and misguided. Knowledge or truth, however, is impartial. Thus it is higher than love, its task being to purify love. Again, there is a connection between truth and God because, while God is love, he is also truth, i.e., God is impartial in that his love goes out equally to all.

The claim that Eckhart is a monist epistemologically, or a nondualist if one prefers the Vedantist term, may not be an exaggerated one. Many times he seems to quite closely identify

God with the universe and, of course, God with the self. One finds a corollary between the association of truth and God in the image of God and the idea of God, as is the case of Anselm. We might conclude that for Eckhart, as for Anselm, God and the idea of God are not two but one; for the idea of God is God, or God and the idea of God are one and the same.

In metaphysics Eckhart was also much less of a dualist than his colleagues. He recognizes, of course, that the world we experience immediately through the senses is marked by distinctions, divisions, contrasts, and opposites. But one must not stop there as most do, any more than one should stop with God on the relative level. We must look into the heart of reality itself.

When one does, one finds a "real is-ness," a "simple unity in which there are no distinctions." Eckhart says that, when one has been purified, even the sense world is recognized as a unity—"when the forces expressed through the five senses are gathered again into the soul, then the soul is one agent by means of which everything is unified." In the realm of reason "opposite[s] are forgotten" and "the whole scattered world of lower things is gathered up to oneness."[29] The disunities and diversities of the phenomenal universe are recognized for what they are, relatives or on the relative level, and they are left behind as the soul, itself now integrated, recognizes the true essence of things as characterized by oneness or nonduality.

In *The Book of Divine Comfort*, Eckhart refers to a "power in nature" that "seeks oneness instead of likeness and loves things only for the sake of the One in them." The essential nature of the universe is associated with God and this accounts for its oneness, since God is himself absolute oneness or unity. Eckhart says that "God gives to all things alike and as they proceed from God they are alike." Furthermore, "God cannot be distracted by the number of things . . . for he is one in One, in which all divided things are gathered up to unity and therefore undifferentiated."[30]

The unity of the universe is due to its having proceeded out of, or having emanated from, God. A statement of his emanation theory, in addition to the one above, is "Angels, men, and creatures all flow out of God in whom their prime origin is" (*Sermons*, No. 23). A created universe implies a deity outside of, and completely separate from, the universe that he had, at one moment in time, created. Eckhart rejects this and makes use of the image of unfolding. The universe is God unfolded. Thus the universe is of the same nature as God himself. Eckhart also conceived of God as analogous to a fountain from which everything both flows and returns. God is the root from which everything springs, and there is in everything a longing to return to or be united with its roots, to use a popular Taoist analogy.

Eckhart also views the universe as being dynamic, not static. It is in a constant process of folding and refolding. The seeking of unity and a return to the source is a part of a continuing drive for self-realization, a movement toward one's true being or Being *per se*, the reaching of the imperfect toward perfection. "Every creature is on its way to the highest perfection" (*Sermons*, No. 27), Eckhart said. Everything is in a state of constant movement until it has attained unity with the godhead wherein it finds rest, quiet, stillness, completion.

The profundity and depth of Eckhart's mysticism is reflected in this distinction between God as absolute and God as relative. In the case of the first, we are referring to God as He is in himself, in the second as He appears to us. In the first instance we are speaking of God before and apart from the emanation of the universe, in the second after emanation. God as absolute is God beyond and without attributes; as relative, God has characteristics such as love, goodness, and knowledge. "God is neither good, better, nor best," Eckhart said, and "God is neither a being nor intelligent and he does not know either this or that. God is free of everything and therefore He is everything." We may attribute characteristics to God on the relative level, although even there it ought to be done cautiously, but not on the absolute level. Eckhart exemplifies the *via negativa* of the mystic who claims that we can only say what the absolute God is not. He does not have attributes, for example. He cannot be named for, as the Taoist says, that which can be named is not the Tao.[31]

Eckhart points out that God as absolute is impersonal or transpersonal, a view held by Vedantism and Vedantists such as Sankara. God on the relative level is personal, a person or manifested in persons and the person of Christ. The absolute God is unmoved, unmanifested, a one or a unity, beyond time and space. As relative, God is in time and space, in nature, in the Trinity and partakes of multiplicity. In the case of God as absolute, opposites are nonexistent. If there are distinctions, they are not actual but only potential, inasmuch as unfoldment has not yet occurred.

For Eckhart, the absolute God, or God before emanation, was pure Being but "When creatures came to be and took on creaturely being, then God was no longer God as he is in himself, but God as he is with creatures." On the absolute level God simply is; he is the Unmoved Mover; on the relative level he acts. "The difference between God and the Godhead is the difference between actions and nonaction," Eckhart says.[32]

The absolute God is a Being without form that Eckhart on occasions refers to as the Godhead. On returning to or merging with it, one becomes formless oneself, "When I return to God," Eckhart says, "I shall be without form and thus my re-entry shall be far more exalted than my sitting out. . . . When I return to the core, the soil, the river, the source which is the Godhead, no one will ask me whence I came or where I have been." One is reminded once more of Taoism and Lao Tzu's theme of returning to the roots of one's existence. Eckhart refers to this primeval state, thus, "Back in the Womb from which I came, I had no god and merely was myself. I did not will or desire anything, for I was pure being, a knower of myself by divine truth. Then I wanted myself and nothing else. And what I wanted, I was and what I was, I wanted, and thus, I existed untrammeled by god or anything else."[33]

Eckhart draws a parallel between the two natures of man and the two levels of God when he refers to himself in terms of "my eternal being and my temporal being." Elsewhere the dualism is stated in the form of "the outward man—the sensual person" and "the inner man—the spiritual person." There is an essential self and accidental self also, of course, the soul as distinct from the body. In the instances above Eckhart is referring to the absolute self on the one hand and the relative on the other, just as he does in the case of God. And in the case of both, the task is to get beyond the relative to the absolute.

Eckhart was very insistent on this point. One should transcend the empirical self and act in terms of the soul. One should go beyond words, recognizing they are but symbols of a reality they transcend. One should not allow oneself to be limited by religious symbol and ritual for this is but religion institutionalized. One must go beyond union with Christ, even, to union with God or the Godhead, of which Christ is a manifestation or, perhaps, emanation. This was contrary to the religion of his Christian brethren and even some Christian mystics who took as their chief end the love of, and union with, Christ. Climactically, one must go beyond God, Eckhart insisted in one of his sermons: "Therefore, I pray God that he may quit me of god."[34] To those of his listeners who did not understand, this must have smacked of heresy indeed!

One clue to Eckhart's ethical thought is his assertion that God is not to be bargained with. In a sermon on "Truth is not Merchandise," he says that, as truth should not be bought, sold, or used as a bargaining chip, neither should virtuous deeds. He labeled as merchants those Christians who "would like to be good people and do their good deeds to the glory of God . . . and yet they do these things so that the Lord will give them something in exchange, or do something they ardently want to have done. . . . They want to give one thing for another and to trade with our Lord but they will be cheated out of their bargain."[35]

Similarly, God is not to be loved for utilitarian reasons. Regarding people "who love God for the sake of outward wealth or inward comfort," Eckhart says, "they do not rightly love God when they love him for their own advantage." How, then, should one love God? Eckhart replies that "the just man loves God for nothing, neither for this nor for that." The just or the virtuous person needs no motive for loving God any more than he does for loving truth, justice, and goodness. He loves them for their own sake. In loving this way one is emulating God. For, "as God, having no motives, acts without them, so the just man acts without motives."[36]

Eckhart's emphasis on "motiveless action" is exactly that found in chapter 2 of the *Bhagavad Gita*. To seek truth, justice, and goodness for utilitarian ends is to lower them from the absolute to the relative level, just as to love God for the same reason is to make God into god. Truth, justice, and goodness, like God, have intrinsic worth. The person who views them in a utilitarian fashion sees them as having only extrinsic worth.

Purity of motive is the centerpiece of Eckhart's ethics. It requires purity of self, and this is one reason Eckhart distinguished between being and doing and gave priority to the first. "People out not to consider so much what they are to do as what they are," he said. "Let them but be good and their ways and deeds will shine brightly" (*Talks of Instruction*, No. 3). This is an example of the "essence precedes existence" concept; this is Eckhart's ethics of being. The outer, the deed, is determined by the inner, the mind, soul, or will; thus, Eckhart's insistence on the purity of the soul. For, if it is purified, and again we are reminded of the *Bhagavad Gita*, one can arrive at a state of being in which one does the good unconsciously, motivelessly, and sacramentally, a state put beautifully by Eckhart in his statement: "When one can do the works of virtue without preparing, by willing to do them, and bring to completion some great and righteous matter without giving it a thought, when the deed of virtue seems to happen by itself, simply because one loved goodness and for no other reason, then one is perfectly virtuous and not before."[37]

One does the good, then, simply because it is the good, and because God wills that one do the good. Our goal should be "neither to seek nor to take our own advantage in any matter, but always to find and procure the advantage of God." We should recognize that God "will not be influenced in the least to give or to do by any act of ours." We are to be like God who, when he acts "does not seek his own. In all his acts, he is innocent and free and acts only out of true love. That is why the person who is united to God acts that way; he too . . . will act out of love and without asking why, solely for the glory of God, seeking his own advantage in nothing, for God is at work in him" (*Talks of Instruction*, No. 21).

This theme is spelled out in Eckhart's essay, "*About Disinterest.*" In it he surprisingly, but with good reason, places disinterest above love. Typically, love is possessive. The lover seeks to possess the object of his love, whether a person or thing. Disinterest, however, rules out this drive to possess and not allow a thing to be what it is. Thus disinterest is superior to love. Eckhart also put disinterest above humility, and this may be surprising, too. The reason, however, is that the person who seeks to be humble is always conscious both of those who are not, and whom he thus consciously disdains, and of his own efforts to be humble, which gives rise to pride. This being so, he is still conscious of himself, and he has not reached that stage or level of disinterested being in which one simply is what one is without being conscious of it. Disinterest, then, is superior to humility also.

What is disinterest? In the first place, it is not, or does not imply, a lack of interest, care, or concern. Disinterest, on the one hand, is a state of being self-contained. It is not a matter of being unaware of, or uninterested in, those around you, but of not being dependent on them, for your self-esteem, for example. Eckhart describes the state of disinterest in several other ways also. It is one in which a person is "dead to the world" because "he has no appetite for any earthly things." The disinterested person is one who lives in terms of his needs and abjures superfluities. He, as Eckhart says, "wants nothing, and neither has he anything of which he would be rid."[38]

Eckhart points to another result of disinterest when he says, "there is, however, no peace except in disinterest." For the person who lives in terms of his needs, as with a nation, does not act selfishly, demandingly, and arrogantly toward others. His or its actions, therefore, are conducive to peace, not war. Eckhart also associates disinterest with objectivity in his statement, "Among men, be aloof; do not engage yourself to any idea you get" (*About Disinterest*). The disinterested person is one who is not so attached or partial to his own particular point of view that he holds to it obstinately and harmfully, even in the face of overwhelming evidence against it.

Does the disinterested person pray? Eckhart answers no. A disinterested man "pure in heart, has no prayer, for to pray is to want something from God." And the disinterested person, again, "wants nothing" and therefore has no prayer. "Or if he prays, he prays only to be uniform with God" (*About Disinterest*). To Eckhart, disinterest is detachment. It is a state of being in which one does not view nature, or the things of the world, in terms of how much he may profit from them. It is that state of being, noted in the *Bhagavad Gita*, in which one is so unaware of himself that he "does not know what God is doing in him"; he simply does the things of God unconsciously. Disinterest is, paradoxically, a state of being without being conscious of being. But then, Eckhart says, only in such a state can God come into the self, soul, or being.

It is significant that Eckhart associates disinterest or detachment with the mystical experience as both a precedent and consequent. In the *Talks of Instruction*, we read, "The truth is that it is not enough that the heart of man shall have its detached moments, in which to seek union with God; there must be a disciplined detachment which precedes and follows (the moment of union) and only in that way may man receive the great things of God and God himself in them."[39]

Eckhart asserts that a state of virtue is achieved in two ways. One is through self-effort, especially as pertaining to the world of affairs. "Above all a person should take care to discipline himself strictly and thoroughly," Eckhart says, "if he is to achieve anything of worth." On the other hand, the virtuous state is reached through the eliminating of self-will. One finds in Eckhart much concern with the will. Inklings of Kant's insistence that the only absolute or final good is a good will are seen in Eckhart's statement that "if you have good will, you shall lack for nothing, neither love, humility, nor any other virtue."[40]

Eckhart took seriously Christ's statements, "Thy kingdom

come, thy will be done" and "not my will but thine be done." Regarding the will and the everyday world, he says "the storms of unrest come of self-will. We should commit outselves and all our minds to the complete undoing of will, to desire only that we may fall in with the good and loving will of God." He describes a pure heart as one which is "unencumbered, unworried, uncommitted, and which does not want its own way about anything but which, rather, is submerged in the loving will of God, having denied self."[41]

Eckhart portrays the highest prayer as one wherein a person says not "Give me virtue or a way" but only "Lord, give me nothing but what thou wilt and dost." Using the theme of surrender, he says, "In general, it is the will of God that we surrender our wills . . . apart from complete surrender of the will, there is no traffic with God." In another instance he turns to the image of merging. "The only true and perfect will is the one that has been merged with the will of God, so that the man has no will of his own. And the more it is so, the more man blends into God."[42]

When asked what the perfect will is, Eckhart replied that the will "is perfect and right when it has no special reference, when it has cut loose from self and when it is transformed and adapted to the will of God." As to the results of giving up self-will, Eckhart asserts that "God never gave himself, nor will he ever, to one whose will is alien to his own. Where God finds His will done, there He gives himself and enters (the world) with all that He is and the more we depart from self, the more (the self giving of God) will be realized."[43]

In the above statements we see Eckhart's emphasis on "reducing oneself to zero" or denying the will, for two reasons, the practical one being that it is more conducive to peace in the world, and the theological one being that it leads to union with God and the doing of his, not one's own, will. The concept of zero is not a negative one to Eckhart. There cannot be a sequence of numbers, for example, without zero as the first one. And a state of zero is not a state of nothingness, because potentiality is there. A vessel, for example, must be empty before it can be filled, or only an empty vessel has the potential of being filled.

For Eckhart man is like the rest of nature in origins. In one sermon he said, "Angels, men and creatures all flow out of God in whom their prime origin is." Man's end is to return to that state of original being, the state in which he existed before being created "when there was no separation between man and God" (*Sermons*, No. 23). Being freed of self-will is one way of doing this. Eckhart draws an analogy between fire and wood and man and God. Just as the fire burns the wood and changes the wood into its own nature, so when man and God are united, man is changed into the very nature of God. Does this mean that the individual has lost all individuality in this union? It would seem so. However, let us not draw a final conclusion at this point.

Blakney, in his translation of Eckhart, suggests that Eckhart's main concern was "the unity of God and man."[44] More recently, Cox writes that "Eckhart's principal preoccupation was the nature of God."[45] Another recent author notes that "the Meister's message about the return or reditus of all things to God" is "the central theme of his vernacular sermons as well as the major component of his scholastic works."[46] One might combine the above three by indicating that the questions Eckhart agonized over concerned the nature of God; God's relation to man and creation, whether a distinct or indistinct one; how man is to relate to God; and the nature of the relationship.

Eckhart's basic premise regarding man is that he is body and spirit[47] or, to use other terminology, has a lower and higher consciousness and, regarding reality that, as has already been noted, everything emanates or comes from one primal source and seeks to return to it. All creation desires unity, the supreme unity being with the source of all that is. In the unification process, the source, as eternally active, reaches down to man, even as man reaches up to it. Thus, the answer to the last question about the nature of the relationship is that it is one of union; if union with God, a sense of selfhood remains; if union with Godhead, none does. The answer to questions two and three is a twofold one. God relates to man and man to God in two ways, to use contemporary terminology, through "the birth of the Son in the Soul" and by "breaking through to the divine Ground."[48]

Eckhart answers the first question by making a basic distinction between God and the Godhead. God is personal being, with attributes, active, creator, of the category of the relative, the "uttered word," the "Trinity which flows out from the unity of the Godhead."[49] We must distinguish this type or level of reality from the second, the Godhead that is absolute, nonpersonal, being per se, without attributes, the ground of all including God, wordless, indescribable, uncreated, undifferentiated, formless, hidden.

Because man's goal or ultimate end is union, we can now ask, in more detail, how it is accomplished. In the case of the personal God, it is done on God's part by the manifesting of Himself in the Trinity of the Father, Son, and Holy Spirit viewed as, among other things, love, such as the love between a father and a son. It is done on man's part by his attaining of a state of nonconscious ethical purity through the practice of detachment or disinterest, love, self-emptying or abandonment, denying of self-will and other virtues. By reaching such purity, man opens himself up to God's manifestation of Himself in the Son; that is, the birth of the Son in the soul occurs.[50]

As to union with the Godhead, Eckhart was much concerned about this. For he found that, while the first view of Divine Reality as personal, in which one is united with God through Christ, was sufficient for the majority, it was not for himself. He could not rest until he had gone beyond that to an experience of the root of all existence, the Godhead itself, or, until he had broken through to the Divine Ground.[51] Such union and breaking through is possible because the Ground acts and in some mysterious way opens itself up to man and his higher consciousness or soul. But the individual must be active also, and his action takes the form of transcending the senses and reason[52] and through intuitive direct insight[53] immediately experiencing the Godhead.

A comparison of the two views of the Divine and union therewith is interesting. In the first instance it is union through a medium and thus can be associated with the notion of the "birth of the Son in the Soul." It is God's "distinct" relation to creation, distinct because it is in the visible person of Christ.[54] It is a union of God and the soul in its formal existence or aspect.[55] It is a union of love because God is love and out of his love for man he sent Christ into the world to save man. It is dualistic because "love implies duality,"[56] a duality of lover and loved or God and man. It is a union in which the sense of individuality remains.

In the case of the second it is an unmediated,[57] ontological union, a union of the essence of the soul with the essence of all being, the Godhead. Union with the Godhead is possible because the soul is grounded in the Godhead, even as is God. Thus the soul "breaks through" to the Divine Ground. It is an "indistinct union" because it cannot be fully described; it is, to use traditional terms, ineffable or noetic. And it was Eckhart's trying to give expression to the ineffable,[58] which, among other things led to his being charged a heretic. It is a union of knowledge on the one hand, but it is more than that. It is a transpersonal, sensual, and rational state of being and is possible because the soul has a higher consciousness. It is monistic and ontological in that knowing and being become one. The knowing process is one in which the knower is both active and acted upon. Thus to know is to become aware of, sensitive to, conscious of, illuminated by. And awareness expands and illumination increases as one reaches deeper and deeper into the recesses of the soul.[59] It leads to stillness, stability, quiescence, loss of individuality, silence, and the peace that "passes all understanding."[60]

We may end by noting that, while he did not deny the latter, Eckhart's is primarily a mystical, not historical, interpretation of the Incarnation,[61] that for him man's return should be to the ultimate Godhead and that it is accomplished through the *via negativa* and the *via interioria*. Unfortunately, his critics either did not understand or did not want to understand this, and this is why he faced the Inquisitors of the Church, as did others before and after him.[62]

Thomas à Kempis

The third medieval mystic to be taken up is Thomas à Kempis. His life, from 1380 to 1471, was a rather uneventful one. He was born in the small town of Kempen, near Cologne, and went to a Brethren of the Common Life school whose religious orientation was Christ- and piety-centered, with little concern for theology and the institutionalized aspects of Christianity. At the age of twenty-five, he became an Augustinian monk and for the rest of his life lived at the monastery of Mount St. Agnes near Zwolle, where he became noted for his devoutness, zeal in prayer, austerity, humility, and thorough knowledge of the Bible, the New Testament portion being his favorite. The work he is most noted for is *The Imitation of Christ*, one of the most widely read books in Christendom.

Thomas seems to have taken a rather dim view of the world. He refers to "these days of fallen Christianity" and says life is filled with vanity, corruption, restlessness, trials, and tribulations. He writes that "we are surrounded on all sides by opponents—after all, remember that the devil slumbereth not, nor is the flesh yet dead. Be, therefore, continually prepared for the contest; for, on the right hand, and on the left, thou art beset with enemies that are never at rest."[63] Like Ecclesiastes, he laments that "the strength of the mighty bring no support; the counsels of the wise and the labors of the learned impart no instruction; the treasures of the earth purchase no deliverance, and the most remote and secret places afford no protection. All persons and things that seem to promise peace and happiness are in themselves vanity and nothing, and subvert the hope that is built upon them."[64]

Thomas declares that we are constantly beset by "our adversary the devil, who never sleepeth, but continually goeth about, seeking whom he may devour." In this world, he says, "all is vanity but the love of God, and a life devoted to His will." He urges us to "abandon the cares and pleasures of this fallen world" for, "whatever I can desire or conceive as essential to my peace cannot be the production of this world, and in this world I seek not for it." And in the last chapter of his book he prays to God, "O protect and keep my soul amidst the innumerable evils which this corruptible life is always bringing forth."[65]

Thomas saw the world as also filled with dualities, antinomies, and contradictions. A basic one is the dualism of heaven and earth or the heavenly and the earthly. He contrasts "the uninterrupted felicity of paradise" with "the darkness, impurity and tumult of the world." He touches on the body/spirit dualism many times. For example, "the delights of the world and the pleasures of sense are either impure or vain," while the "joys and consolations of the spirit alone are holy, substantial and delightful." The patient man is one who constantly "endeavors to bring the body into absolute and total subjection to the spirit." And the "inordinate love for the indulgences of corrupt flesh and blood" is contrary to "the interest of our immortal spirits."[66]

Further antinomies are "the infinite and unchangeable good" in contrast with "that which is finite and perishing." God is "infinite in goodness" while man is "wholly evil." If you are to keep yourself "for eternal life," you must "hate the temporal life." If you are to be "exalted in heaven," you must "humble thyself on earth." How Thomas deals with the dualisms will be noted later.

Thomas's low view of the world is matched by an equally negative view of man. We exist in a "prison of flesh and blood." We lie "bound in the chains of animal passions unwilling to rise above the selfish enjoyments of flesh and blood." We are driven by the "evil appetites and passions of our fallen nature." We demonstrate our evilness by our ingratitude for God's grace "in not rendering back the gift (of his Holy Spirit) with the thankfulness and praise of dependent wretchedness."[67] How he reconciles man's wretchedness with his being created by God and in God's image will be dealt with subsequently.

Thomas warns that we must be careful about the way we live in this world, for a day of reckoning is inevitable. In that approaching day of "universal judgment" or that "great day of universal retribution" we will be asked "not what we have read, but what we have done, not how eloquently we have spoken, but how holily we have lived." His description of purgatory is graphic and detailed:

As thy soul is imperishable, what can the fire of purgatory devour but thy sins. The more, therefore, thou now indulgest thyself, and gratifiest the desires of thy flesh, the more severe must be thy future suffering, and the more fuel doest thou heap up as food for that fire. The pains of that tremendous state will arise from the nature and degree of every man's sins. There the spiritual sluggard shall be incessantly urged with burning stings, and the glutton tortured with inconceivable hunger and thirst; there the luxurious and voluptuous shall be overwhelmed with waves of flaming pitch and offensive sulfur; and the envious, with the pain of disappointed malignity, shall howl like mad dogs; the proud shall be filled with shame, and the covetous straightened in expressible want. One hour of torment there will be more insupportable than an hundred years of the severest penance in this life; there, no respite of pain, no consolation of sorrow, can be found; while here, some intermission of labour, some comfort from holy friends, is not incompatible with the most rigorous discipline.[68]

If the sinful will be punished on the day of judgment, the virtuous, on the other hand, will surely be recompensed. He advocates, therefore, the "patient endurance of evils and wrongs," for:

... then shall the righteous man stand in great boldness before the face of such as have afflicted and oppressed him. Then shall he rise up in judgment, who now meekly submits to the judgment of others; then the humble and poor in spirit shall have great confidence, and the proud shall be encompassed with fear on every side; then it will be evident to all, that he was wise in this world, who had learned to be despised as a fool for the love of Christ; then the remembrance of tribulation patiently endured will become sweet, and all iniquity shall stop her mouth; then every devout man shall

rejoice, and every impious man shall mourn; then shall the morti-
fied and subdued flesh triumph over that which was pampered in
ease and indulgence, the coarse garment shall shine, and the soft
raiment lose all its lustre, and the homely cottage shall be more
extolled than the gilded palace.[69]

Many today would find unacceptable Thomas's counsel that
we suffer the evils and injustices of this life for a future heavenly
reward. This is in part because we live in a milieu which is more
this-worldly-oriented and in which one major task of religion is
believed to be the confronting and overcoming of the injustices
and wrongs people experience here and now. Otherwise, as
Marxist and non-Marxist alike says, religion simply becomes
an opiate.

While this is true, should we not, nevertheless, admit the
possible validity of what Thomas is saying? There are times
when we suffer personal grievances, and, after we have done all
we can to right them without complete success, what do we
do? Do we become bitter and disillusioned, or do we take consolation in a deity who we believe will at some time or other
compensate for the unrighted wrong? Thomas advises us to follow the latter course.

While Thomas paints a picture of the future life of the blessed
and the damned, we are still faced with the question of how to
live here and now. His answer to that question is found in the
title of his chief work; it is by imitating Christ. It would not be
too far afield to call Thomas a Christo-centric mystic, for there
are numerous references to Christ in his writings.

He pictures Christ as the Truth. He is the "teacher of teach-
ers," the "light and lord of angels." Christ is "the Comforter
within." He is to be "the supreme object of our love" and alone
"is to be loved without reserve." He is to be our "chosen friend,
infinitely loved and preferred above all others." To meditate on
him should be "our principal employment." We should depend
upon Christ and not the "caprice of men." He who depends
solely "on his redeeming power turns not aside to vain comforts
nor seeks after any delights of the senses."[70]

If Christ's life is to be imitated, what kind of life did Christ
live? Thomas presents Christ as meek and lowly on the one
hand, and triumphant, crucified, and risen on the other. He was
patient under tribulation. He lived a life of humility and self-
denial. He did not put himself forward. He was "rejected of men
and in the extremity of distress, forsaken by his disciples and

friends." He had "enemies and slanderers." Yet in the end he triumphed over such animosities, transcended such humiliations, and rose victorious over the things of the world.

Thomas warns of the price to be paid for "living a life conformed to the life of Christ." You must "patiently bear whatever befalls thee." You must be willing to "become a fool for the sake of Christ." You will be required to undergo "severe exercises of self-denial" and "endure the most painful labors." But most of all, you must "partake of his suffering on the cross." You must "suffer with Christ and for Christ."[71]

But no matter how hard the life you will be required to lead, live it for the sake of Christ and for the benefits that will accrue in the hereafter. For the glory of Christ "patiently bear whatever befalls thee." Remember that you are living to please Christ and not the world, to do his will, not yours. If you do that, Christ will come and bless you. You will find in Christ the peace the world cannot give, the peace "that passeth all understanding." Moreover, "when Jesus is present," all is well and no labor seems difficult. Be consoled with the truth that "the path of light and glory are found only by servants of the cross." Be then a willing "servant of the cross." For Jesus' sake, take up the cross and follow him.[72]

If we are to follow and emulate Christ, we are to do the same or even more so in the case of God. In the end, God is to be our model. Ultimately God is the one to look up to. His power saves us. His wisdom enlightens us. His goodness envelops us. Thus, Thomas is a God-centered, as well as a Christ-centered, mystic.

Where does Thomas's view of God come from? The answer is the New, much more than the Old, Testament. Thomas rejects the warrior God of the Old Testament who slays and conquers, who is an absolute sovereign, demanding unquestioned obedience and compliance, who rules arbitrarily and chooses whom he will. Thomas pictures God instead, as "righteous and good," and of "infinite wisdom." He is "the Comforter within," our refuge and hope. God is to be loved, not feared, for "he that loveth God with all his heart fears neither death, nor punishment, nor judgment, nor hell."[73]

Thomas says that "true glory and holy joy is found only in thee." In God one finds "supreme and everlasting rest." All blessedness is in God alone. All good proceeds from Him. He is "the author of all the good that nature can dispense." He is a fountain "from whom all good originally flows." He is Himself "infinite in goodness." God is providential, and we are to "wait patiently the disposals of my providence and thou shalt find all things work together for thy good." God pours out His spirit on the "truly thankful and from the proud is taken away that which is always given to the humble." God is "the comfort of the poor and the exultation of the humble." He "raiseth the humble and humbleth the self-presuming." Thomas's emphasis on God and the humble is emphatic in his statement that:

> The humble man God protects and delivers; the humble he loves and comforts; to the humble he condescends; on the humble he bestows more abundant measures of his grace, he reveals the mysteries of redemption, and sweetly invites and powerfully draws him to Himself. The humble man, though surrounded with the scorn and reproach of the world, is still in peace: for the stability of his peace resteth not upon the world, but upon God.[74]

The requirements for union with God and a life of holiness enumerated by Thomas are much like those of other medieval mystics. They include self-abandonment, surrender, denial, conquest, renunciation, and subjection. Self-will is to be abandoned for "all is vanity but the love of God and a life devoted to his will." "To abandon thy own will is the only way to become united with God," Thomas says. Moreover, "he is truly learned who hath learned to abandon his own will and do the will of God." We are to abandon "the cares and pleasures of this wretched world and turn to the lord with all thy heart." Paradoxically, to "abandon all is to possess all."[75]

As for self-denial, Thomas says it is "the basis of spiritual perfection," and "without a total denial of self" one cannot attain "the possession of perfect liberty." One must be careful to "resist and subdue small sins" lest one "insensibly fall into greater." To make progress in the Christian life, one must "restrain all thy senses within strict discipline." The "appetites of the flesh" must be restrained, self-love must be subdued. This is not easy; rather, it requires "long and severe conflicts to subdue the earthly and selfish nature, and turn all the desire of the soul to God."[75]

Given his view of man, Thomas's insistence that union with God is not achieved by man's efforts alone is not unexpected. God's grace is required in addition. Thomas says, along with other Medieval mystics, that, even as man reaches up to God, God in his grace and mercy reaches down to man. Thomas writes that as a person advances in the process of self-mortification, surrender, and renunciation, he obtains "higher degrees of the grace of God" and "if thou press forward with unabated fervor, thou shalt find strength and peace, and through the mercy of God and that love of holiness which his grace hath inspired, wilt perceive thy yoke become daily more easy and thy burden more light."[77]

To the question of God and evil, Thomas gives both a practical and theological answer. The practical is seen in the title of a chapter, "Of the Benefit of Adversity." "Gold is tried in fire," he wrote, "and acceptable men in the furnace of adversity." Adversity reminds us we should not place our trust "in any worldly enjoyment." Further, "to be evil thought of and evil spoken of even when intentions are upright and action blameless" helps to keep us humble and is "a powerful antidote to the poison of vainglory." Third, adversity purifies us. Thomas writes that "temptations, however dangerous and afflicting, are highly beneficial because, under their discipline, we are humbled, purified, and led towards perfection." Also, suffering leads us to have recourse not to human but godly consolations. Adversity, then, leads to a greater trust in God and His providence.

On a theological level, Thomas asserts that the presence of evil in the world does not deny God's omniscience, beneficence, and omnipotence. God knows what is happening to us and will see to it that everything works out all right in the end. Because He is good, whatever God permits to befall us, He "permitteth it to promote the important business of our redemption." Thomas adds that, "no evil, however, is permitted to befall thee but what may be productive of a much greater good" and "though thou permittests me to be exposed to the trial of various troubles, yet thou mercifully superintendest the conflict, and directeth the event for my supreme and everlasting good" (*Imitation*, 306). Evil, then, is not a denial of God's goodness, wisdom, and power.

Thomas distinguishes sharply between the godly and the worldly and insists that they are exclusive of each other. He writes that "thou canst not live to me whilst though seekest delight in the transitory enjoyments of time and sense" and "my grace, which is infinitely pure, like the fountain whence it flows, cannot unite with the love of sensual pleasure, and the enjoyment of the world." In another passage, he writes that "as long as thou are united to an earthly body, thy days will often be full of heaviness and thy heart of sorrow . . . and thou must groan under the power of those carnal appetites that interrupt the exercises of the spirit." And the distinction between God and this world is put most fully and forcefully in a paragraph in the last chapter of *The Imitation of Christ:*

> Wherever I look for support and consolation out of thee I find nothing but weakness and distress: and if thou dost not revive, strengthen, illuminate, deliver and preserve me, the friendship of mankind can give no consolation; the strength of the mighty, bring no support; the counsels of the wise, and the labours of the learned, impart no instruction; the treasures of the earth, purchase no deliverance; and the most remote and secret places afford no protection. All persons and things, that seem to promise peace and happiness, are in themselves vanity and nothing, and subvert the hope that is built upon them; but thou art the supreme, essential, and final good; the perfection of life, light, and love! and the most powerful support of thy servants, is found in an unreserved and absolute dependence upon thee![78]

The contrast between the godly and the wordly or the human and the divine is especially evident in Thomas's view of man, of which more may be said at this point. He follows the St. Paul and Augustinian "utter depravity" view of man that is reflected in his numerous characterizations. We groan under the power of "carnal appetite" and "dark passions." We are more inclined to evil than good. We are poor and destitute in every respect. We are "inconstant and feeble," "changeable as the events of time." We are "tossed by every wave of affliction and driven by every gust of passion." We are subject to "the influence of unredeemed human nature which is ever tending to love of self." Thomas says his sins are "so numerous and aggravated that they have exposed me to everlasting wrath and rendered me unworthy of the society of thy faithful servants, from which I ought to be driven as an object of universal scorn and contempt."[79]

All of this has made us a "stranger and a pilgrim" or a "spirit fallen into a corrupt human body." Our frailty is such that "we are more ready to believe and speak evil of one another than good." We judge persons "as they either oppose or gratify our private views and inclinations." We naturally love those most "whose sentiments and dispositions correspond most without own." Men are "as inconsistent as the wind, and he that is for thee today may tomorrow be against thee." Our natures are such that while "to will is present with me, how to perform that which is good, I find not."[80]

A summary of man's condition is found in Thomas's well-known chapter, "Of the Different Characters and Operations of Nature and Grace." In describing the differences between man's actions when under the influence of nature and grace, he says the following:

> Under nature we are motivated by self-interest and advantage, although we pretend not to be. Under grace we do what is profitable for all; we are concerned about the common good, and we do not act hypocritically. Nature leads us to seek our own gratification, grace to further God's good. Under nature's influence we desire "the exercise of authority and dominion;" under grace we live in submission to God's authority and will.

> By nature our sensual appetites are stimulated; by grace they are subdued. By nature we are fond of receiving honor and applause; under grace we care for only what brings honour and praise to God. Nature courts idleness and rest; grace idleness as the nurse of sin, labour as the condition of life. Nature delights . . . in the splendour of dress; grace puts on " . . . the most plain and humble garments." Nature is concerned with the pleasures and successes of this world; grace does not adhere to " . . . the enjoyments of time and sense."[81]

Nature seeks after that which is perishable; grace seeks the eternal. Nature makes us greedy and selfish, grace benevolent and sharing. Nature seeks her comfort from that which "produces animal delight"; grace has no comfort but in God. Under nature we do the good, expecting recompense, under grace for its own sake. Nature favors the rich, the ostentatious, the powerful; grace the humble, poor, lowly. Nature claims all excellence for herself; grace ascribes all goodness to God. Nature claims wisdom for herself and restlessly pursues the novel and unique. Grace views the wisdom of the world as vain and seeks only the gifts and graces of the Holy Spirit. Such are the different influences of nature and grace.

How did man get into the predicament he finds himself in? Thomas's answer is quite simple—the fall. In speaking of "all the workings of revolted nature, which is disposed to evil from its birth," he writes that "it fell in Adam, and fallen, descended from him to all mankind, who have increased its obliquity by voluntary and habitual sin." We have here the traditional Christian doctrine of original and transmitted sin and the solution Thomas proposes is the traditional one as well. One need quote only two of his statements to demonstrate this. The first is, "In true contrition and humiliation, the hope of pardon has its birth: there the troubled conscience is set at rest; the grace that was lost is found again; man is delivered from the wrath to come; and God and the penitent soul meet together with a holy kiss." Thus this is the way of penance, pardon, and union.

The second is the statement with which Thomas ends his soliloquy on nature and grace:

> Such is the transcendency of grace to nature. She is the offspring of the light of heaven, the immediate gift of God, the peculiar distinction of the elect, and the pledge of eternal happiness; by whose power, the soul is raised from earth to heaven, and from carnal transformed to spiritual. The more, therefore, nature is suppressed and subdued, the more grace lives and triumphs; and by super-added communications of light and strength, "the inward man, is day by day," more and more renewed after the Image of God.[82]

The transformation of man comes through an infusion of God's grace. The ennobling of man is the result of his being renewed in God's image. We see here some universal themes of the mystics; their minimizing of the self and the exulting of that which is not the self; their sense of dependence on that which is greater than oneself; the giving up or giving over of oneself to that being; and the rapture, joy, and plenitude that results.

Kempis's ethics may be called an ethics of grace, one reason being his insistence that whatever good man does is through God's grace and not his own merit. Thomas is very definite about this in his statement, "Do not desire to be admired and praised for the goodness in thee, as if it were thy own. For the praise of being good is the prerogative of God. His goodness alone is absolute and underived, and thou art good, only by the communication of that goodness which from eternity to eternity dwells essentially in him." Other statements are equally pointed: "There is no good dwelling in me that I can call my own"; "there is no goodness in man but what he receives immediately from me"; "whatever good they have, they acknowledge it to be received"; "there is no good of which I am not the principle and centre"; "he that challengeth and appropriateth any good to himself bars the entrance to the grace of God. For the Holy Spirit chooses, for the seat of his influence, a contrite and humble heart"; "how indispensably necessary is thy grace, O Lord! by whose power alone every good work must be begun, continued, and perfected. Without that power, I can do nothing that is acceptable to thee; but with it, I can do all things."[83]

As the statements above indicate, Thomas believes that God's goodness is absolute and underived while man's is derived. Man and God differ in regard to motivation also. Thomas, like Eckhart, believes that God does not need a motive for doing the good. He simply does it. Man, however, acts only if there is a reason for doing so. Thomas lists as "the common motives that influence the conduct of men . . . inordinate effectations, self-will, the hope of reward, and the desire of personal advantage and convenience." And many actions that "assume the appearance of charity (love)" are "wholly selfish and carnal."[84]

Thomas, of course, would have us act from pure motive. One reason is that God can see within and know why a person acts as he does. God, Thomas says, "regardeth more the degree of love with which we act than what or how much we have performed." God's concern, then, is for the motive as much as the act itself, for He knows that a good act can be soiled by an impure motive. Thomas acknowledges the desirability of doing good works. But they should be done for the right motive, namely for the sake of goodness in and of itself. They should not be done in the hope of attaining eternal life; that, according to Thomas, comes from repentance and faith in God through Christ, and not through good works.

For Thomas, the internal and external cannot be separate. Thus, if our "inward principle" is corrupt, our acts that flow from it "must be corrupt also." For it is only out of a pure heart "that the divine fruits of a pure life can be brought forth." It is not to be wondered, then, that Thomas placed so much emphasis on a pure heart or inner purity for, if the heart is pure, one's acts will be also.

Conducive to inner purity is the living of a life of simplicity. If we were to attribute an economic philosophy to Thomas, we might describe it as a philosophy of asceticism and grace. He points out that, as a matter of fact, our "real wants are soon and easily supplied." Man's real happiness "consisteth not in the abundance of things which he possesseth." And such temporal advantages as riches and power "are of no value; their acquisition and continuance are uncertain, and their enjoyment painful, for they are never possessed without solicitude and fear."[85]

As to grace, Thomas says, grace "has no temporal interests to secure, for she desires no greater share of the possessions of time, than is necessary to sustain her in her progress to eternity." Also, grace favors the poor rather than the rich. Moreover, grace "is wholly inattentive to personal profit and convenience, and regards that most which is most subservient to the common good."[86]

Thomas often reiterates the theme of the common good. He exhorted his fellow monks "to be always either reading, or writing, or praying, or meditating, or employed in some useful labor for the common good." He urged that "whatever good thou are truly conscious of, think more highly of the good of others, and thou mayest preserve the humility of thy spirit." He pointed out that "he doth much and well, who constantly preferreth the good of the community, to the gratification of his own will" (*Imitation*, 83).

Thomas's economic philosophy was not shared by many in the medieval period, both outside and inside the church. Interests were becoming increasingly privatized. The wealth of the church was multiplying, and while the medieval period is often said to be more other than this worldly oriented, one wonders about such an assertion.

Inner purity also leads to the use of only good means to achieve one's ends. Thomas specifies at least two instances in which evil means are not to be used. The first is indicated in his statement, "Let not the hope of any worldly advantage, nor the affection thou bearest to any creature, prevail upon thee to do that which is evil." The point here is obvious; we are not to use evil means to advance our temporal welfare.

Thomas becomes more specific in the second instance when he says that God is "not a God of dissension, but of peace; and the interest of peace are promoted by meekness and humility, not by strife and self-exaltation." Concerning Thomas's views on what means are to be used to deal with enemies and the evil doers, several of his statements may be quoted that reflect a combination of Stoicism and the teachings of Christ. Similar to Marcus Aurelius's admonition is Thomas's injunction: "When thou meetest with injury from the violence or treachery of man, exert all thy resolution to drive the thoughts of it from thy heart; but if it toucheth thee too sensibly to be soon buried in forgetfulness, let it neither depress nor vex thee; and if thou canst not bear it cheerfully, at least bear it patiently." Traces of Stoicism are also found in this statement, "it is not by flight, but by patience and humility, that we must become superior to all our enemies."[87]

In comparing nature and grace, Thomas notes that "nature

exults in the extensive interest of numerous relations and friends; glories in dignity of station, and splendor of descent; fawns upon the powerful." Grace, however, "loves her enemies and counts not the number of her friends; she values not the splendor of station and the nobility of birth, but as they are dignified by superior virtue." Thomas may have had in mind Jesus' exhortation, "Blessed are the peacemakers" when he wrote, "The patient man hath, in this world, a true and salubrious purification; who, when he is injured, is more grieved for the sin of the offender, than for the wrong that is done to himself; who can ardently pray for his enemies, and from his heart forgive their offences; who feels no reluctance to ask forgiveness of others; who is sooner moved to compassion, than provoked to anger."[88]

To those quick to take things in their own hands, Thomas cautioned, "If after the first and second admonition, thy brother will not obey the truth, contend no longer with him, but leave the event to God, who only knoweth how to turn evil into good, that His will may be done, and his glory accomplished in all His creatures." And in regard to Jesus, Thomas wrote, "For his sake, and in the power of His love, thy enemies are to be dear to thee, as well as thy friends; and let it be thy continual prayer for all, even for thy enemies, that all may be blessed with the knowledge and love of him."[89]

The statements above reflect a strain of pacifism in Thomas's thought which, like his economic philosophy, was not widely heeded in the medieval period. Reflecting the predominant view was the exhilaration and zealousness of the crusades and crusaders, and the spinning out by theologians of the just war arguments. Thomas, however, urges men to trust in God rather than in power, violence, force, or arms. Follow the teachings and example of Christ who loved and forgave even those who crucified him. Return to the tradition of the pre-Constantine Church when Christians refused to take up weapons and fight in the armies of Rome.

As a final comment on Thomas's ethics, one may note that he was an ethical universalist or absolutist. He speaks of an "infinite and unchangeable good," known only to those few who totally "abandon that which is finite and continually perishing." Clues to how it may be known is found in chapter three of *The Imitation*. It begins with the statement, "Blessed is the man whom Eternal Truth teacheth, not by obscure figures and transient sounds, but by a direct and full communication." "Transient sounds" refers to the "perceptions of our senses" which, Thomas says, "are narrow and dull." "Obscure figures" refers to "our reasoning on those perceptions" that "frequently mislead us." Such statements indicate Thomas's attitude toward knowledge gained through the senses and reason. At best, it is flawed, and at the most, it is limited to the material world.

Thomas, of course, is more concerned about other types and levels of knowledge. How does one come to know Eternal Truth, the Eternal Word, or Eternal Verities. In addition to the "direct and full communication" indicated above, Thomas refers to the knowledge man does not acquire by "labor of study but receives from divine illumination." In another chapter in *The Imitation*, he writes of God: "I am he who exalteth the humble and simple mind, and suddenly impart to it such a perception of eternal truth as it could not acquire by a life of laborious study in the schools of men. I teach not with a clamor of uncertain words . . . I teach in still and soft whispers." In the same chapter he writes, "To some I speak only of common truths; I make myself known to some under the more familiar appearance of human forms; and by a sudden and immediate communication of divine light, open the deepest mysteries to others."[90]

Divine knowledge and knowledge of the greatest import, then, is not known by reason or the senses but through a direct and immediate illumination of the mind or soul. Its source is God, whom he describes by using several similes. Light is one. One becomes aware of one's "fallen state" by "that light with which I, who am the Truth, enlighten thee." God is the origin of "the knowledge that is from above and cometh down from the Father of Light." God is the "eternal Word which condescendeth to teach." God is "that divine principle which speaketh in our hearts and, without which, there can be neither just apprehension nor rectitude of judgment."[91]

For Thomas, truth, like goodness or virtue, exists *a priori*. Man does not create them, he only discovers them. Through a process of self-purification, he lays himself open to them. He makes himself ready to receive them, and they are then given to him.

It is interesting and significant that Thomas closely associates truth and love, or the head and heart. He prays, "O God who art the truth, make me one with thee in everlasting love." He says that "the more a man is advanced in singleness and simplicity of heart, the more sublime and diffusive will be his knowledge which he receives from divine illumination." He points out that God's truths "enlighten the understanding and influence the heart." He notes that "by an intimate and supreme love of me, some have been wonderfully filled with divine knowledge." And God insists, he asserts, that "the flame of divine love should infinitely transcend the sublimest heights of human reason."[92]

For Thomas, truth has ontological overtones. Truth is not simply something one gets. It is a part of a state of being, or a matter of being truthful or attaining a state of truthfulness. It involves a state or attitude of love and compassion. And the greater one's love and compassion, the greater will be one's knowledge.

Thomas's epistemological views should be set within the context of medieval scholasticism. Noted universities were springing up under the jurisdiction of the church. Religious orders such as the Dominicans were becoming leaders in education. Logic, dialectics, and natural sciences were studied along with theology. Men of learning were held in high repute. Classical learning was being revived. Disputations occurred between scholars.

Thomas did not share in the exaltation of scholastic learning characteristic of many of his contemporaries. He did not care for intellectual ostentation. He was concerned not with reconciling orthodoxy and Aristotle, but sinful man with a saving God, man's will with God's, this life and the next. Thus we find him writing, "It is not profound speculations, but a holy life, that makes a man righteous and good, and dear to God," and "I would rather feel compunction (repentance) than to be able to give the most accurate definition of it." Similarly, "If I knew all that the world contains and had not charity, what would it avail me in the sight of God, who will judge me according to my deeds?"[93]

In another chapter, he contrasts "the meek wisdom of an illuminated mind devoted to me" and "the pompous wisdom of a critical and Classical mind." He asserts that "Better is the humble peasant that serveth God than the proud philosopher who, destitute of knowledge of himself, can describe the course of the planets." And to the intellectually arrogant he cautioned, "If thou supposest that thou knowest many things, and has perfect understanding of them, consider how many more things there are which thou knowest not at all; and instead of being exalted with a high opinion of thy great knowledge, be rather abased by a humble sense of thy much greater ignorance."[94]

The last statement indicates one of the ends or purposes of

knowing. It should lead us to be humble rather than proud for the more we know, the more we should realize how little we know. Self-knowledge is a second end. "Let the superior knowledge that is given thee make thee more fearful and more watchful over thyself," Thomas wrote. Third, it should lead to a life of holiness and union with God. Of science Thomas said, "Science, or a proper knowledge of the things that belong to the present life, is so far from being blamable, considered in itself, that it is good and ordained of God; but purity of conscience and holiness of life must ever be preferred before it," and a "humble knowledge of thyself, therefore, is a more certain way of leading thee to God than the most profound investigations of science." Moreover, God's word should be read "not for the reputation of critical skill and controversial wisdom, but to learn how to mortify thy evil passions, a knowledge of infinitely more importance than the solution of all the abstruse questions that have perplexed men's minds and divided their opinions."[95]

In short, know nature or the world not in order to exploit and become rich from it, but only to the degree of sufficiency. Know in order to appreciate. Do not seek knowledge for its own sake. Seek to know only in order to make yourself a more fit vessel for God's purposes in this life and the next.

Thomas believed epistemological humility was of much practical value. It would bring about "rest from an inordinate desire of knowledge." It would lead us to recognize how vain it is "to hunt after honors." It would prevent disagreements coming from intellectual dogmatism for "from the diversity of inclinations and opinions tenaciously adhered to arise dissension among friends and countrymen, nay, even among the professors of a religious and holy life." It would keep us from being pertinacious for "men love to act from their own judgment and are always most inclined to those that are of the same opinion with themselves."[96]

Conclusion

Although there were differences, the medieval mystics had much in common, and it is on that note that I would like to close. They were critical, for example, of both the church and the world, and they sought to cleanse or purify both. They were concerned about how to live a truly Christian life here as well as in the hereafter. Inner purity was a key to such, attained primarily through God's grace rather than self-effort. They believed in God's goodness, providence, and love. They urged people to trust more in God and less in themselves, for God can do things that man cannot. Be illumined by God's grace; let it permeate and radiate out from you, being reflected in all you say and do.

The mystics, if not disdainful of worldly things—power, wealth, privilege, honors—were not attached to or attracted by them. For they recognized that genuine happiness, or beatitude, cannot come from the things of the world, which are subject to change and decay. Real happiness comes through union with God and our fellow human beings. That union is our chief goal in life. Purification or purgation is necessary to reach it, just as joy and beatitude are the result.

The medieval mystics expounded and tried to live by the gentle virtues. Be patient, kind, loving, without envy or jealousy. Return good for evil. Love your enemies. Forgive rather than seek revenge. Be as concerned about the good of others as your own. Empathize with others in their sorrows and their joys. Be humble and do not place yourself in the center of things. For the universe gravitates around God, not you. Let Christ be your model. Seek to imitate Him in all you say and do. Lead a life of simplicity; do not let it be burdened and cluttered up by things. Live in the world without being overwhelmed by it. Do good without thought of reward. To find oneself one must lose oneself. Self-emptying is the way to self-fulfillment. What is true for the individual is true for the church also. To be true to its founder it should give up ostentation, pomp, power, wealth, and privilege. They are incompatible with true Christianity and are contrary to the teachings and example of Christ.

The mystics insisted that the divine is in every person and we should treat everyone thusly. We should recognize the unity, bounty, and oneness of God's creation and seek to become one with it, not exploiting but taking from it only what meets our needs rather than what satisfies our greed. Be good caretakers of that which God has created and given to our supervision.

Finally, for the medieval mystics, the ideal person was not the wise man, the military hero, the entrepreneur, or those in high office, but "the holy man who, inspired by love and respect of God, conforms completely to the will of God."[97]

Notes

1. Thomas Okey, *The Little Flowers, Life and Mirror of St. Francis* (New York: E. P. Dutton & Co.), 380. "For his speech was as a burning afire, penetrat-

ing the secrets of the heart, and he filled the minds of all with amazement, since he set forth no adornments of men's intention, but savoured of the breath of divine intervention."

2. "Oftimes he was rapt in such ecstasies of contemplation as he was carried out of himself, and, while perceiving things beyond mortal sense, knew naught of what was happening in the outer world around him." Okey, *The Little Flowers*, 364.

3. Theodore Maynard, *Richest of the Poor: The Life of Saint Francis of Assisi* (New York: Doubleday & Co., Inc., 1952), 230.

4. Ibid., 235.

5. Ibid., 58.

6. "Christ Jesus crucified, was laid, as a bundle of myrrh, in his heart's bosom, and he yearned to be utterly transformed into Him by the fire of his exceeding love." Okey, *The Little Flowers*, 358.

7. A. C. McGiffert, *A History of Christian Thought*, vol. II (New York: Charles Scribner's Sons, 1954), 233.

8. Ray Petry, *Francis of Assisi* (New York: AMS Press, Inc., 1964), 65.

9. "That he might by all things be stirred up unto the divine love, he triumphed in all the works of the Lord's hands, and through the sight of their joy was uplifted unto their life—giving cause and origin." Okey, *The Little Flowers*, 358.

10. "His affectionate heart had made him kin to all created things." Okey, *The Little Flowers*, 359.

11. Petry, *Francis*, 44.

12. Francis's attitude toward money was much like that of the nineteenth-century mystic saint of India, Ramakrishna. Maynard, *Richest of the Poor*, 117.

13. Petry, *Francis*, 44.

14. The conversation between Francis and his Bishop found on page 90 of Maynard is an amusing example of this.

15. Maynard, *Richest of the Poor*, 115.

16. Raymond Blakney, *Meister Eckhart* (New York: Harper & Row, 1941), 54. Included are Eckhart's *Sermons, Fragments, Talks of Instruction, About Disinterest, The Book of Divine Comfort*, and the *Aristocrat*.

17. Ibid., 131. Compare Matthew Fox, *Breakthrough: Meister Eckhart's Creation Spirituality in New Translation* (New York: Doubleday & Company, Inc., 1980), 140. "I must sometimes point out that the soul wanting to perceive God must forget itself and lose itself. For if it perceives itself, then it does not perceive God." Subsequent references will be denoted by the term *Breakthrough*.

18. Blakney, *Meister Eckhart*, 223.

19. Ibid., 203.

20. Ibid., 114.

21. Ibid., 14. Compare E. College and B. McGinn, *Meister Eckhart, The Essential Sermons, Commentaries, Treatises, and Defense* (New York: Paulist Press, 1981), 258. "If a man were in an ecstasy, as Saint Paul was, and knew that some sick man needed him to give him a bit of soup, I should think it far better if you would abandon your ecstasy out of love and show greater love in caring for the other in his need." The volume is one of the *Classics of Western Spirituality* and further references to it will be denoted by the term *Classics*.

22. Blakney, *Meister Eckhart*, 10. *Classics*, "So a man must be penetrated with the divine presence, and be shaped through and through with the shape of the God he loves, and be present in him, so that God's presence may shine out to him without any effort," 254.

23. Blakney, *Meister Eckhart*, 10. *Classics*, "And in all his activities and under all circumstances a man should take care to use his reason, and in everything he should have a reasonable consciousness of himself his inwardness, and find God in all things, in the highest degree that is possible," 254.

24. Blakney, *Meister Eckhart*, 9. *Classics*, "A man ought not to have a God who is just a product of his thought, nor should he be satisfied with that, because if the thought vanished, God too would vanish. But one ought to have a God who is present, a God who is far above the notions of men and of all created things", 253.

25. Blakney, *Meister Eckhart*, 163.

26. Ibid., 113.

27. Ibid., 157.

28. Ibid., 243.

29. Ibid., 143. For the suggested parallel between Anselm and Eckhart, see "Bishop, Anselm and His Critics," *Journal of Thought* (July 1974), 155–57.

30. Blakney, *Meister Eckhart*, 8. *Classics*, "And so, just as no multiplicity can disturb God, nothing can disturb or fragment this man, for he is one in that One where all multiplicity is one and is one unmultiplicity," 252.

31. "The Tao that can be told of is not the eternal Tao; The name that can be named is not the eternal name. The Nameless is the origin of Heaven and Earth; The Named is the mother of all things." Wing-Tsit Chan, *The Way of Lao Tzu* (Indianapolis: Bobbs-Merrill Co., 1963), 91.

32. Blakney, *Meister Eckhart*, 226. *Breakthrough*, "The Godhead never goes searching for a deed. God and the Godhead are distinguished through deeds and a lack of deeds," 77.

33. Blakney, *Meister Eckhart*, 228. *Classics*, "When I stood in my first cause, I then had no God, and then I was my own cause. I wanted nothing, I longed for nothing, for I was an empty being, and the only truth in which I rejoiced was in the knowledge of myself. Then it was myself I wanted and nothing else. What I wanted I was, and what I was I wanted; and so I stood, empty of God and of everything." 200. *Breakthrough*, "When I stood in my first cause, there I had no God and I was cause of myself. There I willed nothing, I desired nothing, for I was a pure being and a knower of myself in delight of truth. There I willed myself and nothing else. What I willed, that I was, and what I was, that I willed. There I stood, free of God and of all things," 214–5. For Schurmann's translation of the sermon, "Blessed are the Poor," see R. Schurmann, *Meister Eckhart, Mystic and Philosopher* (Bloomington and London: Indiana University Press, 1978), 56.

34. Blakney, *Meister Eckhart*, 23.

35. Ibid., 156–57.

36. Ibid., 241. The notion of loving truth, justice and goodness for their own sake, and God likewise, is brought in Eckhart's sermon, "Woman, The Hour Is Coming." See R. Schurmann, *Meister Eckhart*, 55–58.

37. Blakney, *Meister Eckhart*, 33–34. *Classics*, "When a man finds himself inclined above else to virtue, and if one performs the works of virtue without preparing one's will, and if one carries them out without any special intention

of obtaining some just or important matter, acting virtuously for virtue's own sake, for the love of virtue and no other reason, then one possesses the virtues perfectly, and not until then," 277.

38. Blakney, *Meister Eckhart*, 89. *Classics*, "But a heart in detachment asks for nothing, nor has it anything of which it would gladly be free," 292. I have discussed Eckhart's emphasis on detachment in *Some Aspects of Western Mystical Ethics, The Brahmavadin* (July and October 1972), 138–48.

39. Blakney, *Meister Eckhart*, 33. *Classics*, "Indeed, it is not enough for a man's disposition to be detached just for the present moment when he wants to be bound to God, but he must have a well-exercised detachment from what is past and from what is yet to come. Then one is able to receive from God great things and, in the things, God," 276.

40. Blakney, *Meister Eckhart*, 13. *Classics*, "You can want for nothing if you have a true and just will, not love or humility or any virtue," 256.

41. Blakney, *Meister Eckhart*, 4. *Classics*, 248.

42. Blakney, *Meister Eckhart*, 4. *Classics*, "Only a perfect and true will could make one enter perfectly into God's will and be without will of one's own; and whoever has more of this, he is more fully and more truly established in God," 260.

43. Blakney, *Meister Eckhart*, 74. *Classics*, "God never gave himself or gives himself according to anyone else's will. He gives himself only by his own will. When God finds someone who is of one will with him, he gives himself to him and lets himself be in him, with everything that he is. And the more that we cease to belong to ourselves, the more truly do we belong to this," 276.

44. Blakney, *Meister Eckhart*, xxiii.

45. Michael Cox, *Mysticism. The Direct Experience of God* (Wellingborough: The Aquarian Press, 1983), 99.

46. *Classics*, 47.

47. Blakney, *Meister Eckhart*, *Breakthrough*, 510.

48. Recent studies have focused on these two themes as being central to Eckhart's thought. *Classics*, 47. For a discussion of the *Birth of the Son in the Soul*, see Frank Tobin, *Meister Eckhart: Thought & Language* (Philadelphia: University of Pennsylvania Press, 1986), 94–105, 170–71, 179–80, 182–83.

49. Cox, *Mystics*, 100. Eckhart's distinction between God and the Godhead is discussed in Oliver Davies, *God Within* (London: Darton, Longman Todd, 1988), 45–46 of the chapter on Eckhart.

50. Blakney, *Meister Eckhart*. "In the second place, the soul is purified in the practice of virtues by which we climb to a life of unity. That is the way the soul is made pure—by being purged of much divided life and by entering upon a life that is focused to unity," 173.

51. Eckhart calls this the sixth grade of living—"In the sixth grade, he is 'disformed' and transformed in the divine eternal nature, having achieved full perfection," Blakney, *Meister Eckhart*, 76. *Breakthrough*, "The sixth state is reached when people are formed from and beyond God's eternity and attain a completely perfect forgetfulness of this temporary and passing life, when they are drawn and changed into the divine image," 513.

52. "To reach out for God through the senses is futile. Knowledge derived from the sense concerns only the world of phenomena, the 'show world.' It is the lower consciousness of man that deals with the experience of the senses which is concerned only with the particular and the finite.," T. Katsaros and

N. Kaplan, *The Western Mystical Tradition* (New Haven, Conn.: College and University Press, 1969), 250.

53. "Whether the right term is existence, as Maritain claims, or essence, as it is called by many mystics, all agree that we have here a direct, although negative, knowledge of ultimate selfhood, an immediate awareness of presence to oneself and to the transcendent source of the self. Such a direct intuition bypasses the channels of sensation and judgment by which the awareness of self is usually attained." Louis Dupré, *Transcendent Selfhood* (New York: Seabury Press, 1967, 102. The Hindu Vedantist might prefer the term insight (*darsana*) to the term intuition.

54. The contrast between "distinct" and "indistinct" is one used by B. McGinn in his essay in the book *Mystical Union and Monotheistic Faith*, edited by B. McGinn and M. Idel (New York: Macmillan, 1989), 78. The contrast also is discussed several times in Tobin, *Thought & Language*, 54–55, 63–64, 78–79, 125, 136. The notion that it is an unmediated, indistinct union, that nothing should come between man and God is seen in Eckhart's statement, "But in order that nothing remain hidden from me in God, that all be revealed to me, no likeness nor any image may endure. Indeed, no image will disclose the Godhead or God's being to us. If some image or similitude remained in you, you would never become one with God. Therefore, in order for you to be one with God, no image must be represented in you, and you must not represent yourself in any." Schurmann, *Meister Eckhart*, 134.

55. Idel and McGinn, *Mystical Union*, 17.

56. Louis Dupré in *Mystical Union*, 22.

57. "The soul's agents, by which it acts, are derived from the core of the soul. In that core is the central silence, the pure peace, and abode of the heavenly birth, the place for this event: this utterance of God's word. By nature the core of the soul is sensitive to nothing but the divine being, unmediated. Here God enters the soul with all he has and not in part. He enters the soul through its core and nothing may touch that core except God himself," Blakney, *Meister Eckhart*, 97.

58. Cox, *Mysticism*, 102.

59. "The mystical mind views itself as derived from, and guided by, a higher power. This power destines it to be the link that unites what is only in part with what is wholly and unqualifiedly real. In the process of fulfilling this function, the mind moves from a level of mere consciousness to one in which consciousness coincides with being. All of Western mysticism, and much of what I know of Eastern, consists of a transition from a lower or more superficial to a higher or deeper level in which mind turns into being." Dupré in *Mystical Union*, 21. It is unfortunate that there is such a scarcity of references to the religious and philosophical traditions of India and China in Idel's and McGinn's book. Interesting comparisons are a fertile field of inquiry in future studies of Eckhart. For example, how does the Hindu concept of Brahman with attributes (Sa guna Brahman) and without (Nir guna Brahman) compare with Eckhart's God and Godhead concepts? Also are there similarities between Raj Yoga and Eckhart's way to the Godhead?

60 Blakney, *Meister Eckhart*, 79, "For granting that the soul could not be happy without it (consciousness of its own processes), still its happiness does not consist in that; for the foundation of spiritual blessing is this: that the soul look at God without anything between; here it receives its being and life and draws its essence from the core of God, unconscious of the knowing

process, or love or anything else. Then it is quite still in the essence of God, not knowing at all where it was, knowing nothing but God." *Breakthrough*, 516, "For the first characteristic of blessedness is that the soul sees God without disguise. In this way the soul receives its whole being and life, and creates all that it is out of the depth of God. The soul knows nothing about knowledge or love or anything else. It wishes to be completely at rest and exclusively in God's being."

61. Cox, *Mysticism*, 101.

62. I have drawn extensively on Blakney's translation but have coordinated it with Colledge's and McGinn's and Fox's translations as much as possible. I have also referred to Tobin's book, and to Shurmann's text where he presents and elaborates on three of Eckhart's sermons. Fox speaks somewhat harshly (3) and I believe unfairly, of Blakney's translation and is quite opinionated regarding his own (6). Blakney, relying heavily on Pfeiffer's 1857 translation, recognized the difficulty of authentication. He believed the twenty-eight sermons he included to be "most readily authenticated by reference to the *Defense*" (ix). Colledge and McGinn used the 1936 edition of the *Deutsche Forschungs gemeininschaft* and modestly admitted that "there can never be any final interpretation of Eckhart" (25). The Blakney edition seems to me a sound and readable one that captures the essential spirit of Eckhart's mysticism.

63. John Payne, trans., with an introductory essay by Thomas Chalmers, *The Imitation of Christ in Three Books by Thomas à Kempis* (New York: Robert B. Collins, 1851), 146.

64. Ibid., 306.
65. Ibid., 207.
66. Ibid., 110.
67. Ibid., 147.
68. Ibid., 110.
69. Ibid., 111–12.
70. Ibid., 143.
71. Ibid.
72. Ibid., 295.
73. Ibid., 113.
74. Ibid., 125.
75. Ibid., 234.
76. Ibid., 143.
77. Ibid., 119.
78. Ibid., 306–7.
79. Ibid., 280.
80. Ibid., 291.
81. Ibid., 284–90.
82. Ibid., 290.
83. Ibid., 292.
84. Ibid., 80.
85. Ibid., 102.
86. Ibid., 285.
87. Ibid., 78.
88. Ibid., 110.
89. Ibid., 140.
90. Ibid., 255.

91. Ibid., 61.
92. Ibid., 82.
93. Ibid., 59.
94. Ibid., 60.
95. Ibid., 253.
96. Ibid., 71.
97. Frank Thilly and Ledger Wood, *A History of Philosophy* (New York: Henry Holt & Company, 1957), 235.

4

Quaker Mysticism

WARREN STEINKRAUS

To regard religion as something more than a passing mood like patriotic fervor or to see it as more than a set of explanatory theories like astronomy is almost as uncommon today as it was in the seventeenth-century Great Britain. Although there might be Sabbath prayers for king and country and pious ceremonies for baptism, marriage, and funerals, there was little else at that time that could be called more than formal religion. The Anglican Church was not much more than an adjunct of nationalistic patriotism. Christianity had little to do with daily life. Its precepts were not sought or followed by those in power, not by the wealthy, not by the military, nor by the rulers. If anyone had said that all of life—private, social, economic, political, and even relations among nations—should be governed and judged by the teachings of Jesus, that person would be viewed not just as a fanatic but as a positive menace to all that was accepted and conventional.

Now George Fox (1624–91) was such a menace. His experience of the presence of God was so vivid and persistent that it motivated him to view life in a way almost incomprehensible to his compatriots, but in a way readily comprehended by the humble poor people of his day. Although the simple understood his message and aims, the wealthy and the powerful and the government shunned him and even imprisoned him from time to time. The clergy was affronted by this plain man who came forward with such a new view of religion, and some were as bothered by him as they were another innovator almost a century later, John Wesley (1703–91). Wesley always remained within the established church in leading the Methodist movement, but Fox broke completely with the church and offered a more radical social ethic. He was a seeker who was turned into a finder, notes Henry Cadbury, and he became the chief instrument in the founding of the Society of Friends.[1]

Fox was arrested once in Nottingham in 1649. In his *Journal*, he reports looking at the town from some distance and spying the church, "a great and idolatrous temple." Inside he had heard the priest proclaiming that "the Scriptures were the touchstone and judge by which they were to try all doctrines, religions and opinions." Fox then reports that he was so moved that he cried out, "Oh, no, it is not the Scriptures." Instead it is the Holy Spirit "by which the holy men of God gave forth the Scriptures, whereby opinions, religions, and judgments were to be tried" for the Holy Spirit "led into all Truth and so gave the knowledge of all Truth." As he spoke, the officers came and put him into prison, "a pitiful stinking place."[2]

Here we have the clue to Fox's interpretation of Christianity and to what has come to be known as Quaker mysticism. Unlike traditional Christianity and Judaism, Fox claimed that God spoke directly and immediately to his devotees. Mediation by the church and its ordained clergy or by the Scriptures alone (as Martin Luther maintained) was not necessary. The earnest individual could be in touch with the divine being directly, without any mediation. It was Fox's view that the voice of God spoke to any person who readied himself for it and was "open to it."

His personality was so vibrant, his earnestness so evident and his message so convincing that he began to win converts who joined with him in the Society of Friends. He endorsed the Christian Scriptures and made ample use of them but he consistently argued that, as God spoke in times past to the writers of the Bible, he *still* spoke to receptive persons. Once, when placed on trial for blasphemy, in Lancaster, in October 1652, he made full use of the New Testament to reply to the eight charges against him. The first charge alleged that Fox was in error because he had said that the divinity was "essentially" in him, but Fox replied, noting that the Scriptures say that "saints shall be made partakers of the divine nature" but that does not mean equality or essentiality with God. He appealed constantly to the Christian tradition but did not think that God stopped speaking to humans directly at the end of the biblical age.[3]

The presence of the inner voice was recognized in no less a person than William Penn who, in describing Fox in his Preface to the 1694 edition of the Journal, said that Fox:

... much laboured to open Truth to the people's understandings,
and to bottom them upon the principle, and principal, Christ Jesus,
the Light of the world, that by bringing them to something that was
of God in themselves, they might better know how to judge of him
and themselves. (xliii)

With the conversion of William Penn, the Society of Friends
achieved more status and respect, but that was no guarantee
against reproach and persecution. Penn was the chief agent in
establishing Quakerism in North America. From these beginnings issued forth a line of leaders and thinkers unbroken to the
present time. Quaker mysticism has been kept alive not only
by the repeated experiences of the inner light among ordinary
persons, but it has been promulgated by keen thinkers who have
given the mystical experience both intellectual support and rational understanding.

We shall now examine the nature and character of mysticism
as we see it illustrated in the Society of Friends. We will note
that: (1) it claims to be a purifying factor in the Christian tradition, going to its roots; (2) it implies certain teachings about the
nature of God; (3) it implies commitment to ethical and social
ideals and action; and then (4) we shall trace features and elements in the mystical experience itself.

(1) When George Fox attained his fresh understanding of the
individual's relation to God, it was an idea closely tied in to
the Christian tradition. He never really broke with the general
tradition though he was viewed by outsiders, of course, as a
heretic and nonconformist. His basic teaching was that there is
a light that lights every person, not in the sense of a formal
revelation of ideas or knowledge, but as a kind of insight that
helps one understand the meaning of life and gives one a sense
of mission. In addition, it provides satisfaction and joy to persons whose affiliation with religion might have been conventional, nominal, and unimportant as far as their lives were
concerned. Fox saw religion as the guide to life, its sole organiz-
ing principle, its primary truth. His motivation was so intense
and so persuasive in his own consciousness that he henceforth
sought to govern his life and actions by the spiritual insight
he had attained. When brought before tribunals for allegedly
disturbing the peace, he refused to doff his hat, refused to take
oaths, and indeed asked the constables who struck him on the
face for his "insolence" to strike him yet again. He was plain

speaking, extraordinary, and thoroughly dedicated to what he took to be the demands of God on his life.

Part of the meaning of the Quaker experience can be seen by what it rejected outright from the tradition of established Christianity in England. No special consideration was given to lords and ladies, to royalty or officialdom of any kind. All persons were treated alike; there was no deferential bowing or removal of hats. To the Friends, such breaks with convention were merely instances of recognizing that all humans were of equal value in God's eyes and so must be in theirs as well. Ceremonialism in religion itself was also done away with. Instead of being taken up with the formal business of taking the sacraments, the convert was taught to cultivate the direct awareness of God. Mediation by a church or a priest was not only avoided but seen as detrimental to genuine spirituality. Historic creedal statements and articles of religion were likewise deemphasized for insofar as one makes an issue out of creedal conformity and creedal recitation, one nullifies the essence of religion, for Quakers held that what is vital to faith is the cultivation of the soul's intimate personal relation with God himself. Rufus Jones, a great mystic of the generation just past, remarks: "Mysticism does not have to do with creeds and dogmas. Christianity is broader than any creed. It leaves religious problems and deals with life itself."[4] The Quaker poet, John Greenleaf Whittier, characterizes this distinction in his poem, "The Eternal Goodness" (B. Perry, *John Greenleaf Whittier* [Boston: Houghton, Mifflin and Company, 1907], 107):

> I trace your lines of argument
> Your logic linked and strong.
> I weigh as one who dreads dissent,
> And fears a doubt as wrong.
> But still my human hands are weak
> To hold your iron creeds.
> Against the words ye bid me speak,
> My heart within me pleads.

Furthermore, although surely recognizing human frailty and wrongdoing, Fox and his followers were not obsessed with sin and guilt as were those in the Reformed tradition or within the quietism of Lutheranism. Some orthodox believers were so overconcerned with hidden faults and deep original sin that they took no interest in social responsibility or in stressing the life of personal and group righteousness. The early Quakers as well as most contemporary ones are not egotistically worried about private salvation. Nor do they engage in introspective probing of the sort one finds in the self-conscious, literary, aesthetic religion of Sören Kierkegaard.

Although it is evident that some of the earliest Quakers in Fox's movement made a fuss about being different from others in outward appearances and in speech and other habits, those early self-conscious differentiations did not turn out to be significant among Friends as the years went on; though even today there is some remnant of linguistic practice, the use of familiar forms and pronouns, as well as Christian names in human interchange. But there was no "freezing" of clothing requirements nor opposition to motor cars and electricity—features one still finds in this country among the more rigid sects inspired by Menno Simons. What endured among the Quakers was an emphasis on inner awareness and outward commitment to a conscientious self-giving ethical life. We may note that today it is much harder to become an active member of the Society of Friends than it was in the days of Fox and Penn. There are strict requirements of sincere intention and total commitment. In older times, great numbers were won over and accepted into the Quaker fellowship under circumstances resembling the emotional mass evangelism in some current Protestant Fundamentalism.

It is probably safe to say that in contemporary experience, instead of directly seeking contact with God, there is more of a cultivation of an attitude of waiting and listening, a being open to divine leadings. It is obvious, as in the case with other experience-centered religions, that occasional aberrations will arise unless there is a vital community and fellowship to check extremes of fanaticism. Today's worship experiences are on the whole more subdued than those of the earliest times.

(2) Now the Quaker experience implies certain things about the nature of the Supreme One, of God. It is clear that Fox and the early leaders thought in rather conservative Christian terms about God. They did not feel that they needed any agency or instrument to come into God's presence, however, for God was directly available to all who earnestly sought him. God did not first require that one come to him through Jesus or through the church and its sacraments. Accordingly, Jesus was seen not as a saviour who had by his death and resurrection brought people into a new relation to God. Rather, by his life he showed men what the true relation is between humankind and the divine

and urged that relationship be cultivated. Thus, though Quakers in the early period as well as in the present world never lost reverence for Jesus, he became a model for the ideal godly life, not a sacrifice for inherited sins, a living example of how one might live the life divine, not an intermediary between God and man.

As thinkers began to formulate this relation of the individual to God, they employed the terms immanence and transcendence. Immanence is a term indicating that God is in some sense present in this world, in history and in human life. Transcendence, on the other hand, means that God is above and beyond the natural world though he created it and watches over it providentially. Indeed, a transcendent God might intervene through a miraculous show of power at times. Now it is the transcendence of God in the absolute sense that bothered George Fox and his followers because transcendence implies the need for an intermediary. In the times since Jesus, the historic Catholic Church, both Roman as well as Anglican, saw itself as this intermediary. God, in that view, does not speak directly to persons but lets his purposes be known through selected spokesmen. Quakers felt and feel that God speaks directly to the human soul. There are no authoritarian, select spokesmen.

A theology of immanence, accordingly, developed. The so-called trappings of the church were not viewed as efficacious but seen as hindrances to the valid discovery of God in mystical experience. A theological doctrine of immanence becomes the underpinning of Quaker mysticism. It can readily be seen that if one stresses an immanence doctrine of God's presence in the world, it might be a rather easy step to add that God is also immediately present in human selves. Quakers do speak of "that of God in every man" implying, if one takes the words very strictly, that God is somehow ontically present in human beings—that human selves are the fragments or minor units in an all-encompassing God. That is Pantheism, a view rather indistinctly held by Ralph Waldo Emerson who seems not to have understood the full meaning of immanence. Whittier, his contemporary, and others insisted that God was near to every human being but that each individual self was distinct, existentially, from God. The nearness was construed, normatively, as the nearness of a friend, one who cares for and understands another, one who helps and communicates intimately with another without actually being a literal part of that other. Intimacy and friendship do not mean identity. Similarity of purpose and awareness of God's goodness need not mean that we are literally part of the very being of God. Also, within the framework of traditional Christianity, any such tendency to identify the finite self with the infinite or to view it as a segment or portion of the eternal has been generally viewed as unsound and heretical. Quaker language through the years has not been very helpful on this, though its philosophers like Rufus Jones and Douglas Steere have sought to keep the distinction clear, always emphasizing that the experience of oneness is more crucial that having a clear idea of such distinctness.

But there is another feature of transcendence that must be mentioned and that has to do with the character qualities of God. It is obvious that a distant deity may also be viewed as an austere being, one who is so holy and separate from his creatures that his creatures owe everything to him and must willingly and without question submit to his decrees. This was the kind of Calvinistic view that was prevalent in Puritan circles at the time of Fox. The power and wrath of God were seen as more important traits than his love and friendship. It is true that one can find passages in the Judeo-Christian Scriptures that support such a doctrine of God. At a time when there were early despots, the character of God could be construed as virtually despotic. Of course, not all those outside of the Quaker position took so severe a view. But Fox and his followers opposed Calvinism. They brought God morally and psychologically closer to humans. The more power one grants to a transcendent deity, the less important man becomes and the less important human institutions become. If one thinks of God as near, as primarily loving and forgiving, then it is more likely that one will take more responsibility for the world and for one's life rather than waiting for divine decrees that one must acquiesce in obediently and unquestioningly. Nor have modern Quaker thinkers succumbed to the attractions of the theology of Karl Barth, which is little more than a very sophisticated neo-Calvinism. It shuns the emphasis on and even the value of personal religious experience and insists that one recognize the Word of God as it confronts humans in a world racked by human sins. As the jargon puts it, God confronts modern man in the Christ event, whatever that means. Modern thinking among Quaker mystics could scarcely find a congenial home in such thinking.

(3) Quaker mysticism has from the beginning always implied ethical responsibility both individually and socially. For Fox and his followers, religion came to be interpreted as dedicated sensi-

tivity to the welfare of other persons. Never have the Friends been involved in elaborate religious organizations, but they have without fail cultivated a high ethical sensitivity which, I believe, is unparalleled in any religion of the world, including Buddhism. This feature led the agnostic historian, A. J. P. Taylor to say once that Quakers are "the best thing the human race has produced."[5]

There are no authoritarian ethical pronouncements or teachings on particular matters of government coming from George Fox or any other Quaker leaders. But there are some principles early formulated which are still held today and for which Quakers are well known throughout the world. There are differences of minor sorts among the fellowship. Of course, one's personal life was to be pure, honest, forthright, guileless, and noble. There was to be no deceit of words, no artificiality, no oath-taking. But could one hold slaves? Fox soon came to see, in those early days, that slaveholding or the use of slaves in any sense was totally incompatible with the vision of God. The first protest made by a religious body against slavery was in 1688. If all persons were of inestimable value in God's eyes and all persons could enter into a living relationship with God, no sort of "use" of human beings could be tolerated or countenanced.

John Woolman (1720–73), whose *Journal* is a masterpiece of colonial literature as well as a refined expression of the inner life of a Quaker, was the outstanding early leader in the struggle against slavery in the eighteenth-century America. His own vivid encounters with God, which began at the age of seven when he began "to be acquainted with the operations of Divine Love," and his unswerving trust that there was something of God in every human being, led him soon to see that all mankind were on an equal plane including those regarded as slaves. Slowly and deliberately in his daily word and through his contacts with fellow Quakers, he voiced his disapproval of slaveholding. As a clerk who helped his acquaintances draw up wills and other legal documents, he refused to cooperate with those who wanted to pass on their slaves to their heirs. His witness bore fruit and before long, there was no Quaker in the colonies who owned slaves or supported the institution of slavery.

In his own way, George Fox also saw the incompatibility of the Christian faith and war. When confronted by Cromwell's men who sought him for the army, he said, "I told them whence all wars arose, even from lusts, . . . and that I lived in the virtue of that life and power that took away the occasion of all wars."

One could not respect or love another person by mutilating or killing him at the command of some government or power bent on conquest. Fox's opposition to war was not a negative thing. He wanted to promote the kind of life that took away the cause of wars. This theme is also echoed in the teaching of John Woolman. In his *Considerations on the True Harmony of Mankind* (1770), he tried to get at the root causes of disharmony among people and the circumstances that seemingly made war palatable and "necessary." If human beings would simplify their desires, reduce their wants, and cultivate "a brotherly feeling with the poor,"[6] some of the conditions conducive to war would be removed. The posthumously published essay, "A Word of Remembrance and Caution to the Rich" reveals further insights into the conditions that make for war. "Wealth is attended by power . . . and hence oppression carried on with worldly policy and order, clothes itself with the name of justice and becomes like a seed of discord in the soul."[7] And since Woolman's time, the Quaker witness for peace has continued to grow out of a profound mystical experience as well as a frank recognition of the socioeconomic and cultural factors that promote or make for war.[8]

(4) The effort to describe the mystical experience found in the Quaker tradition may seem as difficult as it would be if we sought to describe the enjoyment of a Bruckner symphony to a person who could not hear, for, on the surface, it appears that there is something quite special about mysticism. The philosopher and psychologist William James, who admitted that his own constitution shut him out from the enjoyment of mystical experiences, nevertheless tried to be receptive and sensitive to reports of mystical experience. He suggested that there were four characteristics of mysticism as he found it through study and observation: ineffability, a noetic quality, transiency, and passivity.[9] Ineffability simply means that the experience itself is beyond verbal description. To speak of a noetic quality means that some sort of knowledge or illumination is present. Transiency suggests that the experience is fleeting, lasting at most an hour or two. Passivity as a trait implies that the mystic, though preparing for the experience, feels as though he or she is grasped by a superior power.

Of course one must never confuse the experience Quaker mystics have with the activities of spiritualists and mediums who, in seances, endeavor to contact dead souls with a view to securing messages to report. Rufus Jones once said that he was very cautious about expecting secret messages from social angels. Nor should one equate a mystical experience with the experience reported by many today which is induced by drugs. If one tests such experiences by the positive effects they usually have on many of those experiencing them, the difference is quite evident.

In the early days of Quakerism, one finds reports of experiences that, to say the least, were unbridled and excessive. Certain persons with apparent mental problems may have found in the teachings of George Fox some support for their own aberrations. In 1656, James Nayler, an early Quaker, presuming his own messiahship, rode into the city of Bristol on a donkey. Others under the influence of the early preaching of Fox rejected all conventions and felt obligated to go naked in the streets. Although his own preaching was partly inspired by visions and for a time emphasized a soon-to-come Judgment Day, Fox later saw the unwisdom of strange behavior and apocalyptic ideas and stressed more the cultivation of true inner sincerity. He also concentrated on social justice, opposing low wages, capital punishment, drunkenness, and cheating in business. He insisted that his followers lead simple lives in their dress as well as in their speech.

The vivid experiences of the early Quakers, including Fox himself, were accompanied by literal physical movements, bodily quakes, and shudderings. So early a writer as Voltaire, not noted for his sympathy to religious experience, had heard of Fox and noting that Fox was "irreproachable in his life and conduct," noted that Fox's disciples "aped very sincerely their master's several grimaces and shook in every limb the instant the fit of inspiration came upon them, whence they were called Quakers."[10] In his essay, "The Oversoul," Emerson noted the physical accompaniments of alleged mystical inspiration and claimed they were "varying forms of that shudder of awe and delight with which the individual soul always mingles with the universal soul" (*Essays* [Boston: Houghton Mifflin Company, 1865], 265). He adds, "The soul answers never by words but by the thing itself that is inquired after." No Quaker of recent years has reported such overt results of mystical experience and it is very doubtful if persons like John Woolman in the eighteenth century or John Whittier in the nineteenth had any "shudderings" whatever.

What has kept the mystical experience of the Quakers away from its early excesses is the fact of the religious community.

When one is in the company of like-minded, sympathetic, and earnest believers, one's experience, while strong and meaningful, will be more subdued without the slightest loss of intrinsic value. In trying to understand striking mystical experiences in Fox and others, the great Quaker scholar-philosopher, Rufus Jones, undertook a diligent study of reports of mysticism going back into the early days of Christianity. From the very beginnings there has been a longing of the soul to have direct contact with what it regards as the highest and the ultimate. Immediate awareness of the Supreme One transcends mere intellectual understanding. One needs no mediating priests or sacraments; one can come into the presence of the Holy Spirit directly. Recognizing the long line of saintly persons who have enjoyed such experiences makes it easier for us today to comprehend what occurred in the life of George Fox. In short, Quaker mysticism did not constitute a revolutionary break with the Christian tradition. It was rather a recovery of a feature of Christian experience that had been lost, even suppressed, and surely ignored by church organization, academic learning, and the so-called establishment.

In his careful survey, Jones frankly admits the dangers of aberrations and excesses. He comments that after he had studied the fourteenth-century mystics, "I see now, as I did not see in the early period, what a large pathological factor has been in the lives of many mystics in the long historical line."[11] With great insight he adds, "In some cases the lack of tightness of mental organization brought with it a touch of genius and allowed a unique quality of light to break through."[12] Not favoring the ecstatic or excessive himself, Jones also notes that "it has been by the highway of health rather than over the bridge of disease that the largest freight of truth has come to us."[13] The recovery of the depth-life of the soul, then, is more fundamental than emotional excitement. The mystics and notably the Quaker mystics are people who, while sensitive to the presence of a large divine life, have felt themselves to be in mutual and reciprocal correspondence or communion with a life-giving spiritual environment. When one notices what issues from such experiences, one is bound to admit their significance and vitality. Nor can one then easily deny their validity. We have it on good authority that the test of the value of a religious experience is to be found in the fruit it bears. And Quaker mysticism has produced truly remarkable results for mankind in human history.

In his lifelong study of mystics, Jones also draws some distinctions between the mysticism he took to be normative and that of others. One of the early Quakers, for example, Robert Barclay, had maintained that the "inner Light," the seed of God, was foreign to man's nature and that one had to be wholly passive in receiving it. Jones makes the point that this dualistic view leaves no basis for the divine immanence for it denies the indwelling light of the soul. The true Quaker principle, we read, is that man's spiritual nature is rooted and grounded in the Divine Life. Accordingly, the truth one receives will not be an injected revelation but will appear as "the genuine fruit and output of a personal life which unites in itself the finite and the infinite in one ever-expanding personality.[14] Furthermore, Jones maintains that those mystics, like the author of *Theologica Germanica*, though insightful in clarifying mystical experiences, are quite incorrect when they accept a system of thought "which empties this world here below of present spiritual significance or which robs the life of a human personality of its glorious mission as an organ of the Life of God here and now and which postpones the kingdom of God."[15] In clarifying the mystical experience of the poet Whittier, Jones shows this very interconnection:

> He was a profoundly mystical person, dwelling deep, listening acutely to the inward voice, sensitively responsive to the flow of inward currents and activity, aware of the eternal in the midst of the temporal. At the same time he had a burning moral passion and he was a fearless champion of causes for the enlargement of human freedom, and the persistent foe of every form of human oppression and of ancient customs which bind and hamper the human spirit.[16]

It is evident that earlier as well as contemporary Quaker mystics would favor these interpretations. One need only recall the social activism of Fox, Penn, and Woolman and note the impact of the contemporary American Friends Service Committee. Mystical experience is cultivated, and it is enriching for those who attain it, but it is not sought for its own sake. One opens oneself to divine spiritual leading and the result is that one must change his or her life and one's method of treating others in the world.

The experience itself is variously characterized. It occurs within the individual's consciousness and within the group. Regarding the group experience, which might take place at one of the weekly meetings, Jones remarks:

> The low breathings of a diviner life passing from soul to soul, like a spiritual contagion, is what ought to happen in Quaker worship and the unification of the entire congregation into one living organic group is the ideal end to be looked for.[17]

Such mysticism is quite meaningless in total isolation. Although the individual may feel a special intimacy with the Supreme Spirit, that intimacy does not gain full meaning until it is related to the group, to a fellowship of kindred spirits. One then begins to distinguish acquaintances who live on the surface of daily affairs from those who have a deeper devotional awareness. The former may be active church leaders with executive skills but "in the X-ray light of Eternity," they are shown to be, says Thomas Kelly, "agitated, half-committed, wistful, self-placating seekers to whom the poise and serenity of the Everlasting have never come."[18] And when one has such spiritual sensitivity, one finds a depth of fellowship with like-spirited persons that is unparalleled—a Blessed Community indeed. There emerges an "amazing group inter-knittedness of God-enthralled men and women who know one another *in Him*, whenever there is a rediscovery of "God's joyous immediacy."[19]

The nurturing of this profound group experience is possible because each member apart from social or economic position or even religious affiliation, has a hunger to be close to God, the Center. "It is as if every soul had a final base, and that final base of every soul is one single Holy Ground, shared in by all. Persons in the Fellowship are related to one another through Him, as all mountains go down into the same earth."[20] Such a fellowship cannot by its very nature be merely a self-regarding, self-enhancing community; it must reach out in ordinary daily relationships and view all human relationship and contacts through God, meeting each person "with a background of eternal expectation and a silent wordless prayer of love."[21] The goal of Quaker mysticism is not, then, any secure awareness of private salvation for time everlasting. It is rather to cultivate the individual's deepened awareness of divine love and to quicken the expression of that love in the close-knit fellowship of dedicated souls—and through them, to the wider world community. It can be thus seen at once why the Quaker spirit is unswervingly dedicated to justice and peace and avoids without exception those more typical human tendencies toward self-seeking greed, exploitation, vengeance, and war.

The private individual's mystical experience within the Society of Friends has been written about by practicing and sincere religious devotees from the seventeenth century to the present. In the days of Fox and Penn, it was understood as uniquely occurring within the framework of Protestant Christianity, but as years passed, thoughtful Quakers found that their experiences were not so very different from those undergone by a line of saintly persons stretching back to the eleventh century of Christian history and even before. In his exhaustive study of what mystics before George Fox were like, Rufus Jones reported, for instance, a succession of remarkable women in Germany, beginning with Saint Hildegarde of Bingen (1098–1179). All were motivated by what they felt to be a unique presence of the Divine. Later came Amaury of Bene, in France, who maintained there was no longer any need of sacraments because the Holy Spirit himself was now present, revealing Himself to persons of a spiritual bent.[22] Then came Meister Eckhart (1260–1327) who was one of the greatest mystics of all history. He urged the cultivation of authentic spiritual experience instead of the dry scholastic learning found in theologians like St. Thomas Aquinas, maintaining that a person may behold God in this life in the same perfection and may be blessed in exactly the same way as in the afterlife. Others, following Eckhart, like Johannes Tauler and Heinrich Suso, similarly emphasized the inner life and direct spiritual communion with God. Jan Ruysbroeck, the Flemish mystic, taught that the inward light was supernaturally infused by the Light from God. And in Great Britain, in the fourteenth century, Richard Rolle and Lady Julian of Norwich felt that the spiritual world order was every bit as real as the visible order. Nor is it confined to any group or geographical location.

Accordingly, Quaker mysticism may best be understood and interpreted when seen in this larger perspective of Christian history. But even this can be enlarged upon because we find a semblance of mysticism in ancient non-Christian thought as well, particularly in such later followers of Plato as Plotinus (205–70) who consciously rejected Christianity in his day. It is not obvious that the transports of ecstasy that Plotinus reports are totally different from those periods of ineffable bliss recounted within the Christian tradition. Indeed, there are even connections between Quaker mysticism and certain loftier aspects of Vedantic Hinduism. Thomas Kelly observes the kinship found in the Westerner who, in moments of adoration, may exclaim, "My God, my Holy One" and the Hindu expression in the *Upanishads* indicating adoration, "O Wonderful, O Wonderful, O Wonderful."[23] In each case the individual is overwhelmed by the presence of the Supreme Presence in the universe. At the same time we must note that with Fox, Christian mysticism came alive in the world of living human beings. No saint before his time challenged the rituals and assumptions of the established religious and social order. He denied drastically the institutions of slavery, economic oppression, and militarism. Previous saints did not make the connections. At least one of them, St. Bernard of Clairvaux, vigorously favored the crusades.

Although the mystical fervor of Quaker mysticism has an ineffable quality, some have sought to show its meaning as the spiritual experience flows out into daily existence. Rufus Jones holds that mysticism produces in us a "lighted luster", and he skillfully portrays how the soul is lighted by the divine life and finds there its true significance and immortality.[24] Douglas Steere, a retired professor of philosophy at Haverford, has written a devotional classic, *On Beginning from Within*.[25] Besides explicating what true saintliness means, he proposed a "New Set of Devotional Exercises" (chapter 3) and clarifies the relation of devotion to theology as well as to the understanding of death. Beyond question, the unsurpassed masterpiece of recent Quaker writing on this theme is Thomas R. Kelly's *A Testament of Devotion*, already quoted.

Kelly gives direct advice on how one may cultivate "The Light Within." Thus, one may order one's mental life, for example, on more than one level at once. In addition to carrying out normal daily affairs, one may at the same time live at a deeper mental level. We may live deep within and "at a profounder level be in prayer and adoration, song and worship and a gentle receptiveness to divine breathings."[26] In spite of lapses, one should persist in practicing such inner nourishment. Kelly advised, "Walk and talk and work and laugh with your friends. But behind the scenes keep up the life of simple prayer and inward worship."[27] And when the guidance becomes more dynamic, we find, he adds, that "we are torn loose from earthly attachments and ambitions . . . and we are quickened to a divine but painful concern for the world" (47). The inner light guides us to a "Holy Obedience." "One burns for complete innocency and holiness of personal life" (65) and then "God's holiness takes hold as a mastering passion of life" (67). One may then achieve a true simplicity of life, the fruit of holy obedience. There develops, says Kelly, "an integral simplification of the whole of one's personality, stilled, tranquil, in childlike trust listening ever to Eternity's whisper" (74). One feels oneself to be a member of "The Blessed Community"—a fellowship of persons who meditate on "The Eternal Now" but also have a deep "Social Concern" that is not a mere humanitarianism nor mere pity. "Social concern is the dynamic life of God at work in the world, made special and emphatic and unique, particularized in each individual or group who is sensitive and tender in the leading strings of love" (111). In discussing this fusion of inner dynamic and social concern, which is the essence of Quaker mysticism, Douglas Steere reports on the closing years of the life of John Woolman in these moving words:

> The dream, toward the end of his life, of his being so mixed with a gray mass of suffering humanity that he could no longer reply to his own name when he was called, was a symbol of the way his life was molded and fashioned beyond any expectation.[28]

When one comes to a grasp of this relationship between inner devotion and its outer expression, one may perhaps then claim to have begun to understand what Quaker mysticism is.

The American Friends Service Committee is the major channel through which Quaker social action rooted in Quaker mysticism finds expression today. Founded in Philadelphia in 1917 at the beginning of World War I by representatives of the several branches of Quakers in America, its original purpose and activity was providing Quaker conscientious objectors alternatives to wartime military service in European countries, France being the first in which they served. Rufus Jones was the committee's early guiding light.[29] Following the war, one of its tasks abroad was the distribution of food to undernourished German children. At the same time, at home, the committee undertook efforts to alleviate distress among Appalachian coal miners. Its activity took two forms: providing immediate relief to persons in need and the setting up of "self-help" projects in order to "restore the dignity and initiative of the recipients".[30]

Just as in the years before and during World War II, the years after saw a steady expansion in the number and types of activities carried on by the committee. During the war, aiding conscientious objectors was a major task, as their numbers had increased significantly between wars.[31] Postwar activities took the form of community centers in blighted urban areas, halfway houses, work camps at home and abroad, programs in mental hospitals, feeding stations on Indian reservations, arbitration of migrant farm workers' claims and raising their living standards and working conditions, improving race relations, interreligious dialogue, helping victims of the Spanish and Chinese Civil Wars, the 1967 Middle East Crisis, and the Korean and Vietnamese wars. A number and variety of peace efforts were undertaken to stop the cold war, reduce armaments, and eliminate the arms race. Much educational work was initiated aimed at resolving misunderstanding and creating positive relations between quarreling groups, factions, and nations, the goal being to avoid conflict and war in the first place.[32] The emphasis on conflict analysis and resolution was based on the Quaker faith "that God's love as witnessed by Christ could operate both in individual lives and in societal patterns."[33] And the community projects at home and abroad which set up were based on the belief that "one of the conditions leading to war in the modern world is the disparity between the wealth of the developed nations and the poverty of the underdeveloped lands."[34]

Since its inception in 1917, the committee has grounded its efforts on the principles enunciated in a 1937 statement: "There are two basic principles in the Society which are greater than any disputes among factions of thought. The first is the principle of peace, i.e., that we should so live as to do away with the occasion for all war. . . .The second ideal is the knowledge that the light of Christ dwells in every man; i.e., no man is better than another; therefore, no person has any right to exploit or use another individual and we're all potential sons of God."[35] These principles reflect the basic Quaker belief in personal witness, the indwelling presence, the dignity and worth and the divine in every person, and equality before God and each other— themes Quaker mystics gladly accepted.

Although not associated directly with the Service Committee and the Quakers, two organizations, which imbibed the Quaker spirit and had Quakers among their founders and leaders, are Oxfam and Greenpeace. Oxfam originated in the Friends meeting house in Oxford in 1942, its objective being "the relief, to the extent that the law for the time being permitted, of famine and sickness arising as a result of the war."[36] Its leaders were concerned about certain aspects of the war, one being the allied blockade of the Continent, which meant "hunger and misery for millions. . . .Greece, above all, was fast descending into famine."[37] Greece thus became the focus of immediate relief efforts.

The initial concern for the European continent was broadened in 1949 to "the relief of suffering arising as a result of war or any other cause in any part of the world."[38] The 1960s marked the second way of achieving the end of banishing hunger. Oxfam evolved into a "development agency" and initiated projects and measures worldwide such as community housing and reforestation and agricultural programs facilitating self-help and preventing famine in the first place. The 1970s saw further growth and an additional emphasis upon education and efforts to promote justice and equality by influencing public opinion and bringing pressure to bear on public officials. A 1974 Oxfam Council's statement sets forth its goal of justice for all through equitable sharing.

Bringing people together in an understanding of their common humanity it is our purpose to strive for the justice, freedom, and equitable sharing of resources without which more than half the world's people are presently deprived of their dignity and self-respect, justice and freedom, so that through the surrender of the obstructive powers and privileges concentrated in the hands of the few, all may become the subjects of their destiny instead of its objects. A sharing of resources, so that the products of the earth and collective labour of its people be distributed to ensure for all the basic human rights of food, shelter, education and reasonable conditions of life.[39]

The following year the council made a paradigmatic statement of its objectives which remain the same today.

Oxfam believes in the essential dignity of people and their capacity to overcome the problems and pressures which can crush or exploit them. These may be rooted in climate and geography, or in the complex areas of economics, politics and social conditions. Oxfam is a partnership of people who share this belief—people who, regardless of race, sex, religion or politics work together for the basic human rights of food, shelter and reasonable conditions of life. We believe that, if shared equitably, there are sufficient material resources in the world to enable all people to find fulfillment and to meet basic human needs. We are committed, therefore, to a process of development by peaceful means which aims to help people, especially the poor and underprivileged overseas.[40]

The 1974 and 1975 Oxfam Council's statements regarding the organization's beliefs, make-up, ends, and methods indicate how the mystical Quaker spirit continues to infuse it. We note the belief in the dignity and worth of every individual, the inherent abilities or capacities of each, the concern for the practical, the emphasis upon fellowship and sharing, the goodness of creation in terms of its sufficiency, the transcending of individual distinctions, the use of nonviolence and living needfully rather than greedily. We might note a further characteristic, as pointed out in the same text, "The Quaker background of many key figures in Oxfam helps them to resolve most differences more tolerantly than other charities . . . Oxfam has weathered most of its heated arguments with the aid of its tradition of preferring to take decisions by consensus."[41]

Greenpeace was started by a group in Vancouver, British Columbia, in 1969 called Don't Make A Wave Committee. It took its present name in 1971.[42] Several of its early organizers were pacifist Quakers. Greenpeace's concerns were two: ecology and the nuclear threat. The antinuclear proponents of Greenpeace were led by Irving Stone, one of the Quaker founders.[43] Their first activity was the sailing in 1971 of the boat *Phyllis Cormack* toward the waters around Amchitka Island in the Aleutians where the Atomic Energy Commission was to detonate a nuclear bomb.[44] The U. S. Coast Guard turned the boat back. The action caught the public's eye, leading thousands to demonstrate at the Canadian-U.S. border. The bomb was detonated eventually but no more followed, and the island became a bird sanctuary.

In 1972, the boat *Vega* was sailed into the waters around the atoll of Moruroa where the French were to undertake atmospheric testing. Its ramming by the French Navy attracted widespread publicity and an outcry against the testing that led the French to stop atmospheric and limit testing to the underground in 1973.

Expanding its fleet in the late 1970s and early 1980s enabled Greenpeace to start dealing with its second concern: ecology. This took the specific form of saving whales and seals from extinction by sailing boats into areas where they were being killed and harvested. First to sail into the North Atlantic where whales were being slaughtered was the boat *Rainbow Warrior*. Other boats sailing to other sites followed. The campaign to save the whales and seals followed the course of the antinuclear campaign. Losses suffered by Greenpeace boats and the harming of their crews attracted widespread public attention and led eventually to consumers' revulsion against wearing furs, a revolt against the fur trade, and national agreements to curtail or end the trade. Continuing ecological concerns led to Greenpeace efforts to prevent the dumping of toxic chemicals in the 1980s by British and Continental factories into the ocean and the rivers of Europe. Such efforts helped the Greenpeace movement then spreading over Europe to achieve a number of successes.

In his book, *Eyes of Fire*, the author wrote,

> The philosophy of non-violent, direct action emerged as a powerful weapon for conservation. Life had to be saved by what the Quakers call "bearing witness." A person bearing witness must accept responsibility for being aware of an injustice. That person may then choose to do something or stand by but may not turn away in "feigned" ignorance. The Greenpeace ethic is not only to bear witness personally to atrocities against life, it is to take direct action to prevent them. Although action must be direct it must also be non-violent.[45]

In this statement we see three emphases familiar to the Quaker: one is bearing witness, i.e., being concerned and not turning away; second is taking action, become actively involved personally; and third, that the action be nonviolent.

A continuing Quaker influence on Greenpeace is seen in these statements, "Though not a pacifist organization it has pacifists in it,"[46] and "Greenpeace still believes essentially in the old Quaker ethic of its founders. It doesn't engage in violence against people or property."[47] The "old Quaker ethic," grounded in the New Testament, is pointed out in the following: "The Society of Friends distinguished sharply between the moral code of the Old Testament and that of the New, a distinction which the Puritans seldom made. Only in that way could Friends defend their doctrines regarding war, ritualistic worship, swearing and other customs."[48] The same author goes on to point out that "Christianity is a religion of love, and genuine love must inevitably be all inclusive," and "the Inward Light is primary and history shows that the Quaker type of religion is especially adapted to create sensitivity to all suffering."[49] We might underline the words "all suffering" and "all inclusive." Quakers included in the *all* not only people but other life forms as well. Fox would not ride on stagecoaches, for he had seen too often how the horses pulling them were misused. Woolman, as he traveled about the country, urged Quakers to take good care of their animals, and he reprimanded all who caused animals to suffer, especially in the winter time. English Friends opposed hunting for sport and believed the abusing of animals evidenced a "deficiency of character."[50]

As noted already, Quakers believe in a providential God of

love who, being immanent in the universe, is found in all aspects and forms of creation. They believe in the individual as a spiritual being, with God-given dignity and worth. Implied by both is the concept of stewardship, namely, that God has entrusted the care of the universe to the children He created. They should nurture it wisely and see that everyone shares equitably in the earth's abundance. While many in such movements as Greenpeace would not go as far as to attribute sacredness to the earth in the Quaker sense, they did believe that the earth and all therein should be respected and treated reverentially and responsibly, that it should not be despoiled, exploited, and used up for immediate gain or profit and that it should be shared in equitably. This might be called an attitude of secular, if not Christian, stewardship, the end being the same. The people in Greenpeace with whom the Quakers worked were motivated by a deep humanitarian commitment which, if not strictly religious, had religious overtones. They exhibited a sense of earnestness, devotion, dedication, devoutness, courage, purpose, sensitivity, integrity, compassion, and personal sacrifice religious in nature. Their expanded vision led to a concern for both persons and other forms of life. They believed in taking only what one needs and leaving the rest for future generations. Like John Woolman, they were keenly aware of the abuse of wealth and power.[51] They broke with the established order, as had Quakers previously. In their case it was their middle-class background and mentality that tended much more to support than criticize the status quo.[52] And they were guided by an inner voice, impetus, or awareness that led inevitably to outer commitment.

Spiritual mysticism has been ever present in the Quaker tradition. It will be so in the future, and its influence will continue to be felt outside as well. Friends do not jealously hoard that spirituality. They are glad for those who would bear witness to the inner light, wherever they are found.

Notes

1. Henry Cadbury, "George Fox's Later Years," Epilogue in *The Journal of George Fox*, ed. J. Nickalls (Cambridge: Cambridge University Press, 1952), 713.
2. Nickalls, ed., *Journal*, 40.
3. Ibid., 134–35.

4. Elizabeth G. Vining, *Friend of Life: The Biography of Rufus M. Jones* (Philadelphia: J. B. Lippincott Co., 1958), 39.

5. A. J. P. Taylor, *A Personal History* (London: Hodder & Stoughton, 1984), 82.

6. John Woolman, essay on *Considerations on the True Harmony of Mankind* in A. M. Gummere, *Journal and Essays of John Woolman* (New York: Macmillian Company, 1922), 439.

7. Ibid., 493.

8. See such pamphlets as *Speak Truth to Power,* published in 1953 and others such as Fleming's *Does Deterrence Deter?* (1962) or Sibley's *Unilateral Initiatives and Disarmament* (1963). There has been a constant and regular supply of articles and pamphlets dealing with prisoners in the Viet Nam War, for example, exposing the fallacies in the White House's thinking on Nicaragua, the Near East, and up to the present. *The AFSC Responds to Apartheid* (1986). Current materials are available from the AFSC, 1501 Cherry Street, Philadelphia, PA, 19102.

9. William James, *Varieties of Religious Experience* (New York: Longmans, Green, 1902), 380–82.

10. Voltaire, *Lettres Philosophiques* in *Harvard Classics,* Vol. 34, 72–4.

11. Rufus Jones, *The Flowering of Mysticism* (New York: Macmillan, 1939), 5.

12. Ibid.

13. Ibid., 7.

14. Vining, *Friend of Life,* 105.

15. Jones, *Flowering,* 184.

16. Rufus Jones, pamphlet, "The Faith of John Greenleaf Whittier," a sesquicentennial celebration publication, reprinted from *Friends London Quarterly* (April 1938), 27.

17. Ibid., 23.

18. Thomas R. Kelly, *A Testament of Devotion* (New York: Harpers, 1941), 79.

19. Ibid., 80.

20. Ibid., 83.

21. Ibid., 88.

22. Jones, *Flowering,* 50. What follows in this paragraph is a brief summary from this source.

23. Kelly, *Testament,* 61.

24. Rufus Jones, *The Radiant Life* (New York: Macmillan, 1944), 1–6.

25. Douglas Steere, *On Beginning from Within* (New York: Harpers, 1943).

26. Kelly, *Testament,* 35.

27. Ibid., 39. Parenthesized numbers following in this paragraph are citations to pages in this book.

28. Steere, *On Beginning,* 51.

29. Margaret Bacon, *The Quiet Rebels* (New York: Basic Books, Inc., 1969), 182.

30. Ibid., 186.

31. C. H. M. Yarrow, *Quaker Experiences in International Conciliation* (New Haven: Yale University Press, 1978), 33.

32. Ibid., 33–50. Organizations and activities included Friends International Centers, Quaker UN Office, British East-West Relations Committee, Student

internships, International Students Seminars, Conferences for Diplomats, among others.

33. Ibid., 33.

34. Bacon, *Quiet Rebels*, 195. Woolman made the same point when remarking on disparities in America.

35. Mary Hoxie Jones, *Swords into Ploughshares* (Westport, Conn.: Greenwood Press, 1937), 316.

36. Ben Whitaker, *A Bridge of People* (London: Heinemann, 1983), 14.

37. Ibid., 15.

38. Ibid., 18.

39. Ibid., 29.

40. Ibid., 30.

41. Ibid., 24.

42. Fred Pearce, *Green Warriors* (London: The Bodley Head, Ltd., 1991), 17–18.

43. Ibid., 22.

44. Ibid., 19. The idea of sailing boats into detonation areas was borrowed from the Quakers who had already done so.

45. David Robie, *Eyes of Fire, the Last Voyage of the Rainbow Warrior* (Philadelphia: New Society Publishers, 1987), 2.

46. John Dyson, *Sail the Rainbow* (London: Victor Gollancz Ltd., 1986), 63.

47. Pearce, *Green Warriors*, 47.

48. Anna Brinton, *Then and Now* (Freeport, N.Y.: Books for Liberal Press, 1960), 198.

49. Ibid., 191.

50. Ibid., 194.

51. John Kavanaugh, *The Quaker Approach to Contemporary Problems* (Westport, Conn.: Greenwood Press, 1953), 242. "We American Friends must rethink our way as citizens of a country which has newly reached political, economic and military power."

52. Charles DeBenedetti, *Peace Heroes in Twentieth Century America* (Bloomington: Indiana University Press, 1986), 263.

5

Varieties of Jewish Mysticism:
A Typological Analysis

ELIOTT WOLFSON

Introduction

ONE might isolate two distinct concerns running through all
the major texts that scholars include in the corpus of Jewish
mysticism.[1] On the one hand, there is the claim to an esoteric
knowledge (whose content will naturally vary from one period
to another) that is not readily available to the masses through
the more common avenues of religious worship, ritual, or study.
This knowledge, moreover, is not attained through ordinary rational means but is transmitted either orally from master to
disciple or is the result of some divine or angelic revelation. To
be sure, those enlightened in either of these ways can then find
the truths and secret meanings hidden within the traditional
biblical and rabbinic texts. The former assumption regarding
oral transmission provided the key term used to designate different forms of Jewish esotericism in the High Middle Ages, for
example, kabbalah, which means tradition or that which is received. Frequently, the esoteric knowledge conveys truths about
the inner workings of the divine world and is therefore theosophical in its orientation.

The second major element identifiable in Jewish mystical literature is the emphasis placed on intense religious experience.
The particular form of this experience varies but usually includes one or more of the following: heavenly ascent, vision of
the divine form, and mystical union. What also distinguishes
the ecstatic experience is the claim that special techniques of a
meditative sort were required to induce the desired frame of
mind. It is in virtue of these techniques—especially those that

involve recitation and/or combination of the letters of divine names—that an important strand of Jewish mysticism bears a strong resemblance to magical practices. Indeed, in some cases it is extremely hard to draw the line between mysticism and magic within the Jewish sources. Those texts that are of an almost purely magical sort are referred to in the traditional literature itself as practical kabbalah *(qabbalah maʿasit)* to be distinguished from the more theosophical or speculative kabbalah *(qabbalah ʿiyyunit).* It must be noted, however, that important theosophical elements are often found in these more practical texts, the study of which has been grossly neglected by scholars. In sum, then, the word mysticism will be used here to refer to those trends of thought in Judaism which lay claim to either an esoteric knowledge of the Godhead (theosophy) or to an intense religious experience of a visionary or unitive sort (ecstasy), though I do not think these two can always be separated in a clear and distinct manner.

Merkavah Mysticism

The first major expression of mysticism within Judaism can be found in the writings that make up the so-called *merkavah* (chariot) or *hekhalot* (palace) corpus. This term is used to designate those texts, composed over a period of about eight hundred years, from the second to the tenth century, which describe in detail the ascent of an individual through the heavenly realms, culminating with an ecstatic vision of the luminous form on the throne located in the seventh palace of the seventh heaven. The vision of the divine chariot was first recorded in the book of Ezekiel, a prophet living in Babylonia in the sixth century B.C.E. Although many of the themes in the biblical prophecy served as the basis for the details elaborated in the *merkavah* corpus, the essential difference between the prophetic theophany and mystical vision is evident. Closer to the spirit of the *merkavah* praxis are remnants of heavenly ascents recorded in Jewish and Christian apocalyptic literature from the second century B.C.E. to roughly the third century C.E.[2] It is generally believed that *merkavah* mysticism is an outgrowth of Jewish apocalypticism, though some important differences are found as well.[3] More difficult to ascertain is the relationship between the *merkavah* mysticism and the esoteric discipline mentioned by the rabbis in the Mishnah, *maʿaseh merkavah* (account of the chariot). It may be assumed that this discipline, as the other ones specified by the rabbis, *ma'aseh bereshit* (account of the creation) and *'arayot* (illicit sexual relationships), was exegetical in nature. Indeed, recent scholarship has argued that the *ma'asehmerkavah*, as understood by the Palestinian rabbis of the first centuries, referred to explication of the literary account of Ezekiel's prophetic vision, involving no ecstatic experience or mystical practice.[4] A striking example of this exegetical-homiletical genre of *ma'aseh merkavah* can be found in the treatise known as *Re'uyot Yehezqel (Visions of Ezekiel)*.[5] Awareness on the part of the rabbis of the distinction between esoteric study and mystical praxis is evident from the following comment: "Many have expounded upon the *merkavah* without ever seeing it" (*Tosefta* Megillah 3[4]:28).[6] Still, it must be said that from some of the legendary accounts of rabbinic authorities engaged in homiletic speculation on the *merkavah*, especially R. Yohanan ben Zakkai and his disciples,[7] it is evident that this form of exegesis was capable of producing states through which the historic event of revelation was relived.[8] Indeed, there is a clear thematic connection linking the Sinaitic revelation and Ezekiel's chariot theophany in rabbinic homelitcal literature.[9] Nevertheless, these experiences do not yet amount to a mystical praxis, at least not as defined as the ascent to the chariot. Whatever pneumatic powers the study of Ezekiel's chariot-vision could impute to the exegete it should be noted, parenthetically, that according to one scholarly opinion midrashic activity in general must be viewed as a means to reexperience the seeing of God at the historical moment of Sinai, i.e., interpretation is an effort to reconstitute the original experience of revelation[10], this study did not constitute a vision of the chariot itself. On the other hand, given the literary and conceptual continuity linking apocalyptic and *Hekhalot*, it is difficult to maintain that the rabbis who lived in the period of the Mishnah were not cognizant of heavenly ascensions to the throne when they spoke of expounding the chariot.

The crucial turning point in the development of *merkavah* mysticism occurs, as Joseph Dan put it, "when active mystical ascent to the divine world replaced passive homiletical speculation in the midrashic manner concerning the chariot envisioned by Ezekiel."[11] It is not known precisely when and where this occurred, but it is likely that the mystical praxis of ascent was cultivated in Babylonia sometime in the Amoraic period (fourth–fifth centuries).[12] The five most important texts that provide descriptions of this mystical ascent are *Hekhalot Zutarti (Lesser Palaces)*,[13] *Hekhalot Rabbati (Greater Palaces)*,[14] *Sefer Hekhalot*, also known as *3 Enoch*,[15] the treatise published by Scholem under the title *Ma'aseh Merkavah*,[16] and a fragment from the Geniza which is referred to by the scribe as *Hotam ha-Merkavah (Seal of the Chariot)* and called by scholars the Ozhayah text.[17] The protagonists of these ascent texts are R. Ishmael, R. Akiva, and R. Nehunyah ben ha-Qanah. While we may say with relative certainty that the use of these rabbinic figures is a mere literary device to transmit the mystical teachings in the name of established authorities, the precise historical and social context of the authors who produced these works is not at all clear. It may be assumed that the texts in the form in which they have been preserved were redacted in the Geonic period, sometime between the seventh and tenth centuries. Not only do the first explicit references to *Hekhalot* compositions occur in Geonic material, but the first account of the mystical techniques employed for ascent is found in Hai ben Sherira Gaon (939–1038).[18] There is, in addition, substantial textual evidence from this period to show that interest in the mystical and magical traditions (especially connected with divine names) continued to have a decisive impact.[19]

It is possible to distinguish two central elements in the *Hekhalot* texts, the mystical ascent culminating in a visionary experience and the adjuration of angels achieved through various magical techniques, as, for example, the technique of putting on or clothing oneself with the divine name.[20] The adjuration of angels in the *Hekhalot* literature is aimed at the understanding of the secrets and treasures of Torah through magical study that does not require the ordinary effort. This aim is related especially in a section apparently appended to *Hekhalot Rabbati* known as *Sar Torah* (the "Archon of the Torah"). Of the two elements enumerated above, it may be said that the former is centered on the heavenly ascension, whereas the latter constitutes, in the words of Peter Schäfer, a "reverse heavenly journey,"[21] i.e., an effort to bring the angel down to earth by means of adjurations that consist of mentioning the divine names and displaying the magical seals which likewise are composed of divine names. Although I do not dispute the need to distinguish between the purely mystical and magical aims present in this corpus, it must be noted that similar magical or theurgical means are employed in the heavenly ascent as well. Moreover, in spite of the recent critique of various scholars,[22] it seems to me that Scholem's insight regarding the centrality of the visionary experience as the major element in the mystical praxis of these texts is an entirely defensible position.[23] The culmination of the ascent is a direct vision of the divine glory *(kavod)* or power *(gevurah)* referred to by several technical terms, including, most prominently, on the basis of Isa. 33:17, beholding the king in his beauty.[24] Although the vision of God is stressed time and again in these texts, it must be noted that one finds as well the opposing claim that God cannot be seen.[25] Scholem already noted this tension when he observed that for the *merkavah* visionaries the enthroned glory is "at once visible and yet, by virtue of His transcendent nature, incapable of being visualized."[26] *Hekhalot* literature thus incorporates the tension, rooted in the biblical tradition, between a visible, corporeal form of God, on the one hand, and the prohibition of seeing God, on the other.[27]

According to the terminology employed in some of the principal texts in this corpus, especially *Hekhalot Rabbati*, the approach to the throne is called *yeridah la-merkavah*, "descent to the chariot," and the mystics who approach *yorede merkavah*, "descenders to the chariot." Most scholars, *pace* Scholem, consider this a paradoxical expression that refers to the act of ascending.[28] I have recently argued, however, that a careful examination of the texts wherein this terminology appears indicates that it refers to an actual descent to the throne.[29] The heavenly journey thus involved an ascent through the seven heavens and the first six palaces of the seventh heaven, followed by entry into the seventh palace and descent to the throne itself. At the time of this descent the mystic stands before the enthroned glory and utters the appropriate praises together with the angels; he is then placed upon a throne alongside of or facing the throne of glory and has a vision of the luminous divine form.[30] The descent to the chariot, therefore, results in a deifying vision. To be sure, as Scholem already observed, there is no *unio mystica* in these texts, for the distinction between God and human is never fully overcome.[31] On the other hand, there is ample evidence to show that the enthronement of the mystic was a central part of this mystical experience, an enthronement that involved a form of quasi-deification. To see God requires that one be made like God, i.e., that one be substantially transformed into a spiritual (angelic) being. The classical example of the apotheosis of a human occurs in the *Sefer Hekhalot* (or *3 Enoch*) where the biblical Enoch (here understood to represent the prototype of the *merkavah* mystic) is translated into the heavenly realm and transformed into the angelic Metatron who occupies a throne alongside of the divine glory. Although this last step is not explicitly taken in the other major texts from this corpus, it is nevertheless clear that the enthronement of the *yored la-merkavah* signifies his elevation to the status of the highest angel in the celestial retinue. It is in virtue of this enthronement that the mystic can see that which is ordinarily hidden from human perception.

The most detailed description of the visualized form of God is given in the cluster of texts known as *Shiʿur Qomah (Measurement of the [Divine] Stature)*. In these texts the reader is provided with graphic details of the various limbs of the body of the enthroned divine figure, the *Yoser Bereshit* (i.e., the Demiurge or Creator), both in terms of names and dimensions.[32] This secret knowledge is said to be revealed to the mystic, either R. Aqiva or R. Ishmael,[33] by Metatron, designated as the "great angel" or the "angel of the divine countenance."[34] Some scholars have conjectured that the core theosophic speculation underlying the *Shiʿur Qomah* tradition distinguished between the supreme Godhead and the secondary demiurgic power (identified as Metatron) who was subject to corporeal measurement.[35] In the texts that are extant no such distinction is immediately evident.[36] On the other hand, there is evidence for such an interpretation of the *Shiʿur Qomah* from later kabbalistic sources.[37] Thus, for example, in a fragment of R. Abraham ben David of Posquiéres (ca. 1125–98) reported by his grandson, R. Asher ben David, we find the following interpretation of the talmudic statement that God wears phylacteries:[38] "This refers to the Prince of the Countenance [i.e., Metatron]. . . .And it is he who appeared to Moses at the bush, and to Ezekiel 'in the semblance of a human from above' (Ezek. 1:26). . . .And this is the secret of the account of creation: 'whoever knows the measurement of the Creator can be assured of his portion in the world-to-come,'[39] and this is [the subject of the verse] 'Let us make man in our image' (Gen. 1:26)."[40] A similar approach is attested in the following statement of R. Isaac of Acre, a kabbalist active in the end of the thirteenth and beginning of the fourteenth century: "I have received a true tradition concerning the fact that this measurement applies only to the created Metatron [i.e., the angelic Metatron] for he is the supernal Adam,[41] but above him the prophet said, 'To whom, then, can you liken God, etc.' (Isa. 40:18). The one who says something contrary to this has not seen the light."[42] Given the alternative approach found in medieval kabbalistic literature to apply the *Shiʿur Qomah* to the sefirotic edifice, it seems to me that the tradition of applying the measurements to the angelic Metatron is an older Jewish esoteric doctrine which the kabbalists did not innovate but rather received as oral lore. Some scholars have also maintained that the *Sh'iur Qomah* is a mystical reading of the description of the Lover in Song of Songs.[43] According to more normative rabbinic modes of exegesis, the Song of Songs was read as an allegorical depiction of God's love for Israel.[44] Given this reading of the text it would stand to reason that the description of the physical body of the Lover (especially in the fifth chapter) should be applied to God and would therefore suggest the corporeal measurements enumerated in the mystical tradition. Other scholars, however, have rejected the proposed connection between *Shi'ur Qomah* and the Song of Songs.[45]

The measurements of the limbs are quite extraordinary, indeed impossible to imagine from a normal human perspective. While the dimensions of the divine body differ according to the different textual traditions, one of the standard measures of the height of the Creator, and that which was most frequently cited by later authors, is 236,000 parasangs,[46] or according to other texts, 2,360,000,000 parasangs.[47] This number is exegetically related in the Aqiban text to the expression *ve-rav koah*, "full of power," in Ps. 147:5, whose numerical equivalence is 236.[48] Similarly, in the sections of the text attributed to R. Ishmael and R. Nathan, the former's student, attached to each of the limbs are what may appear to the modern reader to be a list of meaningless Hebrew consonants which are, in fact, the holy names of God.[49] It has been suggested by some scholars that the astronomical size of the limbs together with the incomprehensibility of the names indicates that the anthropomorphism of this text should be construed as a *reductio ad absurdum* of the very notion of applying corporeal characteristics to God.[50] Whether we accept this interpretation or not, it is clear that the convergence of letter symbolism and anthropomorphism is one of the characteristic features of Jewish theosophic speculation through the ages: one of the primary ways to image the corporeal form of God is through linguistic means, i.e., the limbs of God are constituted by the Hebrew letters.

Sefer Yesirah: Linguistic Mysticism

Another important treatise in the history of Jewish mystical speculation is the *Sefer Yesirah (Book of Formation)*, which is dated anywhere from the third to seventh centuries. While some comments in the treatise suggest that it belongs to the *merkavah* environment, on the whole it stands apart from the rest of the *Hekhalot* corpus. The interest here is not on a mystical ascent culminating with a vision of God, or even magical adjuration of the angels. *Sefer Yesirah* is principally concerned with cosmology and cosmogony, and therefore belongs to the other Jewish esoteric tradition, *maʿaseh bereshit.*[51] The text is extant in three different redactions: the long version, the short version, and that which is incorporated in Saadya Gaon's commentary on it.[52] All versions share the view that the means of divine creativity are the thirty-two paths of wisdom which comprise ten primordial ciphers *(sefirot)* and the twenty-two Hebrew letters. It is possible that originally these were distinct modes of Jewish speculation on divine creativity, which were brought together fairly early in the redactional process. Although the *sefirot* are to be understood as numbers in this context, it must be noted that they exemplify traits hardly befitting numbers in any commonsensical way. Thus, for example, in one of the paragraphs we read that the vision or appearance of the *sefirot* is like a flash of lightning and that they bow down before God's throne. It may be concluded from this passage that the authorship of *Sefer Yesirah* wished to describe these primordial *sefirot* in terms describing the celestial beasts according to the *merkavah* tradition.[53] It is, however, a moot point if this further implies that already in this text the *sefirot* are dynamic potencies within the divine realm that collectively make up the habitation of the divine, or if the author simply wanted to describe the *sefirot* in these terms for a pure literary effect.[54]

The letter symbolism, by contrast, is meant to convey a different idea that has also had a profound impact on Jewish mystics through the ages. The letters, divided into three groups (three mothers, seven doubles, and twelve simples) are not merely the tools of divine creativity, a notion found in more normative rabbinic sources; they are treated in *Sefer Yesirah* as the material stuff of reality.[55] That is, a given thing is brought into life by means of a process of letter-combination for the appropriate letters inform us of that thing's most basic structure. Each of the letters is said to have an impact on three ontological planes: space (*ʿolam*, literally, cosmos), time (*shanah*, literally, year), and the microcosm (*nefesh*, literally, life or soul). Just as other forms of reality are composed of the letters, so, too, the human body. The correlation between letter-combination (through 231 gates of permutation) and limbs of the human body in *Sefer Yesirah* parallels the correlation between letters and the anthropomorphic figure (whose standard measure, as I indicated above, equals 2,360,000,000 or 236,000 parasangs) of the divine described in *Shi'ur Qomah*.[56] Although no explicit connection between the two modes of speculation is made in the earlier sources, it is of interest to note that the two are brought together in subsequent kabbalistic speculation, including, for example, in the Zoharic tradition[57] as well as other sources which, in turn, influenced the version of Lurianic kabbalah expounded in the latter part of the sixteenth century by Israel Sarug.[58] The central role played by letter symbolism is evident in all the main branches of Jewish mysticism, including German Pietism, the ecstatic kabbalah of Abraham Abulafia (1240–ca. 1292), and the theosophic kabbalah.

German Pietism

Merkavah traditions were transported from their Babylonian milieu to the Jewish communities of Europe, most likely through Italy, in the eighth and ninth centuries.[59] But the most important source for the preservation and transmission of these documents were the German Pietists who were active in the Rhineland in the twelfth and thirteenth centuries. The main circle of Pietists was led by Judah ben Samuel ben Kalonymus of Regensburg (d. 1217) and his disciple, Eleazar ben Judah ben Kalonymus of Worms (d. 1240). In addition to preserving the older *merkavah* texts, the Pietists developed their own theosophy which combined *Hekhalot* mysticism, the philosophy of Saadya Gaon (882–942), the writings of Shabbetai Donnolo (b. 913) and Judah ben Barzilai (eleventh–twelfth century), and Jewish Neoplatonism, especially Abraham ibn Ezra (ca. 1092–167).[60] At the center of the Pietistic theosophy is the doctrine of the divine glory *(kavod)* which is largely based on some of the sources mentioned above.[61] A lively discussion in the Pietistic circle revolved around the question of the nature of the glory as it specifically related to the problem of addressing human prayer to a supposedly incorporeal deity. Three distinct approaches can be identified: the glory was a created light extrinsic to God (Saadya); it was emanated from God and therefore attached to the deity (Abraham ibn Ezra); the visible form of the glory is an image within the mind of the prophet or mystic and not an entity outside the mind (Hai Gaon [939–1038] as

transmitted by Hananel ben Hushiel [d. 1055/56]). The Pietists
seem to reject the first opinion and waver between the second
and third.[62] Following the view expressed by Nathan ben Yehiel
of Rome (1035–ca. 1110), itself based on earlier sources, the
Pietists, as may be gathered from the writings of Eleazar of
Worms, distinguished between an upper and lower glory. The
former is an amorphous light, called the "Presence" (Shekhinah) or "great splendor" (hod ha-gaddol), while the latter is
the aspect that assumes different forms within the prophetic or
mystical imagination. Yet, as the Pietists insist, the Creator is
simultaneously outside and inside the image.[63] One can therefore pray to the visible glory—which is an image—for God is
present in that very image.[64] The forms that the lower glory
assumes are multiple in nature, changing in accordance with
God's will and the particular capacity of the given visionary.
The most important of these images is the anthropomorphic
shape suggested already by biblical theophanies including the
chariot-vision of Ezekiel. Furthermore, Eleazar appropriates the
anthropomorphism of the ancient Shi'ur Qomah by applying the
corporeal measurements not to the Creator (as the text explicitly states) but rather to the form that is constituted within the
imagination. Of the many texts that I could cite to illustrate
the point, I will select the following passage from one of
the most esoteric works of Eleazar, the Sefer ha-Shem (Book of
the Name):

> He showed the form of a human countenance (parsuf adam) to the
> heart of the prophet; he saw [it] according to the number of [the
> expression in Ps. 147:5] "full of power" (we-ravkoah) [i.e., 236
> which represent the 2,360,000,000 parasangs attributed to the Cre-
> ator in the Shi'ur Qomah). "Ascribe might to God" (Ps. 68:35). The
> image (temunah) applies only to the human countenance, for he
> imagines His appearance [as an anthropomorphic form]. "Know the
> God of your father and serve him" (1 Chron. 28:9), for according to
> the vision one knows His will and knows the supernal mind (da'at
> 'elyon). . . ."they saw the God of Israel; they beheld God" (Exod.
> 24:10–11).[65]

Eleazar has thus reinterpreted the earlier mystical tradition that
ascribed corporeal dimensions to the divine form. From the vantage point of the Pietistic theology, at least in its exoteric formulation, there is no divine form—God is not a body and therefore
can possess no form or shape—but only that which is apprehended in the mind of the visionary. The measurements spec-

ified in the ancient esoteric work therefore are not attributable to the Creator or even to the glory as it is in and of itself; they represent rather the proportions of the glory as it is visualized through the imagined forms within the prophetic or mystic consciousness. By contrast, according to the writings that Dan has identified as belonging to a second, distinct circle of Pietists, the *Hug ha-Keruv ha-Meyuhad* ("Circle of the Special Cherub"),[66] the measurable enthroned figure is the being designated as the Special Cherub which is the anthropomorphic representation of the invisible, incorporeal divine glory.[67] It must be noted, however, that alongside the exoteric doctrine of the glory the main circle of the Kalonymide Pietists preserved and developed a more esoteric tradition which indeed applied in a more veridical way the measurements of the *Shi ʿur Qomah* to the glory. Thus, for example, in a text attributed by Joseph Dan to Judah the Pious, it is stated explicitly that the measurement of the *Shi ʿur Qomah* is applied "to that which cleaves," an allusion to the glory that emanates from and thus is attached to the One.[68] Similarly, in one context Eleazar writes:

> The essence of the glory is seen above, and a fire of radiance which is unfathomable was opposite the throne. Within [that radiance] the glory is seen in accordance with the will of the Creator, at times like an elder and at times like a youth.[69] The measure of the stature is 2,360,000,000 parasangs, as it is written, "Great is our Lord and full of power" (Ps. 147:5), "full of power" *(we-ravkoah)* numerically equals 236. . . .The stature of the visible glory is 2,360,000,000 parasangs.[70]

Two of the main tenets of the esoteric tradition include the identification of the glory with the Tetragrammaton[71] and the possibility of imaging the letters of this divine name as an anthropos.[72] While this esoteric tradition is alluded to in various Pietistic writings, it is stated more explicitly in *Sefer ha-Navon*, a treatise written by someone who had access to these writings but was apparently not part of the main circle:[73] "The name [YHWH] appears in its letters to the angels and prophets in several forms and radiance and it appears in the image of the appearance of an anthropos it appears 'in the semblance of a human form' (Ezek. 1:26), this refers to the *Shekhinah* and the angel of the glory *(malʾ akh ha-kavod)* which is the Tetragrammaton."[74] Here we come upon a motif that reflects one of the oldest ideas in Jewish esotericism: the identification, or blurring, of the distinction, between the glory, on the one hand, and the angelic being, on the other, which is the anthropomorphic manifestation of the divine.[75] Eleazar himself alludes to this matter when he writes that "the glory is symbolized by the angel which changes to many forms," including most importantly the form of an anthropos.[76] One may also discern from the Pietistic writings that study of the chariot was understood as speculation on the divine names, especially the tetragrammaton.[77] This speculation, moreover, involved a contemplative vision of the name. In some cases it would appear that knowledge of the chariot encompassed a mystical praxis whereby the Pietist ascended by means of meditation upon the divine name.[78] Eleazar thus specifies a series of rituals of purification as a prelude to both the study of the chariot[79] and the activity of mentioning the divine name.[80] It is hardly a coincidence that virtually the same procedure is outlined in these two contexts. It is also evident from Eleazar, as well as other contemporary Ashkenazi material, that the German Pietists cultivated the technique of recitation of divine or angelic names (itself rooted in the older *Hekhalot* literature) in order to induce a state of religious ecstasy akin to prophecy. The technique of recitation of the names and that of letter-combination transmitted in Eleazar had a decisive influence on both theosophic and ecstatic kabbalists active in Spain in the latter part of the thirteenth century.[81]

Another part of the esoteric tradition of the German Pietists involves the use of sexual imagery to characterize processes within the divine sphere. The use of feminine imagery to describe events in the throne-world is present in a cluster of texts that describe the chariot in terms of the structure of a nut. Alexander Altmann was the first scholar to present a systematic account of this material,[82] but it was Joseph Dan who suggested that these texts preserved an ancient esoteric reading of Song of Songs 6:1, "I went down to the garden of nuts," which formed part of the chariot mystical speculation that originated in Babylonia.[83] With respect to the masculine and feminine elements of the nut, Dan proposed that these were innovated by the Pietists, but he categorically denied that the idea of sexual dualism in the divine sphere had any other influence on Pietistic theosophy. He therefore rejects any attempt to see a connection between kabbalistic speculation, which is predicated on a male-female polarity within the Godhead, and German Pietistic theology.[84] More recently, Asi Farber has thoroughly reinvestigated the development of the secret of the nut tradition in the Pietistic corpus. Like Dan Farber she maintains that this represents an older tradition which the Pietists received, but she takes issue with Dan's conjecture that the Pietists themselves added the sexual images. On the contrary, these images were part of the "original" texts, which the Pietists attempted to minimize or even obscure, in some cases by altering the texts. Yet, a careful reading of their own writings shows that there are veiled allusions to the bisexual nature of the divine realm. According to Farber, then, one must distinguish between the "exoteric" side of the Pietistic theology, which attempted to attenuate or suppress sexual images, and the "esoteric" side, which described aspects of the divine in precisely such terms. The esoteric aspect was not fully committed to writing but was transmitted orally.[85]

The feminine quality of the glory is especially evident in the proto-kabbalistic text included in Eleazar of Worms's *Sefer ha-Hokhmah*, the commentary on the forty-two letter name of God attributed to Hai Gaon.[86] In that text the *Shekhinah* is identified as the crown (*'atarah*), prayer (*tefillah* or the Aramaic *selota'*), the divine voice (*bat qol*), the king's daughter (*bat melekh*), the bride (*kalah*) who sits to the left of the groom, God; the tenth kingship (*malkhut 'asirit*) or the tenth *sefirah*. Dan has argued that this text in all probability was not written by Eleazar as it employs terminology and concepts not known from his voluminous writings.[87] It must be pointed out, however, as Scholem himself noted,[88] from a phenomenological point of view the glory does receive in the teachings of the Pietists a dynamic character which is very close to the description of the tenth emanation in the divine pleroma according to kabbalistic sources. Furthermore, Moshe Idel has shown that the elevation of the crown, understood hypostatically, in German Pietistic texts has a decidedly theurgical connotation that bears a close likeness to older midrashic as well as kabbalistic motifs.[89] In a separate paper I have argued that an even more pronounced theurgy is evident in the Pietistic treatment of the commandments.[90] Here I will only briefly summarize the findings of my research. The lower glory, identified as the cherub or the image of Jacob engraved on the throne, is equated with the union of two cherubim which (on the basis of older traditions) correspond to the divine names, YHWH and Adonai, or the two attributes of God, mercy and judgment. Through a complicated numerological exegesis the two names are said to comprise the 613 commandments of the Torah in its totality, the same numerological equivalence of the expression YHWH *'Elohe Yisra'el* ("Lord God of Israel") which is one of the proper names of the enthroned glory. The Pietists draw the obvious theurgical implications: by performing the 613 traditional commandments one unites the two names of God or the glory.

Theosophic Kabbalah

During the same period that German Pietism became an active social and religious force, theosophic kabbalah began to take root in Provence and Northern Spain. The precise origins of kabbalistic speculation remain somewhat obscure, though it is generally assumed that fragments of older documents made their way to Central Europe from the East. Rabbinic writings themselves (aggadic statements contained in the Palestinian and Babylonian Talmuds or in independent collections of scriptural exegeses known as *midrashim*) may be viewed as a repository of ancient Jewish theosophic theologoumena which have been preserved in a very fragmentary form and which were elaborated into a comprehensive and systematic doctrine by the medieval kabbalists.[91] It is also likely that there was a prehistory to some kabbalistic ideas that were transmitted orally in a subterranean fashion. One of the crucial problems in the historical development of theosophic kabbalah is the relationship between Gnosticism, an ancient syncretistic religious movement that flourished in the Mediterranean countries in the first centuries of the common era, and Jewish esotericism. Some scholars maintain that the similarities between these two are purely phenomenological in nature, whereas others insist on an historical connection as well.[92]

Whatever the relationship between Gnosticism and kabbalah, it is evident that in the twelfth century a theosophic conception of God begins to crystallize in Jewish writings. The main elements of this theosophy include the imaging of God in terms of a male-female polarity and the theurgical understanding of normative religious practice such that fulfillment of the traditional precepts increases the stature of the divine structure and, conversely, failure to do so weakens it. Both of these elements are present in the first text dedicated fully to a theosophical-theurgical conception of God, the *Sefer ha-Bahir* ("Book of Illumination"), which presumably surfaced in twelfth-century Provence, though the text obviously contains earlier literary strata.[93] Standard biblical and rabbinic images are here transformed into symbols for the dynamic life of divinity. The presentation of the theosophy is not systematic in the case of the *Bahir* which is, in fact, structured like a traditional midrash.[94] In one section, however, we can discern a fairly cohesive textual unit wherein the ten powers that make up the divine pleroma are called *ma'amarot* (sayings), a reference to the traditional rabbinic notion of the ten *logoi* by means of which the world was created.[95] The authors of the *Bahir* opted for mythical ways to describe these divine grades, referring to them parabolically in such images as crowns, trees, gardens, and the like. The potencies are on one occasion called *sefirot*,[96] the term employed in *Sefer Yesirah*, as we have seen, to designate ten primordial numbers. It was this term that eventually emerged as the predominant denotation of the divine potencies in the kabbalistic literature of the following centuries.

The *Bahir* supplied two important ways of pictorially depicting these potencies: either as a tree[97] or as an anthropomorphic figure.[98] Both of these images had an important influence on subsequent kabbalistic thought, but it is the second that goes to the heart of kabbalah, providing as it does the background for both the theosophical and theurgical axes of the kabbalistic *Weltanschauung*. The *Bahir* interprets the notion of man's being created in God's image (Gen. 1:26) in terms of the divine body, i.e., the limbs of the human correspond to the upper divine limbs (seven[99] or eight[100] are specified and not ten) and as such can influence them through proper or improper action. In virtue of this anthropomorphism one can see continuity between the ancient Jewish mystical speculation and the theosophy expressed in the *Bahir*. The position assumed by the enthroned demiurgical being is now taken by the divine gradations that are visualized in the shape of an anthropos.[101] This cornerstone of kabbalistic thought is well articulated by the anonymous author of the *Ma'arekhet ha-'Elohut*, a work composed in the late thirteenth or early fourteenth century:

Know that a person's physical form is made in the [likeness of the] supernal image *(demut 'elyon)*, and the supernal image is the [sefirotic] edifice, whose essence is *Tif'eret* [the sixth *sefirah*] which is called the anthropos in the chariot. Now that you know the structure of the human form you can comprehend if you have received orally the truth of the prophetic vision seen by the prophets. The rabbis, blessed be their memory, called this vision the measure of the stature *(Shi'ur Qomah)*[102]

It is on the basis of this correspondence between human limbs and those of the divine that the kabbalists assign a central role to the normative life of traditional Judaism,[103] that is, by fulfilling the commandments one strengthens the corresponding limb above in the divine edifice, while neglect to do so or doing what is prohibited causes a blemish above. R. Joseph of Hamadan, a kabbalist writing at the end of the thirteenth or beginning of the fourteenth century, put the matter as follows:

> You already know that man was created in the form of the supernal chariot [i.e., the sefirotic realm]. . . .Each and every limb of man exists from the sparks that originate in the chariot from that very limb, eye from the eye, and so on with respect to all the other limbs. . . .Thus the [sages], blessed be their memory, said, "a limb strengthens a limb."[104] When a person fulfills a commandment he sustains the upper limb and the lower limb but if a person sins with the eye and in a commandment connected to it, he creates, as it were, a blemish in the supernal eye.[105]

The import of kabbalistic theurgy, therefore, can only be understood against the background of the anthropomorphic conception of God, for the impact that one can have upon the divine is predicated on the morphological resemblance between God and human.[106] This anthropomorphism is further accentuated by the kabbalistic identification of the Torah in its mystical essence with the divine edifice (binyan'elohi)—a term employed by R. Ezra of Gerona—or the "holy and pure supernal form" (surah ha-ʿelyonah ha-qedoshah we-ha-tehorah)—according to the location of R. Joseph of Hamadan.[107] The Torah is the shape or image of God, which is construed, by various kabbalists, anthropomorphically. Specifically, each of the laws corresponds to, or derives from, a particular limb in the supernal adamic form which is, at the same time, the Torah. The connection between kabbalistic theurgy and the anthropomorphic conception of Torah as the divine form is brought out in the following passage of R. Joseph of Hamadan:

> The Torah is the shadow of the Holy One, blessed be He. Happy is he, and blessed is his lot, who knows how to direct the limb corresponding to a [supernal] limb, and a form which corresponds to a [supernal] form in the holy and pure chain, blessed be His name. Insofar as the Torah is His form (surato), blessed be He, He commanded us to study Torah in order to know the pattern of the supernal form (dugmato shelsurah ha-ʿelyonah).[108]

The view of Hamadan is expressed in slightly different terms by Menahem Recanti, an Italian kabbalist writing in the first part of the fourteenth century: "The commandments are one entity, and they depend upon the supernal chariot [i.e., the sefirotic realm] each and every commandment depends on one part of the chariot. It follows that God is not something extrinsic to the Torah, nor is the Torah outside of God. . . . Thus the kabbalist say that the Holy One, blessed be He, is the Torah."[109]

At this juncture it must be noted that many of the kabbalists living in the High Middle Ages could not speak unqualifyingly of God as possessing a form or body, let alone masculine and feminine traits. Thus, we frequently find in kabbalistic literature the ascription of anthropomorphic characteristics to the sefirotic realm followed by the caveat that this anthropomorphism should not be taken in any literal sense to imply a belief in God's corporeality. A typical account of the kabbalists' reluctance to accept the anthropomorphic implications of their own thinking may be found in the following passage from Recanati, which is based, in turn, on Joseph Gikatilla:[110]

> The true essence of the Creator, may he He be elevated and blessed, is not comprehended by anyone but Him. . . . If so we must contemplate the [corporeal] attributes found in Scripture and in the words of the rabbis, blessed be their memory, e.g., hand, foot, ear, eye, and the like. . . . Do not think that the eye is the form of a [physical] eye, or the hand in the form of a [physical] hand. Rather these things are inner matters in the truth of the reality of God, blessed be He, from which is the source and the flow that goes out to all created things. There is no similarity between God and us from the vantage point of substance or form . . . for He has no image in the created things. The intention [of these anthropomorphic expressions] rather is that the form of our limbs become symbols *le-dimyon simanim)* for the supernal, hidden matters which the mind cannot grasp.[111] . . . Since God, may He be elevated and blessed, wanted to benefit us, He created in the human body certain wonderful and hidden limbs which are in the form of symbols for the [divine] chariot. If a person merits to purify one of his limbs, that limb will be like a throne for the inner supernal limb that is called by the name eye, hand, and the like.[112]

To speak of divine limbs, accordingly, means only to refer to the divine powers *(sefirot)* in the terms with which we describe the human body. These terms are symbols *(simanim)* for the divine reality which we cannot know in any essential manner.

It should be noted that this approach is very close to Scholem's presentation of kabbalistic symbols as "an expressible representation of something which lies beyond the sphere of expression and communication."[113] The description of God's body or the mating of male and female does not tell us anything about God's true essence for the latter is unknowable. Although there is ample support for such an understanding of the function of religious symbol in kabbalistic texts such as the one cited above, I suggest that this is a reflection of the historical period in which kabbalah emerged as a literary force, and not indicative of its "originary" doctrine.[114] Underlying the ideational matrix of the kabbalah is the mythological belief in the divine body, which was expressed in earlier Jewish mysticism as well, producing the seemingly bizarre speculations of the *Shi'ur Qomah* tradition. In spite of repeated qualifications found in kabbalistic texts, some of the more esoteric elements of kabbalah are intensely anthropomorphic in nature. This includes the literary units of the *Zohar*, which present the most recondite teachings about the Godhead, the *Idra Rabba* (Great Gathering) and *Idra Zuta* (Small Gathering), as well as the mythic theosophy promulgated in the sixteenth century in Safed by Isaac Luria and his disciples largely based on the doctrine of the divine countenances *(parsufim)* elaborated upon in the *Idrot* sections of the *Zohar*.[115]

The literature of theosophic kabbalah spans an extensive period and incorporates many different aspects of Jewish esotericism. One may, however, legitimately isolate speculation on the ten *sefirot* as the distinctive doctrine of this tradition. These *sefirot* are characterized in various ways, but perhaps the most central characterization is that of light. According to one of the accepted etymologies in thirteenth-century kabbalah, the word *sefirot* is said to derive from the word *sappir*, which means sapphire, conveying therefore the notion of luminosity.[116] The centrality of the light symbolism is attested in any number of sources, deriving from either a gnostic-mythological background or a Neoplatonic one.[117] The former is evident in *Sefer ha-Bahir* and in other kabbalists whose thought can be said to emerge out of the ground of midrashic and *Hekhalot* literature. The latter influence is felt particularly in the systematic account of the emanation of the ten spiritual lights out of the *Ein-Sof*, the ineffable Infinite, which is first articulated in the Provençal kabbalah, especially as it appears in Isaac the Blind, and his disciples, Asher ben David, Ezra ben Solomon, and Azriel ben Menahem of Gerona. One of the distinctive features of the Zoharic literature (which had a critical impact on subsequent kabbalistic theosophy) is that it combines the mythic and more philosophical approach.

The *Ein-Sof* and the *sefirot* represent two aspects of the one God: the former is the nameless, boundless ground of being that assumes personality in the dynamic sefirotic structure. Though multiple the *sefirot* form one organic unity and are said to be connected to the Infinite "like the flame bound to the coal" *(Sefer Yesirah 1:7)*. Another image utilized by kabbalists from the same source to depict the unity of the *sefirot* is the expression to the effect that "their end is fixed in their beginning and their beginning in their end." For the most part classical kabbalah depicts the process of emanation of the *sefirot* as issuing forth out of the Infinite like rays of light from the sun. However, there is also evidence for another important motif concerning the primordial withdrawal or contraction *(simsum)* of light before the process of emanation could unfold. Allusions to this idea are found in some thirteenth-century kabbalistic sources,[118] but it was expanded into a systematic doctrine in the sixteenth-century kabbalah of Moses Cordovero (1522–70)[119] and Isaac Luria (1534–72).[120] Kabbalists also differed with respect to the question of the ontological status of the *sefirot* vis-à-vis the Infinite, with some maintaining that the *sefirot* are the essence ('asmut) of God and others asserting that they are instruments or vessels *(kelim)* into which God infuses His infinite light.[121] The opposition between the essentialist and instrumentalist views was dialectically resolved in various ways by sixteenth-century kabbalists, such as Solomon Alkabez (1505–76) and his student, Moses Cordovero,[122] who suggested that the *sefirot* were both God's essence and vessels.

Finally, it should be mentioned that another essential doctrine in kabbalistic thought concerns the realm of unholy or demonic forces that structurally parallel the holy realm of *sefirot*.[123] Although there is some speculation concerning an attribute of evil (personified as Satan) within the divine realm in *Bahir*,[124] as well as some other evidence that early kabbalists had a tradition about demonic forces (both R. Isaac the Blind[125] and Nahmanides[126]), it was in the kabbalah developed in Castile in the second half of the thirteenth century that such speculation was elaborated as an explicit doctrine.[127] The teaching regarding the unholy forces in the writings of the Castilian kabbalists, e.g., Isaac ben Jacob ha-Kohen, Moses ben Simon of Burgos, and Todros ben Joseph Abulafia, had a decisive influence on the *Zohar* which abounds with different accounts of the struggle between the holy and the unholy.[128] As scholars have noted, in the *Zohar* itself one can discern two distinct tendencies: on the one hand, there is clear evidence of a more dualistic posture according to which the forces of light are pitted against the forces of darkness (called the *Sitra Ahra*, i.e., the Other Side), whereas, on the other, there is a more monistic strain in *Zohar* which sees all of the forces as related in a cosmological chain and the ultimate religious ideal being containment rather than separation.[129] This tension is evident in subsequent stages of Jewish mystical thought as well. The more mythological descriptions of the destruction of the primordial forces of evil (unbalanced forces of judgment) or the elimination of impurity from the divine thought[130] had a decisive influence on latter kabbalah, especially the teaching of Isaac Luria concerning the triadic myth within the Godhead consisting of contraction (*simsum*, the breaking of the vessels (*shevirat ha-kelim*) and the consequent formation of the shells (*qelippot*) and the fall of the sparks (*nisosot*), and restoration (*tiqqun*) or liberation of the fallen and entrapped sparks.[131]

Although the main interest of kabbalists was clearly to speculate on and develop the metaphysical intricacies of their doctrine, underlying these theosophic speculations is a deeply experiential component, a point generally missed in scholarly accounts. Scholem's assessment may be considered rather typical. After acknowledging that ecstatic mystical experiences may "lie at the bottom of many Kabbalistic writings"[132] and, moreover, that "the visionary element of mysticism which corresponds to a certain psychological disposition breaks through again and again,"[133] Scholem concludes: "But, on the whole, Kabbalistic meditation and contemplation take on a more spiritualized aspect."[134] What Scholem intends by "spiritualized aspect" is made clear in another passage where he is even more emphatic in his denial of the visionary element in theosophic kabbalah. "The concentration on the world of the *Sefirot* is not bound up with visions, but is solely a matter for the intellect prepared to ascend from level to level and to meditate on the qualities unique to each level. If meditation activates at first the faculty of imagination, it continues by activating the faculty of the intellect."[135] For Scholem kabbalah is, first and foremost, an intellectual discipline which provides one with knowledge of the divine and its relationship to man, particularly the Jewish people, and the world. Kabbalistic texts, according to Scholem's reading, place primary emphasis not on experience, not to mention *unio mystica* which Scholem signals out as being lacking even from kabbalists of a more ecstatic nature,[136] but rather on theory, a body of esoteric lore, a specific program of study characterized by a system of symbolism and a derivative method of exegesis. An important alternative to the Scholemian approach can be found in Moshe Idel who has both reconsidered the importance of *unio mystica* in Jewish texts[137] and paid far greater attention to the experiential side of kabbalistic thought, including specific meditative or contemplative techniques intended to induce religious ecstasy.[138] I should here like to emphasize that the study of the *sefirot* itself as viewed from within the tradition was considered to be an exercise in visualization. Support for my contention is illustrated in a striking way in the following passage extant in manuscript:

> Therefore I will explain the ten *sefirot*, the divine principles, according to the kabbalah so thay one may cleave to them, as it is written, "This is my God and I will glorify Him" (Exod. 15:2), [the word *we-ʾanvehu*, "I will glorify Him," can be read as] I and He *(ʾani wehuʾ)*. When one cleaves to them [the *sefirot*], the divine Holy Spirit enters into him, in all his sensations and all his movements.[139]

The illuminative nature of kabbalistic gnosis is also apparent in the following description in an anonymous commentary on the *sefirot* that was, in all probability, written in Castile in the latter part of the thirteenth century:[140]

> I will enlighten you and lead you in this way, to inform you of the mystery of unity *(sod ha-yihud)* through which the King is unified and the knowledge of His truth through which He is elevated, and to show you the force of His comprehension, the wealth of the glory of His splendor and His kingdom, the majesty of the splendor of His greatness in all the places of His dominion. I will show you the splendor to secure you in the supernal crown [the first *sefirah*], to cover you in the splendor of the faithful wisdom [second *sefirah*], to open for you the gates of understanding [third *sefirah*], to cleave to the attributes of mercy, strength and beauty [fourth-sixth *sefirot*], to take delight in eternity, majesty, the foundation and the crown [seventh-tenth *sefirot*]. Then your soul will don the garment of splendor and beauty, grace and love, and you will be crowned with the resplendent light that surrounds the Presence, and this is the mystery in which is contained the mystery of the upper and lower knowledge.[141]

There is sufficient evidence to show that kabbalists developed and propagated relatively simple mystical techniques in order to induce visions of the divine lights or colors. In the case of some kabbalists, such as David ben Yehudah he-Hasid and other members of his school, the technique of visualizing colors within the imagination was part of the mystical intention of prayer. The imagined colors were not to be confused with the *sefirot* themselves, the visualization of which was forbidden, but were viewed rather as the electrum *(hashmal)* or cover *(levush)*[142] of the particular *sefirah* and therefore capable of being visualized. According to another tradition closely connected with the previous method of spiritual visualization, one is instructed to imagine the letters of the Tetragrammaton vocalized in a specific way and contained within a circle of a particular color corresponding to the appropriate *sefirah*.[143] While the *Zohar* abounds in light imagery in its different characterizations of the divine emanations, influenced especially by the writings of a group of mystics known as the *Hug ha-ʾlyyun* ("Circle of Speculation"),[144] two specific, rather simple, techniques are mentioned in order to induce visual experiences. The first involves the rolling of the closed eyes which produces three colors within the mind that correspond either to the three central *sefirot* in and of themselves;[145] or as reflected in the last of the *sefirot*, the *Shekhinah*.[146] The second technique, which is rooted in an ancient Jewish procedure to induce prophetic vision,[147] involves placing a dish of water in sunlight so that one may watch the shadows cast upon a wall. This visualization results in a state of mystical comprehension or meditation upon the *sefirot*.[148] In a passage from his *Shaʿar Yesod ha-Merkavah*, a commentary on Ezekiel's chariot vision, Moses de León mentions both techniques together, indicating that they achieve the selfsame result: "When the eye is closed and rolls around a concealed splendor is seen momentarily. . . . So it is by the supernal creatures [i.e., the three central *sefirot*]—they are the splendor of the speculum that shines which does not settle down to be seen, but rather 'runs to and fro' (Ezek. 1:14) as the revolving of the water in a plate when faced against the light of the sun."[149] It should be noted that the use of a bowl of water as a medium to induce a vision of the divine glory is also known from the German Pietistic literature.

The visionary aspect of kabbalistic gnosis is epitomized in one of the terms that the mystics use to refer to themselves, *maskilim*, the enlightened, a term derived from the biblical verse that speaks of the enlightened shining like splendor of the firmament (cf. Dan. 12:3). As employed by kabbalists this title is meant to highlight the fact that mystical knowledge is a special sort of illumination. Thus, in one text in *Zohar* we read:

"And the enlightened will shine" (Dan. 12:3). Who are the enlightened? Those who know how to contemplate the glory of their master and know the secret of wisdom.... They shine like the upper splendor. It says "the enlightened" *(ha-maskilim)* rather than the knowers *(ha-yod'im)*, for these verily are they who contemplate the inner, hidden secrets which are not disclosed or transmitted to every person.[150]

By exegetically disclosing the secrets contained in Scripture the kabbalist uncovers the lights hidden within the text which is, mystically conceived, the divine image.[151] From that vantage point it may be said that scriptural interpretation is itself a revelatory mode, i.e., when one meditates on the text one is effectively contemplating the divine form.[152] Perhaps one of the boldest expressions of this is found in Joseph Hamadan: "Therefore the Torah is called by this name [Torah] for it elucidates the pattern of the Holy One, blessed be He the Torah, as it were, is the shadow of the Holy One, blessed be He inasmuch as the Torah is the form of God He commanded us to study it so that we may know the pattern of the upper form [the sefirotic realm]."[153]

The correlation of divine light and the letters of Scripture is substantiated by kabbalists by means of the numerical equivalence between *raz,* secret, and *'or,* light.[154] To comprehend the mystical meaning of Scripture is to behold the light of the divine gradations. A fairly typical account is given by Cordovero: "The mysteries of Torah are verily the splendor of the firmament, and when a person is occupied with the secret of the mysteries of Torah he opens the supernal sources in the secret of their unity by means of the voices of Torah."[155] In slightly different words Abraham Azulai, the seventh-century kabbalist, elaborates on the same point: "There are great lights in the Torah and they are its secrets, and there are several secrets which are still concealed, for they have not yet been revealed in the world; therefore the Torah is hidden and its light has not been disseminated. When the people below in this world bring to light secrets of the Torah, they cause that very matter above, which is hinted at in the secret of the Torah, to be revealed and to be disseminated."[156] The virtual identification of Torah with the divine, on the one hand, and the further specification of the luminous nature of the letters of Torah, on the other, provides us with one of the most frequently recurring themes in the kabbalistic literature. In the case of eighteenth-century Hasidism this developed into a technical meditative technique centered on the cleaving of one's thought to the infinite light contained in the letters of the Torah as well as those of the traditional prayers.[157]

Ecstatic Kabbalah

In the latter part of the thirteenth century, at the time when theosophic kabbalah was flourishing, there emerged as well an alternative kabbalistic tradition with a different focus. The main exponent of this tradition was Abraham Abulafia.[158] Whereas the theosophic kabbalists focused their attention on the hypostatic potencies that made up the divine realm, Abulafia turned his attention to cultivating a mystical system that could assist one in achieving a state of *unio mystica* which he identified as prophecy. He thus called his system "prophetic kabbalah" *(qabbalah nevuʿit)*, though scholars have also referred to it as ecstatic kabbalah insofar as it is aimed at producing a state of mystical ecstasy wherein the boundaries separating the self from God are overcome. Abulafia adopted the understanding of prophecy found in the philosophical writings of Moses Maimonides (1135–1204), who in turn was influenced by Islamic thinkers such as Alfarabi and Ibn Sina,[159] to the effect that the prophet receives an overflow from and thereby attains a state of conjunction with the Active Intellect, the last of the ten separate Intellects in the cosmological chain. For Abulafia, too, prophecy can only be attained when one is in a state of intellectual conjunction, a state that can come about only when the soul is freed from the bonds of the body. Thus, e.g., he writes in his treatise ʾOr ha-Sekhel ("Light of the Intellect"): "The connection of human existence with the divine existence during intellection—which is identical with the intellect in [its] existence—until he and He become one [entity]."[160] The union between human and divine intellects is so complete that in this state the individual can utter with respect to God, "He is I and I am He."[161]

What distinguishes Abulafia's mystical system from the more rationalist approach of Maimonides is that he introduced specific techniques in order to bring about this state of conjunction or union *(devequt)*. The main techniques consisted of letter-combination (in three stages: written, oral, and mental) and recitation of the divine names that involved as well special breathing exercises and bodily postures.[162] Abulafia referred to his "science of letter-combination" *(hokhmat ha-seruf)*, also identified as the "path of names" *(derekh ha-shemot)*, as the true account of the chariot (the term *merkavah* deriving from the root *rkb* which, in one of its conjugational forms, can mean to combine).[163] Idel has attempted to locate the Abulafian technique of recitation of names as an ecstatic exercise in the history of Jewish mysticism, beginning with the merkavah texts of late Antiquity and culminating in some of the writings of the German Pietists. Moreover, Idel has drawn our attention to some striking parallels between Abulafia's system of letter-combination and Eleazar of Worms, whose works Abulafia himself on occasion mentions by name.[164]

Although Abulafia gives preference to the auditory mode over the visual, accusing the theosophic kabbalists of focusing primarily on the latter,[165] in his own system visionary experience plays a critical role. For Abulafia not only is the esoteric wisdom of the divine chariot brought about by knowledge of the various combinations and permutations of the names of God, but vision of the chariot itself consists of the very letters that are constitutive elements of the names. The ecstatic vision of the letters is not simply the means to achieve union with God: it is, to an extent, the end of the process.[166] The culminating stage in the *via mystica* is a vision of the letters of the divine names, especially the Tetragrammaton, originating in the intellectual and imaginative powers. These letters are visualized simultaneously as an anthropos. Gazing upon the divine name is akin to beholding the divine form as constituted within one's imagination. This vision results from the conjunction of the human intellect with the divine, but, like all prophecy, following the view of Maimonides and his Islamic predecessors, there must be an imaginative component. The latter is described either as the form of the letters or that of an anthropos. Both of these are figurative depictions of the Active Intellect who, in Abulafia's writings, is also personified as Metatron. In some sense, as is pointed out most emphatically in the anonymous *Shaʿare Sedeq* ("Gates of Righteousness"), written by a disciple of Abulafia, the image is a reflection of the individual prophet or mystic, an externalization of his inner self to the point of identification of the human intellect and the Active Intellect, personified as an anthropomorphic shape or the letters of the name.[167] With respect to the possibility of envisioning the letters as an anthropos, there is again an interesting parallel between Abulafia and the German Pietists as discussed above. The corporealization of the letters of the name in the shape of an anthropos represents, in my estimation, one of the cornerstones of kabbalistic thought which has its roots in ancient Jewish esotericism. Although it lies beyond the confines of this essay to substantiate my claim in detail, let me underline the essential point that the letters assume an anthropomorphic form. This renders problematic Scholem's general claim that Christian and kabbalistic doctrines of (visual) meditation should be distinguished on grounds that "in Christian mysticism a pictorial and concrete subject, such as the suffering of Christ and all that pertains to it, is given to the meditator, while in Kabbalah, the subject given is abstract and cannot be visualized, such as the Tetragrammaton and its combinations."[168] Scholem's point concerning the centrality of the passion for mystical visions in Christianity is well taken, but his characterization of the subject of visual meditation in kabbalah as always being abstract needs to be qualified. The visualization of the letters of the name as an anthropos in German Pietism, Abulafia, and theosophic kabbalists indicates that in the Jewish mystical tradition as well the abstract can be rendered in a pictorial concrete image in the contemplative vision.

The ecstatic kabbalah had an important influence on the history of Jewish mysticism. In the last decade of the thirteenth century a circle of Abulafian kabbalah was established in northern Palestine.[169] From this circle, which combined Abulafian mysticism with Sufic ideas, derived several works, including *Liqqute ha-RaN* (the teachings of Rabbi Nathan) and the anonymous *Sha'are Sedeq*.[170] It is likely, moreover, that two important theosophic kabbalists, Isaac of Acre and Shem Tov ibn Gaon, were influenced by this circle and thus assimilated ecstatic kabbalah within their respective theosophical traditions.[171] In the sixteenth century Abulafian kabbalah began to have a pronounced effect on some of the major kabbalists in Safed, e.g., Solomon Alkabez, Moses Cordovero, Elijah de Vidas, and Hayyim Vital, and at the same time in kabbalists in Jerusalem, e.g., Judah Albotini and Joseph ibn Zaiah.[172] The influence of Abulafian kabbalah is also quite evident in eighteenth-century

Hasidic literature, deriving directly from Abulafian manuscripts or indirectly through the writings of Cordovero and Vital.[173]

Conclusion

Jewish mysticism is not a monolith that can easily be defined or characterized. On the contrary, a plethora of different intellectual currents have converged to give shape to mystical trends within Judaism. Although I do not think that we can speak of an "essence" of Jewish mysticism in some abstract and general manner, it is still possible to isolate certain "core" phenomena that have informed the religious mentality of Jewish mystics through the ages. We can thus establish the specific phenomenological contours that set Jewish mysticism apart from Islamic, Christian, Buddhist, or Hindu mysticism. This is not to deny that in given historical periods there may have been an influence of an external system of belief upon Jewish mystics. The point I am making rather is that discernible within the large corpus of texts identified by scholars as belonging to Jewish mysticism is a set of distinctive experiences, practices, and doctrines that are uniquely part of the Jewish esoteric traditions. In the opening section I broadly distinguished the speculative-theosophical and the ecstatic-experiential orientation in Jewish mystical sources, but the fact of the matter is that these are frequently very difficult to separate. The mystical (or magical) praxis employing the divine names may have an underlying theosophical context which renders the praxis effective. On the other hand, a theosophical tract may be implicitly visionary such that the content of the theosophy is not simply a matter of study or exegesis but serves as a means for the communion, or perhaps even union, of the mystic with the Godhead.

Notes

1. My typology here is influenced in part by the description given in the entry on Jewish Mysticism to appear in *Harper's Dictionary of Religion*, ed. W. S. Green, co-authored by R. Keiner and myself. The categories employed in that context as well as here, correspond, more or less, to the three phenomenological typologies of Jewish mysticism operative in Moshe Idel, *Kabbalah: New Perspectives* (New Haven, 1988): the theosophical, theurgical, and the ecstatic. To be sure, Idel's phenomenology is based on the research of previous

scholars, including Gershom Scholem (see especially *Major Trends in Jewish Mysticism* [New York, 1956], 124). However, whereas his precedessors saw these typologies as they were manifest in thirteenth-century kabbalah, Idel casts his net more widely and places these types within a larger framework of Jewish literary history. The reader should be aware that this essay was written in the spring of 1990. Much progress has been made in the study of Jewish mysticism that I have since taken into account in publications.

2. The classical study on the motif of heavenly journey remains W. Bousset, "Die Himmelsreise de Seele," *Archiv für Religionswissenschaft* 4 (1901): 136–69, 229–73. For recent surveys, see A. F. Segal, "Heavenly Ascent in Hellenistic Judaism, Early Christianity and Their Environment," in *Aufsteig und Niedergang der Römischen Welt*, Principat II, 23 (1980): 1333–94; M. Smith, "Ascent to the Heavens and the Beginning of Christianity," *Eranosjahrbuch* 50 (1981): 403–29; J. D. Tabor, *Things Unutterble: Paul's Ascent to Paradise in Its Greco-Roman, Judaic, and Early Christian Contexts* (Lanham, MD, 1986), 57–111. A useful bibliography on matters pertaining to apocalyptic literature can be found in D. Hellholm, ed., *Apocalypticism in the Mediterranean World and the Near East* (Tübingen, 1989), 795–825.

3. Scholem, *Major Trends*, 43; I. Gruenwald, *Apocalyptic and Merkavah Mysticism* (Leiden, 1980); M. Himmelfarb, "Heavenly Ascent and the Relationship of the Apocalypses and the *Hekhalot* Literature," *Hebrew Union College Annual* 59 (1988): 73–100.

4. See E. E. Urbach, "The Traditions about Merkabah Mysticism in the Tannaitic Period," in *Studies in Mysticism and Religion Presented to Gershom G. Scholem* (Jerusalem, 1967), 1–28 (Hebrew section); D. Halperin, *The Merkabah in Rabbinic Literature* (New Haven, 1980): and idem, *The Faces of the Chariot* (Tübingen, 1988), 11–37.

5. The text was published by I. Gruenwald, *Temirin*, 1 (Jerusalem, 1972): 101–40.

6. For a study of this passage, see N. A. Van Uchelen, "Tosephta Megillah III, 28; A Tannaitic Text with a Mystic?" *Jerusalem Studies in Jewish Thought* 6 (1987): 87–94 (English section).

7. See J. Neusner, "The Development of the *Merkavah* Tradition," *Journal for the Study of Judaism* 2 (1971): 149–60; N. Séd, "Les traditions secrètes et les disciples de Rabbanan Yohanan be Zakkai," *Revue de l'Histoire des Religions* 184 (1973): 49–66; Halperin, *Merkabah in Rabbinic Literature*, 107–40.

8. See the article of Urbach referred to in note 3.

9. See I. Chernus, *Mysticism in Rabbinic Literature* (Berlin, 1982); Halperin, *Faces of the Chariot*, 17–23, 141–49, 289, 322.

10. For an extreme formulation of such a position, See D. Boyarin, "The Eye in the Torah: Ocular Desire in the Midrashic Hermeneutic," *Critical Inquiry* 16 (1990): 532–50. See idem, *Intertexuality and the Reading of Midrash* (Bloomington, Ind., 1990), 110, 118–22.

11. J. Dan, "The Religious Experience of the *Merkavah*," in *Jewish Spirituality from the Bible through the Middle Ages*, ed. A. Green (New York, 1986), 292.

12. For an earlier dating, cf. G. Scholem, *Jewish Gnosticism, Merkabah Mysticism and the Talmudic Tradition* (New York, 1960); M. Smith, "Observations on Hekhalot Rabbati," in *Biblical and Other Studies*, ed. A. Altmann (Cambridge, MA, 1963), 155–60.

13. A critical edition of the text was published by R. Elior, *Jerusalem Studies in Jewish Thought*, Supplement 1 (1984). See also ed. P. Schäfer, *Synpose zur Hekhalot-Literatur* (Tübingen, 1981), §§335–74, 407–26, 496–97.

14. *Synopse*, §§81–306.

15. H. Odeberg, *3 Enoch or the Hebrew Book of Enoch* (New York, 1973); *Synopse*, §§ 1–80. An English translation by P. Alexander is included in *The Old Testament Pseudepigrapha*, ed. J. Charlesworth (New York, 1983), 1:223–315.

16. Scholem, *Jewish Gnosticism*, 103–17; *Synopse*, §§544–96. Prior to Scholem (though he neglects to mention it), fragments of this text were published by A. Altmann, "Liturgical Poems in the Ancient Hekhalot Literature," *Melilah* 2 (1946): 1–24 (in Hebrew). Two English translations are now available: N. Janowitz, *The Poetics of Ascent* (Albany, 1989) and M. Swartz, *Mystical Prayer in Ancient Judaism: An Analysis of Ma'aseh Merhovah* (Tübingen, 1992).

17. The text was first published by I. Gruenwald, "New Fragments from the Hekhalot Literature," *Tarbiz* 38 (1968–69): 356–64 (in Hebrew). See also ed. P. Schäfer, *Geniza Fragmente zur Hekhalot-Literatur* (Türbingen, 198), 103–5.

18. See Scholem, *Major Trends*, 49.

19. See H. Graetz, "Die mystische Literatur in der gaonäischen Epoche," *Monatsschrift für Geschichte and Wissenschaft des Judenthums* 8 (1859): 67–78, 103–18, 140–52; E. E. Hildescheimer, "Mystik and Agada im Urteile der Gaonen R. Scherira und R. Hai," *Festschrift für Jacob Rosenheim* (Frankfurt am Main, 1931), 259–86.

20. See Scholem, *Major Trends*, 77–78. Concerning the ritual of being clothed in the name, see also G. Scholem, *On the Kabbalah and Its Symbolism* (New York, 1969), 136–37.

21. P. Schäfer, *Hekhalot-Studien* (Tübingen, 1988), 282.

22. Ibid., 285–89; Halperin, *Faces of the Chariot*, 370–75.

23. I. Gruenwald, *From Apocalypticism to Gnosticism* (Frankfurt am Main, 1988), 184: "The main aim of Merkavah mysticism still seems to me to be the vision of God." This represents a substantial change from Gruenwald's earlier view that the theoretical denial of the possibility of seeing God is the main position taken by the *Hekhalot* authors; See *Apocalyptic and Merkavah Mysticism*, 94. On the centrality of visionary experience in these texts, see I. Chermus, "Visions of God in Merkabah Literature," *Journal for the Study of Judaism* 13 (1982): 123–46.

24. See S. Leiter, "Worthiness, Acclamation and Appointment: Some Rabbinic Terms," *Proceedings of the American Academy of Jewish Research* 41–42 (1973–74): 143–45; R. Elior, "The Concept of God in Herkhalot Literature," in *Binah: Studies in Jewish Thought*, ed. J. Dan, vol. 2 (New York, 1989), 1001, 106–8.

25. See view of Gruenwald referred to in note 23.

26. Scholem, *Major Trends*, 66.

27. See Elior, "The Concept of God," 108–10.

28. Scholem, *Jewish Gnosticism*, 20, n. 1; idem, *Major Trends*, 47; Gruenwald, *From Apocalypticism to Gnosticism*, 170–73; I. Chernus, "The Pilgrimage to the Merkavah: An Interpretation of Early Jewish Mysticism," *Jerusalem Studies in Jewish Thought*, 6 (1987): 5 (English section). For some other views regarding this expression, *yeridah la-merkavah*, cf. P. Bloch, "Die *Yorede Mer-*

kavah, die Mystiker der Gaonenzeit, und ihr Einfluss auf die Liturgie," *Monatsschrift für Geschichte und Wissenschaft des Judentum,* 37 (1893): 25; Gruenwald, *Apocalyptic,* 145, n. 15; J. Dan, "Three Types of Ancient Jewish Mysticism," The Seventh Annual Rabbi Louis Feinberg Memorial Lecture in Judaic Studies (University of Cincinnati, 1984), 34, n. 29; Halperin, *Faces of the Chariot,* 226–27.

29. E. Wolfson, *"Typology of Ecstasy and Enthronement in Early Jewish Mysticism,"* in *Mystics of the Book: Themes, Topics and Typologies,* ed. R. Herrera (New York, 1993), 13–44.

30. Cf. *Synopse,* §§ 227, 233, 236, 411; *Geniza-Fragmente,* 105.

31. Scholem, *Major Trends,* 5, 55–56.

32. See M. Cohen, *The Shiʿur Qomach: Liturgy and Theurgy in Pre-Kabbalistic Jewish Mysticism* (Lahman, MD, 1983), 99–109.

33. In the extant, *Shiʿur Qomah* texts, a third rabbi, Nathan, who was a student of R. Ishmael, is mentioned, but in this case, Metatron is not the one who directly transmitted the esoteric knowledge to the mystic. See Cohen, *The Shiʿur Qomah: Liturgy and Theurgy,* 86–87.

34. Cohen, *The Shiʿur Qomah, Liturgy and Theurgy,* 124–28.

35. Scholem, *Major Trends,* 65–66; G. Stroumsa, "Form(s) of God: Some Notes on Metatron and Christ," *Harvard Theological Review* 76 (1983): 269–88.

36. On the actual roles played by Metatron in the extant *Shiʿur Qomah* texts, see Cohen, *The Shiʿur Quomah: Liturgy and Theurgy,* 124–37.

37. The attribution of the *Shiʿur Qomah* to Metatron also seems to be implied in a passage from the commentary on the various names of Metatron probably composed by one of the German Pietists. See J. Dan, *The Esoteric Theology of the Ashkenazi Hasidism* (Jerusalem, 1968), 220–23, esp. 223 (in Hebrew). Regarding this commentary, see also idem, "The Seventy Names of Metatron," *Proceedings of the Eighth Congress of Jewish Studies, Division C* (Jerusalem, 1982): 19–23.

38. Babylonian Talmud, Berakhot 6a.

39. This statement is found in the fragments of *Shiʿur Qomah;* cf. *Synopse,* §§ 711, 953.

40. The Hebrew text was published in *'Osar Nehmad* 4 (Vienna, 1863): 37; and See Scholem, *Origins of the Kabbalah* (Princeton, 1987), 212–15.

41. Concerning the traditions that link Enoch-Metatron and Adam, see M. Idel, "Enoch Is Metatron," *Jerusalem Studies in Jewish Thought* 6 (1987): 151–70, esp. 156–57 (in Hebrew). French translation in Ch. Mopsik, *Le Livre Hébreu d'Hénoch ou Livre des Palais* (Paris, 1989), 381–406. English translation in *Immanuel,* 24/25 (1990), 220–40.

42. Isaac of Acre, *Sefer Meʾirat ʿEinayim,* ed. A. Goldreich (Jerusalem, 1981), 40. The text is cited in Menahem Siyyoni, *Perush ʿal ha-Torah* (Jerusalem, 1964), 9a, and from there in Isaiah Horowitz, *Shene Luhot ha-Berit* (Warsaw, 1862), part 2, "Torah Shebikhtav," 46d.

43. A. Jellinek, *Bet ha-Midrash* (Jerusalem, 1967), vol. 6, xxxxii; Scholem, *Major Trends,* 63; idem, *Jewish Gnosticism,* 38–40, and the appendix (in Hebrew) of S. Lieberman to the same volume, 118–26. See also G. Scholem, *Kabbalah* (Jerusalem, 1974), 17.

44. See E. E. Urbach, "The Homiletical Interpretations of the Sages and the Expositions of Origen on Canticles, and the Jewish-Christian Disputation," *Scripta Hierosolymitana,* 22 (1971): 247–75. See also the recent analysis

in Boyarian, *Intertexuality and the Reading of Midrash*, 105–16, who calls for the need to contrast the rabbinic reading as *mashal* and the allegorical exegesis prevalent in Christian authors such as Origen.

45. M. Gaster, *Studies and Texts in Folklore, Magic, Mediaeval Romance, Hebrew Apocrypha and Samaritan Archaeology* (London, 1928), vol. 2, 1333; Cohen, *The Shi'ur Qomad: Liturgy and Theurgy* 19–20, 22–23, 27–28, 31, 111–12.

46. M. Cohen, *The Shi'ur Qomah: Texts and Recensions* (Tübingen, 1985), 31–32; L. Nemoy, "Al-Qirqisani's Account of the Jewish Sects and Christianity," *Hebrew Union College Annual* 7 (1930): 350.

47. Cohen, *The Shi'ur Qomah: Texts and Recensions*, 27. See 127, where the measurement of the height of the divine body is given as 2,300,000,000 parasangs, but it is clear from the context that the intended sum is really 2,360,000,000, for the measurement from the seat of the glory upward is given as 1,180,000,000, and the measure from the seat of the glory downward is the same, making a total of 2,360,000,000. See Cohen, *The Shi'ur Qomah: Liturgy and Theurgy*, 155–56, n. 80. See also 'Otiyyot de-Rabbi 'Aquiva' in *Batte Midrashot*, ed. S. Wertheimer (Jerusalem, 1980), 2:370, where the measure of the body of the divine Presence *(gufo shel Shekhinah)* is given as 2,360,000,000 parasangs.

48. Scholem, *Major Trends*, 365, n. 86; Cohen, *The Shi'ur Qomah: Liturgy and Theurgy*, 93, 104, 107.

49. Ibid., 103.

50. J. Dan, "The Concept of Knowledge in the The Shi'ur Qomah," in *Studies in Jewish Religious and Intellectual History Presented to Alexander Altmann on the Occasion of His Seventieth Birthday*, eds. S. Stein and R. Lowe (University, Ala., 1979), 67–73.

51. Another important text of this genre, also transmitted as part of the *Hekhalot* corpus, is the *Seder Rabba de-Bereshit* (cf. *Synopse*, §§ 428–67, 518–40, 714–27, 743–820). This text will not be discussed here. For an extensive analysis, see N. Sed, *La Mystique Cosmologique Juive* (Paris, 1981).

52. See I. Gruenwald, "A Preliminary Critical Edition of Sefer Yezira," *Israel Oriental Studies* 1 (1971): 133–34.

53. Scholem, *Major Trends*, 76; I. Gruenwald, "Some Critical Notes on the First Part of Sefer Yezira," *Revue des Étude juives* 132 (1973): 495; P. Hayman, "Some Observations on Sefer Yesira: (1) Its Use of Scripture," *Journal of Jewish Studies* 35 (1984): 171.

54. This interpretation is enhanced by the thematic connection of *Sefer Yesirah* with the Pseudo-Clementine Homilies noted by several scholars. See H. Graetz, *Gnostizismus and Judentum* (Krotoschin, 1846), 110–15; G. Scholem, *On the Kabbalah and Its Symbolism*, 172–73; S. Pines, "Points of Similarity Between the Doctrine of the *Sefirot* in *Sefer Yezira* and a Text from the Pseudo-Clementine Homolies: The Implications of This Resemblance," *Proceedings of the Israel Academy of Sciences and Humanities* 7 (1972): 63–242.

55. G. Scholem, "The Name of God and the Linguistic Theory of the Kabbala," *Diogenes* 79 (1972): 71–76.

56. See M. Idel, *Golem: Jewish Magical and Mystical Traditions on the Artificial Anthropoid* (Albany, 1990), 12–14.

57. See E. Wolfson, "Anthropomorphic Imagery and Letter-Symbolism in the Zohar," *Jerusalem Studies in Jewish Thought* 8 (1989): 147–81 (in Hebrew).

58. See Idel, *Golem*, 150–54.

59. See ed. B. Klar, *The Chronicle of Ahimaaz* (Jerusalem, 1974), 12; Dan, *The Esoteric Theology*, 16–20; Scholem, *Kabbalah*, 33.

60. See J. Dan, *The Esoteric Theology*, 20–29, 39–40, 114–16. The influence of another Jewish Neoplatonist, Abraham bar Hiyya (d. a. 1136), is especially evident in those texts which Dan attributed to an independent circle of Pietist, the *Hug ha-Keruv ha-Meyuhad* (see below, n. 66). See G. Scholem, "Reste neuplatonischer Spekulation in der Mystik der deutchen Chassidim und ihre Vermittlung durch Abraham bar Chija," *Monatsschrift für Geschichte und Wissenschaft des Judentums* 75 (1931): 172–91; Dan, *The Esoteric Theology*, 157, 204–5.

61. See Scholem, *Major Trends*, 111–16; J. Dan, *The Esoteric Theology*, 104–70. For an English summary, see J. Dan, *Jewish Mysticism and Jewish Ethics* (Seattle, 1986), 48–57; idem, "The Emergence of Jewish Mysticism in Medieval Germany," in *Mystics of the Book*, 57–95.

62. Cf. Dan, *The Esoteric Theology*, 169–71.

63. Cf. text attributed to Judah and published by J. Dan, *Studies in Ashkenazi Hasidic Literature* (Ramat-Gan, 1975), 83 (in Hebrew); Eleazar of Worms, *Sefer ha-Shem*, MS British Museum 737, fol. 320b; idem, *Sha'ar ha-Sod ha-Yihud we-ha-'Emunah*, ed. J. Dan, *Temirin*, 1 (Jerusalem, 1972), 155.

64. The Pietists did not only come up with a theological response to the theoretical problem of prayer but developed a unique exegetical approach to the liturgy which may have had mystical implications. See J. Dan, "The Emergence of Mystical Prayer," in *Studies in Jewish Mysticism* eds. J. Dan and F. Talmage (Cambridge, Mass., 1982), 85–120.

65. MS British Museum 737, fol. 373b.

66. Cf. Dan, *Studies*, 89–111 (originally published in *Tarbiz* 35 [1966]: 349–72); *The Esoteric Theology*, 50–53.

67. Cf. Dan, *The Esoteric Theology*, 156–64.

68. Dan, *Studies*, 154.

69. This is based on the earlier rabbinic tradition concerning the main theophanous forms assumed by God at the splitting of the Red Sea and the revelation at Sinai. Cf. *Mekhilta de-Rabbi Ishmael*, ed. H. S. Horovitz and I. A. Rabin (Jerusalem, 1970), 129; *Pesiqta de-Rav Kahana*, ed. B. Mandelbaum (New York, 1962), 12:24, 223; *Pesiqta Rabbati*, ed. M. Friedman (Vienna, 1880), 21. 100b–101a. See J. Goldin, *The Song at the Sea* (New Haven, 1971), 126–27; A. Green, "The Children in Egypt and the Theophany at the Sea," *Judaism* 24 (1975): 453–56; A. F. Segal, *Two Powers in Heaven: Early Rabbinic Reports about Christianity and Gnosticism* (Leiden, 1977), 33–57.

70. Eleazar of Worms, *Sod ha-Merkavah*, the ("Secret of the Chariot"), published as *Sode Razaya'*, ed. I. Kamelhar (Bilgoraj, 1936), 31.

71. Dan, *The Esoteric Theology*, 135–36.

72. Dan, *Studies*, 153–54, 169.

73. Dan, *The Esoteric Theology*, 60.

74. Dan, *Studies*, 119–20; and see idem, *The Esoteric Theology*, 135, n. 20.

75. See J. Fossum, *The Name of God and the Angel of the Lord* (Tübingen, 1985), 177–191, 319–20; S. Pines, "God, the Divine Glory and the Angels according to a Second-Century Theology," *Jerusalem Studies in Jewish Thought* 6 (1987): 1–14 (in Hebrew); E. Wolfson, "The Secret of the Garmet in Nahmanides," *Da'at* 24 (1989–90): xxv–xlix.

76. *Sha'ar ha-Sod ha-Yihud we-ha-'Emunah*, 151–52.

77. Cf. *Sefer ha-Shem*, MS British Museum 737, fol. 201a. On the especially esoteric nature of meditation upon (or indeed magical use of) the names in the writings of the German Pietists, see Dan, *The Esoteric Theology*, 19, 28, 74.

78. Cf. *Perush ha-Merkavah*, MS Paris, Bn héb 850, fol. 49f.

79. Ibid., fols. 57a–58b. In another context, Eleazar specifies similar techniques of purification (i.e., ritual immersion and the donning of white clothes) as a prelude to the study of *Sefer Yesirah*. In this case the matter of purification is connected to the potential use of the ancient Jewish esoteric work for the purposes of creating a golem, an artificial anthropoid. See Scholem, *On the Kabbalah and Its Symbolism*, 184–85; Dan, *The Esoteric Theology*, 53, 63, 214; Idel, *Golem*, 56–57.

80. *Sefer ha-Shem*, MS British Museum 737, fol. 166a. See Scholem, *On the Kabbalah and Its Symbolism*, 136; Dan, *The Esoteric Theology*, 74–76.

81. See M. Idel, *The Mystical Experience in Abraham Abulafia* (Albany, 1988), 16–17, 22–23; idem, *New Perspectives*, 98–103.

82. A. Altmann, "Eleazar of Worms' Hokhmath ha-Egoz," *Journal of Jewish Studies* 11 (1960): 101–12. See *Major Trends*, 239, where Scholem briefly mentions the symbol of the nut in Eleazar.

83. J. Dan, "*Hokhmath ha-'Egoz*, Its Origin and Development," *Journal of Jewish Studies* 17 (1967): 75–77.

84. Ibid., 77. Dan has steadfastly maintained his position over the years; see his "A Re-evaluation of the 'Ashkenazi Kabbalah,'" in *Jerusalem Studies in Jewish Thought* 6 (1987): 137–38.

85. A. Farber, "The Concept of the Merkabah in Thirteenth-Century Jewish Esotericism—Sod ha-'Egoz and its Development" (Ph.D. diss., Hebrew University, 1986), 101–23.

86. The text has been published and discussed by several scholars. See Scholem, *Origins*, 184–87; Dan, *The Esoteric Theology*, 118–28; idem, "The Emergence of Mystical Prayer," 113–15; Idel, *New Perspectives*, 195; Farber, "The Concept of the Merkabah," 231–44.

87. See references to Dan in preceding note. Another important consideration raised by Dan is the fact that pseudepigraphy is not a feature generally employed by the main circle of Pietists.

88. Cf. Scholem, *Origins*, 186–87, 213.

89. Cf. Idel, *New Perspectives*, 160–61.

90. E. Wolfson, "The Image of Jacob Engraved Upon the Throne: Further Speculation on the Esoteric Doctrine of German Pietism," in *Masser'ot Studies in Kabbalistic Literature and Jewish Philosophy in Memory of Prof. Ephraim* Gottlieb, ed. M. Oron and A. Goldreich (Jerusalem, 1984) 131–185 (in Hebrew).

91. See Idel, *New Perspectives*, 128–36, 156–72.

92. Ibid., 30–32.

93. Scholem, *Origins*, 49–198.

94. J. Dan, "Midrash and the Dawn of Kabbalah," in *Midrash and Literature* eds. G. Hartman and S. Budick (New Haven, 1986), 127–39.

95. *Sefer ha-Bahir*, ed. R. Margaliot (Jerusalem, 1978), §§ 141–70. See also §§ 118, 138.

96. Ibid., §§ 124–25.

97. Ibid., §§ 95, 119.

98. Ibid., §§ 82, 168, 172.

99. Ibid., §§ 82, 172.

100. Ibid., § 168. It should be pointed out, however, that even in this case, where eight limbs or bodily parts are specified, there is an effort to collapse the eight into seven, for the torso *(guf)* and phallus *(berit)* are considered as one.

101. See A. Altmann, *Studies in Religious Philosophy and Mysticism* (Ithaca, 1969), 189–94.

102. *Ma'arekhet ha-'Elohut* (Jerusalem, 1963), ch. 10, 137b, 142b–144a.

103. Altmann, *Studies*, 14–16.

104. For the background of this expression, see Y. Avida, "Limb Strengthening a Limb," *Sinai* 29 (1951): 401–2 (in Hebrew). On its use in kabbalistic literature, see A. Altmann, "Regarding the Authorship of *Sefer Ta'ame ha-Miswoi* Attributed to R. Issac ibn Farhi," *Kiryat Sefer* 40 (1965): 275 (in Hebrew); Idel, *New Perspectives*, 185.

105. M. Meier, "A Critical Edition of the *Sefer Ta'amey ha-Mizwoth* ("Book of Reasons of the Commandments") Attributed to Isaac ibn Farhi / Section I—Positive Commandments" (Ph.D., diss. Brandeis University, 1974), 428. See the parallel texts from the anonymous *Sefer ha-Yihud*, also composed at the end of the thirteenth century by an author who had great affinity with Joseph of Hamadan, discussed by Idel, *New Perspectives*, 184–85.

106. Cf. MS Oxford 1943, fol. 28b (regarding this text, see G. Scholem, "Index to the Commentaries on the Ten Sefirot" [Hebrew], *Kiryat Sefer*, 10 [1933–34]: 512, n. 127): "This is one of the great traditions pertaining to the matter of kabbalah. Know that a person is made in the image of the supernal *sefirot*, as it says, 'Let us make man in our image, after our likeness' (Gen. 1:26), for there are supernal potencies *(ioah 'elyonim)* called hand, foot, eye, and head. . . . Similarly in man there is an eye, foot, and [other] limbs. This is the import of the dictum of the rabbis, blessed be their memory. "The Torah speaks in the language of man' [cf. Babylonian Talmud, Berakhot 31b, and parallels]. In any event these *[sefirot]* are potencies *(kohot)* and not limbs *('evarim)*. The limbs of man are called in accordance with these potencies. . . . Thus you find in many places that many kabbalists call the *sefirot* the supernal Adam *('adam ha-'elyon)*, and the lower man *(ha-'adam ha-tahton)* is sanctified through his limbs . . . and then his limbs will be bound and joined to the limbs of the supernal Adam, and he himself will be called holy. . . . If, God forbid, a person . . . follows the obstinacy of his heart and defiles his limbs, all of them or some of them, it is considered as if, God forbid, he blemishes the limbs of the supernal Adam."

107. See Scholem, *On the Kabbalah and Its Symbolism*, 44–46; Idel, "The Concept of the Torah in Hekhalot Literature and Its Metamorphoses in Kabbalah," *Jerusalem Studies in Jewish Thought* 1 (1981): 58–84 (in Hebrew). See also I. Tisby, *The Wisdom of the Zohar* (Oxford, 1989), 1080–81.

108. Meier, "A Critical Edition," 58.

109. M. Recanati, *Sefer Ta'ame ha-Miswot ha-Shalem*, ed. S. Lieberman (London, 1962), fols. 2a–b. See Idel, *New Perspectives*, 189–90.

110. Cf. Gikatilla, *Sha'are 'Orah*, ed. J. Ben-Shlomo (Jerusalem, 1981), 1:49–50.

111. See reference to Gikatilla in preceding note. Cf. the anonymous text in MS JTS Mic. 1804, fol. 75a. On the use of the word *siman* in this technical way, see also *Sefer ha-Yihud*, MS Paris BN hef 825, fol. 206a.

112. M. Recanati, *Commentary on the Torah* (Jerusalem, 1961), fols. 37b–c.

113. Scholem, *Major Trends*, 27. See also I. Tishby, *Paths of Faith and Heresy* (Jerusalem, 1982), 13 (in Hebrew); J. Dan, *The Early Kabbalah* (New York, 1986), 9–12. For a criticism of Scholem's emphasis on the "inexpressibility" of the sefirotic realm as being essential to kabbalistic symbolism, see Idel, *New Perspectives*, 231–32.

114. See Scholem, *Origins*, 211, who considers anthropomorphism in the case of the kabbalists to be of an apologetic tone. The kabbalists, too, Scholem insists, "undoubtedly maintained the absolute spirituality of the First Cause," but, on account of their "gnostic convictions," they became "the advocates of popular religion and of the faith of the common man," which involved an anthropomorphic conception of the deity.

115. See G. Scholem, *Von der mystichen Gestalt der Gottheit* (Zurich, 1962), 7–48.

116. See Scholem, *Origins*, 81; idem, *Kabbalah*, 99–100.

117. See Tisby, *The Wisdom of the Zohar*, 290–92.

118. See Scholem, *Major Trends*, 260, 410, n. 42.

119. See J. Ben-Shlomo, *The Mystical Theology of Moses Cordovero* (Jerusalem, 1965), 98–99 (in Hebrew); B. Sack, "The Doctrine of Simsum in R. Moshe Cordovero," *Tarbiz* 58 (1989–90): 207–37 (in Hebrew).

120. See Scholem, *Major Trends*, 260–64; idem, *Kabbalah*, 129–35.

121. See Scholem, *Kabbalah*, 101–2; E. Gottlieb, *Studies in the Kabbala Literature* (Tel Aviv, 1976), 223–31; Idel, *New Perspectives*, 136–44.

122. See J. Ben-Shlomo, *The Mystical Theology of Moses Cordovero*, 100–15; B. Sack, *The Mystical Theology of Solomon Alkabez* (Ph.D. diss., Brandeis University, 1977), 15–62 (in Hebrew).

123. For a discussion of the doctrine of evil in kabbalah, see Scholem, *Von der mystichen Gestalt der Gottheit*, 49–82.

124. See S. Shahar, "Catharism and the Beginnings of the Kabbalah in Languedoc: Elements Common to Catharic Scriptures and the Book Bahir," *Tarbiz* 40 (1971): 483–509 (in Hebrew).

125. See Scholem, *Origins*, 289–99; M. Gavarin, "The Problem of Evil in the Thought of R. Isaac the Blind and His Disciples," *Da'at* 22 (1987): 29–50 (in Hebrew).

126. R. Moses of Burgos attributed traditions regarding the demonic powers to Nahmanides and his teacher, R. Judah ben Yaqar. See G. Scholem, "R. Moses of Burgos, the Student of R. Isaac," *Tarbiz* 3 (1932): 276–77, 279–80 (in Hebrew). See also the statement of R. Isaac of Acre in his *Sefer Me'irat 'Einayim*, ed. A. Goldreich (Jerusalem, 1981), 190: "I have heard from the pious one, R. David Cohen, may God protect him, that R. Todros ha-Levi, may his memory be blessed, used to say to him that there is a great matter on the side of the *sefirot*, surrounding [them] from the outside, which is not perceived by those kabbalists who are enlightened with respect to the ten *sefirot*. He did not want to explain his words to him. Afterwards he said to him: 'Know that, in truth, R. Moses ben Nahman, may his memory be blessed, alluded to this in [his commentary on] the section *Naso'* in the matter of the *sotah* [i.e., a woman suspected of infidelity].' After he told me these things I investigated the matter and found that he was referring to Samael and his faction."

127. See G. Scholem, "The Traditions of R. Jacob and R. Isaac, Sons of R. Jacob ha-Kohn," *Madda'e ha-Yahadut* 2 (1927): 193–97; see also the reference above, n. 123. And See J. Dan, "Samael, Lilith and the Concept of Evil in Early Kabbalah," *AJS Review* 5 (1980): 17–41; Y. Liebes, "The Messiah of

the Zohar," in *The Messianic Idea in Jewish Thought: A Study Conference in Honour of the Eightieth Birthday of Gershom Scholem* (Jerusalem, 1982), 124–28 (in Hebrew); M. Oron, "Was the Kabbalah in Castile a Continuation or a Revolution?—A Study of the Concept of Evil in Castilian Kabbalah," *Jerusalem Studies in Jewish Thought* 6 (1987): 383–92 (in Hebrew).

128. See Tishby, *The Wisdom of the Zohar*, 447–546.

129. See E. Wolfson, "Left Contained in the Right: A Study in Zoharic Hermeneutics," *AJS Review* 11 (1986): 27–52; idem, "Light through Darkness: The Ideal of Human Perfection in the Zohar," *Harvard Theological Review* 81 (1988): 73–95.

130. See M. Idel, "The Evil Thought of the Deity," *Tarbiz* 49 (1980): 356–64 (in Hebrew).

131. See I. Tishby, *The Doctrine of Evil and the Kelippah in Lurianic Kabbalism* (Jerusalem, 1952; in Hebrew); idem, "Gnostic Doctrines in Sixteenth-Century Jewish Mysticism," *Journal of Jewish Studies* 6 (1955); 146–52.

132. Scholem, *Major Trends*, 121.

133. Ibid., 122.

134. Ibid.

135. *Kabbalah*, 370.

136. See *Major Trends*, 122–23.

137. See Idel, *New Perspectives*, 59–73.

138. Ibid., 74–111.

139. MS Paris BN héb. 843, fol. 37a.

140. See G. Scholem, "Index to the Commentaries on the Ten Sefirot," 18.

141. MS Milan. Biblioteca Ambrosiana 62, fol. 118a.

142. The precise connection between electrum *(hashmal)* and cover *(levush)* is not clear, though it may be suggested that underlying this association is the numerological equivalence found in other kabbalistic sources between the words *hashmal* and *malbush* (also meaning cover or garment).

143. See M. Idel, "Kabbalistic Prayer and Colors," in *Approaches to Judiasm in Medieval Times*, ed. D. R. Blumenthal, vol. 3 (Atlanta, 1988), 17–27.

144. M. Verman, *The Books of Contemplation: Medieval Jewish Mystical Sources*, Albany, 1992.

145. Cf. *Zohar* (1;97a *(Sitre Torah)*; 2:23a–b, 43b; Moses de León, *Sheqel ha-Qodesh*, ed. A. W. Greenup (London, 1911), 123.

146. *Zohar*, 1:18b.

147. Cf. M. Idel, "On The Metamorphosis of an Ancient Technique of Prophetic Vision in the Middle Ages," *Sinai* 86 (1980): 1–7 (in Hebrew).

148. Cf. *Zohar Hadash*, 39c–d; Moses de León, MS Munich 47, fol. 380a, cited by G. Scholem, "Eine unbekannte mystische Schrift des Mose de Leon," *Monatsschrift für Geschichte und Wissenschaft des Judentums* 71 (1927): 118–19, n. 5; idem, *Sheqel ha-Qodesh*, 113.

149. MS Vatican Biblioteca Apostolica ebr. 283, fol. 170a.

150. *Zohar Hadash*, 105a *(Matnitin)*.

151. See n. 107.

152. See E. Wolfson, "The Hermeneutics of Visionary Experience: Revelation and Interpretation in the *Zohar*," *Religion* 18 (198): 311–45.

153. Meier, "A Critical Edition," 58.

154. See Scholem, *On the Kabbalah and Its Symbolism*, 63; for other references, including earlier sources for this numerology, see Wolfson, "The Hermeneutics of Visionary Experience," 337, n. 61.

155. *Tiqqune Zohar 'im Perush 'Or Yagar*, vol. 1 (Jerusalem, 1972), 82.

156. *Hesed le-Avraham* (Bene-Beraq, 1986), fol. 12b.

157. J. Weiss, *Studies in Eastern European Jewish Mysticism* (Oxford, 1985), 56–68.

158. For an exposition of Abulafia's sytem, see Scholem, *Major Trends*, 119–55; Idel, *The Mystical Experience in Abraham Abulafia* (Albany, 1988); idem, *Studies in Ecstatic Kabbalah* (Albany, 1988); idem, *Language, Torah, and Hermeneutics in Abraham Abulafia* (Albany, 1989).

159. See F. Rahman, *Prophecy in Islam: Philosophy and Orthodoxy* (Chicago, 1958).

160. Translated in Idel, *Studies in Ecstatic Kabbalah*, 67. I have slightly modified the translation.

161. Idel, *The Mystical Experience*, 127.

162. Ibid., 13–54.

163. See Scholem, *Major Trends*, 143; Idel, *The Mystical Experience*, 21; idem, *Language, Torah and Hermeneutics*, 50–52.

164. Ibid., 14–24; *New Perspectives*, 97–103.

165. See Idel, *The Mystical Experience*, 77–78.

166. Ibid., 30–37, 100–105.

167. A major portion of the text dealing with the ecstatic techniques is rendered in Scholem, *Major Trends*, 146–55.

168. Scholem, *Kabbalah*, 371.

169. See Idel, *Studies in Ecstatic Kabbalah*, 91–101.

170. Ibid., 73–89.

171. Ibid., 112–22.

172. Ibid., 95–96. See also Scholem, *Major Trends*, 124, 378, n. 14.

173. See Idel, *New Perspectives*, 62–73. The influence of Abulafia on Hasidism in discussed in more detail in idem, "Perceptions of Kabbalah in the Second Half of the Eighteenth Century," *Journal of Jewish Thought and Philosophy* 1 (1991): 55–114.

6

American Indian Mysticism

PAULA ALLEN

> I live, but I will not live forever.
> Mysterious moon, you only remain
> Powerful sun, you alone remain,
> Wonderful earth you remain forever.
> —Kiowa Warrior Death Song

THE study and practice of their various spiritual paths have occupied American Indian peoples of hundreds of communities for thousands of years. Their traditions are as varied as the lands where they live, as varied as the tribes are from one another, and as multitudinous as the variety of spiritual disciplines practiced by various spiritual societies within each tribe. It is not really possible to give a full account of traditions of such variety and multiplicity—certainly not in a brief essay. Although a vast number of works have detailed the spiritual traditions of various communities or, more properly, of individuals within these communities, few scholars of mystical traditions have written about American Indian spiritual disciplines within the context of world mystical traditions.

For the most part, non-Indians are familiar with those tribal groups which the media have focused on—mostly the Plains peoples, whose mysticism is unique, and which tends to center (in present practice at least) on Sun Dance, Sweats, Pipe-holding, circularity, Peyotism, and a new being usually referred to as The Great Spirit. Some of this present practice is deeply affected by Christianization and acculturation; some of it is at least two centuries old, and much is even older. There is a seeming homogeneity in what is written and taught by spiritual practitioners among Plains peoples who include Lakota, Pawnee, Kiowa,

170

Crow, Winnebago, Cheyenne, Commanche, Tonkawa, Otoe, Kickapoo, Sac and Fox, Hunkpapa, Crow Creek, and more. But the apparent uniformity of the mystical tradition among them is more apparent than actual, and more important than uniformity is the rich diversity of spiritual practice among individuals within these groups and from group to group.

Nor do the peoples of the Plains have much in common as regards mystical practice with the tribes that inhabit the other regions of what is now the United States. Pueblos have their own ways, and their ways vary from Pueblo to Pueblo; Navajos have their own ways, and while there is a certain congruence in mystical understandings among all members of the Dine (Navajo), there is variation from locale to locale in the Navajo Nation. Other Southwestern groups such as the Yaqui, Papago, Pima, Apache, Mohave, Chemahuevi, and Yuma practice traditions that are each particular to themselves, and again, the traditions practiced within each group vary further among various subgroups in each given culture.

Similarly the peoples of the Southeastern United States (many of whom have a majority of their people living in Oklahoma because they were forced to move from their homelands by order of the United States in the early part of the nineteenth century) have mystical traditions that vary widely from group to group and among subgroups within them. Some of the tribal nations included here are the Cherokee, Chickasaw, Creek, Choctaw, and Seminole. The same must be noted for the tribes of the Northeast, the Prairies, California, the Northwest, and the West, areas that encompass hundreds of groups and subgroups, some large, some tiny, but each devoted to a spiritual way that differs markedly from that of its racial kin. Truly, to speak of "American Indian mysticism" in itself creates a seriously false impression. Particular in mystical matters, there is no "Indian" way. There are many ways that are followed with devotion by contemporary American Indian peoples, ways that reach back into time immemorial, and that remain vital and valid even after centuries of assimilationist policies practiced by the United States and the Christian churches.

Although it is safe to say that tribal mystical practices are as varied as the tribes are, it is possible to hazard a few generalizations about tribal mysticism as practiced by Native American people for the past several hundred years, as long as we keep in mind that any generalization is only accurate in a limited way.

It is reasonably certain that all view the land as holy—as vital, intelligent, and mystically powerful, infused with supernatural vitality. The native concept of land includes meteorological phenomena such as wind, rain, clouds, thunder, hail, snow, ice; geophysical features such as mountain ranges, rivers, lakes, ponds, waterfalls, seas, canyons, mounds, bluffs, and rock formations; and nonhumans such as birds, insects, reptiles, and mammals. Always included as holy in one way or another are sky, sun, earth, and certain constellations (these vary from group to group). All feature various disciplines that are practiced by seekers and holy people and to some extent virtually every individual is one or the other, and in some sense many are both.

Among the disciplines widely practiced are dreaming, vision-seeking, purification, fasting, praying, making offerings, dancing, singing, making and caring for sacred objects, and living a good and varied life—usually considered central to spiritual seeking. Oftentimes certain foods, activities, and relationships are eschewed for strictly limited periods or for entire lifetimes, and these restrictions are dictated by tradition or by the spirit people themselves and are determined by the nature of the person's "power" and the requirements of the deity and spirit he or she serves.

Fundamentally, mysticism among American Indian peoples is based on a sense of propriety, an active respectfulness for the powers (these are People, not of the human or animal communities but Holy People [YEI] or nonmortals) that inform the world and the people's lives, on a ritual comprehension of universal orderliness and balance, on a belief that a person's every action, thought, relationship, and feeling contributes to the greater good of the universe or to its suffering. Thus a human being is required to live in such a way that balance is maintained and furthered, and disorder (also perceived as disease) is kept within bounds. That is not to say that properness or respectfulness is seen as a passive process, but that one's active efforts in every area of one's private and communal life aid the powers in functioning for us and through us to keep all of us, human and nonhuman alike, whole and in harmonious equilibrium. We are responsible for that equilibrium—that is the proper activity of human beings (or "two-leggeds" as some tribal languages phrase it). Other orders of creatureliness have other tasks. Only if each species occupies itself with the tasks that are proper to its being can the universe function in life-enhancing ways. When any species fails to meet its obligation to the All-that-is, everyone suffers—human, animal, plant, and nonmortal kingdoms alike.

Pretty Shield, the elderly Crow (Wise One) Medicine Woman Frank Linderman interviewed at length in the 1920s or 1930s, told him a story about the chickadees, one about mice, one about the magical antelope, one about the entities she referred to as a Person, and one about her own medicine animal, the ants. Her story about the chickadee was occasioned by Linderman whistling the chickadee's spring song as he entered the place where the interviews were to be held. She asked him if he knew the chickadee well, and he said he did, though in the ensuing conversation he found he didn't know they had several tongues that grew or shortened by season and shaped the different songs they sang at different times in the year. She told him how when she was very small she had been walking with her grandmother when they came upon some chickadees. Because she knew that the birds had been stealing fat from the meat the women were drying on racks in the village, and "because they were full they were all laughing," the child decided to throw some dry buffalo-chips at them to see them all fly. Her grandmother told her she had been wrong to do that and picked up the little girl and carried her to a nearby bush where the scattered chickadees had landed, and apologized to the birds by saying that the child would never throw anything at them again and asking them to forgive her because she didn't know any better. Then she told Pretty Shield a story about how she had lost a good friend because "the woman had turned the chickadees against her."

> My grandmother's name was Seven-stars. . . . She was a Wise-one [a Medicine Woman]. She would have only black horses; and her medicine was the chickadee.
>
> She and another woman, whose name was Buffalo-that-walks, had built a fire among some bushes, and both were working on robes that were pegged to the ground, with the fire burning between them. . . .
> A chickadee flew into a bush beside Buffalo-that-walks. "Summer's near, summer's near," he said, over and over, while he hopped about in the bush.
> Buffalo-that-walks was a cross woman. "Be quiet," she said to the little chickadee. "Don't you believe that I have eyes. I can see that the summer is near as well as you can. Go away. You are bothering me."[1]

The chickadee persisted in his conversation until the woman threw a stick at him. The bird dodged the stick and said to Buffalo-that-walks:

"Yes, I suppose I do bother you,". . . And now I will bother you a
little more. You are going to be wrapped up in that very robe you
are making so soft. I came here to tell you this, and you threw a
stick at me."
Then the chickadee flew to a bush that was near my grandmother.
"Summer's near, summer's near," he said, as though there was
nothing else he could think about. [Seven stars] picked up her
little girl. The chickadee had made her afraid. "I threw no sticks
at you," she said, starting toward her lodge with her child in her
arms.[2]

Her friend tried to convince Seven-Stars to stay, saying that
she should ignore the chickadee because he'd say anything, but
Seven-Stars told her friend not to say such things and went to
her own lodge. Later she brought some good fat to the bush
where she thought the bird would find it, and he did. According
to Pretty Shield, the chickadee

. . . came while yet my grandmother was there. "Don't worry," he
told her, picking at the back-fat. "You are not in this trouble. You
have nothing to worry about. It's the other one."
Buffalo-that-walks died that very night, and they wrapped her in
that very robe, as the chickadee had said. Grandmother told me
that as soon as Buffalo-that-walks was put away the village moved,
and that the dead woman's man did not go with the village. He
stayed behind to mourn for his woman. While he was sitting by
the tree that held his woman's body the chickadee came to him.
The man smoked deer-tobacco, offering his pipe to the chickadee.
"I am sorry that my woman mistreated you," he said. "I wish you
would be my friend, chickadee." The little bird sat on the man's
hand, and talked to him. "I am small," he said. "My strength is
not great. I only run errands for the big ones, and yet I can help
you. In the morning a person will come to you. Listen to what he
has to say. I must go about my own business now."[3]

As the chickadee promised, the man was visited by a powerful
Spirit bird who said he would be the man's helper because he
was sorry for what his woman had done. The following spring
another chickadee came to Seven-Stars and told Seven-Stars to
meet her at the creek. After doing a sweat and making herself
ready to speak to the chickadee, Seven-Stars met her and she
told Seven-Stars her future and the importance of every creature
tending to its own work everyday. The chickadee flew higher
and higher into the air—

Straight up it went, growing larger and larger and larger, until it was as large as a war-eagle [mountain, or golden eagle]. "See, it called down . . . there is great power in little things." And then [Seven-Stars] saw that the bird held a buffalo calf in each of its taloned feet. "I am a woman, as you are. Like you I have to work, and make the best of this life," said the bird. "I am your friend, and yet to help you I must first hurt you. You will have three sons, but will lose two of them. One will live to be a good man. You must never eat eggs, never. Have you listened?" asked the bird, settling down again and growing small.[4]

A tribal mystic is a person who is conversant with certain mysteries and a person who can achieve certain effects in reality as a result of his or her conversance with those mysteries. Unlike the Western mystical tradition, tribal people experiencing mystical states seldom focus on their emotions as part of the content or proof of their state (though the individual may experience a whole range of affects in reaction to what occurs during an ecstatic trance or vision); rather tribal mystics are engaged in mental states that are intertwined with physical and physiological states, both in terms of cause and effect, and visionary experiences are either directly a requirement for some ritual activity the individual is engaging in or a prelude to a life as a holy person, conjurer, healer, singer, doctor, priest, or shanan (these various English terms refer albeit imperfectly to specific types of spiritual practitioners in tribal systems).

For instance, in their discussion of sacred ways of knowledge, Beck and Walters say the following about "ecstatic states."

In a state of ecstasy or altered consciousness an individual may find that he/she may lose the ability to think or speak in an ordinary way. Other means of perception and communication take over them. . . . For example, individuals who have experienced once or many times this kind of altered consciousness find that they can, without previous experience, compose songs, see into the future, foretell events, see into a body or into an illness, and even fly.[5]

For tribal mystics, altered states do not so much convert into emotive personal experience as into physical experience or experience with a direct effect on the physical, so that a person, as a consequence of entering an ecstatic state, can do something actual. Thus the practitioner might locate game for the hunt; call game toward the hunter; excise a disease-bearing object from a patient's body; "teleport" a lost saddle or rifle from wher-

ever it was to the room where people have gathered for the
recovering-lost-articles session; empower an object, that is, create a talisman or amulet; create a rainstorm; or perform a wide
variety of effects in the material world. Alice Marriott, the anthropologist who spent much time among Kiowa and Cheyenne
women, tells a wonderful story about one such event, which I
shall briefly recount. An elderly Kiowa woman named Spear
Woman, on hearing from her son and granddaughter Leah that
there were buffalo at Ft. Lawton, said she wished she could see
the buffalo once again. She needed to see them, she said, because
long ago she had failed in her part of a ritual, and was the one
that kept the buffalo from coming back. She had been scared of
them and had "thought them back into the hole in the ground"
that they had originally emerged from. She wanted to tell them
how sorry she was to keep them shut up down there, and since
she was old she needed to see them right away or "soon it will
be too late."

Her son decided there was just enough gas to make the
hundred-mile round trip (this was during World War II and gas
rationing was an ever-present consideration). But Spear Woman
was not willing to just get in the car and go. She spent four days
preparing everything just right. She said, "You owe respect to
buffalo. They kept us alive," when Leah did not want to sham-
poo the car's upholstery. Finally everything was arranged to
Spear Woman's satisfaction, and dressed in her best clothes, her
face painted in the old ritual way, she planted herself firmly on
the good Pendleton blanket she had placed over the car seat and
gave Leah, who was driving her to Ft. Lawton, the signal to go.
When they arrived at Ft. Lawton it was midday, and the buffalo
were resting, staying out of the hot noonday sun. The women
had lunch and rested until the shadows were long. Finally Spear
Woman told Leah it was time to go and see the buffalo.

There was a little draw ahead of them, across the blueing prairie,
and there was something dark moving along it. Spear Woman saw
it before Leah did. "There they are. You'd better stop. I'll call
them this way."
She stood up in the car and lifted her voice out of her throat, not
loud, but clear and high and true. It ran across the grass to stop
the herd and turn them, and Leah understood why women always
went on the hunts in the old days. It was to draw the herds to
them with their voices. No man had a voice that could do that.
The buffalo had changed their course, and were moving jerkily along

and up the draw. They were coming nearer, and Spear Woman called to them again. They actually began to hurry then.
Spear woman stood in the car beside her granddaughter. Tears ran down her face, and her mouth tasted salt, but she was singing; she who had never made a song before found words in her heart and sang them aloud.

> Once we were all free on the prairies together.
> Blue and rose and yellow prairies
> We ran and chased and hunted
> You were good to us.
> You gave us food and clothes and houses.
> Now we are all old.
> We are tired.
> But our minds are not tired.
> We can remember the old days.
> We can say to each other,
> Those times were good.

Something had happened to the buffalo. They were near to the fence, now, but they had stopped. The clear, high call they had obeyed; the song puzzled them. The herd broke apart, shuffling and snorting against the wire, and Spear Woman, dropped from her song, stared at them.
Then she saw. They were yearlings, little more than calves. And she had been singing to them about the old days. The tears were still on her cheeks, but she began to laugh. She laughed and laughed.
. . . and Lean stared at her, in wonder and fright.
"Of course you don't understand my singing," Spear Woman said. "Of course you don't know what it's about when I sing about the old days. You're just calves. You don't remember. You were born inside the fence, like my own grandchildren."
Then she sat down in the car and waited to be driven home.[6]

In the old days, most, if not all of the members of a given tribal society were initiated in at least a few of the methods of achieving mystical awareness. Fasting; praying; dancing; dressing in a ceremonial manner; participating in rites of healing, hunting, medicine, and food gathering and preparation were common features of everyday life, and every child learned how to do them. In every tribal society girls were trained in the mystical responsibilities that fell to every woman, and they were at least aware that special mystical states and responsibilities were privy to certain holy women and female ritual leaders. Similarly every boy learned his spiritual and mystical responsibilities and was at least aware as an observer of the special states that certain men on certain occasions experienced, though, as in the case of the girls, the boys might not know much more than that about those special states and persons. However, each gender was put through whatever formal initiations adult members of their society were required to undergo before they could take their place as adults in that society. In the case of persons with "mixed" gender status, some of the initiations might be those more appropriate to members of the opposite gender, some might be those appropriate to his or her own gender, or they might all be those of the opposite gender with something extra (for those who would become especially connected with the mysteries as cross-gendered or other-gendered members of the society).[7]

In the present day members of a given tribal society still undergo initiations, though many are not raised in a traditional manner and so do not experience formal initiation, or do so later in life rather than in childhood.

Although there are numerous examples of initiatory rites, including the special rites for young women practiced by ancient and contemporary Apaches,[8] the rite practiced by many of the Pueblo and exemplified in this account from the Hopi gives an idea of one such method used to introduce the young into the consciousness of and direct experience with the sacred that will enable them to be full adult members of their communities. This ceremony, called Kachinyungta or the Kachina Society ritual, lasts for four days. The first three consist of dancing and other readying activities in the kiva (a round underground chamber reached by two ladders—one on the outside that leads to the opening in the top of the chamber then a longer one that reaches to the floor inside). White Bear, a Hopi man, recounts the event as he remembers it from his own boyhood:

> ... The evening of the fourth day—Piktotokya [Piki-Making Day][9]—we were taken to the Ahl Kiva for Kachinyungta, the Kachina Society ritual.
> There were a lot of us, boys and girls, the boys on the north side of the lower floor, the girls on the south side. We were all stripped naked, holding blankets around us. . . .
> We did not have long to wait. The Powamu Chief[10] came in, wearing a white cape and carrying a long rod with a crook on top and several Corn Mothers[11] [Chochmingure] tied to the bottom. Standing between the fire-pit and the hoop, the Kachina Chief sang to us of world we left behind. The story told of one wicked woman who corrupted most of that world, boasting that she would take so many turquoise necklaces from men for her favors

she could wind them around a ladder from her kiva so long it reached to the end of the pole. . . .

At the end of the song each boy or girl in turn was led out and made to step inside the large hoop or ring of feathers. The Powamu Chief and the Kachina Chief moved the ring up and down over [the child's body] from head to foot four times. When [the child] stepped out of the ring, several Kokoyemsim [Mudheads] came out from behind our godfathers on the upper level and made a circle around [the child]. Carrying Corn Mothers in each hand, they moved from [the child's] feet to head four times, making him [or her] grow. . . .

Just as the Mudheads were running back behind our godparents, I heard a dreadful noise on top of the kiva. I knew the moment had come. The two Hu'whippers and their mother Angwushahai'i had arrived. Circling the ladder entrance four times, they were lashing the ladder poles and the straw nuts in what seemed an uncontrollable fury. We all trembled with fear, though my godfather had told me I was not to be whipped.[12]

The whipping started immediately. A sponsor led out a boy to the middle of the floor, and one of the whippers struck him four times. Then a girl was led out and whipped . . . they aren't easy lashes. I could see the blood running on one boy who had always been disrespectful to his elders, and I was glad I had been polite. But sometimes a godfather will get sorry after a blow or two and take the rest of the lashes. It was a noisy ordeal, the Whipper Mother encouraging the whippers to strike harder, the godfathers and godmothers yelling about favoritism, the children screaming loud with fear and even louder when their turn came, and all the yells and noises of the kachinas. Finally it was over. The Kachina Chief said, "I am Father of all of you, yet as a father I have failed to protect you as my children, and it makes me sad to see this happen to you." He warned us never to tell anyone what we had seen, or the kachinas will punish us even harder.[13]

So, while in the West mysticism is a kind of special experience that only a few are familiar with, in tribal societies mysticism is as normal as supper, and like supper, some mystical events are more intense and powerful than others. That is, for tribal peoples some mystical experiences are just supper, such as everyone on the block eats, while some are holiday dinners, replete with special clothing, special setting, decoration, manners, and menu. Some of the more popularized versions of American Indian mystical experiences that are quite popular among Americans treat the subject of Indian mysticism from a Western point of view, giving the impression that these states

are uncommon, eerie, superlatively extraordinary, and characterized by abnormal states of unconsciousness.

But tribal testaments indicate quite otherwise. Although paranormal events are reported, they appear to be accepted as part
of normal experience—to be expected under ritual circumstances. I should say that few of these events are recorded for
white eyes, largely because Western sophisticates are unpre-
pared to accept the events and the person who recounts them
with the equanimity one would give to Thanksgiving dinner.
Linderman, who recounted Pretty-Shield's experiences, remarks
that he found recording the dreams of old Indians "bewildering. . . . Trying to determine exactly where the dream begins and
ends is precisely like looking into a case in a museum of natural
history where a group of beautiful birds are mounted against a
painted background blended so cunningly into reality that one
cannot tell where the natural melts into the artificial."[14] Because he believed there is a clear division between mind and
material "reality," Linderman looked for a clear boundary de-
marking the dream from the waking experience. But to tribal
traditionals such divisions do not exist, at least not in the sense
that they do for Western people, nor is there a clear line between
sacred and secular for them.

Because this is so, they live each day in the arms of the sacred,
aware that whatever they do will have repercussions far beyond
the merely psychological and personal precisely because everything is sacred or infused with Spirit and Mind and that, in a
very real sense, dream is what we live every moment, which is
why Indian people believe we must all do our daily work and
make this life as good as we can. Holy Persons are more benevolent toward those who meet their ordinary obligations with
awareness of the extraordinary nature of mortal existence than
toward those who choose to be careless and disrespectful in their
daily lives even if they meditate and pray mightily on occasion.

For tribal peoples then, spirituality and mysticism are com-
munitarian realities. The community and every individual
within it must ever be mindful of the human obligation to spirit,
to balance, and to the relationship (or kinship) that exists among
all beings, so that all might prosper. The sick have an obligation
to be well, the weak must become strong, the selfish must become able to share, the narcissistic must learn to put other's
interests on a par with their own, and all members of a community must live in a good way, mindful of the power and mystery
that fills and surrounds them and be able to cooperate with it.

Those women and men who in Native America can be categorized as shamans, singers, priests, wise ones, conjurers, or holy people (the variety of names reflects not only local parlance but points to distinctions among methodologies of the sacred applied by different practitioners) are in consciousness and competence analogous to saints, yogis, masters, shamans, prophets, and swamis in Eastern and Middle Eastern traditions. Their ability to manipulate extraordinary energies and forces, their ability to travel to distant places either in or out of the body by means other than mechanical transportation or on foot, their ability to see and know the supernatural as well as the natural world in its multitudinous interactions are in effect similar to those attributed to practitioners of the sacred in the Old World.

What they do cannot really be described as psychic, because they are manipulating the laws of the universe understood as sacred, powerful, or beyond the ordinary realm of people who may otherwise be able to exercise paranormal abilities. Nor can these practitioners be compared to mediums or "channels" as they are presently characterized in the United States. Among these adept, mystic competence and experiences are to be found operating at a level beyond the ken of most tribal peoples even though they are, as a group, inclined to the mystical by genetic and cultural heritage. We're talking mega-spirituality here!

There is a somewhere that I call "Mythic Space" where the powers they draw from reside. The practitioner learns to enter this "space," more and more deeply to inhabit it, and to bring from it to her or his work what energies are needed for the good of the people. Entering this space, which in its center or heart is "the creation," takes a certain kind of training as well as an inborn temperament. The training that is growing up in a tribal world is basic to the rest but is only the beginning. Certainly the next stages are easier to master from a securely mystical social foundation, but the individual must go on from there should he or she find himself or herself compelled to do so. The compulsion to continue along the arduous path of the sacred can come in many forms: happenstance, vision in which one is commanded to by a Spirit Guide, affinity for such pursuits evidenced from early childhood or suddenly arising for a variety of reasons or no "reason" at all, tradition, or heredity. There are many stories about how a person becomes involved in the mythic life of the people—and their variety point to the infinitude of ways that one can stumble into a mystic path from which there is, perforce, no return. Those who are so caught by the supernaturals have a number of choices—again these are as much dictated by temperament and circumstance as by "free will" as Western people understand the term—but the actions the person takes, the decisions of the Spirits to whom the human is accountable, the exigencies of history and tradition— may draw the practitioner farther and farther along the Path of Power and Beauty, or may dump her or him back into "normal" life at any point. She or he may be fully endowed with whatever power was mastered during the sojourn into other lands or may lose much of what was gained. As far as I can tell the overriding factor seems to be "what time it is," or, in other words, how her or his practice melded in the long run into the overall gestalt *(kopishtaya)* of the hemisphere as seen from the point of view of the "folks in the next room"—the powers of the planet and solar system.

The realms of existence are multiple, and it is these various realms that the practitioner enters and learns to "live" in, that determine the nature and extent of the powers available for his or her use. For tribal people, knowledge and power are always connected, as Essie Parrish the Pomo Dreamer notes:

> The Creator has placed everything in a great storehouse— everything that has happened or will happen to mankind is there. All knowledge is placed there. This knowledge is let go or given to the people through the shaman in different ways, at different times and in different places. When the Creator sees there is a need for knowledge-power, the Creator provides this to the shaman for [her] people.[15]

What sorts of events might cause a person to walk the path of power? In some traditions, accidentally stumbling upon a sacred society (group of practitioners dedicated to certain, specific mystical pursuits) engaged in ritual activities means the hapless individual has "been drafted" into that society. He or she (depending upon the society) will be required to learn the ways of the society and to participate in its activities on public and private occasions. Usually the membership in societies such as these is secret, or as secret as anything can be in the tightly interconnected communities that characterize Native America, but the obligation to participate is non-negotiable. In the way of the ancients there are no accidents on the path of the sacred, so what appears to be happenstance in ordinary terms is considered to be "ordained" in mystical terms.

The accidental, unwilled nature of this tradition and others like it points to the fact (or belief, if you must) that the spiritually powerful are more often chosen than choosing, and that once chosen, an individual cannot refuse without suffering severe penalty to self, loved ones, and even the entire group. It also heavily implies that an individual cannot decide to be a spiritual practitioner, that no amount of seeking, studying, praying, working, trying, begging, bargaining, or paying will get an unchosen chosen. If the powers are uninterested, the power does not come.

Material gathered from the Lakota about the heyoka and/or "contraries," a number of accounts from the Pueblo, the nature of the great visions of Black Elk, Handsome Lake, Quanah Park, Wawka, and Sweet Medicine all attest to the quirky nature of spiritual blessing upon hapless mortals. Among the Lakota, *hanblecheya* is a tradition practiced at least once upon a time by most if not all, but not all were granted seemingly miraculous power. Although those who want power often engage in a variety of active endeavors to court the power's attention, such activity is no guarantee of success. The capriciousness of the situation puts me in mind of a Stephen Crane poem I learned in high school:

A man said to the Universe, "Sir, I exist!"
"However," replied the Universe, "that fact does not create in me
A sense of obligation."
(Joseph Katz, ed., *Poems of Stephen Crane* [New York:
Cooper Square Publishers, 1966], 102)

Although it is true that all human beings have obligations to the right working of the Universe, the universe is in no way compelled to respond to ways humans might find felicitous. She is not required to respond at all. Of course, in tribal terms, universe is an inaccuracy. The universes, the powers, the multiplicities would be more accurate expressions in English. Monotheism is no part of archaic tribal belief, though since colonization and Christianization, many or perhaps most refer to "The Great Spirit" (a term foisted on tribal people by missionaries, even in their own tribal languages) as though that was the term the elders had used before history happened to the native peoples. The only term I have uncovered in elder traditions is that of the Ojibway (and perhaps akin Algonquin peoples such as the Chippewa), Kitche manitou, or Great Spirit. But as I understand it, the term referred to a particular manitou (Holy Person or Immortal) who was extraordinarily BIG. Huge. Vast. Massive. That is, the Big Manitou (manido, in some spellings). Kitche means large, huge, big, and in the eighteenth-and nineteenth-century usage, great was one English synonym for big, one usually preferred by gentlemanly Anglo-American writers.

Another way in which one might find themselves walking the good road might be brought about by personal tragedy that the individual reacts to so intensely that he or she is catapulted into nonordinary worlds and gains the attention of the spirits. Or the person might suffer from a life-threatening illness, enter a coma, be abandoned in the wilderness for one reason or another, be abducted by a Holy Person, or be simply commanded by a voice "from nowhere" as it were.

The great Teacher Sweet Medicine of the Cheyennes, the wichasha wakan Black Elk of the Lakota, Handsome Lake, the prophet of the Seneca, Bear Maiden and Snake Maiden of the Navajo, Kochinnenako of the Western Keres Pueblos Wawoka of the Paiutes, Essie Parish of the Kashia Pomo—all are examples of what might be called "spirit seizure."

Sweet Medicine, a long ago person, murdered a member of his band. It is said that the murder was accidental, but however it happened he was banished in accordance with the laws of the Cheyenne people. Banishment from a group meant banishment period. One who was banished could not go to a neighboring tribe for shelter, because only perpetrators of a serious crime were banished, and no one else would want such a one living among them. So Sweet Medicine, left helpless and alone in the wilderness, went to the Wichita Mountains to live out his life or what he could manage to salvage of it. There he was taken in by supernaturals, and they instructed him in their ways. After four years he was transformed. He was given the laws of the new religion (Life Way) to take back to his people and charged with the duty of instructing them in how to live in a good way.

Returning to the people he was welcomed into the sacred lodge (a place of amnesty for any one requesting it, even ones who have been banished) where he told the council of his experiences and his charge. Matters were arranged so that he was able to teach the people, and he lived a long time among them— several generations—until the teachings were firmly established among them. Before his death he warned them about the coming of the whites, and prophesied that they would lose their way, falling into bad habits foisted upon them by the newcomers. He said that should that happen they would be extinguished as a people.

Handsome Lake was in his adulthood at the close of the American Revolution which saw the Seneca reduced to penury under the "Law of Conquest" that the Americans claimed applied to the Iroquois in what had, according to the United States, become the United States. In the Americans' view the Iroquois had been allied with the British (they weren't, but that's another story). The white traders to the Seneca (as to many other tribes) made a habit of bringing what they liked to call "fire water" to Indian country and treating the Indians around to a "party" whose main intent was to reduce the natives to comatose drunkenness. In this condition they could not defend themselves from merchantly predators, government agents, land speculators, or other ruffians. Many in that terrible period succumbed to grief and the severe deprivation brought on when the Americans sacked their villages, salted their fields, and ran them off into the forests; they became alcoholic—perhaps in an attempt to put something in their stomachs and to protect themselves from the bitter cold of the long winter. Handsome Lake was one of these. During one bout when he remained for a long time in the snows and nearly lost his life, he received a vision that in its detail and clarity is similar to that of Sweet Medicine long before. It featured a Holy Person, a "blue" man, according to Handsome Lake.

The Code of Handsome Lake or Gaiwaio, as it is known to the Six Fires of the Iroquois Confederacy, is the vision that prescribed the new ways in which the people were to live under conquest. Again, this man, a prophet as was Sweet Medicine, brought Sacred Laws to the people at the command of Holy People who had taken responsibility for their survival in the transition from the old ways to the new.

Like Handsome Lake, Black Elk is a postcontact medicine person. He died in the 1950s, and his story (or at least pertinent parts of it) have been rendered in John G. Neidhart's account *Black Elk Speaks* (Lincoln: University of Nebraska Press, 1961). When Black Elk was a small boy, he suddenly fell into a comatose state for several days. During this time he experienced a vision, that is, he was taken in an "out of the body state" to a supernatural realm where he witnessed a number of events. These events were seen in the Lakota way, and their mundane significance became apparent as the boy's life unfolded. Among

other things, the child saw the defeat of his people at the hands
of the whites, saw the "hoop of the nation" broken. He also saw
it mended, and whole, operating in concert with many hoops.
The vision is thought to apply to the term of his life and years
beyond his lifetime, and even though he lamented before Neidhart that he had failed in his given task to bring about the mend-
ing of the hoop, many believe that he did not fail. And his
lament was a proper one, because a heyaha (like many Native
Americans) never prays from a boastful place but from a place
of humility in which they make it clear to the powers that they,
the "shamans' or medicine people, are less than nothing—poor,
pitiable, inadequate, without ego or accomplishment before the
Holy People. It is a convention, that prayerful stance, and it is
one that is to be found among mystics the world over. As a
consequence of his great vision, Black Elk possessed shamanic
powers of various sorts, including Elk power which made him
virtually irresistible to women. He also had spiritual responsibilities to discharge during his life. History happened. The
Plains Wars, which ended with the Massacre of Black Kettle's
band at Wounded Knee in 1892, broke the hearts and the backs
of the People. But their great vision and their spirit was not
broken, as the supernaturals had shown Black Elk. But over the
century since then they have made each of the painful descents
and ascents the Holy People showed him. Some wonder if this
next few years will see the final scene of his vision, the scene
where the hoops of the nations are whole again, and the People
once again live in vigor and peace.

Abduction is an event that in as far as I know is mostly confined to women, generally (though not always) unmarried, sometimes outcasts for reasons often left obscure, or in some sense
left unprotected. (Deer Woman stories from the Southeast and
more recently Oklahoma are the only exceptions to this that
I'm aware of.) The Navajo mythic account of the abduction of
Snake Woman and Bear Woman, which gives rise in the end to
the major Chantway systems of Dine (the Navajo people), is a
classic example of how abduction becomes the major path by
which a woman becomes a practitioner of the sacred. It was
during the war (which one is not important, though oftentimes
the speaker refers to the most recent conflict), and two men
from the enemy abducted two maidens during a raid on their
village. Taking them to the cliffs away from the fray, they led
them deep into ancient ruins. These ruins, built in the old way,
are several stories tall, entered from above. Taking the young

women to the lower levels, once used for food storage, they spent the night having intercourse with their captives. In the morning when they awoke, the young women saw only bones, and among them either a bear or a snake. Dismayed at their discovery they are nonetheless compelled to leave the ruins by the magical creatures, called Snake Man or Bear Man. Later they separate, Bear Man taking his captive one way, Snake Man another, but each takes the young woman in his thrall to his mother. There the young woman is subjected to numerous tests, most of which she fails (which constitutes the teaching method of the supernaturals) until the time comes when she is considered by her teacher, the mother of her supernatural captor, to have achieved competence. At that time she is sent back to her people to give them the Chantway she has earned the right to sing and bestow. Beauty Way is the Chantway Snake Woman transmitted, and Night Way is the Chantway Bear Woman gave.

Once the woman has transmitted this knowledge and its attendant power to the appropriate people, she returns to the mountains where as a Holy Person her continued existence in the knowledge and power of the people who abducted her functions as a source of the power that enables the Chantways to work their healing power on the ill.

There are stories of Kochinnenako (Yellow Woman) that feature her abduction by Whirlwind Man who takes her under threat of death away from her village to the mountain abode of his mother. My favorite Yellow Woman account is one about her seduction of (and by the way, as it is mutual) by Summer man. The people are very hungry, as they have been living under the governance of Winter Man, Yellow Woman's husband, and his provisions are sparse. They live mainly on a diet of cactus. One day, when Yellow Woman is out gathering some cactus, she looks up to see a handsome young man (he's a Person, as Pretty-Shield would say) who engages her in talk about her pursuit. When she tells him of their hunger, he tells her that where he comes from they have plenty. Then he asks her to invite him home with her to meet her parents (an oblique proposal), and she says she will go ask them if they want to receive him. Briefly, they are glad to entertain the Magical Man from the South (Summer), and they welcome him into the village. When her husband, who is returning from some sojourn, notices that the snows around the village are melting, he knows something's up. Discovering that Summer Man has been there and has been courting his wife, Winter Man challenges him to a duel. After

a ritually prescribed time has past, they engage in a contest
that eventually Summer Man wins. He, of course, gets to marry
Yellow Woman, too—sharing her with Winter Man—seven
months for him, six months for Winter (the Keres year has thir-
teen months), and the people prosper. In this spiritual event,
Yellow Woman serves as the agent of power through which certain needs of the people are met. Of course the story is about
supernaturals, or their charged representatives both human and
nonhuman, but again the idea that the supernatural world lives
next to the human and that certain agents are empowered to
move freely into the one to bring its energies to play in the
other are detailed here.

As may be seen from these accounts, when a person engages
in concourse with the other realms—"countries" or "worlds"
as some tribal practitioners identify the various universes—she
or he generally receives instruction that is composed of tests
and failures or experiences that are seldom explained in what
Westerners would think of as intellectually satisfying ways. She
or he is given strict rules to obey either on certain occasions or
for the rest of his or her life, or both and usually is given a
specific task or tasks to carry out among the people on return
to mundane existence.

Spiritual life among tribal peoples can confer many benefits
upon the practitioner ranging from the respect of the people
demonstrated in their providing for the material needs of the
practitioner to their active fear and awe of her or him, but it
also entails certain sacrifices and numerous responsibilities that
can be burdensome and even devastating. Essie Parrish comments that the dreaming kept her awake at night! And both
Pretty Shield and Mount Wolf Woman, both wise women, but
of different tribes, comment on certain foods they had to forego
and other constraints on their behavior required by their power.
Having a power to guide your life generally entails living to a
greater or lesser extent in ways that differ from others in your
community, and for people who treasure community greatly,
this in itself can be difficult, if not painful. However, as all
attest, failure to follow the prohibitions set down by the power
who guides the practitioner will inevitably result in consequences suffered not only by the practitioner but by those close
to her or him, even by the entire community.

To my mind, four aspects of the mystic tradition among native
peoples are characteristic: seduction (which includes taking care
of or earning), gambling, multiplicity of personal experience,

and humor. I suppose these four seem particularly illuminating because they stand in such stark contrast to American Christian spiritual practice. In many ways they seem to be in direct conflict with Christianity and Christian mysticism.

Seduction is the term I use to refer to the traditions of seeking power. In a nutshell, the mode of preference is seduction. The seeker uses a multiplicity of seductive ploys to attract the attention of a Holy Person, as a lover might employ a variety of ploys to attract the attention of the beloved. But while in Sufism, say, the seductive nature of the quest is clearly about passionate, unending desire (witness the plethora of tales about Majnun and Laylee), the tribal mode is more frequently represented as hunting, feeding, clothing, gift giving, and pleading that is believed to eventually compel the reciprocal response of a power (should one such be so inclined). Bold deeds, riotous adventures, unflinching self-abnegation and cooperative nurturing, terrifying risk-taking with personal wealth, life, and welfare, a willingness to try everything and to live on both sides of "Law and Order"; devoted and determined giving, working for, feeding, clothing, nursing, helping with everyday chores—all done without expressly asking, or being asked, and without intrusion on the privacy of the one who is being courted—unhuman patience, inner stillness, almost unmoving watching, waiting, listening, learning—all while seeming to be otherwise occupied and virtually indifferent to outcomes—all mark the kind of seduction I am referring to. A seeker courts power in the same way that a hunter courts his prey. With infinite care, timely stalking, and complete disregard for personal comfort, the slow steady chase, accompanied with numerous gifts such as pollen and turquoise laid in the prints of the prey, smokes offered to his/her greatness, and prayers that coax the power into communication with the seeker/hunter progresses. A lucky hunter-seeker will eventually cajole and flatter the power into agreement and will secure her or his aim.

Mountain Wolf Woman describes one variant (hers) of this mode: She tells about the importance of being good to old people because, as she says, "The thinking powers of old people are strong and if one of them thinks good things for you, whatever he wishes for you, you will obtain that good fortune. That is what they [the traditionals, the older ones] always said."[16] She says this because she believes it, but also because she is courting a certain old man she calls, respectfully, her grandfather (he was actually her brother-in-law as well as the son of her mother's paternal grandfather's brother, which in the European kinship system, would make him her first cousin twice removed). But because she sought and got sacred information from him, which implies a respectful relationship, she properly refers to him as grandfather. That he intensely desires good things for her was important because he had knowledge she wanted. To get it, she had to work for it, which she did in the following ways.

> I used to give things to this old man. He wore buckskin moccasins, he always wore Indian shoes. He did not like hard-soled shoes, so I used to make buckskin moccasins for him. He appreciated whatever I did for him. If I ever went to a town and there was a secondhand store I always looked at the pants, big pants, and if a pair seemed the right size, and a shirt, I bought them. I would give them to him. "Grandfather," I used to say to him, "I brought these things for you."
> "O, granddaughter," he used to say, "you are doing a great kindness." Quite often I did things of that sort for him. I often fed him. If he were coming by on the road when it was close to mealtime I would call to him, "Grandfather, come and eat."
> "Oh, good!" he would say. He would come and eat there and he would be so grateful.
> Sometimes if there was a coat that seemed the right size, one of those nice overcoats, if I could afford things of that sort I would buy them and give him such things.[17]

Eventually, she buys him a small stove, and installs it in his "tarpaper wigwam." He is very grateful, she notes. At that juncture he asks her what she wants, noting that she has given him food, and even clothing, and has treated him very well, doing many kindnesses for him. As she has sufficiently earned recompense—the recompense that the old man has known all along she was after—he finally acknowledges that she has made sufficient payment, and shown sufficient payment, and shown sufficient determination, sensitivity, awareness, and competence to indicate what he owes her and that she will not take the power lightly or misuse it foolishly or selfishly.

She tells him, somewhat indirectly, as is proper in the Indian way for the most part, that she likes the Indian medicines and has a need for them as well as knowledge that they are truly useful for healing ailments. He tells her that she has asked for something valuable, and that, as he is getting old and probably no one in his family wants his knowledge, he is willing to pass it on to her. All of which is another indirection. Much information, face-saving and implication is conveyed in his, as well as her, phrasing. Having said that, he continues:

> ... A long time ago when you were a little girl this was meant to occur. Way back then you were working for it. [The information and power to use it.] When mother used to give medicines to the white people you used to help her by being her interpreter. Since that time these medicines were going to be yours. You have been working for them since long ago. You have been working for this. Today it has come about.
> It is good. You will prescribe Indian medicines. I used to do this; now you will do it. The power will all be yours. You are not yet holy, but these medicines are holy. . . . These medicines are going to talk to you. If someone sets his mind on you, that is, he is going to buy medicines from you, you will know it before they come to you. And when they come to you, say to them, "You will be cured." If you put your mind to it intensely, that is where you will have your power. . . . You are going to be a medicine woman. You are going to cure sickness. This rebounds to your honor, my granddaughter.[18]

Gambling is a much favored native pastime, simple and complex gambling games are to be found in every region and community. Because, for traditionals, nothing is that is not inextricably intertwined with the sacred, therefore, gambling is a way of conversing with the powers, testing one's favor with them, and earning favor from them. In many respects it is connected with hunting and gathering, with successful ritual and courtship of suprahuman energy, with war in the sense of war as a sacred path rather than war as a defensive or conquesting operation, with gaining and practice of healing power, rain making, success in food gathering and production, and prayer. In a Western framework, such an identification of chance and luck with mystic discipline may seem jarring, but in a tribal matrix, it harmoniously blends with other strands of the sacred. Gambler Myths (narratives of power that interconnect with dances and chants of power) abound, and those who are successful gamblers are seen as possessing a particular relation with the sacred that is to be both envied and treasured. Often such a power, like other powers, is used for the benefit of the people. It, like the powers of healing, dreaming, or prophesying, must be used unselfishly lest it turn on the lucky person and bring him or her to grief, along with loved ones or the entire community. Even the Pueblos of the Southwest, otherwise congenitally conservative, have gambler stories and gambling games. The persistence of this feature of native life has translated in the widespread presence of bingo games on American reservations. The games function wholly within the tradition; they bring good fortune, prosperity, and community cohesion—or so it is hoped.

What I have termed "multiplicity of experience" is another important feature of native mysticism. One good example of this discipline is given by John Fire Lame Deer in his autobiographical account published as *Lame Deer, Seeker of Visions* (New York, Simon and Schuster, 1972) with editor Richard Erdoes. In his time, John Fire is a rodeo rider, a tribal policeman, an outlaw and hard drinker, a spiritual teacher, a political activist, a philosopher, a healer, and a shaman. By his account, having experiences on various (and contradictory) sides of life are indispensable to developing the balanced outlook that must underlie every perception and activity of one who deals in the sacred. One-sided development is likely to prove dangerous to the community as well as to the adept, or so the tradition goes, and hardihood of temperament is requisite for sane wielding of the vast amounts of sacred power a shaman regularly manipulates.

Mountain Wolf Woman, too, exhibited in her checkered career an appetite for a variety of experience. She was married two or three times, busied herself in a number of occupations in addition to mothering and grandmothering, lived in a number of locales, and she is a devoted and active practitioner of a variety of religious paths. All these experiences strengthen her and make her able to be a medicine woman and a wise woman.

Finally, humor—this most sacred of native qualities informs every tradition I am aware of. Black Elk speaks of its integral part in the Lakota traditions he is conversant with, as does Lame Deer—though the latter, probably because his words are recorded, in English, into a tape recorder and then simply transcribed and properly punctuated, capitalized, etc., gives an account of his spiritual odyssey sprinkled liberally with humorous comment. The story Alice Marriott recorded about Spear Woman also testifies to the humor that goes with the respectful as an equal partner in her encounter with the reservation buffalo. Among many traditions the presence of clowns—often referred to in English as "sacred clowns" in order to highlight the necessary relationship between humor and power—is a normal part of various sacred dances, and the oral tradition (when left relatively unmarred by the translator's tendency to separate what he or she perceives as jokes from true spiritual material) mixes the hilarious with the terrifying, the amusing with the serious with the judicious sense of a consummate artist. Anything that is sacred is laughable, but let me hasten to add that the laughter is not to demean or degrade but is one mode of expressing satisfaction and fulfillment. Certainly, joking, like gambling and like the day-to-day recognition that human life is always and forever lived within the matrix of the sacred, is one of the most finely developed arts among native traditionals. It is as though they think that anything worth doing is worth a good joke.

In all the rich tapestry of native spiritual practice and bewildering variety of spiritual paths that can be traveled by native people throughout the Americas, the land of our mother and all her children—including the immortals, the nonhuman persons who are also her children and our elder siblings (as are all the other species—mineral, plant, and animal)—is primary and forever. It is for her we live, and by her will we make, do, pray, and seek. Known as Turtle Grandmother to some, Grandmother Spider and her sacred sisters to others, earth and her sisters, galaxy and her multitudes, tradition and her varieties are the source and aim of human and nonhuman intelligence in its multitudinous spiritual and mortal forms alike. It is in recognition of this fundamental truth that the old Kiowa sang his death to him (another variant of the seduction theme). It is a good song, one we are fortunate to have been given. In return, we must live each day, each event, each turn of fate and happenstance, loved or disliked, comforting or painful, funny or aggravating (and everything in between and beyond these) with whatever balance and immediacy we are capable of. It is our obligation to do so. And our primal right. And in this way, we can also sing in the face of our own transition from here to there, "wonderful earth, you remain forever."

Notes

1. Frank B. Linderman, *Pretty Shield, Medicine Woman of the Crows* (Lincoln: University of Nebraska Press, 1972), 156.
2. Ibid., 157.
3. Ibid., 157–58.
4. Ibid., 159–60.
5. Peggy V. Beck and A. L. Walters, *The Sacred Ways of Knowledge, Sources*

of Life (Tsaile RPO, Navajo Nation, Arizona: Navajo Community College Press, Curriculum Development Center, 1977), 101–2.

6. Alice Marriott, *The Ten Grandmothers* (Norman: University of Oklahoma Press, 1945), 285–89.

7. Will Roscoe, *The Zuni Man-Woman* (Albuquerque: University of New Mexico Press, 1991), 123–46.

8. Inez Talamantez, an Apache woman as well as professor of religious studies at the University of California, Santa Barbara, has published important firsthand accounts and scholarly studies of this major Apache ceremonial.

9. Piki bread is a special bread made of blue corn meal mixed with water to a consistency of pancake batter, then spread by hand in paper-thin sheets on a sizzling hot slate-stone and lifted off (again by hand) and rolled into smallish loaves. It's delicious.

10. The Powamu is one of the two major societies that every Hopi joined.

11. A Corn Mother is a sacred or powerful ear of corn dressed in certain feathers and kept by certain clan women who "feed" it daily. Among many Pueblos, every infant is given his or her own particular Corn Mother in order that he or she stay attuned to Earth Woman or Corn Woman, the goddess of the Earth, though the ones referred to here do not seem to be personal but rather Society Corn Mothers.

12. White Bear would not be whipped because he and a few others had been selected to join the Powamu rather than the Kachina Society, and children chosen for the former, who were generally keenly disposed to serious religious pursuit, were not whipped. Frank Waters, *Book of the Hopi* (New York: Baltimore Books, 1963), 213.

13. Ibid., 217–19.

14. Linderman, *Pretty Shield*, 11.

15. Essie Parrish, as noted by Beck and Walters (*The Sacred*, 185), uses "The Creator" in the sense that the "All Powered" or "The Unseen" is used in other traditions.

16. Mountain Wolf Woman, *The Autobiography of a Winnebago Indian*, ed. Nancie Oestreigh Lurie (Ann Arbor: University of Michigan Press, Ann Arbor Paperbacks, 1966), 61.

17. Ibid., 61–62.

18. Ibid., 63–64.

7

The "Feminine" Mode of Mysticism

SANDRA A. WAWRYTKO

A rarely asked, but nonetheless significant, question within the study of mysticism has to do with the effect of gender upon a mystic's experiences. Are women mystics somehow different from mystics who are men? Is there a difference in the quality or content of their experiences? Steven T. Katz has observed: "The subject of the particular nature of women's mystical experience, if indeed there is something specific and individuating, is one of great interest, given the large role women have played in mystical, especially Christian mystical, traditions."[1] Thus far two issues of *Studia Mystica* have been devoted exclusively to the topic "Women and Spirituality."[2]

Any distinctions that might be uncovered between men and women mystics undoubtedly would be influenced by a variety of factors—cultural, social, psychological, even political and economic. But before determining the relative importance of any of these factors, we must establish whether a "feminine" mode of mysticism indeed does exist. If it does, its parameters need to be defined. These tasks can best be accomplished by examining the reports of women mystics and comparing them with the accounts given by their male counterparts, as a means of distinguishing recurrent themes and tendencies. From the Greek Pythia to Hawaiian kahunas, from African shamanesses to the Roman Sibyl, history attests to the mystical experiences of women across cultures. In the Islamic tradition we encounter the Sufi saint, Rabia (died 801); at least one woman disciple is mentioned by name in the Upanishads; the works of the Chinese poetesses hint at a "higher" state; Tibetan Buddhism chronicles a long line of accomplished female practitioners; and the native American tradition continues to support the cultivation of "medicine women."[3]

Unfortunately, we are unable to make full use of the above resources due to the lack of available materials authored by the women.[4] So we must content ourselves in this study with the records that do exist. These records mainly are to be found within the Christian tradition and specifically within the medieval Christian tradition. In addition, contemporary Western sources as well as the non-Western traditions of Buddhism, Taoism, and Hinduism have been consulted.

Defining Feminine Mysticism

Some scholars already have scouted out the territory we are concerned with here and have contributed their own assessment of feminine mystic characteristics. These analyses can serve as a useful starting point for our own study. For example, writing in 1941, Gershom G. Scholem notes the absence of "feminine influence" in Jewish mysticism, with the result that it "remained comparatively free from the dangers entailed by the tendency toward hysterical extravagance which followed in the wake of this influence," as expressed in "mystical autobiography and subjectivism."[5] We are left with the impression that Judaism had no need for women mystics—and was very fortunate not to have been bothered by their pernicious presence.

Women who sought to follow the mystical path found little encouragement from their family or culture. Most were actively dissuaded from such a life, and even denounced for abandoning the "proper" womanly roles of wife and mother. The experience of Mirabai (ca. 1498–1546), who eventually fled from her family's acts of coercion, is typical:

> The colors of the Dark One [Krsna] have penetrated Mira's body;
>   all the other colors washed out.
> Making love with the Dark One and eating little, those are my
>   pearls and my carnelians.
> Meditation beads and the forehead streak, those are my scarves
>   and my rings.
> That's enough feminine wiles for me. My teacher taught me this.
> Approve me or disapprove me: I praise the Mountain Energy night
>   and day.
> I take the path that ecstatic human beings have taken for
>   centuries.
> I don't steal money, I don't hit anyone. What will you charge me
>   with?

> I have felt the swaying of the elephant's shoulders; and now you
> want me to climb on a jackass? Try to be serious.[6]

We can only speculate on the numbers of women who lacked
the resolve of Mira and other women mystics. Succumbing to
overwhelming social pressures, their voices were forever si-
lenced and their experiences melted into oblivion, never to be
retrieved by later generations.

Others have been more receptive to the feminine element.
The Christian mystic Henry Suso reports a vision in which he
embraces "Eternal Wisdom" as his bride.[7] Correspondingly, the
ninth-century Tamil poetess Antal addresses the god Krsna as
consort, and her sensuous verses are permeated with expressions of feverish longing to unite with him. She stands
as an exemplar of this highly evolved genre of Hindu poetic
mysticism.:

> The feminine approach to the beloved is so compact of the element
> of surrender that several men saints, including Nammalvar and Tir-
> umankai Alvar, composed songs in which they put themselves in
> the place of love-sick gopis pining for Krsna. What is unique, how-
> ever, about Antal's *Nacciyar Tirumoli* is the depth of what has been
> termed "Tamil anthropocentrism," evidenced in her ability to de-
> scribe divine longing in terms of human love between woman and
> man.[8]

Mystics of the Vajrayana school of Buddhism identified *prajna*
or wisdom as feminine and *karuna* or compassion as masculine.
Realization of the "mind of enlightenment" was represented in
terms of sexual symbolism as an orgasmic union of these two.[9]
Accordingly, male practitioners routinely focus their meditation
on *dakinis,* "skygoers," as manifestations of the feminine while
women practitioners visualize a male guide *(daka).* In each case
the guide often is embodied in a consort who participates in
sexual practices aimed at enlightenment.[10]

Writing from a contemporary perspective, Carol Christ argues
that women's different experiences in society, in combination
with biological differences (such as the mothering potential),
determine differences in the way spirituality is expressed.
Christ's conclusions are based on a survey of six contemporary
women writers, culminating in what she terms "a phenomenological description of a common pattern in women's spiritual
quest, derived from literary analysis and reflection on the relation of experiences depicted in literature to life."[11] More suc-

cinctly, Agnes Whistling Elk, a modern day medicine woman, argues "enlightenment is arrived at in a different way for a woman than for a man. . . . For me to teach a man, I have to reverse everything;" she defies a woman to "Teach the next ten men you meet how to have a baby."[12]

Christ has identified three key components of women's spirituality:

1. *"experience of nothingness,"*
2. *"Mystical awakenings* in nature,"
3. *"new naming* of self and world."[13]

According to Christ, each of these elements has a special meaning for women. Due to the adverse effects of social conditioning, women "experience emptiness in their own lives—in self-hatred, in self-negation, and in being a victim; in relationships with men; and in the values that have shaped their lives." Because women have less to lose then men, having less access to power and prestige in society, they can more readily reject conventional approaches in life, thus "opening themselves to the revelation of deeper sources of power and value."[14] Consequently, the mystic's "dark night of the soul" is almost second nature to women. Agnes Whistling Elk seems to speak of this experience when she refers to the "power of void, of woman."[15]

Similarly, Christ argues, the traditional roles assigned to women encourage the habit of receptivity which is at the heart of mystical oneness.[16] Moreover, women benefit from a lack of rigid ego boundaries, which do not develop in childhood due to the daughter's identification with the mother. In sharp contrast, the son experiences a sense of otherness with regard to the mother very early on. The end result of this double standard, according to Christ is that "identification, sympathy, and mystical experiences are easier for them [women] to achieve."[17] Or, as Allione puts it, "Women tend to have a natural affiliation for the receptive states of meditation, intuitive knowing and compassion."[18]

There is, however, a problem with such analyses that assert the special talents of women as mystics. The implication being made is that women are not only naturally adept at and culturally groomed for mysticisim but actually more suited to its pursuit than men. Why, then, have women mystics been a minority in most, if not all, cultural traditions (so much so that one is hard-pressed to identify individual women mystics within some

groups—Judaism and Taoism for example)? From the enthusias-
tic remarks cited above we would expect quite the opposite to
hold true—namely we would expect the mystical sphere to be
dominated by women.[19] And how are we to explain the fact
that the widely held definitions of mysticism provided by such
authorities as William James, R. C. Zaehner, and Evelyn Underhill are in general equally adequate for describing the experiences of men or women, as Christ herself admits.[20]

Shifting her ground somewhat, Christ attempts to isolate two
truly unique elements of women's spirituality: "women's
grounding in the powers of being often leads to newfound self-
awareness and self-confidence," and "the great power is often
experienced in nature."[21] The tentativeness of these observations, as indicated by the qualifying word "often," leaves room
for many exceptions and makes these two elements unsuitable
for our purposes. Nor has Christ resolved the question of the
source of any difference along female/male lines—are these differences genetically inherent or merely culturally induced?
What we need are criteria for a feminine mode of mysticism
with broad applicability to a wide range of religious and cultural
traditions. So, although Christ and others have pointed out the
way to us, they have not traveled it to the end.

My own review of writings by and about women mystics suggests an alternative approach, one that reaffirms many of the
above insights while going beyond them as well. To begin, rather
than referring to gender differences—women versus men—I pro-
pose we refer only to feminine characteristics set in contrast to
masculine ones. This change in terminology leaves open the
inevitable borrowing from each category by individuals of both
genders. So a mystic who happens to be a man may be seen
to display feminine characteristics without contradicting our
thesis, just as a woman mystic may give evidence of masculine
tendencies.[22] Although mystics with "feminine" orientations
are much more likely to be found among women and "masculine" mystics are overwhelmingly represented by men, the
feminine/masculine boundary is not irretrievably drawn by gender restrictions. In this way we avoid perpetuating the dangerous
Freudian myth that "anatomy is destiny" and leave more op-
tions open to both men and women in their mystical endeavors.

Secondly, I would like to suggest that the basis of the femi-
nine/masculine differences lies not so much in a different quality of mystical experience as it does in a difference of emphasis,
in stylistic expression, which often reflects the individual mys-

tic's social and educational background. This can be made clearer by a survey of the main concepts that have been identified as common to mystical states by John C. Clark (as derived from Clark's survey of the work of William James, W. T. Stace, M. Laski, and F. C. Happold):

1. knowledge, significance
2. unity, belongingness
3. eternity, the eternal now
4. light (a sensitivity to externals)
5. body sense (an internal focus)
6. joy
7. freedom.[23]

Although all seven concepts can be found in mystic accounts, feminine mystics show a definite preference for the concepts of unity, body sense, and light. However, perhaps the most pervasive characteristic among those with a feminine orientation is the element of joy, indicative of a grounding in the emotions. To this must be added joy's polar extreme and complement—pain, which frequently serves as a prelude to joy for the feminine mystic, most especially among the Christian mystics.

The identification of the resounding keynote of emotion as feminine is supported by Walter T. Stace's account of the two variable factors that give rise to "different cultural types of mysticism," namely, "intellectual interpretation of the experience" on the one hand and "emotional tone" on the other. Most significantly, Stace observes that the degree of emotionalism varies even within a single culture, due to individual personality types. By way of example for his theory of mystic duality, Stace cites the case of Teresa of Avila to represent "hyperemotionalism" and that of Meister Eckhart or Buddha as "calm serenity."[24] Stace's choice of examples demonstrates the natural parting of the ways that occurs in terms of the level of emotion expressed by a mystic—the feminine being at the high end of the scale and the masculine at the low end (with a corresponding reversal of emphasis with regard to intellectual elements—high in the masculine and low in the feminine). As expressed by Agnes Whistling Elk, for the feminine mystic "knowledge is not enough . . . knowledge sits in your head like uncooked food on a stove."[25]

Let us expand upon the definitions of the proposed feminine mystical elements:[26]

joy—the guiding principle of *EROS,* expressed as a nonrational, feeling response which encompasses the extremes of joy or ecstasy along with pain and fear and also may be manifested in terms of sexuality and erotic imagery;

light—*RECEPTIVITY* to externals leading to an openness to the mystical experience, a willingness to surrender to, to be possessed by, a higher power;

unity—*ALL-IS-ONE-NESS,*[27] the recognition that *THE INNER IS THE OUTER,* that complete unity is possible because no real distinction exists between the mystic who is experiencing the divine and the source of the mystical experience;

body sense—*THE LINK WITH NATURE,* a sense of the body as a source of connectedness with the "external" world through our physical experiences,[28] as a possible source of mystical stimulus (what Stace has termed "extrovertive mysticism"[29]).

Each of these points can be illustrated more concretely through the work of women mystics who fall within the feminine category. All of the key elements of feminine mysticism are clearly evident in one of the most significant religious movements of the medieval period in Europe, the "Gottesfreunde" (Friends of God):

Eros—characterizations of the group as "hysterical," "pathological, and "repressed;"[30]

Receptivity—the ideal of "self-renunciation, or a ceding of self-will to God's will;"

All-is-one-ness—belief in "the action of the Spirit in all believers" and the "feasibility of the *unio mystica;"*

The link with nature—in a negative sense, recognition of the importance of the body in one's spirituality as seen through the need for mortification of the flesh, amounting in some cases to self-torture; the women in the movement were known especially for "austerities and penitential sufferings, as well as some instances of highly subjective and erotic accounts of the mystical life."[31]

Many critics, unsympathetic to their feminine mode of mysticism, have dismissed the school as not worth serious attention. Since the medieval women mystics tended to write in the vernacular (having limited access to the educational opportunities required to master the theological standard of Latin), their audience usually was limited to common people. Through the use of down-to-earth metaphors their mystical experiences become, if not accessible to all, at least somewhat more comprehensible. Many were in fact illiterate and thus typically relied upon male secretaries to record their experiences.[32] But their literary deficiencies have been interpreted as an advantage by some: "When we consider the originality of both Teresa [of Avila] and Catherine [of Siena] as writers, our wonder is twofold: First, there is the wonder that these women could write so masterfully without academic discipline; second, we wonder whether the absence of training was not in effect freeing."[33]

Similarly, in Japan the religious activities of women largely have been confined to the "Little Tradition" of grass-roots, popular movements rather than the rarefied realm of philosophical and academically respectable "Great Tradition" encompassing Buddhism. Since Buddhism is itself an import, Japanese women are more closely identified with the indigenous traditions of Shinto, inclusive of shamanistic possession by *kami*. Thus, their mystical experiences tended to be channeled through such less highly regarded avenues of expression. Even today their involvement in Buddhism has been negligible. Dedicated nuns tend to inhabit only the fringes of Buddhist religious practice, in positions subordinate to priests and monks (following the pattern of gender discrimination practiced within Catholicism).

In what follows each of the four proposed feminine elements has been examined, as reflected in the texts describing the experiences of women mystics:

I.   The Method of Feminine Mysticism: EROS
II. The Attitude of Receptivity: Openness to the Beyond
III. The Encompassing Quality of Mystical Union: All-is-One-ness
IV. The Embodied Mystic: The Link with Nature.

The results of the overall examination are summarized in the closing section, which includes some indication of how a study of feminine mysticism contributes to the general topic of mysticism.

I. The Method of Feminine Mysticism: *EROS*

As noted above, the most distinctive and pervasive element of feminine mysticism is eros, manifested as both passionate outpourings and erotic overtones in imagery. Thus Underhill describes the Catholic women mystics as "possessing a rich emotional life and, largely by means of that emotional life, actualizing and expressing their communion with the spiritual world."[34] Agnes Whistling Elk declares, "true power is love," and tells a story in which a visionary female figure states: "No woman is worthy until she follows her heart."[35]

A feminine incorporation of emotion is found in Mahayana Buddhism, which emphasizes the need for compassion *(karuna)* in combination with wisdom *(prajna)*. In Tantric Buddhism the power of the emotions is mobilized on behalf of enlightenment, based on the realization that it is more productive to transcend the passions than to suppress them.[36] Even the deities partake of the emotional dimension of life. Describing a vision of a dakini who is the embodiment of feminine wisdom, Allione characterizes her as "fearless yet compassionate, ecstatic yet grounded, and above all she was inviting me with her confidence and her joy."[37]

The emotional content of feminine mysticism also may include negative elements. The Tantric pantheon includes "wrathful" deities along with benign ones, while ecstasy often accompanies pain and fear. This lends credence to the assumption that a masochistic element is inherent in the feminine outlook. However, such judgments must be made carefully, and only after having taken into consideration the overall context of the symbolism, without artificially isolating the negative emotions. During peak experiences the extremes of agony and delight can be indistinguishable.

Although, as Stace has observed, love has a distinctive role to play for the Christian mystics,[38] the function of this deep emotion for feminine Christian mystics is even more distinctive. A long tradition exists in Western thought of the soul as a feminine entity (derived from the Greek psyche and the Latin anima, both of which are feminine nouns). For the Christian,

God's loving, personal relationship with the individual soul was epitomized by the imagery of Solomon's Song of Songs, which has as its subject the longing of a lover for her beloved.[39] The use of passionate erotic language was transposed to the spiritual plane, and it is in this light that the language of the feminine mystics must be understood.[40]

Thus, Teresa of Avila speaks of her "rapture, or elevation, or what they call the flight of the spirit, or transport . . . ecstasy," the effects of which are felt and manifested in her soul and body simultaneously; Catherine of Siena describes the "hungry longing" of her heart for God.[41] God addresses Julian of Norwich with suggestive language: "It is I whom you love; it is I whom you delight in; it is I whom you serve; it is I whom you long for, whom you desire; it is I whom you mean; it is I whom am all;" Julian's comment to the experience is "the joy in that revelation surpasses all the heart could wish for or desire."[42]

The theme of God as lover and the soul as the beloved is developed even further by other mystics. Simone Weil reports the first time "Christ came to take possession of me," while she was reciting a poem entitled "Love."[43] In a vision prior to her death Angela of Foligno relates how God "showed me the Bridegroom, the Eternal Word. . . . And the Word entered into me and touched me throughout and embraced me."[44] Margery of Kempe tells of having been commanded to "boldly call me Jesus, your love" and experienced a marriage to God,[45] while Catherine of Siena became Christ's fiancée at age twenty-one.

An entire school of mysticism known as the *brautmystik* or "bride mysticism" school was spawned in medieval Europe by such visions. Additional influences and refinements came from the romance and conventions of courtly love. A fine example of this trend is found in the writings of Hadewijch, including an aptly named piece, "The Perfect Bride." In Hadewijch's poem, "Love's Seven Names," the experience of divine love is depicted through erotic symbolism interwoven with the conventions of Christian doctrine:

> Calm reigns at last,
> When the loved one receives from her Beloved
> The kisses that truly pertain to love.
> when he takes possession of the loved soul in every way,
>
> Love drinks in these kisses and tastes them to the end.
> As soon as Love thus touches the soul,

She eats its flesh and drinks its blood.
Love that thus dissolves the loved soul
sweetly leads them both
To the indivisible kiss
The same kiss which fully unites
The Three Persons in one sole Being.[46]

Mechtild von Magdeburg belongs to this same tradition; she "does not shrink from using even the most daring sexual symbols in speaking of her intimacy with God and Christ." In her small book, *The Flowing Light of Godhead*, she describes in exquisite verse disrobing her soul, devoid of any false sense of modesty before the divine; she then happily follows her Lord into his chamber, with nothing now standing between them.[47] Bernard gives evidence of these feminine tendencies when he depicts the soul as a bride "to be introduced by the King [God] into His chamber, to be united with Him, to enjoy Him."[48]

The erotic symbolism of the soul's relationship to God is not confined to Western sources. One of the most famous such "love affairs" is chronicled in the story of Krishna and Radha. As an expression of the bhakti (devotion) religious tradition in Hinduism, a series of songs was written detailing the intimate relationship between the divine husband and his beautiful bride:

From the time our eyes first met our longing grew.
He was not only the desirer,
I not only the desired:
passion ground our hearts together in its mortar.[49]

Yet another practitioner of *bhakti*, Dadu, employs a similar image to convey his longing for God, as a faithful wife longs for her absent husband:

In my yearning desire for the Beloved I break into song day and
   night;
I pour out my woes like the singing-bird.
Ah me! Who will bring me to my Beloved?
Who will show me his path and console my heart?
Dadu saith: O Lord, let me see thy face, even for a moment, and
   be blessed.[50]

But even in the depths of these delights, or perhaps because of those very depths, searing pain is experienced by the love-struck mystics. Sister Seraphique de la Martiniere asks God to be gentle with her "or I shall expire under the violence of your love."[51] In contrast, Therese Martin strives to be a "victime d'amour," that is, a victim of love.[52] Jane Lead's Jesus declares "I resolve to grasp in with Love-violence, this my fair, wise, fair and noble Bride."[53] Both Catherine of Siena and Teresa of Avila received "the wound of divine love," which is defined as "a heightened manifestation of the love-union with God; an ineffable ecstasy resulting from a special grace."[54] Loren Hurnscot's description is typical here: "I was burning and consumed for hours in the love of God. . . . The deepest bliss, the burning love of God."[55] Another woman speaks of being loved by God "to distraction;" he "took out her mortal heart, placed it inside of his own and inflamed it, and then replaced it in her breast."[56] Antal focuses on the fickleness of her beloved, by whom she feels abandoned:

> I am caught,
> pulled by the noose
> of the lotus eyes which gleam
> in his cool dark face, this game he plays
> have you seen this radiant lord?[57]

The paradoxical coupling of agony and ecstasy is explained by Julian of Norwich in terms of the two planes of God's "blessed love"—the lower being "pains and passions, sympathy, pity, mercy and forgiveness" while the higher is "the most tremendous and marvellous joy."[58] Apparently the first plane must be passed through to attain the second, perhaps to make our joy more meaningful and more intense. One of Teresa of Avila's most provocative passages in this regard involves an encounter with a beautiful male angel who pierces her heart with a golden spear tipped with fire—"he left me completely afire with a great love for God. . . . I had no wish to see or speak with anyone, but only to hug my pain, which caused me greater bliss than any that can come from the whole of creation."[59] Teresa also reports a certain ambivalence at the onset of a mystical experience, being besieged by conflicting emotions of fear and love of God, although in the end it is "a fear overpowered by the deepest love, newly kindled."[60] Mirabai confirms this experience, adding evocative images from nature:

> When you offer the Great One your love,
> At the first step your body is crushed.

Next be ready to offer your head as his seat.
Be ready to orbit his lamp like a moth giving in to the light,
To live in the deer as she runs toward the hunter's call,
In the partridge that swallows hot coals for love of the moon,
In the fish that, kept from the sea, happily dies.
Like a bee trapped for life in the closing of the sweet flower,
Mira has offered herself to her Lord.[61]

Alternate models for a personal relationship with God also have been explored by feminine mystics. Julian of Norwich draws a parallel between herself and Mary, mother of Jesus: "for Christ and she were so oned in love that the greatness of her loving was the cause of the greatness of her pain."[62] A maternal role is in fact assumed by some of the mystics in their visions. Jesus appears to Margaretha Ebner and Adelheid Langmann as a baby whom they caress and even suckle at their breasts.[63] Taoist mystic Sun Bu-er (born 1124 C.E.) internalizes this relationship in terms of interdependent temporal (child) and primal (mother) energies to be cultivated during meditational practice: "When the child is well nourished, it can benefit the mother."[64] Commentator Chen Yingning ascribes special powers to women here based on their unique procreative capacity: "If women follow the potential to create a human being, they become pregnant; if they reverse that potential to go to the way of immortals, then they can cull medicine and restore elixir."[65]

Most importantly, the Passion of Christ serves as both incentive and model for the feminine mystic. Henry Suso advises Elsbet Staegel to "imitate the suffering life of Jesus Christ."[66] Indeed, the mystic's life on earth is compared to that of Jesus on the cross, in that one is "dying with him in our pains and passion."[67] And so it is that they "made life one long agony, not to appease God, but to be like Christ who had suffered for them—to imitate Him was life to them."[68]

Following the model of Jesus as sufferer, the degree of joy experienced by the feminine mystics often seems to exist in direct proportion to their degree of suffering. In a vision Jesus appears to Julian of Norwich and declares, "It is a joy, a bliss, an endless liking to me, that ever I suffered passion for thee: and if I might suffer more, I would suffer more."[69] Julian is more than willing to return the divine favor, asking God to grant three requests: "bodily sight of the Passion of Christ" as a means to share in his suffering empathetically, as did Mary; "a bodily sickness" as a means of purification; and most importantly, "three 'wounds' of sorrow for sin; of suffering with Christ; and of longing for God."[70] Several of the mystics, such as Catherine of Siena and Gertrude, felt themselves specially honored with the stigmata—a duplication of the wounds of Jesus on the cross.

In extreme cases suffering surpasses joy in importance, and the two actually become inseparable. Such suffering, says Elizabeth of Dijon, has been raised from the mere finite level to that of the infinite; it is thus the "very pith of love," "love brought into action." Elizabeth declares, "I know that suffering is the revelation of love, and I hasten towards it. There I am certain to meet my Lord and to dwell with him."[71] The soul then "eagerly longs to suffer," for "suffering is delight and pleasure is wearisome."[72] A like-minded mystic asserts "nothing but pain makes my life supportable."[73] Taken to their extremes, pain and ecstasy become indistinguishable:

> The sky and the strong wind
> have moved the spirit inside me
> till I am carried away
> trembling with joy.[74]

The method of the feminine mystic, then is steeped in eros, passionately expressed love. Often erotic imagery was chosen to convey their experiences, a logical extension of the metaphor of the beloved soul relating to a lover God. This experience culminates in a spiritual marriage consummated by a mystical union. At the opposite pole, ecstatic bliss emerges as the extreme of pain, and in some cases pleasure and pain become indistinguishable. The force of God's love was experienced in direction proportion to this exquisite suffering, for which a model was found in the love of Mary and the Passion of Christ.

II. The Attitude of Receptivity: Openness to the Beyond

The feminine attitude toward an intimate relationship with God is reactive rather than active. Although generally assumed to represent passivity, receptivity seems a more accurate choice of terms. The term receptivity conveys the essentially positive meaning of being open to and receiving externals so essential to the feminine response to mystical experience. The attentions of the divine are not mere passively "put up with" or endured but are welcomed, just as the bride welcomes the bridegroom.

Only an unhappy or ambivalent bride could be said to be passive in such a situation.

The very language of feminine mystics reflects a receptive attitude. Within the Sufi tradition Rabia is credited with reorienting the standard approach to divine love by recognizing God's active and initiating role in the love relationship: "God's love precedes man's love, which means that man can never begin to love God unless the initiative comes from God."[75] We are urged to "yield ourselves up to His guidance. Be perfectly pliable then in His dear hands;" the soul experiences " a surrendering of her will," so she "yielded to Him each thing He asked" with "swift obedience" and is rewarded with "wondrous blessedness."[76] Similarly, Madame Guyon describes her "state of acquiescence and resignation" resulting in "an entire loss of what regards myself."[77] A more detailed report is offered by Mrs. Jonathan Edwards: "The glory of God seemed to swallow up every wish and desire of my heart . . . God had graciously given me an entire resignation of his will . . . I found a perfect willingness, quietness, and alacrity of soul in consenting that it should be so if it were most for the glory of God."[78] In a more austere vein, Antoinette Bourignon heeds the commands of a divine voice to "forsake all earthly things by abandoning her worldly goods as well as her family.[79]

By comparison, male, and masculine, mystics tend to espouse an active, even aggressive role for the soul in her relationship to the divine. In the first chapter of the *Spiritual Marriage*, Jan van Ruysbroeck depicts "the inward lover of God" as possessing, rather than being possessed by, God, and refers to his love as "adhering and active."[80] The outgoing attitude of the soul is equally evident in the work of Meister Eckhart, who speaks of the soul as actively "flowing full-flood into the unity of the divine nature."[81] Such language stands in sharp contrast to Simone Weil's description of mystical experience as allowing one "to remain where one is, motionless, in expectation."[82]

The receptivity of the feminine mystics is further shown in the way they talk about the records of their own mystical experiences. For example, Hildegard of Bingen sees herself as a *homo simplex*, a mere mouthpiece for the divine word; Elizabeth of Schonau echoes these sentiments by referring to herself as "a poor earthen vessel" intended to contain the divine "Light."[83] Catherine of Siena views herself "in the valley of humility" but also is assured by God that this is the way to come to a knowledge of the divine, while Teresa of Avila says the irresistible force of God's will "imprints in us great humility."[84] Hence, Agnes Whistling Elk advises, "Learn to receive, learn to hold."[85]

> Effortlessly,
> Love flows from God into man,
> Like a bird
> Who rivers the air
> Without moving her wings.
> Thus we move in His world
> One in body and soul,
> Though outwardly separate in form.[86]

This receptive, even vulnerable, stance is met on God's part with a maternal attitude. God is "the kindly loving Mother that witteth and knoweth the need of her child and keepeth it full tenderly as the kind and condition of Motherhood will."[87] The maternal aspect is even more prominently in evidence outside of Christianity. The Great Mother is honored within Tantric Buddhism as "source of dharmas," "Mother of all Creation," "Mother of the Buddhas," also known as Tara.[88] Descending into a womblike cave as part of a mystical initiation, Andrews reports, "I felt an enormous protection within these walls, as if I could fall back into the arms of the Great Mother."[89]

The nontheistic character of Buddhism allows the mystic to assume the maternal role, as in the case of Zen practitioner Myodo Satomi (1896–1978). Having previously engaged in shamanistic spirit possessions, Myodo notes the contrast of these with her *satori* experience:

> I myself unmistakably became Amenominakanushi-no-Okami [a Shinto "deity"]. This went one step beyond the spheres of kami possession or "oneness of kami and person" which I had hitherto known. In the next moment, the room shrank and the universe was transformed into its essence and appeared at my feet. "Ah! The beginning of the universe—right now! . . . Ah, there is no beginning!"
> The next moment, the whole world became a deep blue, glowing and rippling, the magnificent whole. "Ah! I gave birth to Buddha and Christ! . . . The unborn, first parent . . . that's me! I gave birth to me! I was what I am before my parents were born!"[90]

This enlightenment experience is confirmed by a Zen Master as "two cracks in a rice paper."[91] Later, when Myodo realizes the final kensho ("seeing the self"), she portrays herself as a lost child who has returned to her original home.[92]

The receptivity of the feminine mystic thus represents an attitude of openness to the divine, an affirming acceptance of what God—or one's inmost spiritual nature—has to offer. For some this willingness to receive the experience is characterized as a surrender or yielding. The image of a bride welcoming her bridegroom is utilized here, as is the image of a child under the devoted care of her mother or even one's own primal maternity. In each case positive results are anticipated. The power beyond evoked a reaction in loving response to its activity. Feminine mystics thereby are made vessels and extensions of the divine.

III. The Encompassing Quality of Mystical Union: All-Is-One-Ness

If feminine mystics are more tentative than masculine ones about asserting themselves in their relationship with the divine, they also are more assertive in their statements about the intimate nature and sweeping extent of mystical union. While Jan van Ruysbroeck cautions that in the union with God "the creature never becomes God, nor does God ever become the creature," Teresa of Avila boldly asserts "it is quite clear what union is—two different things becoming one."[93] In various visions God speaks in the same way. Julian of Norwich is told—"I have ever been with thee, and now seest thou me loving, and we be oned in bliss;" Margery of Kempe hears "I am a hidden God within thee," "God is in thee and thou art in him."[94] Hadewijch observes, "He is in me and I in Him."[95] Similarly, Agnes Whistling Elk instructs a female disciple "dream to the great mother. Your lap is her altar."[96]

Another common theme among the feminine mystics is that of the transformation of the soul through the agency of divine love, by which God "makes of her [the soul] another himself."[97] Hence, Catherine of Genoa declares, "My Being is God, not by some simple participation but by a true transformation of my being."[98] Madame Blavatsky agrees—"Behold! thou hast become the Light, thou has become the Sound, thou art thy Master and thy God."[99] Communion with the divine allows us to assume God's role. The soul "knows and enjoys with God the most holy things."[100] "It is the Divine Being who thinks, loves, and lives within me."[101]

The transformative power of love is also a creative power. "When you say 'I love you,' you are saying, 'I transform you.'

But since you alone can transform no one, what you are really saying is, 'I transform myself and my vision.'"[102] In some cases the transformation wrought by love amounts to an obliteration of the self. The soul, says God in a vision, "dies to itself wholly, daughter, in order that it may flex itself more and more upon Me, it is no longer itself that lives, but I."[103] The actual process by which this occurs is explained by Malwida von Meysenburg in terms of an experience at the seashore, leading to her own definition of prayer as a "return from the solitude of individuation into the consciousness of unity with all that is, to kneel down as one that passes away, and to rise up as one imperishable."[104]

A keynote of the mystical experience for the feminine mystic thus is an encompassing sense of belongingness, a sense that all is indeed one in and through the divine. It is at this point that the inner being becomes identified with the outer being, both figuratively and literally. To quote medicine woman Ruby Plenty Chiefs, "Inward is outward."[105] Or, we may say that there is a revelation that this unity always has been the case but previously had been obscured. Such experiences, which can be traced back to early shamanistic possessions, remain prevalent within many sects of Japanese popular tradition, dominated by women as both founders and members. The "allocentric commitment" entailed extinguishes ego and allows another's viewpoint to be adopted by the spirit host *(aite no tachiba ni nanu)*.[106]

The relatively minor role played by knowledge for the feminine mystic now becomes more understandable, because one must concentrate on coming to be one and realize oneness with the divine rather than on coming to merely know it in an intellectual sense. The union with God comes about through eros, the heat of emotional energy, a love that unites in bliss, not through the cold agency of intellect. For the masculine mystic this approach seems a confused inversion of the facts. Indeed, many women mystics have been criticized, even discounted, due to what has been perceived as their deficiency of knowledge. The typical masculine view assumes that love is logically prior to, thus less advanced than, knowledge and is expressed as follows: "When the goal of love is consummated, what is left? Perfect knowledge is at once possession and being. You are what you know."[107] In other words, loving in the absence of knowing is deemed impotent.

From the feminine point of view, however, the knower/

known distinction itself precedes the experience of union that accompanies love. Since the inner is assumed to be the outer, there is no need for verbal expression, which would constitute a monologue rather than a dialogue. The critical evaluation of the work of Teresa of Avila put forth by Stace rests on the assumption that by focusing on love she has not gone far enough, has not achieved the supreme heights of knowledge:

> She writes with much vivid detail of the physical or bodily accompaniments of union and rapture. This information is interesting and valuable. But of the inward spiritual life she actually tells us very little, in spite of making great preparatory gestures for doing so. Nor has she any power of psychological analysis—or, indeed, of analysis of any kind. . . . She was unable to cope with any sort of subtle distinctions. She was, in fact, a wholly nonintellectual person.[108]

Let Teresa now speak for herself, in the very kind of passage that Stace faults as being lacking in "psychological analysis:" "The will must be fully occupied in loving, but it cannot understand it loves; the understanding, if it understands, does not understand how it understands, or at least can comprehend nothing of what it understands. It does not seem to me to be understanding, because, as I say, it does not understand itself. Nor can I understand this."[109] Judged by masculine standards Teresa's account may seem deficient. But given a feminine context of evaluation, what she says is quite appropriate and clear. The knower/known distinction has been transcended, as has understanding, along with the need to understand in an intellectual sense.

If union with the divine is the end sought by the mystic, then any means to that end which proves successful should not be either discounted or underrated. Eros is the guiding principle of Teresa's mystic method, and so it colors her experiences with subtle shades of emotionalism, even occasional sensuality. Nonetheless, she does appear to have attained the goal of unity—a fact that not even Stace can deny.[110] If we accept the feminine approach to the divine as a legitimate alternative in mysticism, we also must accept what Teresa has to offer us on her own feminine terms and judge her accordingly.

Perhaps the best response and defense, which can be offered on Teresa's behalf, as well as on behalf of feminine mystics, comes from the works of Julian of Norwich. Attempting to answer her own question as to the meaning of her experiences,

Julian receives clarification in a vision: "Love was his [God's] meaning. Who showed it to you? Love. What did he show you? Love. Why did he show it? For love. Hold onto this and you will know and understand love more and more. But you will not know or learn anything else—ever."[111] For the feminine mystic, what is truly important is the understanding that surpasses all understanding, the understanding that there is something to be desired even above and beyond understanding itself—namely, love. For "knowledge is a kind of wall that has to be torn down in order to experience illumination."[112]

The all-is-one-ness element in feminine mysticism can be summarized by a comparison between two uses of a light/window image. John of the Cross states that "the soul is like the window: the Divine light of the Being of God is unceasingly beating upon it, or, to use a better expression, the Divine light is ever dwelling in it."[113] An insurmountable dualism of soul and God is implied in this masculine phrasing; oneness does not reign on the ultimate level. When Teresa of Avila applies a similar image, however, a quite different approach is taken, reflective of the fundamental difference between feminine and masculine modes of mysticism. Teresa describes union with God "as if in a room there were two large windows through which the light streamed in: it enters in different places but it all becomes one."[114] Here the feminine truth that all-is-one is explicitly put forth as a nondualist position, which Stace associates with eastern mysticism, as distinguished from the dualism inherent in Western (masculine) religions. The apparent inconsistency in Teresa's position, which upsets Stace's neat geographical dichotomy between East and West, he is unable to explain except in terms of what he interprets as her lack of intellectual ability and philosophical awareness.[115]

IV. The Embodied Mystic: The Link with Nature

The final element that delineates feminine mysticism concerns body sense or internal focus. Feminine mystics display a keen sense of their own bodies—whether in a positive way, as an additional means of acquiring mystical experience, or in a negative way, through an ascetic denial of the interfering desires of the body. In both cases they are affirming the key role of our physical form as either participating in or hindering mystical union. Thus we can accurately characterize feminine mystics as embodied souls, or souls who, for better or for worse, experience in and through their bodies.

A testimony to the body's function for feminine mystics comes in its being called "the trysting place of God and their truest selves."[116] Teresa of Avila illustrates in her writings the positive participation of the body during mystical union, repeatedly mentioning how her raptures affect her both physically and spiritually,[117] which amount to "a chaste yet highly physical expression of the fullness of spiritual enjoyment."[118] Teresa concludes that God "has so deep a love . . . He seems not to be satisfied by literally drawing the soul to Himself, but will also have the body, mortal though it is, and befouled as is its clay by all the offenses it has committed."[119] Greater respect is shown for the physical form by the Tibetan Buddhist Nangsa Obum who declares, "The precious human body is like a rare flower, Difficult to find," and who returns from an untimely death when the Lord of Death instructs her, "If you have a mind that always thinks of Dharma you will become enlightened. But the best thing is to have both outer and inner practice of Dharma," that is, her mystical insights must be implemented through her material existence.[120]

Others likewise have recognized the value of the senses. Mechtild von Magdeburg refers to her five senses as "waiting maids" who prepare the bride (soul) for the meeting with the divine bridegroom.[121] Similarly, Agnes Whistling Elk advises "understand things with all of your being, with all of your senses."[122] Tantric Buddhism, of course, has long recognized the potential of the senses as a means to the end of liberation, qualifying it as a quintessentially feminine form of mysticism.[123]

When the mystic makes love with God, both body and soul participate in the "delightful inebriation," which denies dualism and reasserts oneness, such that the model given in *The Song of Songs* aptly has been described as "a praise of erotic love, of the ecstasy of delight in embodiedness."[124] Virginia Woolf seems to have felt something of this bodily rush in a peak experience following from having concluded one of her literary works: "How physical the sense of triumph and relief is! I certainly felt at the end, not merely finished, but rounded off, completed."[125] Some even advise exclusive reliance upon the physical—"hear only with your body. Clear your mind."[126]

A further indication of the importance of material being for feminine mysticism is the fact that many women mystics had their initial spiritual experiences under circumstances in which the body served as catalyst. For example, Margery of Kempe first had visions of Jesus as a beautiful young man during a postpartum depression. Several others were "visited" during periods of life-threatening illness, including Teresa of Avila, Margaretha Ebner, Adelheid Langmann, Mechtild of Magdeburg, and Soeur Therese de L'Enfant-Jesus. The traditional isolation of women during menstruation is explained by Agnes Whistling Elk as a positive, rather than a negative, indicator and an appropriate point for them to evoke mystical experiences: "Women in their moon have set themselves aside because it is their power time, their time to look within and feed their inner strength."[127]

Concern with the material aspect of life also is reflected in the social activism of many women mystics. Simone Weil is credited with the "conviction that a contemplation of the social scene can be a form of purification."[128] Going beyond mere contemplation to concrete action, religious people sought to relieve suffering by founding orders and convents dedicated to serving the needs of the poor and the ill. During the period of upheaval prior to and during the Reformation in Europe, many women advocated reforms quite different from the approach found in the Inquisition and "holy" wars. Catherine of Siena advocated that the advice she received from Jesus be followed so that the church would be reformed "not through war, not through the sword and violence, but through peace and calm."[129]

Nor is the wider world of nature neglected by feminine mystics. Their views represent a reversal of the masculine approach, which "associated spirituality with a separateness from nature and all that it represents, in terms of birth, death, children, and so on."[130] Both Rose of Lima and Francis of Assisi exemplify "the Christian mystics of nature"[131] who are supportive of the feminine outlook. Their sensitivity to nature is echoed by many others. Julian of Norwich exclaims "I saw God in a point . . . by which I learned that he is in all things;" she often makes use of concrete natural objects to present her concepts of the divine, including water, rain, the sea, and even a hazelnut.[132] Our contemporary sense of rootlessness, Simone Weil contends, is due to our having "lost contact with the divinity in the world itself."[133]

This is not, however, a problem among feminine mystics, for they find the glory and mystery of the divine reflected in the glories and mysteries of nature, however mundane that experience of nature may seem to outsiders. A sampling of such experiences follows:

In every other respect it was an ordinary commonplace day. Yet here, in this everyday setting, and entirely unexpectedly (for I had never dreamed of such a thing), my eyes were opened and for the first time in all my life I caught a glimpse of the ecstatic beauty of reality.[134]

That indescribable sense of the inflooding, enfolding, brimful-filling of God's love, and the knowledge that the material universe, the atmosphere, world, body are screens of mercy, which in our fallen state are there as a protection. There is no least corner in the universe where God's love is not.[135]

Every flower spoke to me, every spider wove a miracle of intricacy for my eyes, every bird understood that here was Heaven come to earth. . . . Whether I sat, whether I walked, He was there—radiant, burningly pure, holy beyond holy.[136]

I felt there was a real exchange of energy between my body and the earth . . . I felt a very real connection as we were breathing the same air in exactly the same rhythm.[137]

The force of cosmic correspondence, a mutual reflection of nature's macrocosm with the microcosm encompassed by individual human experience, is particularly prevalent among poetically inclined Chinese and Japanese mystics:

> My mind is like the autumn
> In the heartland of Chan;
> I earnestly sit in mental work
> From midnight and noon.
> Fish and dragons are lively,
> While the waves are still
> There is just the moonlight remaining
> In the eternal sky.[138]

> Watching the moon
> at dawn,
> solitary, mid-sky,
> I knew myself completely:
> no part left out.[139]

A spirit living firmly, and fruitfully, within the body speaks to us in these words, embracing sensuality for the sake of spirituality:

Even if only in our daily amazement, wondering yearning, joyful expectation and stunned delight at nature's bounteous gifting us with dazzling color, scent and sound, we know the Beloved is near. We see His blood upon the rose, know God in the diamond eye and flashing wing of a bluebird, while the white night awes our timid, quivering souls.[140]

The verse Antal is frankly sensual in its evocation of the longed for Lord:

> Do they smell of camphor
> or of the lotus bloom?
> Do they taste sweet
> his sacred lips of coral hue?
> O white conch
> from the fathomless sea,
> I long to know,
> tell me the taste,
> the fragrance of the
> lips of Madhavan
> who broke the elephant's tusk.[141]

Finally, mention must be made of the negative expression of the link with nature among feminine mystics. The argument could be made that these individuals not only feel no link with nature but actually repudiate the very existence of such a link, as demonstrated by their physical austerities, even self-tortures. However, what is proven by their great efforts is the power of the body, its potential to stand in the way of spiritual development. The stronger its pull, the greater must be the austerities practiced; the vehemence of their self-denial is a good indicator of their fear of the power that must be repressed. And so we have stories of nuns who beat themselves with iron scourges, slept on stones, doused their food with cold water, and even denied themselves the sight of the beauties of nature[142]—all out of fear of their own sensuality. Hence, it seems significant that many of the women ascetics of the early Christian church in Egypt were former courtesans, Thais being one of the most famous of this group.

The link with nature, then, is an important aspect of feminine mysticism. It can be expressed either at the level of the individual body or that of nature in general. In a positive sense it affirms the role of sense experiences in furthering and supporting mystical union. In a negative sense, it recognizes the power of sensuality as a distraction or impediment to spirituality. Concern for the concrete aspects of life also is reflected in social activism and reform as championed by many feminine mystics. The value of our material existence is implied in their striving to better the in the world condition of their fellow beings.

V. Conclusion

We began our discussion with an attempt to define the parameters of feminine mysticism. Our tentative outline of key elements in the feminine mystical mode included four points out of the seven main concepts recognized in mysticism—joy (representing an emotional orientation expressed through eros or love); a sensitivity to externals (an attitude of receptivity, openness to the experience of the divine); unity or belongingness (following the assumption that all-is-one, the inner is the outer); and body sense (a recognition of the link with nature on both an individual and a cosmic plane). Each of these elements grows from and supports the others. An emotional outlook on life, guided by love, leads naturally to receptivity to the divine lover. Once we are united with the divine we have an immediate experience of our oneness in the mystical union, surpassing intellectual understanding. And since the inner (the soul, the beloved) is now congruent with the outer (the divine, the lover), we can trust our physical senses, our bodily feelings as verification and support of mystical oneness.

A survey of accounts provided by mystics who adopt a feminine mode—primarily women—demonstrates the presence of each of these elements. What emerges is a coherent picture of the world from the feminine perspective, a picture heavily influenced by a variety of factors—the life experience of women in terms of their biological and social roles, cultural conditioning, educational limitations, etc. Having been relegated to subordinate functions in society, these women brought with them to the mystical experience an awareness of that status, as reflected in their passivity/receptivity and occasional masochism. At the same time, their relationship to the divine afforded them consolation as well as a transcendence of the barriers posed by social conventions.[143]

Drawing upon their personal resources for images to convey their experiences, the women mystics show a preference for the model of interpersonal relationships to explain their relationship to God the lover/spouse, God the father, God the mother. However, these conventional images are revitalized and transformed by their emotional depths. They speak the language of the senses in describing the ecstasies—and agonies—of the divine love, a love that burns and engulfs, which can induce fear along with delight. They relate to the human dimension of a God who loves, nurtures, and suffers in ways paralleling their own loving, nurturing, and suffering.

Unfortunately, the contributions of many women mystics have not been fully appreciated due to an inability on the part of the masculine-oriented to see their unique priorities as feminine mystics. The masculine mystic primarily is concerned with the concepts of knowledge, eternity, and freedom in Clark's list. The other concepts, while not necessarily omitted, tend to receive much less emphasis. However, to criticize the feminine mystics for not meeting the expectations of the masculine mode of mysticism is like saying that my cat is a terrible dog because she does not perform the functions proper to a dog—does not guard the house, fetch bones, display profuse affection on demand, etc. By the same token, my dog is a failure as a cat, being incapable of purring, climbing trees, or exhibiting feline independence. Or, it is like criticizing the work of the great haiku poet Basho because it fails to meet the criteria of a Shakespearean sonnet. Of course, by haiku standards, Shakespeare is equally incompetent. Cat and dog, haiku and sonnet, feminine and masculine mysticism—each offers valuable insights and potentials to those willing to listen.

Finally, to dismiss the uniqueness of the feminine mode of mysticism is to close ourselves off from the full resources of an important heritage, well deserving of our attention. Nor should we ignore what can be learned from studying the way masculine elements are interwoven in the work of those who use a predominantly feminine mode of mysticism. The interplay of feminine and masculine emphases in mystics who are men likewise is deserving of consideration. Only when we have sympathetically surveyed all mystical resources will we be able to judge whether the mystical experience is indeed one, though its expression may be many.

Notes

1. Steven T. Katz, "Recent Works on Mysticism," *History of Religions* 25, no. 1 (August 1985), 80.

2. *Studia Mystica* 3, no. 4 (Winter 1980) and 15, no. 1 (Spring 1982).

3. Rabia is mentioned by Annemarie Schimmel, "Sufism and Islamic Tradition" in Steven T. Katz, *Mysticism and Religious Traditions* (New York:

Oxford University Press, 1983), 132–33. Rabia also is the subject of Margaret Smith's *Rabia the Mystic and Her Fellow Saints in Islam* (1928; Cambridge: Cambridge University Press, 1984).

In the *Brithadaranyaka Upanishad* a conversation occurs between Maitreya and her husband Yagnavalkya in which she asks to be instructed in "the way to immortality" (as quoted by Walter T. Stace in *The Teaching of the Mystics* [New York: New American Library, 1960], 35–37). There is every indication that Maitreyi intends to follow up on the advice given to her.

As for the Chinese dimension, we get a glimpse of probable mystical experience in the poem" To the tune of 'The Honor of a Fisherman'" by Li Ch'ing-chao (1084–1151):

> The heavens join with the clouds.
> The great waves merge with the fog.
> The Milky Way appears
> Turning overhead.
> A thousand sails dance.
> I am rapt away to the place of the Supreme,
> And hear the words of Heaven,
> Asking me where I am going.
> I answer, "It is a long road, alas,
> Far beond the sunset."
> I try to put it into verse But my words amaze me.
> The huge roc bird is flying
> On a ninety thousand mile wind.
> O wind, do not stop
> Until my little boat has been blown
> To the Immortal Islands
> In the Eastern Sea.

A similar image is employed by Yu Hsuan-chi in the ninth century, in "Living in the Summer Mountains:"

> I take a leisurely ride
> In the painted boat,
> And chant poems to the moon.
> I drift at ease, for I know
> The soft wind will blow me home.

From *The Orchid Boat: Women Poets of China*, trans. and eds. Kenneth Rexroth and Ling Chung (New York: McGraw-Hill Book Company, 1972), 41, 18. The lives of six Tibetan mystics, practitioners of Buddhism, are recounted by Tsultrim Allione in *Women of Wisdom* (London: Routledge & Kegan Paul, 1984). The centuries-long tradition of native American women is reflected in a trilogy of books by Lynn V. Andrews: *Medicine Woman, Flight of the Seventh Moon: The Teaching of the Shields*, and *Jaguar Woman and the Wisdom of the Butterfly Tree* (New York: Harper & Row Publishers).

4. For example, of the forty-eight mystic poets included in Stephen Mitchell, ed., *The Englightened Heart: An Anthology of Sacred Poetry* (New York: Harper & Row, 1989), only seven are women.

5. Gershom G. Scholem, *Major Trends in Jewish Mysticism*, 3rd rev. ed. (New York: Schocken Books, 1941), 37–38.

6. "Why Mira Can't Go Back to Her Old House," trans. Robert Bly and included in Mitchell, *The Enlightened Heart*, 77.

7. See David Baumgardt, *Great Western Mystics, Their Lasting Significance* (New York: Columbia University Press, 1961), 58–59.

8. Vidya Dehejia, *Antal and Her Path of Love: Poems of a Woman Saint from South India* (Albany: State University of New York Press, 1990), 34.

9. See E. K. Neumaier-Dargyay, *The Sovereign All-Creating Mind The Motherly Buddha: A Translation of the Kun byed rgyal po'i mdo* (Albany: State University of New York Press, 1992), 28.

10. See Allione, *Women of Wisdom*, 25–42.

11. The writers surveyed are Kate Chopin, Margaret Atwood, Doris Lessing, Adrienne Rich, and Ntozake Shange. Carol Christ, *Diving Deep and Surfacing: Women Writers on Spiritual Quest* (Boston: Beacon Press, 1980), 138, n. 1.

12. As quoted by Lynn V. Andrews, *Flight of the Seventh Moon: The Teaching of the Shields* (San Francisco: Harper & Row Publishers, 1984), xi, 14.

13. Christ, *Diving Deep*, 119–20.

14. Ibid., 13. The case of Nagsa Obum, a victim of spousal abuse, illustrates Christ's point:

> When I look at my husband,
> I think of the fluttering flag on the roof.
> Even though he is my husband he is not stable.
> He believes what other people say before hearing my side.
> Thinking this, renunciation arises in this woman.

Allione, "*The Dakini Principle*," 87.

15. Quoted by Andrews, *Flight of the Seventh Moon*, 186.

16. Christ, *Diving Deep*, 19.

17. Ibid., 20.

18. Allione, *Woman of Wisdom*, 17.

19. Two alternate arguments remain open here for Christ and her supporters. First, that men mystics receive attention not so much because they are more adept than women as because they manage to do it all, while for women it is so natural as to barely merit any notice. On the other hand, one could argue that women mystics consistently have been undervalued or even ignored due to the tyranny of masculine standards of judgment. Although possible, neither of these lines of argumentation seems especially productive in terms of the advance of mystic wisdom.

20. Christ, *Diving Deep*, 20–21.

21. Ibid., 21–22.

22. For a fuller discussion of feminine/masculine differences, see Sandra A. Wayrytko, *The Undercurrent of "Feminine" Philosophy in Eastern and Western Thought* (Washington, D.C.: University Press of America, 1981), especially the first chapter. See also Sandra A. Wawrytko, "A Provocative Alternative to Social Values: The 'Feminine' Complement to the Dominant 'Masculine' Perspective," in *The Social Context of the Person's Search for Meaning*, ed. Norman N. Goroff (Hebron, Conn.: Practitioner's Press, 1985), 70–92.

23. John H. Clark, *A Map of Mental States*, chapter 2, "Mysticism" (London: Routledge & Kegan Paul, 1983), 20.

24. Walter T. Stace, *The Teachings of the Mystics* (New York: New American Library, 1960), 130–31.

25. As quoted by Andrews, *Flight of the Seventh Moon*, 22.

26. The framework of the feminine perspective, including the principle of eros and the keynotes of receptivity, all-is-one-ness, and the link with nature, is drawn from Wawrytko, *The Undercurrent of Feminine Philosophy.*

27. R. C. Zaehner proposes a similar term, "pan-en-hen-ism'" in *Mysticism: Sacred and Profane An Inquiry into Some Varieties of Praeternatural Experience* (London: Oxford University Press, 1957), 28.

28. As Christ explains it, "women's bodily experiences of menstruation, pregnancy, childbirth, and lactation, combined with their cultural roles of caring for children, the sick, the dying and the dead have led to the cultural association of women with the body and nature" (22). In this case of feminine mystics attitude toward the body is of greater importance than cultural expectations, since their experiences take them beyond the usual constraints of either the physical or social worlds. Equally noteworthy is the fact that many of the most renowned women mystics lived a life of celibacy, thereby excluding them from many of the primal female experiences listed by Christ without reducing their potential for mystical experience.

29. Stace, *Teachings of the Mystics*, 15.

30. Valerie M Lagorio, "The Medieval Continental Mystics: An Introduction," in *An Introduction to the Medieval Mystics of Europe: Fourteen Original Essays*, ed. Paul E. Szannach (Albany: State University of New York Press, 1984), 161–193.

31. Ibid., 172. See also Rufus M. Jones, *The Flowering of Mysticism: The Friends of God in the Fourteenth Century* (New York: Macmillan Company, 1939), especially 172–75.

32. Given the noble birth of many of these women, there are notable exceptions to such educational deficiencies, including Elsbet Staegel (see Jones, *Flowering of Mysticism*, 171), Gertrude, and Catherine of Siena (see Lagorio, "Medieval Continental Mystics," 171, 185). In many cases, these women simply underestimated their own talents and so delegated the task of writing to men despite their obvious qualifications to speak for themselves (Hildegard of Bingen and Brigitta of Sweden are examples here; see Lagorio, pp. 163, 182).

33. Mary E. Giles, "The Feminist Mystic," included in her ed., *The Feminist Mystic and Other Essays on Women and Spirituality* (New York: Crossroad, 1982), 29.

34. Evelyn Underhill, *The Essentials of Mysticism and Other Essays* (New York: E. Dutton & Company, Inc., 1960), 176.

35. As quoted by Andrews, *Flight of the Seventh Moon*, 130, 36.

36. See Allione, *Women of Wisdom*, 40.

37. Ibid., xxix.

38. Stace, *Teachings of the Mystics*, 131.

39. See Bernard's "Sermones" in *Cantica Canticorum, Sermon on the Song of Songs; On the Song of Songs*, trans. Kilian Welsh (Spencer, Mass.: Cistercian Publications, 1971).

40 Mystical eroticism is included in the second of the three categories into which Evelyn Underhill divides mystics, based on the kinds of symbols they resort to in discussing their experiences. The three groups are identified as: "Divine Transcendence and the idea of pilgrimage," mutual desire and symbols of love," and "Divine Immanence and symbols of transmutation" in *Mysticism: A Study in the Nature and Development of Man's Spiritual Consciousness* (New York: The Noonday Press, 1955), 125. For a fuller discussion of Underhill's second category, see also 128, 136–40.

A more detailed account of the religious use of erotic symbolism can be found in Goeffrey Parrinder, "Visions, Raptures and Sex," in his *Mysticism in the World's Religions* (London: Sheldon, 1976), 169–74. Among male mystics this feminine orientation also can be found on occasion, as in Ramon Lully's *Libre d'Amic e Amat (The Book of the Lover and the Beloved* trans. E. A. Peers, New York: Macmillon Company, 1923) and Bernard's *De diligendo Deo (How God Is to Be Loved)*, ed. Hugh Martin, trans. W. Harmon van Allen (London: SCM Press, 1959).

It is interesting to compare the Tantric and Christian trends of mysticism with regard to erotic language and imagery. While the Tantric practitioner makes explicit use of sexuality, eroticism apparently plays little or no role in their descriptions of mystical ecstasy. For example, the "marriage" of a yogini and yogi, ritual intercourse is described as "unifying profound cognition [the feminine] and skillful means [the masculine]" (Allione, *Women of Wisdom* 170). Contrastingly, for Christian mystics, the taboo on explicit sexuality seemingly has led to a proliferation of implicit eroticism, such as found in the writings of Teresa of Avila (see excerpts below).

41. Teresa of Avila, *The Life of Teresa of Jesus: The Autobiography of St. Teresa of Avila*, trans. E. Allison Peers (Garden City, N.Y.: Doubleday & Company, Inc., 1960), ch. xx, 189; Catherine of Siena, *Dialogue*, 63, as quoted by Lagori, "Medieval Continental Mystics," 191.

42. Julian of Norwich, *Showings* or *Revelations of Divine Love*, as quoted by Ritamary Bradley, "Julian of Norwich: Writer and Mystic" in Szarmach ed. *Medieval Mystics of Europe*, 214.

43. Simone Weil in *Seventy Letters*, ed. Richard Rees (New York: Oxford University Press, 1965), 142, as quoted by Kathryn Hohlwein, "Armed with a Burning Patience: Reflections on Simone Weil," in Giles, *The Feminist Mystic*, 153.

44. Angela of Foligno, *Memoriale de fra'Amaldo*, 262–63, as quoted by Lagorio, "Medieval Continental Mystics," 180.

45. Margery of Kempe, as quoted by Maureen Fries, *An Introduction to the Medieval Mystics of Europe*, ed. Paul E. Szavnach (Albany: State University of New York Press, 1984), 220, 222.

46. Hadewijch, *Poems in Couplets*, 11.113–24, 355, as quoted by Lagorio, "Medieval Continental Mystics," 177.

47. Baumgardt, *Great Western Mystics*, 28.

48. Bernard, *Sermones de diversis VIII:9*, as quoted by Maurice Valency in *In Praise of Love* (New York: Macmillan, 1961), 22.

49. *In Praise of Krishna: Songs from the Bengali*, trans. Edward C. Dimock, Jr. and Denise Levertov (Garden City, N.Y.: Anchor Books, 1967), 41.

50. *Psalms of Dadu*, No. 17, *Pad*, 151, as quoted by W. G. Orr in *A Sixteenth-Century Indian Mystic* (London: Lutterworth Press, 1947), 66.

51. Sister Seraphique de la Mariniere from Bougaud's *Historie de la Beinheureuse Marguerite Marie* (1894), 125, as quoted by William James, *The Varieties of Religious Experience: A Study in Human Nature* (New York: Collier Books, 1961), 225.

52. Underhill, *The Essentials of Mysticism*, 209.

53. Jane Lead, *A Fountain of Gardens Watered by the River of Divine Pleasure, and Springing up in all Variety of Plants*, I, 69–71; 118; 77–78, as quoted by Catherine F. Smith, "A Note on Jane Lead with Selections," *Studia Mystica* 3, no. 4 (Winter 1980), 81.

54. Lagorio, "Medieval Continental Mystics," 170.

55. Loren Hurnscot, *A Prison, A Paradise* (1959) as quoted by Anne Fremantle, *The Protestant Mystics* (Boston: Little, Brown, 1964), 367.

56. An account of the life of Margaret Mary Alacoque, Bougard, 145, as quoted by James, *Varieties* 273.

57. "We Saw Him There in Vrindavan," as cited by Dehejia, *Antal and Her Path*, 128.

58. "Julian of Norwich," as quoted by Bradley, 214.

59. Teresa of Avila *Autobiography*, chapter xxix, 274–75.

60. Ibid., chapter xx, 192.

61. Trans. Jane Hirschfeld and included in Mitchell, *The Enlightened Heart* 79.

62. Julian of Norwich as quoted by David Knowles, *The English Mystical Tradition* (New York: Harper & Brothers, 1961), 127.

63. See quotes from these mystics in Baumgardt, *Great Western Mystics*, 78, n. 1.

64. Su Bu-er, in trans. Thomas Cleary *Immortal Sisters: Secrets of Taoist Women* (Boston: Shambhala, 1989), 26.

65. Cleary, *Immortal Sisters*, 33. Running throughout the entire Taoist canon are prominent images of Tao as nurturing mother to be emulated, including the creation of an immortal spiritual embryo by inner alchemy that is given birth through meditational practice.

66. Henry Suso in a letter to Elsbet Staegel, as quoted by Jones, *Flowering of Mysticism*, 172.

67. Julian of Norwich, as quoted by Bradley, *Julian of Norwich* 213.

68. Jones, *Flowering of Mysticism*, 174.

69. Julian of Norwich, as quoted by Bradley, *Julian of Norwich* 213.

70. Julian of Norwich, as quoted and discussed by Knowles, *The English Mystical Tradition*, 121.

71. Elizabeth of Dijon as quoted by Hans Urs Von Balthasar, *Elizabeth of Dijon: An Interpretation of Her Spiritual Mission*, trans. A. V. Littledale (New York: Pantheon, 1956), 66.

72. Catherine of Siena, *Dialogue*, 144, as quoted by Lagorio, *The Medieval Continental Mystics*, 190.

73. Margaret Mary Aloque, in a letter quoted by James, *Varieties*, 249.

74. Uvavnuk, Netsilik Eskimo shamaness of the late nineteenth and early twentieth century; included in Mitchell, *The Enlightened Heart*, 123.

75. Rabia focuses on Sura 5/59 of the *Koran*—"He loves them and they love Him"—as the basis for her insights on love. Schimmel, *Sufism and Islamic Tradition*, 132.

76. Hannah Whitall Smith, *The Christian's Secret of a Happy Life*, as quoted by Fremantle, *The Protestant Mystics*, 272–73.

77. Madame Guyon, as quoted by James, *Varieties* 231.

78. Mrs. Jonathan Edwards, as quoted by James, *Varieties*, 224.

79. Antoinette Bourignon, as quoted by James, *Varieties*, 257–58.

80. Jan van Ruysbroeck, as quoted by Stace, *Teachings of the Mystics*, 162.

81. Meister Eckhart, *Another Sermon*, as quoted by Stace, *Teachings of the Mystics*, 156. Eckhart presents an interesting example of the merging of feminine and masculine trends, meriting closer examination. Although the remark just quoted has masculine force to it, at other times his statements have a very feminine feel of all-is-one-ness and receptivity—"The eye by

which I see God is the same as the eye by which God sees me. My eye and God's eye are one and the same—one in seeing, one in knowing, and one in loving, *Sermon 23;* "The soul will be most perfect when it is thrown into the desert of the Godhead, where both activity and forms are no more, so that it is sunk and lost in this desert where its identity is destroyed," *Sermon 22;* as quoted by Stace, *Teachings of the Mystics,* 157, 156.

82. Simone Weil, *Seventy Letters,* 137, as quoted by Hohlwein *Armed With a Burning Patience,* 156.

83. As quoted by Lagorio, *The Medieval Continental Mystics,* 163, 166.

84. Catherine of Siena, *Dialogue,* 29, as quoted by Lagorio, 186. Teresa of Avila, *Autobiography,* chapter xx, 192.

85. Agnes Whistling Elk, as quoted by Andrews, *Flight of the Seventh Moon,* 21.

86. Mechthild, trans. Jane Hirschfeld, and included in Mitchell *The Enlightened Heart,* 65.

87. Julian of Norwich, as quoted by Underhill, *The Essentials of Mysticism,* 197. For a fuller discussion of the maternal aspect of God within Christianity, see Ritamary Bradley, "Mysticism in the Motherhood Similitude of Julian of Norwich" and Valerie M. Lagorio, "Variation on the Theme of God's Motherhood in Medieval English Mystical and Devotional Writings," *Studia Mystica* 8, no. 2 (Summer 1985), 4–37. See also Caroline Walker Bynum, *Jesus as Mother: Studies in the Spirituality of the High Middle Ages* (Berkeley: University of California Press, 1982).

88. Allione, *Women of Wisdom,* 22–24; see also 176–78. See also Neumaier-Dargyay.

89. Andrews, *Flight of the Seventh Moon,* 100.

90. *Passionate Journey: The Spritiual Autobiography of Satomi Myodo,* trans. and annotated by Sallie B. King (Boston: Shambhala, 1987), 75–76.

91. King, *Passionate Journey,* 94.

92. King, *Passionate Journey,* 107.

93. Jan van Ruysbroeck, *The Adornment of the Spiritual Marriage,* chapter 8, as quoted by Stace *Teachings of the Mystics,* 170. Teresa of Avila, *Autobiography,* trans. J. M. Cohen (Harmondsworth: Penguin Books, 1957) chapter xviii, 174.

94. Julian of Norwich and Margery of Kempe, as quoted by Knowles, *The English Mystical Traditions,* 130, 144, 146.

95. Hadewijch, Letter 9, as quoted by Lagorio, *The Medieval Continental Mystics,* 176.

96. Agnes Whistling Elk, as quoted by Andrews, *Flight of the Seventh Moon,* 78.

97. Catherine of Siena, *Dialogue,* 25, as quoted by Lagorio, *The Medieval Continental Mystics,* 186.

98. Catherine of Genoa, *Purgation & Purgatory* and *Spiritual Dialogue,* as quoted by Dorothy H. Donnelly, "The Sexual Mystic: Embodied Spirituality," in Giles, *The Feminine Mystic,* 127.

99. H. Blavatsky, *The Voice of the Silence,* as quoted by James, *Varieties,* 330.

100. Angela of Foligno, *Memoriale de fra' Amaldo,* 124, as quoted by Lagorio, *The Medieval Continental Mystics,* 179.

101. Lucie-Christine, as quoted by Underhill, *The Essentials of Mysticism,* 224.

102. Agnes Whistling Elk, as quoted by Andrews, *Flight of the Seventh Moon*, 156.

103. Teresa of Avila, *Autobiography*, chapter xviii, 179.

104. Malwida von Meysenburg, as quoted by James, *Varieties*, 311.

105. Ruby Plenty Chiefs, as quoted by Andrews, *Flight of the Seventh Moon*, 96.

106. See Takie Sugiyama Lebra, "Self-Reconstruction in Japanese Religious Psychotherapy" in Takie Sugiyama Lebra and William Lebra, eds., *Japanese Culture and Behavior: Selected Readings*, rev. ed (Honolulu: University of Hawaii Press, 1986).

107. Joscelyn Godwin, *Mystery Religions in the Ancient World* (San Francisco: Harper & Row, 1981), 31.

108. Stace, *The Teachings of the Mystics*, 175.

109. Teresa, *Autobiography*, chapter xviii, 180.

110. Stace writes of Teresa, "It is certain that she has reached up to the supreme enlightenment of the unitive life," *Teachings of the Mystics*, 175.

111. Julian of Norwich, *Showings*, as quoted by Bradley, *Julian of Norwich*, 207.

112. Agnes Whistling Elk, as quoted by Andrews, *Flight of the Seventh Moon*, 191.

113. John of the Cross, *The Dark Night of the Soul*, as quoted by Stace, *The Teachings of the Mystics*, 188.

114. Teresa of Avila, *The Interior Castle*, "Spiritual Marriage," as quoted by Stace, *The Teachings of the Mystics*, 185. In this same passage Teresa also uses the image of rain falling into a river to convey all-is-one-ness—"there is nothing but water there and it is impossible to divide or separate the water belonging to the river from that which fell from the heavens," 115. Stace, *The Teachings of Mystics*, 126–29. Zaehner likewise draws a distinction between Christian mystical experience and "pan-en-henic" experience (see n. 23 above). Those Christian mystics who indulge in nondualist imagery Zaehner assumes are only "speaking figuratively or in poetry" or else are unorthodox (29). An alternate explanation is that they simply favor the feminine mode of mysticism.

116. Donnelly, *The Sexual Mystic*, 133–34.

117. For examples, see Teresa of Avila, *Autobiography*, chapter xx, 192, 197, 199.

118. Bernard Soulie, *Tantra: Erotic Figures in Indian Art* (Freiburg-Geneva: Productions Liber SA, 1982), 51.

119. Teresa of Avila, *Autobiography*, chapter xx, 192.

120. Quotes from a folk drama based on the life of Nangsa Obum, as quoted by Allione, *Women of Wisdom*, 126, 92; see also 113.

121. Mechtild von Magdeburg, as quoted by Baumgardt, *Great Western Mystics*, 28.

122. Agnes Whistling Elk, as quoted by Andrews, *Flight of the Seventh Moon*, 83.

123. Agehanada Bharati states, "What distinguishes tantric from other Hindu and Buddhist teaching is its systematic emphasis on the identity of the absolute *(paramartha)* and the phenomenal *(vyavahara)* world when filtered through the experience of *sadhana;*" the *Tantric Tradition* (Garden City, N.Y.: Anchor Books, 1970), 18. It is interesting to note that Teresa of Avila has been included in the school of "Christian Tantrism" by modern exponents of

Hinduism. In the company of Ignatius Loyola, founder of the Jesuits, it has been said of Teresa that "instead of eradicating all sensuality from their behavior, . . . [they] adopted it fully and turned it to advantage in the pursuit of asceticism;" Soulie, *Tantra*, 51, 55.

124. Donnelly, *The Sexual Mystic*, 132, 134.

125. Virginia Woolf, *A Writer's Diary*, February 7, as quoted by Fremantle, *The Protestant Mystics*, 327.

126. Agnes Whistling Elk, as quoted by Andrews, *Flight of the Seventh Moon*, 24.

127. Agnes Whistling Elk, as quoted by Andrews, *Flight of the Seventh Moon*, 77.

128. Hohlwein, *Armed with a Burning Patience*, 154.

129. Catherine of Siena, *Dialogue*, 159, as quoted by Lagorio, *The Medieval Continental Mystics*, 187.

130. Allione, *Women of Wisdom*, 20. Allione is referring here to the views of men in spirituality; however, our present emphasize indicates a rephrasing of this to transcend mere biological gender.

131. Baumgardt, *Great Western Mystics*, 51.

132. Julian of Norwich, as quoted by Bradley, *Julian of Norwich*, 208; see also Bradley's discussion of Julian's analogies, 207–12.

133. Hohlwein, *Armed with a Burning Patience*, 156.

134. Margaret Prescott Montague, *Twenty Minutes of Reality*, as quoted by Fremantle, *The Protestant Mystics*, 320.

135. Hurnscot, as quoted by Fremantle, *The Protestant Mystics*, 368.

136. Katherine Trevelyan, *Through Mine Own Eyes*, as quoted by Fremantle, the *Protestant Mystics*, 362.

137. Andrews, *Flight of the Seventh Moon*, 79. The Link with nature is indicated further by the various visions Andrews experiences under the stimuli of nature (a waterfall, a cave, a canyon, etc.) and the lessons she learns from her "helpers" (including a squirrel, a raven, crystals, a bear, and pebbles). At several points Nangsa Obum compares herself to other creatures of nature—a snow lion, a deer, a fish, a bird, a flower—and is referred to by others in the same terms; Allione, *Women of Wisdom*, 108–9, 118–19, 122, 124–25,

138. Zhou Xuanjing (twelfth century), as quoted by Cleary, *Immortal Sisters* 82–83. The explanatory note appended to the poem is worth quoting:

> Autumn, when the leaves fall from the trees, is a classic Chan Buddhist metaphor for the riddance of mental clutter. Midnight and noon are common Taoist symbols for key points in meditation: Midnight is the point of utter stillness and silence followed by the gradual dawning of new awareness; noon is the point where full awakening is consummated and begins to reintegrate with the ordinary world. Fish and dragons are the ordinary and extraordinary faculties in the mind; the stillness of the waves refers to emotional detachment from the vissicitudes of events. The "eternal sky" represents the openness cultivated by Taoists to allow the "moonlight" of the original mind to shine clearly.

139. Iwmi Shikibu (974–1034), trans. Jane Hirshfeld with Mariko Aratani, included in Mitchell, *The Enlightened Heart*, 40.

140. Donnelly, *The Sexual Mystic*, 136.

141. Antal, "White Conch from the Fathomless Sea," in Dehejia, *Antal and Her Path of Love*, 99.

142. Detailed descriptions of their "cruel castigation and self-inflicted tor-

ment" can be found in the biographies of the sisters, compiled by Elsbet Staegel; see Jones, *The Flowering of Mysticism*, 173–75. See also Margaret Smith, "Asceticism and the Monastic Life among Women," chapter 3 of her book, *The Way of the Mystics: The Early Christian Mystics and the Rise of the Sufis* (1931; London: Sheldon Press, 1976), 34–46.

143. An interesting comparison can be made here between the religious experiences of women and those of blacks in American society. Both groups historically suffered the effects of discrimination and restricted movement within society, due in one case to sexism and in the other to racism. This predicament often led them to seek solace in a higher, more just power. As Paul Radin observes, "What the slave desired was a status that he himself had ordained, not a fictitious one imposed from without. Such a status he could only secure in the realm of dreams, fantasies, and visions." Radin, "Status, Fantasy, and the Christian Dogma: A Note about the Conversion Experiences of Negro Ex-Slaves," Foreword to Clifton H. Johnson, ed., *God Struck Me Dead: Religious Conversion Experiences and Autobiographies of Ex-Slaves* (Philadelphia: Pilgrim Press, 1969), viii. The difficulties encountered by women in pursuit of a life of spirituality have been almost insurmountable at times. For example, Nangsa Obum was ridiculed, threatened, and beaten by her own family and her husband's family in an effort to dissuade her from practicing Dharma. The response she received when she first approached her guru reflects the low regard accorded women:

> If you are an incarnation of Tara, you can be accepted.
> But ordinary girls cannot practice Dharma,
> A beautiful young woman like you will find it hard to practice.
> So you had better go home.
> If you cut your hair your parents will be angry with me.
> I did not invite you here, you had better go back!

Allione, *Women of Wisdom*, 120. Only by threatening suicide was Nangsa finally accepted as a disciple.

8

Chinese Mysticism

KUANG-MING WU

THIS essay explicates Chinese mysticism in the following three parts. First, the notion of "mystical a priori" is critically developed by dialogue with Tillich, Stace, and Aristotle, thereby characterizing Chinese mysticism as predominantly a mystical sentiment. Then, specific manifestations of the Chinese mystical a priori are illustrated by way of explaining (i) the Classic of Change, (ii) the Five Cosmic Agents and the Chinese Almanac, (iii) Chinese Medicine, (iv) the Taoist Pantheon, (v) Ch'i and geomancy, (vi) Shen, (vii) human interactions with gods, (viii) the mystical in Confucianism, (ix) the Heaven, (x) history and myths, (xi) Ch'eng (sincerity), (xii) Li (ritual, decorum), (xiii) Jen (humanness). Finally, a brief conclusion sums up the entire essay.

General Characteristics

There is a difference between mysticism as an ism separate from philosophy, business, and the like, on the one hand, and mysticism as an atmosphere, tone, color or characteristic which pervades all our daily activities, on the other. Chinese mysticism in a deep sense is of the latter kind.

To be sure, there is Chinese mysticism of the former kind as well, as in popular religious Taoism, divination, astrology, geomancy, and shamanism. But these are not the only kinds of mysticism in China. Chinese mysticism as a whole is less of a divinatory manipulation of milfoil stalks and frenzied shamanic dance than the mystical awe that permeates human integrity and activities, as well as the disclosure of the as–is of things. William James said somewhere that, for Western philosophy, empiricism is mysticism, for our empirical investigation of things is based on our deep mystical assumption that what we know is true of things. For Chinese philosophy, it can be said that mysticism is empiricism, for the Chinese mystical sentiment has its pervasive empirical significance in morality, politics, arts, martial arts, cooking, medicine, and the like.

In defense of such a peculiar character of Chinese mysticism, the following consideration can be offered. Usually the mystics avoid being autobiographical; self-advertisement of occultism is said to be foreign, if not contrary, to the truly mystical spirit. This is understandable once we realize that the mystical is ineffable. To delimit, identify, and advertise the mystical is to efface the ineffable; noisily to point at the ineffable is to miss it.

But if this describes mysticism, then mystical experience can no longer be called (identified as) an ism, but can only be alluded to as an elusive special quality pervading thoroughly our daily ongoings. Mysticism is less a noun, a realm, than an adjective, an atmosphere. If Walter T. Stace rightly excludes esoteric mysteries of paraphysic occults (such as telepathy, telekinesis, clairvoyance, precognition, spiritualism) from the properly mystical,[1] then Stace should also have noted that what he called extrovertive mysticism (the mystical is everywhere) is the higher and truer mysticism than the so-called introvertive mysticism (the mystical is within the self).

For in extrovertive mysticism the ineffable pervades everything; in introvertive mysticism the ineffable is found within the self, leaving the world alone. The latter is to delimit the mystical as something peculiar as occultism does. This point is consistent with Stace's observation that representative mystics condemn unethical retreats from sorrows of our fellow men into private ecstasy. Such retreat is another bifurcation of the mystical from the nonmystical.

In fact, if extrovertive mysticism is everywhere, it includes introvertive mysticism as well, for "everywhere" includes the self. But then extrovertive mysticism abolishes the extro-introvertive distinction. If the distinction is valid in mysticism, then the distinction vanishes; mysticism is mysticism, and nothing more can be added.

From this we can also understand the paradoxical expressions among the mystics. On the one hand, they say their experience is beyond expression; on the other, they do use words to describe their experience. Describing their experience as indescribably mystical means that their experience is "immediate," that is, not mediated by our usual forms and categories of experience. But "experience" means precisely something mediated by experiential categories, as Kant and Katz[2] said.

When the mystics use words to convey their experience of no experience, their words are so paradoxical that the words do not convey anything at all. Such paradoxical expressions perhaps tell us that the ordinary are not discarded but charged with the mystical, which is yet different from the ordinary.

All this consideration applies to Chinese mysticism. For Chinese mysticism the mystical is its start (the regulative principle), its finish (the purpose), and its guarantor (the protector). To describe Chinese mysticism amounts to describing the entire Chinese philosophy and religion from such perspective.

What does such pervasive mysticism mean? Let us consider Paul Tillich's confusion on the meaning of mysticism (sensitive as he is). On the other hand, he produced a most beautiful (though unrecognized) passage on what he called a "mystical a priori":

> In both the empirical and the metaphysical approaches ... the a priori which directs the induction and the deduction is a type of mystical experience. Whether it is "being-itself" (Scholastics) or the "universal substance" (Spinoza), whether it is "beyond subjectivity and objectivity" (James) or the "identity of spirit and nature" (Schelling), ... whether it is "absolute spirit" (Hegel) or "value creating process" (Whitehead) ... —each of these concepts is based on an immediate experience of something ultimate.... Idealism and naturalism differ very little in their starting point .... Both are dependent on a point of identity between the experiencing subject and the ultimate which appears in religious experience or in the experience of the world as "religious." The theological concepts of both idealists and naturalists are rooted in a "mystical a priori," an awareness of something that transcends the cleavage between subject and object.[3]

This is to stress the universal character of mystical experience.

On the other hand, Tillich called the Christian Incarnation the *only* unique point of identity of the absolutely concrete and the absolutely universal.[4] This is because he distinguished this Incarnation from mysticism which renders the "objective side ... accidental ... by devaluating every medium of revelation and by trying to unite the soul directly with the ground of being, to make it enter the mystery of existence without the help of a finite medium."[5] Thus, he takes mysticism to be simply the introvertive one.

Sadly, the meaning of mysticism militates his insight expressed in the phrase, "mystical a priori." If he were to take mysticism to mean the mystical a priori in every human activity and thinking, he would have to recognize that the "finite medium" shines with the "mystery of existence;" otherwise, it is not "medium." The genius of mystical experience ("direct union of the soul with the ground of being") lies precisely in the unity of the finite with the infinite, to see the one *in* the other. Nothing is devalued. "If there is a knowledge of God, it is God who knows himself through man,"[6] who then is not denied but sanctified *as man*. If there is an "ecstatic union of man and God," man is man rendered transparent, not man transcended. Magic is "direct, physical unmediated sympathies and influences between" gods and men.[7] Mystical experience, in contrast, is "experience by participation"[8] in this point of identity, which does not need to devaluate the medium and make the concrete irrelevant.[9]

All in all, if mysticism is participation in the identity of the concrete and the universal, the finite and the infinite, the medium and the message, then "directness" of mystical experience harmonizes with its "mediation," and the a priori of the mystical in Chinese thinking is explained as something essential in all human experience. And if such is extrovertive mysticism, then extrovertive mysticism is vindicated as not only viable, but also inclusive of introvertive mysticism as well.

In sum, we must assume an affinity and interaction of a sort, such as co-responses or correspondence, between the macrocosm of our environment and the microcosm of our psychophysical self. Even pure mechanism and pure mentalism must assume such interaction and affinity between our self and our world.

Such an assumption cannot, however, be either validated or invalidated, simply because the proof requires the very assumption. Yet without this unprovable assumption, we cannot live in the world. The assumption is something mystical, appropriately to be called the "mystical a priori."

Since Socrates, philosophers in the West have tried to understand how the mystical a priori is possible—Plato, Aristotle, Descartes, Hume, Kant, Hegel, Wittgenstein. In China, the mystical a prior is less examined and analyzed than treasured, systematized, and applied—Yin-Yang, the Five Elements (or

Agents), reverently applied in almanac-astrology, historiography, music, morality, politics,[10] medicine,[11] military strategy,[12] arts,[13] and occult.[14]

To say that the West tries to understand the mystical while the Chinese simply treasures it and lives in it is simply to describe the predominant facts in the respective worlds of intellectual pursuit. Both approaches are necessary to do justice to the mystical a priori of our life. This essay is written for the promotion of both.

What is this mystical a priori? First, the "mystical," then the "a priori," must be explained.

To begin with, the salient features of the "mystical" must be counted. Two features have already been mentioned: ineffable and beyond. The mystical is *ineffable*, that is, elusive and indescribably, expressible only in poetic and paradoxical allusions. This is because the mystical is *beyond* our usual linguistic expression and understanding. In China, the mystical is the concrete. It cannot be exhaustibly understood because the concrete is the experiential, that with which we are in *direct* contact, and reflective understanding is possible only at a cognitive distance. There is an *absence* of subject-object dualism in the mystical-concrete; we *are* our situation to be understood.

The epithet, "nondualistic," would have been appropriate were it not already used by Buddhism,[15] for to say "one" already rejects the more-than-one, thus implies a dualism. But Chinese mysticism does not oppose or transcend the many in the concrete, as Buddhism does. Nor does Chinese mysticism bring *down* the supreme deity, the exalted ancestor, the vital pervasive moral force, the Heaven. Instead, Chinese mysticism lets us realize that the world *is* up there without nullifying the distinction between the ultimate and the concrete; the distinction is reverently *accepted*. Such is the meaning of the mystical absence of dualism in which all is in direct contact with all, experiencing one another.

This brings us to the final feature of the mystical in China, that the mystical is *all*-pervasive, serving as the unifying principle of life of all.

All this is the mystical a priori in China in the following senses.

Those five points above (a) constitute that in *terms* of which the Chinese people understand the world. These points constitute their cosmology by which they take their daily moral, political, even commercial and culinary bearings. These points (b) cannot be challenged without collapsing the entire cultural edifice in China, and yet (c) cannot be validated either, because they are themselves that in terms of which things are justified and made meaningful.

Thus, those five features of Chinese mysticism are what Aristotle called the "first principles," equivalent to the law of identity at the base of all arguments. They are the laws of Chinese identity. They constitute the "metaphysical beliefs"[16] or backbones of Chinese civilization.

Before we go into a specific description of Chinese mysticism, one more notion must be clarified.

What does "direct" mean when we say that mystical experience is direct experience? Steven T. Katz followed Kant and vigorously argued that it is impossible for any human experience to be "direct and raw," that is, pure and unmediated by our experiential categories.[17] This seems to conflict with the mystics' claiming that they see the light and hear voices without physically seeing or hearing. Katz's interpretation of experience precludes any understanding of mysticism from the outset.

Katz's stance is that of common sense, as Kant's was. Let us shift our perspective and join what Aristotle and Michael Polanyi split, turning Kant, Katz, and Stace outside in. We will then understand what "direct" means in an experiential context.

Aristotle distinguished theoretical knowledge (*theorea*— knowledge by thinking) from practical knowledge (*phronesis*— knowledge by doing). Kant distinguished transcendent knowledge (knowledge of the outside world) from the transcendental categories (*our* frame of reference in terms of which we understand the world). Polanyi distinguished focal awareness (on something) from the tacit dimension of our experience, what is taken for granted, in terms of which we do other things. "We attend from something [(tacit)] for attending to something else [(focal)]."[18] Stace distinguished extrovertive mysticism which finds the One in the external world, from introvertive mysticism which finds the One in the self.

Usually thinkers split the self and the not-self, valuing the not-self higher than the self. This is why we find it difficult to understand mysticism which *unifies* both in mutual participation. Where Kant misled us is that his transcendental categories of experience give us the impression that we have all but lost our spontaneity, as if we were constantly putting questions to

nature as we experience it, and "asking" is a conscious delibera-
tive activity. This stance may well have come from Aristotle
who valued theoretical knowledge higher than pragmatic, because the former can be explicitly, precisely, and deliberatively
formulated, while the latter cannot.

What is revolutionary in Stace and in Polanyi is that they
reversed our value preference and valued the introvertive-tacit
dimension of our experience higher than the extrovertive-focal.
Sadly, Stace went too far in stressing the inside at the cost of
the outside; Polanyi tend more to split than to join the focal
and the tacit. In life and in mysticism, it is the *joining* that
counts. The following neat summary hides the problematic in
our project of understanding Chinese mysticism—to split or to
join, and which pole to stress:

SELF	*NOT-SELF*	
pragmatic	theoretical	Aristotle
transcendental	transcendent	Kant
tacit	focal	Polanyi
introvertive	extrovertive	Stace
involuntary	voluntary	human experience

"Direct experience" is not raw and unmediated, cut off from
conscious ratiocination and categories of experience. Direct experience means rather a taking *in* of things and experiences,
rendering all of them as spontaneous and "involuntary" as our
heartbeat. To grow into ourselves means to expand the area of
such direct experience, joining more and more of our "not-self"
into our "self."

This fact can easily be observed in the child. The child grows
by stretching his conscious attention toward walking, talking,
writing, acting, and (later) all sorts of behavior and skills. The
child is said to have "grown" when we see him internalizing—
incorporating all these and turning them into involuntary, nonconscious activities, which are now part of himself.

Mysticism expands on this process of growing things into oneself, by first turning what no child needs learning into the objects of concentrated learning, such as breathing, sleeping,
moving, feeling, and sensing, as well as thinking. And then mysticism teaches us to learn ourselves into breathing from our
soles, sleeping without dreaming, flying as if without wings,
knowing as if without knowing, feeling without feeling, doing

without doing; in a word, becoming the new child whose area of the "self" is much fuller than the child.

What seems in mysticism like rejection of what we commonly treasure (knowledge, culture) is really to shock us out of our evaluative habit, stop us from valuing the not-self higher than the self, and incorporating more and more of the not-self into the self, which is now nonexistent to the self. And so, paradoxically, looked at from the self, the self is now dissolved precisely because the not-self is incorporated into the self. Everything is now transparently "direct."

As a result, we come spontaneously to respond to *whatever* comes. In other words, the self absorbs all the not-self, which is now completely eliminated. What cannot be held *(wu k'e nai ho)* is now part of what we cannot help but do and be *(pu te i)*. Fate becomes destiny, what is inevitable is now what ought to be, and we welcome whatever comes with the child's excitement. Divine naturalness *(shen hua)* describes such a situation, and the *I Ching*, among others, is to help us respond in such natural spontaneity. This is mysticism, at least Chinese mysticism.

Now we are ready to go into specific items of Chinese mysticism, one by one. Items I and II are shared by Confucianism and Taoism. Items III through VIII concern Taoism. Items IX through XIV concern Confucianism.

Specific Features

The I Ching

The *I Ching* (the classic of change) has been regarded highly by students of Chinese thought (both mystical and metaphysical) to which the *I Ching* has a close relation throughout.

The very character, *i*, signifies "change," picturing either the chameleon *(hsi i)* whose head changes its color twelve times every twelve hours, or the sun *(jih)* and the moon (*yueh*, written as *wu*) succeeding each other.

The activities of things are here looked at from a bipolar perspective, Yin and Yang, the quiet and the moving, the shady and the sunny, mutually succeeding one upon another. The dynamic interchange is symbolized by combining broken lines (Yin) and unbroken lines (Yang) into a six-lined cipher called "hexagram" *(kua)*. Each hexagram symbolizes one pattern of things' dynamic

interchange. The *I Ching* has sixty-four different hexagrams,
each of which is accompanied by an explanation that is itself
profoundly vague and evocative. The first hexagram is all unbroken lines, signifying the "heavenly creativity" *(ch'ien)*. The last
hexagram is made up of three pairs of Yin-Yang lines (counting
from bottom), signifying the "yet to complete" *(wei chi)*, the
inexhaustible vitality of nature, the Great Ultimate.

These hexagrams are supposedly (1) "simple and easy to
understand," *(chien erh i chih)* meaning, presumably, intuitively obvious, (2) "changing and interchanging *(pien i)* everywhere" as in weather and in births and deaths, and (3) "not-
changing" *(pu i)* in positions (the heaven is high; the earth is
low) and in the pervasive elan of births and rebirths *(sheng
sheng)* by mutual influences and responses *(kan ying)*.

Each of those sixty-four patterns of change comes alive, that
is, becomes relevant to a specific situation ('here and now"),
when a person obtains a specific hexagram (and its explanation)
by divinatory manipulation of milfoil stalks. Then he gets an
hexagramic advice, which *he* at the moment interprets for his
specific situation in a specific manner, as to what to do and how
at that moment. And so the effectiveness of the *I Ching* lies
at the intersection between the sixty-four hexagrams and the
personal interpretation in a specific situation. The book is alive
to the extent that we are.

The significance of the Classic of situational Changes can be
seen in the following four points:

1. The hexagrams capture the patterns of the interactions,
correspondings, between human affairs and their environment,
the human and the "heavenly" (the natural), the earth and the
heavens, the Yin and Yang. Such correspondence and co-
respondings are called "vitality" (natura naturans?) *(sheng sheng
pu i)* that brings beings into existence. There is unity among
the individualities of things, the one in the many, the many in
the one, ever changing, never ceasing.

2. An event is a coming-to-pass of happenings, a chancing
upon each other of several trends of things. Life is wave after
wave of such chancing-together *(chi hui)*. Hexagrams portend
patterns of such waves as auspicious or otherwise. Man's happiness depends on such waves but is not locked in them. Even
when a hexagram shows a situation auspicious, I myself can
ruin it if my responses to it are not appropriate; even when a
hexagram portends inauspiciousness, I can obtain happiness

with my appropriate responses. My life is a "math-meet" *(chi hui)* between what portends and what I respond with.

3. Thus appropriateness is what is crucial. Appropriate responses bring appropriate happiness in every situation. I must (a) know my particular place *(chih wei)* in the dynamic scheme of things, (b) realize my right time *(chih shi kairos)*, the right juncture in the correlative changes among things and situations, and (c) discern the workings *(yen chi)* of the nature of things thereby. Such threefold intimation of things enables me never to "push the river" of things but ever poised, ready to hit what is right *(chung cheng)* in the trends of the times, as to when to advance, when to retreat, when to arise, when to let go *(chin, t'ui, ch'un, wang)*.

4. To assist us in doing so, the *I Ching* was devised out of "the Diagrams of the (Yellow) River" *(ho t'u)*, which was reputed to be given to and deciphered by the legendary sage King Fu Hsi, while he was observing the patterns of hair-twirls on the back of the Dragon-Horse which arose out of the Yellow River. Such a myth vividly portrays the correspondence of man's appropriate behavior and nature's patterns of change.

As was mentioned above, the *I Ching* is structured in ciphers of sixty-four hexagrams, that is, sixty-four variations of a three-paired set of broken and unbroken lines, and can be interpreted freely. Historically there had been six hermeneutic traditions in China on this Classic, constituting the six schools on the *I Ching*. They are number-symbolism *(hsiang shu)*, augury *(chi hsiang)*, Taoism, magic-alchemy *(t'u shu)*, Confucianism *(ju li)*, and historiography *(shih shih)*. It is important to note that while such interpretive endeavors flourished, they also developed Chinese metaphysics. Thus the *I Ching* at the crossroad of man-nature interaction also occasioned and paralleled the development of Chinese philosophy.[19]

The Five Agents (or Elements) and the Chinese Almanac

Western philosophy started with Thales in ancient Greece, who claimed that "things" are varying forms of one primary and ultimate element, water. Aristotle then conceived things in terms of four "causes"—matter, meaning (aim), force, and form—and classified Thales as one of the philosophers of material cause.

If one cosmic element were to expand into five, each of which functions as four causes, the Chinese Five Elements-Agents are obtained. Furthermore, these elements are in two orders of dynamic mutuality: the "mutual birthing" (yang) order, and the "mutual overcoming" (yin) order. In the *first* order, Wood gives birth to Fire, Fire to Earth, Earth to Metal, and Metal to Water, and the cycle starts over again after Water giving birth to Wood. This order typifies the first half of the year when nature blossoms forth. In the *second* order of mutuality, Water overcomes Fire, Fire subdues Metal, Metal conquers Wood, and Wood wins over Earth, and the cycle starts again after Earth overcomes Water. This order symbolizes the wintering second half of the year.

The Five Elements have further cosmic implications, such as directions, colors, seasons, as follows:[20]

Element:	Wood	Fire	Earth	Metal	Water
Direction:	East	South	Center	West	North
Colour:	Blue	Red	Yellow	White	Black
Season:	Spring	Summer	Late Summer	Autumn	Winter
Numbers and					
Heavenly Stems (yin)	8, i	2, ting	10, chi	4, hsin	6, suei
(yang)	3, chia	7, ping	5, wu	9, keng	1, jen
Climate:	Windy	Hot	Humid	Dry	Cold
Mountains:	T'ai-shan (in Hunan)	Heng-shan	Sung-shan	Hua-shan (in Hopei)	Heng-shan
Planets:	Jupiter	Mars	Saturn	Venus	Mercury
Sound:	Shouting	Laughing	Singing	Weeping	Groaning
Musical Note:	chüeh	chih	kung	shang	yü
Virtues:	Benevolence	Propriety	Faith	Righteousness	Wisdom
Emotions:	Anger	Joy	Sympathy	Grief	Fear
Animals:	Dragon	Phoenix	Ox or Buffalo	Tiger	Snake and/or Tortoise
Viscera:	Liver	Heart	Spleen	Lungs	Kidneys
Orifices:	Eyes	Ears	Mouth	Nose	Anus and Vulva
Tissues:	Ligaments	Arteries	Muscles	Hair and Skin	Bones
Flavour:	Sour	Bitter	Sweet	Pungent	Salt
Odour:	Rancid	Scorched	Fragrant	Rotten	Putrid
Emperors:	Fu Shi	Shen Nung	Huang-ti	Shao-hao	Shüan-hsü
Their Assistants:	Chü Mang	Chu Jung	Hou-t'u	Ju-shou	Hsüan-ming

Such a scheme applies both to the objective macrocosm of the universe and to the subjective microcosm of an individual. This is a map of the world, facilitating our engineering of the patterns of change around and within us.

Because the right timing is essential for such cosmic maneuver, the Chinese calendar was developed. Linked to the four seasons, the length of the month is determined by the moon cycle. The calendar has sixty years as one cycle. The cycle of sixty *(hua chia tzu)* is formed as the least common multiple of twelve Earthly Branches *(ti chih)* and ten Heavenly Stems *(t'ien kan)*. This sixty-year cycle serves the same purpose as our century of years. C. A. S. Williams quotes from Mayers's *Chinese Reader's Manual*, II 296, saying:

> According to the *Yüeh ling chang chü* [in] the *Record of Rites*, the invention of this system is due to Ta Nao, 27th Century B.C., who studied the properties of the five elements and calculated the revolving motions of the Tou constellation, Ursa major, and thereupon devised the combination above named for . . . giving names to days. By joining the first of the twelve to the first of the ten signs, the combination *Chia-tzu* is formed, and so on in succession until the tenth sign is reached, when a fresh commencement is made . . . . The cyclical signs play a great part in Chinese divination, owing to their supposed connection with the elements or essences which are believed to exercise influence over them.[21]

We can see how much the calendar has to do with stars and planets. Each planet and star symbolizes a specific omen according to how it appears in the sky. "The appearance of comets, and eclipses of the sun and moon, are believed to have a malign influence over the affairs of men."[22]

Medicine

Active correlation, that is, correspondences and co-respondings, between the macrocosm of our universe and the microcosm of our selves (life, body), are expounded and expressed in the Yin Yang interaction, the Five Elements-Agents, and the *I Ching*. This active correspondence is the framework of Chinese medicine. Shih Shou-t'ang of the Ch'ing dynasty started his book, *The Original Principles of Medicine (i yuan)* (1861) as follows:

> Man is naturally endowed with the breaths of Yin Yang and the Five Elements between Heaven and earth, to all of which man conforms in every situation. [And this is the health of man.] Man's sickness is analogous to failure of rightness in the Yin-Yang [relation] within the Heaven and earth. Therefore, we must understand the Heaven and earth in order to understand man. The *I Ching* said, "The way

of establishing heaven lies in the Yin and the Yang; the way of establishing earth lies in the soft and the tough." For the substances of the soft and the tough came from the concentration of the breaths of the Yin and the Yang. Therefore . . . nothing with the breaths is not from heaven; nothing with the shape [of a thing] is not from earth. . . . . Talking about man, whatever is above the diaphragm, such as the lungs, the heart, and the pericardium (hsin pao lo), symbolizes heaven; whatever is below the diaphragm, such as the liver, the gall bladder, the spleen, the stomach, the intestines, the kidneys, the triple burner (san chiao), the bladder, symbolizes the earth. The [former realm] is governed by the breaths of heaven; the [latter] is governed by the breaths of each . . . . Therefore I say: the human body is one small heaven-and-earth. (My translation)

Similarly, Hwang Fo-mi of Chin dynasty started his *Classic of Acupuncture* (the earliest book on acupuncture) (282 A.D.) by rehearsing our births from the heaven and earth and then said:

Therefore to nourish our life we must conform to the four seasons and follow the cold and the hot, harmonize emotions and settle peacefully in our habitation, set ourselves to the rhythm of the Yin-Yang and harmonize the tough and the soft. (My translation)

The entire system of Chinese medicine is based on the cosmology of the I and the Yin-Yang, and there is no reason offered for such a base. If such body-cosmos correspondence is not to be characterized as "mystical," then I do not know how else to characterize it.[23]

Taoist Magic

Although lacking an organized "church," Taoism has been the cult of the masses, whatever the ruling classes may do or think. Its culture revolves around divination, magic, medicine, and the everyday ceremonies of life, and provides a background to Chinese art and thought.

The Taoist magic diagrams *(t'u)*, talismans *(fu)*, and patterns *(ke)* are visual art products and magic forms with which the Chinese people communicate with the spirit world, thereby to influence the workings of the invisible forces of nature for human benefit. Taoist magic is a sort of primitive science geared to changes of stars and seasons, envisioned in agricultural terms such as planting and harvesting. Such magical engineering is aimed at curing sickness, blessing marriage, easing childbirth, and guarding against the calamities of fire and pestilence.

This magical science helps us humans harmonize with the energies of the universe that act upon us and within us, such as the polar Yin and Yang, complementary powers of nonbeing and being, which constantly shape each other as silence and sound, space and shape. Harmonization takes place when we can discern within the turbulent daily occurrences the Great Ultimate, the Whole, the mystery of all mysteries, the Tao, the Way things go. All magical practices of palmistry, physiognomy, geomancy, alchemy, herbal medicine, acupuncture, the arts of movement such as T'ai Chi Ch'üan and kung fu, and the like, are, ultimately speaking, the practices of such cosmic-concrete harmony of man with the universe in which he lives and has his being.

The main source available today of Taoist magic diagrams, talismans, and charms is in the esoteric volumes of *Tao Tsang*, originally published in 1190 and republished in 1436 (early Ming dynasty) after Kublai Khan of the Yüan dynasty burned many of its volumes in 1281.

The present version of the *Tao Tsang* consists of seven sections ("caves") with supplements, in fifty-five hundred volumes. The collection has more than fifty million characters and several thousand diagrams, most of which are ancient canonical forms over two thousand years old, rooted in the shamanism of the second millennia B.C.

The shaman is a person with a skill to freely contact and incarnate spirits, usually by songs, dances, drums, narcotics, and diagrams of talismans, calligraphy, charms.

The diagrams are produced by illiterate villagers, recluses, and hermit scholars, Taoist exorcist-priests, faith-healers, sorcerers. Most of them are anonymous, for the powerful talismanic forms are to be treated with reverence and reservation.

These diagrams were originally the most perishable visual art products of China. Some were drawn in the dust with a stick or a finger, others on paper to be burned at the magic rite. The perishability is symbolic of the principle of Eternal Change of the universe.

The principle of cosmic change is the One, the Whole, the Great Ultimate *(t'ai chi)*, which produces the polarity of Yin (the shade, negative, female, soft, watery, earthly, still, and so on) and Yang (the light, positive, male, tough, fiery, heavenly, moving and so on). Each pole contains at its center the seed of its opposite, to which it changes. Such complementary polarity in its/their interaction gives birth to the Five Dynamic Elements from which all events and things come forth, as was described above.[24]

Ch'i and Geomancy

Ch'i is the Chinese understanding of the vitality of change of and in the universe, somewhat like "ether" was in the early period (seventeenth century) of Western science. Perhaps ether taken as the works of the elan vital can characterize ch'i, for ch'i is not only the etherlike medium of change and identities of things but also is the workings of change, its vitality, the "vital breathing energy" coalescing to form things and dispersing to let things dissolve into vacuity. Thus, ch'i is the inner pure thrust of all changes and things, the workings of the original elan of life-and-death which breathes itself from one life to another.

Such vital *breath* gives energy to man, life to nature, movement to water, growth to plants. It is exhaled by the mountains as clouds and mists. Burning incense lets the smoke rise to represent the cosmic breath of life. The Taoist breathing exercise circulates and invigorates our ch'i, to maintain our personhood, and to banish evil. Strengthened in ch'i, some Taoists were said to charm the stream to drop its water level, quiet dogs' barking, light up the dwelling without burning it, and so on. Such miraculous feats are understandable once we realize that ch'i pervades everywhere, and he who masters and embodies the Tao of ch'i can influence things' ch'i with his own.

Geomancy *(feng-shui)* has a lot do to with such human interaction with natural ch'i. Feng-shui originally meant the climatic changes produced by moral conduct of people through the agency of the celestial bodies. Later it became the art of adjusting the sites and orientation of the abodes of the living (houses, cities) and of the dead (graves), so as to harmonize them with the current of the cosmic breaths (ch'i) exhibited in mountains and hills (yang), valleys and water (yin), and the movements of the heavenly bodies. The dousing-rod and the astrological compass are used to define the geomantic system which determines the most auspicious sites, heights, shapes, and orientations of dwellings. In this way the good luck of families and communities is fixed. Artificial alteration of natural forms has a good or bad effect according to the new forms produced. And by means of talismans and charms, the unpropitious character of any particular topography may be counteracted. The dead are affected by and able to use the cosmic ch'i to the benefit of the living, so that it is to the interest of the family to secure and preserve the most auspicious environment for the grave and the ancestral temple, as well as the home.

For instance, for a grave, a wide river in front, a high cliff behind, with enclosing hills to the right and left, would constitute a first-class geomantic position. Houses and graves face the south, because the annual animation of the vegetable kingdom (with spring and summer) comes from the south and the deadly influences of winter from the north. The symbolic figures on the roofs, the pictures of spirits on the doors, and stone images erected before tombs, produce an auspicious aura in which the cosmic ch'i may generate favorable feng-shui.

Shen

Shen is also a commonly used term in Chinese thinking and especially in mystical operation, together with ch'i. Shen has three meanings:

1. What draws out *(shen)* everything as it is, giving birth to things as they are, the elan vital of the universe, as described in Chapter Fifteen of the Chuang Tzu (15/20).[25]

2. What shen (as noun) does to man is also his shen (as adjective), his vitality and spiritedness. Lack of human shen (one of the Three Treasures in human health) leads to unconsciousness or insanity. Human shen is the alertness, the luster in the eye, the vitality behind *ching*, the source of life, and *ch'i*, the ability to activate movements of life. Chapters 11, 14, and 15 in the *Chuang Tzu*, for instance, describe the human shen and how to cultivate it.

3. The demonic wonders one can perform, when being at one with shen, is also shen (as adverb), divine spiritedness, as in an artwork. This is almost like the Socratic Demon, though without its foreboding, forbidding connotation. Chapter 19 in the *Chuang Tzu* is a collection of such marvels, various extensions of the Cook's story in chapter 3.

The final meaning (3) originates in the union of the first two (1, 2) perhaps, but the union is less a Faustian selling off of one's identity than an invigoration of one's deepest vitality, the "force of human personality" (Kaptchuk), which somehow echoes (in affinity) with the cosmic elan vital. It is the Socratic demon with a positive implication of sharpening of one's awareness, sensitivity, and versatility with things, enabling one to be an expert as divine as the creator gods who are also called shen.

Heraclitus expressed this cosmic depths of the spirit of a person when he said, "You could not discover the limits of the soul, even if you traveled every road to do so; such is the depth of its meaning (logos),"[26] though Heraclitus may not have meant what is meant here. Traveling every road is to travel the world in all its divine meanings. Our inability to discover the limits of the soul signifies that the soul is coequal with the cosmos, in which it is. Our discovery of the work is through our probings into the depths of ourselves. To reveal and release such depths of ourselves, which echo the world, is the description of the Tao of the Cook-Butcher who attained the divinity *(shen)* of his skill in the loosening up (releasing?) of the ox, in chapter 3 in the Chuang Tzu.

This leads us to a consideration of our body as related to the cosmos. Our body is also governed by the principles of the Great Ultimate; Yin-Yang, and the Five Elements. When Yin and Yang were formed out of the primordial confusion (*hun-tun*, chaos), the light Yang went up to form Heaven and the heavy Yin went down to form Earth. Analogously the human head is heavenly with the Yang spirits and the feet are earthly, accommodating the Yin spirits. The primordial Yang filled us at birth, waxing (with our growth) into the peak of maturity. As senescence sets in, Yin increases, until we die when the balance of Yin and Yang cannot be maintained, and Yin and Yang in us are separated.

Yin and Yang are symbolized by the trigrams K'an and Li respectively, which in turn are manifested in the heavenly influences of Ch'ien the furnace, and the earthly influences of K'un the crucible. The furnace is the "subtle fire" of the body, and the crucible is the bodily center which transforms energy, forming the elixir of life by combing K'an and Li.

In any case, shen and ch'i are the principles governing Chinese thinking as above, applied to medicine and Taoist magic, to win over the Yin-Yang harmonies and happiness. Some post-Han Taoist cults even proposed giving birth to a new man *within* oneself, the immortal soul that leaves the mortal body when this worldly life is over to join the spirit world. This is the result of inward concentration of life forces (K'an and Li), aided by talismanic magic, enveloped in the fire of transformation.[27]

Being within us and around us, such vital forces of shen and ch'i are difficult to deal with unless objectified. And so the Taoist spirit world came about. Tens of thousands of zoomorphic and anthropomorphic gods, spirits, and demons appeared, drawn from ancient Chinese nature-worship, hero-cults, and ancestor-worship.

The Taoist Pantheon

There are gods of the Prior Heavens and gods of the Posterior Heavens. The gods of the Prior Heavens do not change, being in the abode of transcendent and eternal Tao, representing the sources of life, primordial breath, and blessing in the Posterior Heavens. The Taoists worship gods of the Posterior Heavens where seasonal change and Yin-Yang interaction happen. These gods are those of the Heavens, those of this world of nature and man, and those of the underworld beneath the oceans. In the Taoist spirit world, "bribery" and power of accumulated "merits" exist. Bribery by "paper money" are given to Kuei-demons and Shen-spirits in the nether world.

Before death the Yang part of a man's soul is hun, and after death, it is shen. The Yin part of the soul before death is p'o, and after death it is *kuei*, which is demonic, and becomes harmful if the man has not been properly buried because (for instance) of drowning or violence, seeking vengeance on people.

According to Taoist beliefs, the Yin soul is divided into seven emotions while the Yang soul has three parts responsible for virtues; together they correspond to the Five Elements, four seasons, four directions and so on. Man has relation with the many layered Taoist pantheon, which is further complicated by sectarian teachings in geomancy, alchemy, medicine, and so on, about the unity of the round Heaven and square Earth, nature worship of sacred mountains and indoor dwarf plants, the vague cosmic ch'i, self-cultivation through breathing exercises and prolonged sexual activities that symbolize (if not reenact) the cosmic unity of the Yin and the Yang.

Human Interactions with Gods

In such mystical context, people participate in the activities of the gods who fill the universe; people use "godly" activities to influence gods and to placate them, as well as to become "godlike." We make our impacts on the gods by the way we conduct ourselves (following the *I Ching*'s advice), by the way we position ourselves in our environment (following geomantic and astrological advice), and by mystical writings, music, and dances.

Writings by mystics and shamans have talismanic power more significant than in the West because of the Taoist intimacy in interdependence between the spirits and the material world. The Taoist mystics in direct contact with the spirits' world composed talismans of special invocatory power. The sensitive Chinese writing brush is one of the most ingenious inventions of Chinese culture, legislating graphology with strict calligraphic rules. Such rules are deified purposely with waves and curves to express supernatural unorthodoxy of the written amulets and tablets that protect us against death or wounding in battle, in travel, against crocodiles, insects, winds, waves, tigers, illness, demons. The strong esoteric influence of the strip-format survived in the Chinese and Japanese hanging paintings.

Graphic compositions other than calligraphy are trance-drawings, diagrams, charts, whose mystical potency was so venerated that the inspired painters and calligraphers were generally taken as communicators with spirits.

Magic *dance* is an art of movement that invokes and influences the cosmic change, which is, in turn, embodied by the dancers to be transmitted to the whole community. The heavenly spirits were reputed to have instructed the limping Emperor Yü the magic dance which gave command over the spirits of nature. Such hopping dance handed over to the Taoist shaman sorcerer in trance traces with his feet a vortex or a spiral of magic, corresponding to astrological constellations.

Such dance is of course accompanied by *music,* which together with words, costume, and movement constituted the traditional opera, in which change, movement, and energy swirled into a virtual microcosm to bring together the human world and the world of spirits.

The occult art also Taoistically established "no statement" to enable a statement. The "no statement" was the artistic, mystical framework in which statement *(yang)* blended in with calligraphic "emptiness" *(yin).* The musical pause, the momentary stillness in dance, the enclosed emptiness in calligraphic composition or painting—they were the negative yin element contributing to the representation of the Great Ultimate of the universe. Such yin element symbolizes (partakes of) the vague uncertain future in our destiny, always changing, always flexing toward novel turnings.

The Taoist magic offers in this manner an inner vision, a

flexible frame of significance, in which to communicate with the spirits that inhabit our body and our universe. Talismanic calligraphy lets the Taoist extract the cosmic emblems from within the project around himself into a meditative cosmic mandala, with himself at the center. Such a mandala can be represented by an *empty* circle, the whole, Great Ultimate, in perfect equilibrium which nothing, neither joy nor sorrow, can harm.

The *spirit* of philosophical Taoism remains the central mystical core (mystical a priori) in the talismanic occult, which is, in fact, one of the manifestations of Taoistic philosophy, exhibited in naturalness, the vita flow of ch'i, shen, oneness with what there is and so on. Talismanic magic embraces both the symbolic noise of the firecrackers of the popular festivals and the Taoist hermit's meditation. Meditative stillness blends in with vigorous dance swirls in multiple perceptual symbolisms. Together they dissolve time and space in the great unity of the Tao of the heaven and the earth.[28]

The Mystical in Confucianism

Roger T. Ames persuasively demonstrated that *wu-wei*, traditionally taken to be a Taoist concept, played an important role in Confucian political theory.[29] This example is only one among many which show the common undercurrent, the mystical a priori, shared by Taoism and Confucianism. At the bottom of its moralism, Confucianism also starts, envelopes itself, and ends in the mystical unity of man and nature, the individual and the cosmic environment. To be in line with this unity is right and happy; to be out of it is wrong and disastrous.

In the following some salient Confucian notions are examined. They shall show the same mystical undercurrent that runs in Taoism.

At the base of all Confucian thinking is the notion of the unity of Heaven and man *(tien jen ho i)*, through both of which the same Tao runs.

Heaven is here synonymous with nature *(tzu jan, t'ien)*, and nature with the natural-inborn *(hsing)*. Going after *(ch'iu)* one's own nature which has been lost is to become one with the universal Tao. For "all things are already complete in oneself *(fan shen tzu ch'eng)*," Mencius declared. One should examine oneself and be sincere and the joy of being at one with all things will come of itself *(Mencius 7A4)*.[30]

Thus, man is the great of all things *(wan wu chih ling)*, as Chou Tun-i said, echoing the standard sentiment since time immemorial in China. This means not so much the Baconian supremacy of man over things as an intuition that man has special access to knowing nature, that man can co-respond with nature, influencing nature contrivedly and being influenced by nature intelligently, more than anything else in the universe. Thus, it is not wrong but off focus to characterize Chinese philosophy as "humanism" and *then* qualify it as "the humanism that professes the unity of man and heaven" as Wing-tsit Chan alleges when he starts his celebrated *A Source Book in Chinese Philosophy*.[31] Rather, Chinese philosophy should be described as first and foremost centered in the Heaven-man harmony, *in* which man occupies a unique (though not supreme) place.

In this context, it is natural to see that what *we* think and feel and do, in genuine sincerity *(ch'eng,* authenticity), corresponds with what is real. This is a Hegelian unit of rationality and realty with a vengeance. There exists a sort of energy-and-thrust in us *(ch'i)* that corresponds with, and is part of, the cosmic elan *(hao jan chih ch'i)*. To realize this truth and to strive to realize it in our person is to become the true man *(ch'eng jen)*.

After all, the core and essence of humanity *(jen)* is the core and the essence of *(jen)* all things; "the Heaven and man are of one body," as all the Neo-Confucians asserted. But they were just echoing the age-old Chinese sentiment, repeatedly expressed in the *Five Classics*, the *Four Books*. Neo-Confucians, such as the two Cheng brothers and Wang Yang-ming, elaborated this sentiment into a metaphysical scheme. This is what *Mencius* casually called the "single basis or origin" (3A5) which gave birth and conferred the final approval on the cosmic holism in Chinese psychology (thing about human nature), moral endeavors and speculations (five Constant virtues), interpersonal mutuality (Five Relations), and political structure (as patterned after the family relations).

The Heaven

Is the Heaven and the divine *(shen, ti)* (they are synonymous) personal? Yes, it is, in the sense that it has the characteristics of personhood such as intelligence and will, though whether the divine is singular or plural is not debated in China, especially not in philosophy, nor is the divine creation of all things admitted. Furthermore, although the divine is personal in the above sense, we men respect and keep our distance *(ching yuan)* from it, which is shrouded in awesome mystery.

Is the divine sphere rationally comprehensible? Yes, in the sense that it responds to our moral behavior. The divine sign *(fu ming)* of rulership is conferred on him who is morally worthy. And the will of Heaven changes according to how the moral man obeys the moral codes. Yet such rational correspondence between good fortune and good behavior is not exactly mathematical, manifesting many (almost musical) variations, as shown in the *I Ching* and in the divine significance of music. The divine-heavenly is inscrutable also in the sense that we do not understand the basis on which the correspondence obtains, nor do we understand the suffering of the good. What we *are* convinced of is that soon the select few will emerge, endowed with the mission to rectify the world. They are sagely kings, heroes, worthies.

History and Myths

In China, the universe is reasonable; the cosmic reason is not mathematical but historical. That is, the universe is not chaotically irrational, but orderly and reasonable in the patterns of its history.

The cosmic history is in the final analysis intertwined with the history of mankind, and has morals for man. The universe has a story to tell us, and such a story is true and good for us. This conviction originates the cosmic story of the golden past, the historical myths that admonish our present and guide our future. The Confucian literati-officials described the historical mistakes to warn and remonstrate with their rulers. And the myths of the sagely kings and devilish rascals came into being.

Taoism in fact thrives on a satirical manipulation of counterfactuals into stories which yarn out the never-never-land that *had better* come true, shocking our factual world into realizing its own senselessness. The Confucian Utopia of "the under-heaven public" *(t'ien hsia wei kung)* described in the *Li Chi* (Li Yun chapter) is amazingly similar to *Chuang Tzu*, the Taoist's description of the "World (or Age) of Perfect Virtues" especially in chapter 12. Chinese people thus use history and myths as an active point of orientation for guiding their activities. Such myths are "true" because of their mystical a priori, to wit, the past, the present, and the future are on the same realm of the affinity of the self with the cosmos, of the human with the divine-heavenly.

Ch'eng (Sincerity, Authenticity)

Chinese grammar expresses the correlation of subjective truthfulness with objective truth, when the Chinese language means by ch'eng both "sincere" and "truly."

(a) Ch'eng as meaning *sincerity* with cosmic significance is brought out well in the "Great Learning," which Chu Hsi (a famous Neo-Confucian) took out of *Li Chi* (one of the *Five Classics*) to make into one of the *Four Books*. The passages goes as follows:

> What is meant by "making the will sincere" is allowing no self-deception, as when we hate a bad smell or love a beautiful color. This is called satisfying oneself .... Only when he [the inferior man] sees a superior man does he then try to disguise himself, concealing the evil ... in him. But ... other people see him as if they see his very heart .... "What ten eyes are beholding and what ten hands are point to—isn't it frightening?"[32]

(b) Ch'eng as showing *truth*, that is meaning "truly," "is in truth," "is in fact," is exemplified in *Mencius, Chuang Tzu*, and others:

> "You are *in truth* (ch'eng) a man of Ch'i" (*Mencius* 2A1).
> "I regard non-action as *true* (ch'eng) joy" (*Chuang Tzu* 18/11).[33]

(c) Furthermore, ch'eng is so active in its force that its implication stretches far into the future to form an if-then construction, "if indeed," "if in fact":

> "*If indeed* (ch'eng) things were like this then the people would return to him as [surely as] water flows downwards" (*Mencius* 1A6).
> "*If in reality* (ch'eng) rulers in their undue fondness for knowledge lacked Tao then the whole world would be thrown into confusion" (*Chuang Tzu* 10/34).[34]

Now, given the above usage of ch'eng, and thus the Chinese thinking about the relation between the ch'eng-inside and the ch'eng-outside, it is natural for ch'eng to be elevated to one of the pivotal notions that expresses the unity of subjective authenticity and cosmic concord.

Of course, we have no guarantee that what we honestly say and think to be is always "true," that is, always so in fact; we do make some honest mistakes. But unless it is possible for our honest saying to be true, we can say nothing valuable anymore; in fact, the entire saying becomes futile—for our dishonest saying can hardly be true, and all our sayings become nothing-saying.

It is this twofold point—no guarantee that honest saying is true saying, yet without such unity of honesty with truth somewhere in the world, no saying is worthwhile—that makes ch'eng, as the unity of inner-truthfulness and outer-truth, *mystical* (in the teeth of honest mistake) and *significant* (in the teeth of the collapse of "saying" and thinking). This mystical sense is beautifully expressed by Max Picard in his *The World of Silence:*

> In the fables of the Golden Age . . . men understood the language of all animals, trees, flowers, and grasses . . . . This language climbed upwards toward the vault of heaven . . . . It formed an arch . . . and all the sounds of . . . nature met together . . . . Every single voice entered in and became a part of it, and therefore every voice was understood. This heaven of the languages was the homeland of all voices; they all came to themselves and to each other in this heaven. This language was unobtrusive despite its powerfulness, as unobtrusive as silence itself.[35]

This is the cosmic ch'eng-language, the heart-to-heart talk throughout the world.

What is special about ch'eng is that the sentiment is built into the very core of Chinese thinking, the cornerstone especially of the "Doctrine of the Mean" and Neo-Confucianism. They said in effect that sincerity-saying is sincerity vibrated out of the totality of our beings. And since our beings are the product of the unity of the breaths of Heaven and Earth, whatever honestly and truly vibrated out of ourselves must be an honest reflection of actuality of the universe. Ch'eng thus reflects the mystical a priori of our thinking, saying, and being. What William James said in his lone moment is echoed through the history of Chinese philosophy. He said, "The recesses of feeling, the darker, blinder strata of character, are the only places in the world in which we catch real fact in the making."[36] James unwittingly hit the core of sincerity in China, where to be sincere is to be creative, not just passively corresponding with actuality. In expressing ("saying") something sincerely, that something is accomplished. Sincerity is at the root of things; it is at its root the principle of creation, hence the principle of expression of our being.

Such a principle of creation is both human and cosmic. To "be sincere" is heaven; to "sincere it" is human, says the *Doctrine of the Mean*. Sincering-it is an active principle of self-examination and its meticulous practice, to ensure that any mistake (honest or otherwise) be eradicated by extensive studies, accurate inquiries, careful meditation, clear discernment, and earnest practice (chapter 20).

All this active transitive sense of sincerity belongs to being human. As perceptual mistakes can be corrected only by more careful perception, so honest mistakes can be corrected only by more sincere examination. Such active sincerity is that with which human beings participate in the cosmic sincerity, ever creating.

Heaven and earth continually create by sincerity, as chapters 25 and 32 of the *Doctrine of the Mean* magnificently describe it.[37] The laws of nature do not deceive, nor can they be mocked. We humans survive and thrive to the extent that we embody in our daily living such a cosmic principle of creative sincerity, as chapter 22 of the *Doctrine* said.

Human creation is first of all ourselves in our inner motivation, then the members of our community. All this is the root and core of *ethics* in China. Then, extending such ethical principle of creative sincerity we come to forming a social concord, the so-called *political* community, the state. Politics is based on this cosmic sincerity, as repeatedly described in chapters 20, 24, 27 and others, in the *Doctrine*, as well as the entire *Great Learning*. The pivot of politics lies in *sincering (ch'eng chih)* what one professes, the "rectification of names" *(cheng ming)*.

The essence of politics *(cheng)* then is correctness*(cheng)*, especially active correct correspondence between the name and its counterpart in actuality, *making* them correspond with each other.[38] This is the so-called Rectification of Names. To call oneself "ruler," one must become truly rulerlike *(chün chün)*. To call oneself "father," one must become truly fatherly *(fu fu)*. To become so is to head for social concord, for it is to conform to the way of nature as it professes to be. To produce the conformity of name with what the name professes is to have the Tao under-heaven *(t'ien hsia yu tao)*; to lose such conformity (active-creative sincerity) is to have no Tao under-heaven *(t'ien hsia wu tao)*. To embody Tao under-heaven is synonymous with universal peace and concord; not to embody Tao under-heaven is social chaos.

It is abundantly clear that to have such political philosophy we must have at its basis the *unity* of man with nature and its Tao; such unity has been expressed as active-creative sincerity, correctness, rectification of names. And such unity cannot be proven; it can only be assumed.

Li (Ritual Decorum)

Another key Confucian notion is *li*, the rite-decorum of society and of the cosmos.

Li is our correct mode of living-as-ourselves. *Yüeh Chi* says, "Manifested, there is li and yueh, hidden, there is spirit and divinity" *(kui shen)*. Chu Hsi says of this passage that what is spiritual-divine is what is alive of the universe, the active principle of nature that "bends and stretches" *(ch'ü shen)*. To manifest it is decorum and music. Music is a reflection of the orderly rotation of day and night, opening-closing *(he pi)* of the Yin and the Yang, flowing everywhere. Decorum is the reflection of their orderliness and distinctions. The sincerity of li is the harmony of yüeh.

Therefore, li is the reflection of the order of the universe, the central warp *(chung ching)* of nature, as music is its harmony. To practice li amounts to returning home to the original order of nature in our daily comportment. Li is the true regulation of human behavior in the sense that it comes directly out of the nature principle *(li)* in the inner grain of our personhood and our social and daily affairs. To go home to such vital orderliness is to bring everyday social affairs to their ingrained vibrant orderliness.[39]

This is what explains the *magic* of a handshake, as noted by Herbert Fingarette when he said:

> I see you on the street; I smile, walk toward you, put out my hand. ... And behold—without any command, stratagem, ... special tricks, ... you spontaneously turn toward me, return my smile, raise your hand toward mine. We shake hands ... by spontaneous and perfect cooperative action. Normally we do not notice the subtlety and amazing complexity of this coordinated "ritual" act .... Just as an aerial acrobat must ... posses (but not think about his) complete trust in his partner if the trick is to come off, so we who shake hands ... must have (but not think about) respect and trust.[40]

Politeness pervades all things, keeping them alive as they are. To conform to such politeness-as-ritual-of-the-cosmos is to perform the ritual of life. As such, li is the gist of all human virtues, the manifestation of, if not being synonymous with, *jen*, humanness. "Human life in its entirety finally appears as one vast, spontaneous and holy Rite: the community of man."[41] We may add that such "community of man" is the community that is the heaven and earth.

Jen (Humanness)

Jen is the "vital-originative intentionality (sheng i) of the universe, the "seed" of life, according to Che'ng I, the Neo-Confucian. As such, jen is at the kernel of everything, and is the core of *our* nature. A paralyzed hand is the hand of not-jen; jen is the vitality of our body and our mind.[42] Thus, although we have no medical irregularity within us, when we see a baby about to crawl into a well, we feel sudden pain in us. Such alarmed pain is the manifestation of our commiserative heart, said *Mencius* (2A6). To know how this connection between the baby and our heart obtains, and where it came from, is to know jen, said Yang Shih (1053–1135).[43]

Such feeling of commiseration manifested in our action is virtue. To know jen and to act jen is to be at one with everything. This is the cosmic-mystical rationale of morality, freely and everywhere operative. This is why Confucius could afford to describe jen as the ideal human and freely changed his description of what jen is, sometimes as so difficult that even the sage only approximated it, sometimes so near to us that as soon as I desire jen, it is here, sometimes as being loyal, sometimes as being agile *(min)* and quick in our deeds. This is also why Mencius equated jen the humane with the human *(jen)*, and even with ideal government described as "jen-government," where the emperor shares *(t'ung)* with his people what he desires, extending *(t'ui)* what he loves toward them.[44]

Other key notions come to mind. *I* is both situational appropriateness and personal uprightness. *Li* is both the principle to which things should conform and their inner grains to which they naturally tend. *Ming* is both what is endowed by nature and the givens in the situation to be observed. There are others such as *liang chih* (innate knowledge) and *ching* (earnestness).

But enough has been said about a crucial point in Chinese mysticism. All these notions manifest the basic merging point, the mystical unprovable rapport, between the personal and the cosmic, on which Confucianism bases itself.

Conclusion

Needless to say, the above sweeping survey of various aspects of Chinese culture in their mystical atmosphere is just that, a "sweeping survey," more illustrative than exhaustive. But even from such a rough survey, we can see that, unlikely as it is, the Chinese pragmatic approach to life and the world has a mystical a priori, a mystical point of rapport between the human subject and the cosmic whole.

On this mystical basis, Confucianism developed spatially, adding one excellence on to another, striving to capture and to expand that cosmic humanism, as schematized in the *Great Learning*. No wonder Confucianism developed in the sphere of morality and politics, even bureaucracy.

In contrast, Taoism developed temporally, following the trend and letting go of things as they are, as illustrated in the *I Ching*. And so Taoism naturally deepened itself into the arts and religion, even occult.

Confucianism is the outward flourishing, and Taoism is the inner composure, of our meditative contacts with the Heaven and earth. Every Chinese is Confucian in his daily pursuits and Taoist at heart in his personal depths. Every Chinese is a pragmatic mystic.

Notes

1. Walter T. Stace, *The Teachings of the Mystics* (New York: The New American Library, 1969), 10. Incidentally, my campaign for "extrovertive mysticism" counters Stace's preference for introvertive mysticism. Also, someone may demür to my carping so much at thinkers in the West. I beg him/her to see how entirely Western such a critical stance of mine is. Thinkers in China, much less the mystics there, seldom argue in this manner.

2. Steven T. Katz, ed., *Mysticism and Philosophical Analysis* (New York: Oxford University Pres, 1978), 22–74.

3. Paul Tillich, *Systematic Theology*, vol. 1 (Chicago: University of Chicago Press, 1951), 9.

4. Ibid., 16–17.

5. Ibid., 140.

6. Ibid., 172.

7. Ibid., 213.

8. Ibid., 44.

9. Ibid., 140.

10. In many ways these aspects of Chinese culture are presented in the Chinese Classics, as they appear in the following English versions: James Legge, trans., *The Chinese Classics*, 5 vols. (reprint; Hong Kong: Hong Kong University Press, 1960); James Legge, trans., Ch'u Chai and Weinberg Chai, ed., *I Ching: Book of Changes* (New Hyde Park, N.Y.: University Books, 964); Richard Wilhelm and Cary F. Baynes, trans., *The I Ching: Book of Changes* (Princeton: Princeton University Press, 1967); Evan Morgan, trans., *Tao: The Great Luminant: Essays from Huai Nan Tzu* (New York: Paragon Book Reprint Co., 1969); Roger T. Ames, *The Art of Rulership: A Study in Ancient Chinese Political Thought* (Honolulu: University of Hawaii Press, 1983), esp. 165–209, translation from the *Huai Nan Tzu*, chapter 9; the *Chou Li*, the *Ch'un Ch'iu Fan Lu, Lu Lan Shih Erh Chi, Chou Pi Suan Ching, Lo Shu Chen Yao Tu, Shan Hai Ching, Tzu Ch T'ung Chien*. Cf. Hiraoka, Teikichi, *E Nanji ni Arawareta Ki no Kenkya* (Tokyo: Liso Sha, 1968); Philip Rawson and Laszlo Legeza, *Tao: The Chinese Philosophy of Time and Change* (London: Thames and Hudson, 1973); Laszlo Legeza, *Tao Magic: The Chinese Art of the Occult* (New York: Pantheon Books, 1975); Khigh Alx Dhiegh, *The Eleventh Wing: An Exposition of the Dynamics of I Ching for Now,* A Delta Book (New York: Dell Publishing Co., 1973); Raymond Van Over, trans., *Chinese Mystics* (New York: Harper & Row, 1973); etc.

11. *Nei Ching; I Yuan; Chen Chiu Chia I Ching; Pao P'u Tzu; Pen Ts'ao Ching; Shang Han Lun; Pen Ts'ao Kang Mu; Shan Hai Ching;* Ted J. Kaptchuk, O. M. D., *The West That Has No Weaver: Understanding Chinese Medicine* (New York: Herder & Herder, 1971); William R. Morse, *Chinese Medicine* (New York: Paul B. Hoeber, 1934); Hoshio Manaka, M.D. and Ian A. Urquhart, Ph.D., *The Layman's Guide to Acupuncture* (New York and Tokyo: Weatherhill, 1973); Al Chung-liang Huang, *Embrace Tiger, Return to Mountain— The Essence of T'ai Chi* (Moab, Utah: Real People Press, 1973); Ma Chi-jen, *Chung Kuo Hi'i Kung Hsueh* (Shan Hsi: K'e Hsueh Chi Shu Ch'u-pan She, 1983).

12. The famous Seven Books belong here: *Sun Tzu, Wu Tzu, Ssu-ma Fa, Wei Liao Tzu, Li Wei Kung Wen Ta, Huang Shih Kung San Lueh, Liu T'aoi.* Cf. *Shih-i Chia Chu Sun Tzu* (Shanghai: Ku-chi Ch'u-pan She, 1978).

13. *Wen Hsin Taio Lung* is the most famous document in this sphere. See also Lin Yutang, *The Chinese Theory of Art: Translations from the Masters of Chinese Art* (New York: H. Putnam's Sons, 1967). There is a beautiful description of the cosmology of Chinese language, poetry, painting, and music (similar to that of the *I Ching* and *Tao Te Ching*) by Francois Cheng in his *Chinese Poetic Writing* (Bloomington: Indiana University Press, 1982), x–xiv, 1–22.

14. Popular religious Taoism, palmistry, alchemy, etc.

15. However, Chinese mysticism differs from the Buddhist kind. Buddhism denies differences in objects, denying even the denial of differences—hence, nonmonism. Buddhist nonmonism is the denial denied. Chinese nonmonism is acceptance of both the denial and the acceptance.

16. Cf. Stephen E. Toulmin, Ronald W. Hepburn, and Alasdair MacIntyre, *Metaphysical Beliefs* (London: SCM Press, Ltd., 1957).

17. See n. 2.

18. Michael Polanyi, *The Tacit Dimension* (Garden City, N.Y.: Doubleday & Co., 1967), 10. Cf. his *The Study of Man* (Chicago: University of Chicago Press, 1963); *Personal Knowledge* (New York: Harper Torchbooks, 1962); Marjorie Grene, ed., *Knowing and Being* (Chicago: University of Chicago Press, 1969); with Harry Prosch, *Meaning* (Chicago: University of Chicago Press, 1975).

19. For more details, see n. 10.

20. The chart is from Legeza, *Tao Magic*, 11.

21. C. A. S. Williams, *Outlines of Chinese Symbolism and Art Motives* (New York: Dover Publications, Inc., 1976), 104–5; cf. 280, 380.

22. Ibid., 29. For more details, see n. 10.

23. For more details, see n. 11.

24. For more details, see Legeza, *Tao Magic*, 10–17.

25. Fukunago, Mitsuji, *Soshi* (Tokyo: Asahi Shinbun Sha, 1966), vol. 2, 345–50; Hsu, Fu-kuan, *Chung Kuo I-shu Ching-shen* (Taipei: Hsueh-sheng Shuchu, 1976).

26. Diels, Fragments, No. 45; Burnet, Fragment, No. 71; Philip Wheelwright, *Heraclitus* (New York: Atheneum, 1971), 58–59; Fragment, No. 42.

27. For more details, see Lu K'uan Yu, *Taoist Yoga: Alchemy and Immortality* (New York: Samuel Weiser, Inc., 1975).

28. For more details, see Legeza, *Tao Magic*, 30 and *Tao*, 55–71.

29. Roger T. Ames, *Rulership*, 29–64.

30. Wing-Tsit Chan, *Sourcebook in Chinese Philosophy* (Princeton: Princeton University Press, 1963) 79.

31. Ibid., 3.

32. Ibid., 89–90.

33. James Legge, trans., *Sacred Books of China* (New York: Dover Publications, Inc. 1962) Vol. 2, 3.

34. Cf. W. A. C. H. Dobson, *A Dictionary of the Chinese Particles* (Toronto: University of Toronto Press, 1976), 152. I modified some of his translations. He has more examples.

35. Max Picard, *The World of Silence* (South Bend, Ind.: Regnery/Gateway, Inc., 1952), 56.

36. As quoted in E. R. Dodds, *The Greeks and the Irrational* (Berkeley: The University of California Press, 1964), 1.

37. Chan, *Sourcebook*, 108–114.

38. Confucius, *Analects*, 12/11, 17, and 13/3 are the most representative of this line of thinking.

39. *Chu Tzu Yu Lei*, 87, 95.

40. Herbert Fingarette, *Confucius—the Secular as Sacred* (New York: Harper Torchbooks, 1972), 9–10.

41. Ibid., 17. This, his concluding statement, is almost a verbatim quotation from the *Book of Rites*.

42. *I Shu*, 2, 3, 11, 18.

43. *Yang Kui-shan Hsien-sheng Chi*, 11,26.

44. *Analects*, 6/22, 7/30, 12/2–3, 14/4, 6. *Mencius*, 1A7, 1B5, 2A1, 7B16. For more details, see Yamaguchi, Satsujo, *Jin no Kenkyu* (Tokyo: Iwanami Shoten, 1937); Takeuchi, Teruo, *Jin no Kogi no Kenkyu* (Tokyo: Meiji Shoin, 1964).

9

Mysticism in a Buddhism Context

LESLIE KAWAMURA

TRADITIONALLY, scholars have discussed mysticism according to the four marks outlined by William James in his Gifford Lectures (1901–2) delivered in Edinburgh. According to James, experiences that are characterized by *ineffability, noetic quality, transiency,* and *passivity* are mystical experiences That is, mystical experiences are said to be ineffable, because they cannot be described; *of noetic quality,* because one gains knowledge through such experiences; *transient,* because these experiences do not last long; and finally, *passive,* because these experiences occur to the one who is experiencing them.[1]

Although these marks may be useful in discussing "mystical experiences," they are not unique to "mystical experience" alone, because they are attributes commonly found in ordinary experiences. If such attributes were to define a particular experience as a "mystical," then all experiences comprising the world of ordinary people (in contrast to the so-called world of the mystics) would have to be "mystical." To state it another way, if those attributes that are common to ordinary experiences are the attributes that define an experience as "mystical," then the so-called "mystical experience" would be none other than a normal experience and so there would be nothing special about it. But that should not cause us great concern, for life is itself a *wonder* and to that degree always *mystical.* Moreover, because every experience in life is characterized by this *wonder,* there is no need to particularize an experience as mystical.[2] In other words, there is no mystical experience, i.e., there is no mysticism-as-such[3] and still only mysticism prevails. At first glance, this may impress one as paradoxical; yet writers of mysticism, such as Robert S. Ellwood, state:

Not all these experiences may be mystical by a strict definition. Yet however, it is defined, it does not appear that mysticism is a rare and exotic experience limited to monasteries or to a few favored souls. Rather, it is common to ordinary streets and houses, a part of ordinary life if not of every life.[4]

Thus, it is clear that a mystical experience, whatever it may be, need not be extraordinary and can be, indeed, a common phenomenon. However, we should also keep in mind that common phenomena do not arise in a vacuum. Whatever experience may constitute one's encounter with life, it should be remembered that those experiences always take place within a certain cultural and historical context. Consequently, the experiences that constitute human existences are not abstract concepts— i.e., some static kind of thing—that can be discussed outside of an historical/cultural context. According to Gershom Scholem, there is a need to understand the

> ...contextual qualifications concerning mysticism. Mysticism ... historically comprises more than the experience, even though this experience lies at its root. No thing as mysticism in the abstract exists .... But the perception that mysticism has a history and historical context is very important, particularly because mysticism's claim to contact with transhistorical reality has often so fascinated observers (as well as mystics themselves) that some ignore the importance of its historical context.[5]

It seems reasonable, therefore, to accept that the term "mysticism" is meaningful only insofar as it is used in a conventional sense *(vyavahara)*, that is, within an historical context. It follows, then, that to have any significance at all within a Buddhism context, *mysticism* must necessarily be paradoxical, because no human experience can be reduced to any kind of a static, substantive, reality-as-such. This chapter will explain how, within a Buddhism context, "mysticism" does not refer to a special kind of reality, beyond the ordinary world, actual or psychological, but that it does refer to the world of ordinary human existence.

Historical Context

There has been a tendency among scholars of religious pluralism to be somewhat uncritical when they discuss Buddhism within a religious pluralistic context. Consequently, before a discussion on *mysticism* within a Buddhism context can be properly addressed, it is important to understand the term *Buddhism* in its proper context.[6]

We often find scholars discussing Buddhism as if it were a single, consistent system. However, an investigation into different Buddhist systems will show immediately that all of the systems that developed throughout its history are uniquely different and to that extent, it is only within the context of a specific Buddhist system that certain claims can be made. Yet, however much these systems vary, insofar as they are called "Buddhist systems," there must be a common element among them.

When one looks into the life of Siddhartha Gotama (ca. 550 B.C.E.), the historical figure to whom all credit for the historical basis of Buddhism is given, one finds that the salient feature that made Siddhartha different from all of this contemporaries was his realization of reality through an awakening experience *(bodhi)* that he gained in his meditative practice *(dhyana* or *samadhi)*. Although this is not the place to go into great details about Siddhartha's life, it may be helpful to discuss, in summary, the significance of Siddhartha's realization and its content. By so doing, we will be able to establish what it is that constitutes a system as a Buddhist one[7] and thus understand how all ordinary human experiences are mystical and thus are in no need to be singled out and particularized as "mystical."

The religio/philosophical milieu into which Siddhartha was born and in which he lived was a Brahmanical one. At this time, the people of India believed that human beings were born and reborn through a cycle of existences *(samsara)* owing to the kind of life they led in their previous lives *(karma)*. In order to overcome the thrust of karmic tendencies, a person had to endeavor to improve one's lot, but this could take many lifetimes. It took myriad lives to be born into human existence, and it would take as many lives to be born in heaven among the gods *(devas)*. These repeated births and deaths were possible because at the base of and underlying each individual existence was *atman* (a self), eternal and unchanging *(nitya)*, which when released *(mutki)* from its various rounds of existences *(gati)* would become one with the Absolute *(brahman)*.

Siddhartha's reason for giving up his aristocratic existence as the prince of the Sakya clan and renouncing the world was to find a way by which he would overcome his rounds of existences. He went from teacher to teacher, but none could tell him how to overcome old age, sickness, and death.

He went through the most severe ascetic practice of self-mortification in the hope that a solution would be found. Finally, determined to find an answer to his quest, he sat under a Sal tree vowing not to move until he had found his answer. In deep concentration (*dhyana* or *samadhi*), he realized *(bodhi)* that life's suffering *(duhkha)*—i.e., old age, sickness, and death—was inextricably linked with the manner in which human existence itself was constituted. He came to the realization:

1. that all of life's frustrations *(duhkha)* originate from human desire *(trsna)*, i.e., the desire to transform transiency *(nitya)* into something permanent;
2. that everything is without substantial basis *(an-atman)*, because transiency means an uninterrupted flow, like a stream; and
3. that equanimity *(santa)* results from the extinction of the frustration *(nirvana)*.

This realization *(bodhi)* which must be the common element of all schools of Buddhism and which has been characterized as the realization of transiency, nonsubstantiality, and of dissatisfaction or frustration, has been transmitted as the three characteristics of reality *(dharmoddana)*.[8] But what is the reason for accepting transiency, nonsubstantiality, and so on as the defining characteristics of reality?

Usually, transiency is understood in respect to something existing. That is, something is accepted first to exist and then that which has been accepted to exist is believed to undergo change. However, "transiency" cannot be understood in this manner within a Buddhism context, for there, it is the reverse. Within Buddhism, it is the dynamics of change, i.e., transiency, that gives the basis for existence, and for that matter, nonexistence. This principle is known as *pratityasamutpada* (interdependency) and *pratityasamutpada* is a shorthand way of stating that it is the dynamics of change, i.e., transience, that brings a thing into existence or takes it out of existence. Consequently, it would not be accurate to speak about something undergoing change; on the contrary, it can be said only that there is "a coming into being" and " a going out of being"—i.e., an arising and an extinction. This fluctuation between arising and falling (extinction) is the basis for the occurrence of existence or nonexistence and gives both existence and nonexistence their open possibilities *(sunyata)*.[9]

Siddhartha's realization that all forms of existences and nonexistences arose interdependently *(pratityasamutpada)* further reinforced his realization that transiency, nonsubstantiality, dissatisfaction, bliss, and open possibilities that comprised and characterized reality were not communicable to others simply because those who wanted "essence" in existence would be not only unable to, but would also be unwilling to, see the reality *(satya)* of those characteristics. Even though there is nothing mystical or transcendental about those characteristics of reality, in view of the discussion above, we would have to conclude that when reality is seen in that manner by a person who has awakened to (realized) *pratityasamutpada*, that person has a different perspective of reality than the person who desires permanency. That is, given the transient nature of existence and nonexistence, for the awakened person, it would be difficult, and even mystical, to see reality as some unchanging, substantial existence. This means that, for a person who has awakened *(buddha)* to the reality of relativity *(pratityasamutpada)*, there can be no underlying, unchanging substance that makes reality what it is. Reality simply *is*. It is not something. This realization *(pratityasamutpada)* must be fundamental to any form of Buddhism, and, consequently, any system that claims to be a Buddhist system must be based upon this principle.

The First Turning of the Wheel of Dharma

Siddhartha, who realized the reality of *pratityasamutpada* and thus became an awakened one *(buddha)*, did not venture out immediately to expound the contents of his awakening experience. Instead, he sat quietly at the place of his awakening, reflected over the steps that led him to the awakening experience, and enjoyed fully the impact of the experience *(dharma)*. During this period of sitting, reflecting, and savoring, he must have thought about with whom this experience could be shared. And at the same time, he must have thought about the futility of trying to explain this experience to some other person. He thought it futile, because in all probabilities no one in the world who is tormented by self-love and pride would comprehend transiency and would accept the nonsubstantiality of one's own existence.[10]

In spite of this initial hesitation,[11] it is well known that Siddhartha did, indeed, go to Sarnath where he sought out and met the five ascetics who were his former colleagues and to whom he shared his awakening experience. This act of sharing his experience is known as the "First Turning the Wheel of Dharma" *(dharma-cakra-pravartana)* and is related as the doctrine of the four aspects of reality *(catvary arya-satyani):*

> (1) frustration; (2) its cause; (3) the cessation of its cause; and (4) the path leading to a heightened awareness—as seen by an awakened person.[12]

Along with this message of the "four aspects of reality" is the equally important message of the "middle path" *(madhyama-pratipad)* which is the message that the extreme views of nihilism and eternalism, existence and nonexistence, etc. must be avoided if one wishes to overcome the thrust of *duhkha* (pain, suffering, frustration, dissatisfaction). *Duhkha* is not a concept, although it takes language to point to it. *Duhkha* is the dynamics of existence itself which defies and is beyond any linguistic definition. The point behind Buddhist practice is to see (realize) *duhkha*—that is, when *duhkha* is explained in the Buddhist texts, one understands that therein *duhkha* is not some pain or frustration that can be scrutinized. To the degree that pain or frustration remains a concept and not a reality experienced by a particular individual, to that degree there is no "practice of Buddhism" for that individual.

According to the Buddhist way of seeing life, human existence is like a locus—a focal point from which and to which all forms of forces radiate and converge. This is the meaning of *pratityasamutpada* (interrelated co-arising) and the manner in which any individual sees one's "place," "position," or "locus" is created and determined by this process that comprises one's historicity. In the words of John V. Alpcznyski:

> All human experience of reality is conditioned by the form of indwelling in which it is actualized. By dwelling in their cultural frameworks, individuals are enabled to make the accustomed natural integrations of daily living or of specialized theoretical disciplines insofar as they tacitly rely on the assumptions of these frameworks. When these integrations are expressed linguistically

they become instances of explicit knowledge justifiable or falsifiable (at least potentially) within the given form of indwelling.[13]

Because individuals cherish their own egocentric demands, they are unwilling to give up their fixed beliefs or what has been referred to above as "the given form of indwelling." So long as one insists on staying with "the given form of indwelling" and tries to rationalize the authenticity of one's own biased view, there will be no resolution to one's frustration and anxieties.

Although the above discussion may paint a rather bleak picture of human existence, it need not be so negative provided the arising of incidents such as anxiety are seen in a different light. That is, for example, without anxiety one could never realize the feeling of relief from anxiety. This is not to say that unless one is anxious one cannot be happy, for happiness could occur without a person being anxious. But for a Buddhist, the way of understanding happiness would be the same as the way of understanding anxiety. That is, without anxiety, there could be no happiness and without happiness there could be no anxiety.

Because joy or happiness is itself transitory and without substantial existence, it is bound to perish. When joy or happiness perishes, then one will become troubled over the loss of joy or happiness. When one is troubled over the loss of joy or happiness, then one will find oneself in a dissatisfied state. When one is truly immersed in, not only simply acknowledging, dissatisfaction then, for the first time, one will make a "turn about" (paravrtti) in one's life.

The oscillation between joy and dissatisfaction and between dissatisfaction and joy is none other than transiency that underpins our existence. The same idea has been vividly described by a Japanese haiku poet, Issa,[14] who lived during the Tokugawa Period (1600–1867), a period in which the bourgeois culture[15] flourished. Among his many Haiku poems are these:

> Y-no-na-ka-waji-go-ku-no ue-no ha-na-mika-na
> Ah, worldly existence is the viewing of cherry blossoms amidst the infernal of hell.
> Sa-ku ha-na-no na-ka-niu-go-me-ku shu-jo ka-na
> Sentient beings squirm amidst the blooming flowers.[16]

The simplistic presentation of the haiku poem in fifteen syllables makes it difficult to translate these poems with all of their implications; however, Issa is describing the human situation which is very much like viewing cherry blossoms in the spring. When one is in the midst of myriads of cherry blossoms, one can easily forget the very ground of transiency on which one is standing. Therefore, Issa says that our life is like viewing cherry blossoms in the midst of the infernal of hell. When one realizes that one's existence is like the dew drops that fall from the cherry blossoms, then even in the midst of the beauty of the flowers—i.e., the enjoyments of life—one faces anxiety attacks; therefore, sentient beings are squirming with anxiety and frustration even though they are in the midst of the beauty of life.

It has already been pointed out that not until one is immersed in anxiety that the reality—not the concept—of dissatisfaction becomes of concern. When dissatisfaction is a real concern, then just as one must do something when one's hair is on fire,[17] one will do something about the frustration. When one is actively engaged in the removal of anxiety or frustration, one is actively living Buddhism.

Buddhist Interpretation of Mysticism

For a Buddhist, life is the dynamics of change, i.e., the very fact of transiency, and owing to this transiency there arises all of life's potentialities. These potentialities are best described as our biological and metabolical operations that constitutes life. These biological and metabolical processes will operate in-the-manner-that-they-will irrespective of how I or you wish them to function although, because human being are total systems, i.e., mentally and physically inseparable, how we think will affect how the bodily functions take place, and how the bodily functions take place will affect how we think.

When we attempt to define or to interpret life, we must realize that the definition or interpretation of life that we derive is nothing more than a mental construct in regard to an ongoing process that cannot be reduced to some idea or thing. This means that the "lived experience" is not what is expressible in words, although we constantly communicate what we think through words.[18] This act of communication has become such a commonplace phenomenon with us that there is little room to negate the belief that if any idea can be communicated then it must have a reality behind it or that it must refer to some concrete reality. In the words of Robert S. Ellwood:

> We must then be aware of the basic characteristics of mysticism as it is experienced . . . . Someone simply had a feeling of really *experiencing* something. Understandably, this led us to believe that something must have been there to be experienced. When we see a cat with our physical senses, we naturally assume a cat is there; when we experience something extraordinary with the mind, we likewise tend to assume something more than the mind, at least the ordinary mind, is there.[19]

Because of the principle of belief in the reality of "essence," we begin to think that if an experience is "ineffable" then it possesses a "mystical something." That is, we believe that a certain "unusual experience" is beyond expression and therefore has something "mystical" about it, i.e., it is a mystical experience. On the other hand, a certain "usual" experience can be expressed and therefore has something "nonmystical" about it, i.e., it is an ordinary experience. But the fact of the matter is this: an experience (i.e., reality) is "ineffable" by virtue of the fact that what is real needs no explanation. All human experiences, whether usual or unusual, are beyond expressions, not because they have some mystical element about them, but simply because the reality of experience is within the domain of change, i.e, it is transient. Wherein transiency prevails, therein, there is "no thing-as-such" *(sunyata)* to which language can refer. What *is* simply *is;* it is not *a* this or *a* that.

When one examines how experiences take place, one will quickly realize that all experiences are uniquely individualistic insofar as whatever constitutes experiences is felt (known) within the confines of a particular process comprising an individual, and not outside a particular individual, i.e., among individuals in general.[20] This means that I cannot experience what you are experiencing, and you cannot experience what I am experiencing. Even if I were to claim that I understand what you are experiencing, all that I am saying by such a statement is that I *am going through* and *am aware of* a situation in which I believe I understand the experience through which you are going. At best, any claim for a comprehension of another person's experience is a statement about one's own belief about that experience and is not a statement about the reality of another person's mind. Because I have been ingrained to think that another can have the same idea as the one I hold, the suggestion that someone *could know* what I am thinking is sufficient condition to trigger a belief in me that someone *does indeed know* what I am thinking and vice versa. But, as pointed out above, experience is a very private and an individualistic event; consequently, we may know by awakening to how an experience is constituted and learn through that experience, but we cannot convey the constituents of our knowledge through language to another with any degree of certainty. What we convey are categories of interpretations which, according to Robert Ellwood, explains "mysticism":

> ... mysticism is more a category of interpretation than experience, though the interpretation may be immediate with the experience. Its interpretation may seem self-evident as the experience occurs and may even deepen the experience for the experiencer. In other words, the explanation becomes inseparable from the experience.[21]

What Ellwood fails to see here is that explanations do not constitute the reality of an experience, although explanations are the real linguistic means by which the categories (i.e., ideas) of an experience can be transmitted others. How the others interpret this "interpretation" of mine will depend, not only on how comprehensive my linguistic presentation is, but also on what comprises the historicity of the recipient individual. Whether that individual will interpret my activities—mental, physical, and linguistic—as "mystical" or not will be determined not by whether my activities *are* in fact "mystical" but on whether the interpreter in fact *interprets* them to be so. How anyone who understands that reality is just simply interdependently originating and thus simply ordinary could interpret any event as "mystical" is, of course, simply mysterious.

Conclusion

Finally we can express what mysticism means within a Buddhism context. Mysticism is the wonder that comprises individual, ordinary, and everyday existence, made up of and making up one's experience owing to activities that are interdependently arising. In short, it is the interdependently arising activities that are interpreted as personal existence *(passivity)* through which one becomes aware of one's self and one's constructed world *(noetic)*, in spite of the very dynamic, transforming process constituting a reality *(transiency)* that is in need of no expression *(ineffable)*.

Notes

1. For a full discussion on several approaches to mysticism, see Robert S. Ellwood, Jr., *Mysticism and Religion* (Englewood Cliffs, N.J.: Prentice-Hall, Inc., 1980), 1–26. He discussed James's view in particular under what he calls "psychological and sociological approaches." See page 15.

2. According to Robert M. Gimello, "All mystical experiences, like all experiences generally, have specific structures, and these are neither fortuitous nor *sui generis*. Rather they are given to the experiences, at their very inception, by concepts, beliefs, values, and expectations already operative in the mystic's mind . . . . Were one to subtract from mystical experience the beliefs which mystics hold to be therein confirmed and instantiated, all that would be left would be mere hedonic tone, a pattern of psychosomatic or neural impulse signifying nothing. Surely such mindlessness is not what those who take the matter seriously mean by mystical experience." See his paper, "Mysticism in its Contexts," in *Mysticism and Religious Traditions*, ed. N. Katz (New York: Oxford University Press, 1983), 62.

3. In the words of Gershon Scholem: "There is no mysticism as such, there is only the mysticism of a particular religious system, Christian, Islamic, Jewish mysticism and so on." This view has been expressed by Hans H. Penner in his Article, "The Mystical Illusion" in Katz, *Mysticism and Religious Traditions*, 92.

4. Ibid., 2.

5. Ibid., 21.

6. The need to study mysticism in a particular context has been clearly stated by Hans H. Penner. See his article, "The Mystical Illusion" in N. Katz, *Mysticism and Religious Traditions*, 94, where he states: "When we review the history of texts on mysticism we observe that at the beginning mysticism was defined in rather straightforward terms. With the passage of time and greater attention to the subject, things have changed; now mysticism eludes all attempts at definition. The various attempts at defining mysticism clearly suggest that there simply is no identifiable subject for study. The reaction to this state of affairs has been the development of studies in particular mysticism."

7. The Buddhist systems that developed in later years in India, China, Tibet, Burma, Sri Lanka, Japan, and other Asian countries were considered to be "Buddhist" systems, however different one may have been from another, because each one accepted the principle of interdependent co-origination *(pratityasamutpada)*. The principle of interdependent co-origination is the foundation upon which Siddhartha's awakening experience is based.

8. By adding bliss *(ananda)*, which arises when dissatisfaction is overcome, four defining characteristics of reality are defined. By adding open-ness *(sunyata)*, reality can be seen in view of five defining characteristics. Regardless of whether three, four, or five characteristics are counted, it is not that there are three separate realities—the one reality of interdependent co-origination *(pratityasamutpada)* is seen from these different perspectives.

9. The term *sunyata* has been translated "emptiness," but here I have used the term "open possibilities" instead in order to connote that at any instant life is open to an infinite source of possibilities. This means that the very fact of transiency and nonsubstantiality offers no basis for the occurrence or fulfillment of anticipated expectations; consequently, momentariness implies a pregnant open-ness.

10. Gadjin M. Nagao, *Bukkyo no Genryu (The Origin of Buddhism)*, Asahi Culture Book Series No. 39 (Osaka: Osaka Shoseki, 1984), 74. In this book, G. Nagao gives an excellent historical introduction to the life of Siddhartha, the development of Buddhism in India, and its basic doctrines.

11. This hesitation to express the contents of his "awakening" experience is know as *tusnimbhava* (silence) of the Buddha. For further explanation of this idea, see Troy Wilson Organ, "The Silence of the Buddha" in *Philosophy East and West* (Honolulu: The University of Hawaii), vol. IV, No. 2, July 1954, 125–40. See also Gadjin M. Gagao's excellent article, "The Silence of the Buddha and Its Madhyamic Interpretation" in *Indogaku Bukkyogaku Ronso (Studies in Indology and Buddhology)*, ed. Gadjin M. Nagao and Josho Nozawa (Kyoto: Hozokan, 1955), 137–51.

12. Our encounters with books on Buddhism always refer to *catvary aryasatyani* as the "Four Noble Truths." However, I have rendered this into English by the phrase, four aspects of reality as seen by an awakened person, because it would be self-contradictory for a Buddhist system to claim "truth," given the presuppositions of transiency, nonsubstantiality, open-ness, etc. Further, to consider:

1. *duhkha* (transitoriness, open-ness, nonsubstantiality as the basis of our pain, suffering, frustration, and dissatisfaction);
2. *samudaya* (the inertia of *duhkha*, i.e, its occurrence as the cause and condition for its occurrence and nonoccurrence);
3. *nirodha* (extinguish, quieting); and
4. *marga* (the path as the "going toward and the enactment of" the supreme attainment, i.e., liberation)

as "noble truths" seems to miss the mark.

13. See John V. Apcznyski, "Mysticism and Epistemology," *Studies in Religion* 14, no. 2 (April 1985), 201.

14. For a description of Issa's life, see Y. Fujikawa, *Shinsen Myokonin Den* (Tokyo: Daizo Shuppan Sha, 1971), 161–62.

15. For a good summary of this period in Japanese history that covers all of the forms of art, drama, poetry and prose, philosophy, and culture, see H. Paul Varley, *Japanese Culture: A Short History* (New York: Praeger Publisher, 1973), chapter 7.

16. The original Japanese Haiku appears in R. Fujikawa, *Shinsen*, 180.

17. The analogy of one's clothes or hair on fire has been explained by Nagarjuna in his text, *A Letter to a Friend (Suhrllekha)*. See my *Golden Zephyr* (Emeryville, Calif.: Dharma Publishing, 1975), 77.

18. It is interesting to note that everything that constitutes our knowledge can be expressed in linguistic form. Any idea or thing that cannot be expressed through some linguistic form is incomprehensible and hence not knowable. This seems to indicate that "knowledge" and "experience" need not be coincidental; in fact, from a Buddhist Logic perspective, language and experience

are as far apart from each other as water and oil. It is for this reason that what is expressed in language is always moments removed from the experience itself. See B. Matilal, "Mysticism and Reality: Ineffability" in *Journal of Indian Philosophy* 3, nos. 3/4 (September/December, 1975), 215–52. On page 228 he states:"a mystic usually tries to explain or express in language, at a later time, *what* he has experienced rather than the *experience itself.* The supposedly paradoxiality, in that case, would apply to the 'content' of the mystical experience, i.e., the Ultimate Reality."

19. See Ellwood, *Mysticism and Religion*, 21.

20. We can recall the claim of Humpty Dumpty in Lewis Carroll's *Alice's Adventures Through the Looking Glass*, ed. S. H. Goodacre (Berkeley: University of California Press, 1983), 66, when he said to Alice: "When *I* use a word, . . . it means just what I choose it to mean—neither more or less."

21. See Ellwood, *Mysticism and Religion*, 29.

10

Hindu Mysticism

BINA GUPTA and CHRISTOPHER LUCAS

Hɪɴᴅᴜ thought is striking for its richness and sheer diversity. Encompassed within a tradition extending over the span of nearly two and a half millennia is a broad array of religious and philosophical perspectives. Virtually all major viewpoints and doctrines are represented in its canonical works, not to mention the addenda of succeeding centuries.[1] Yet it is the very scope of Hinduism that makes its exegesis so challenging.

Even the word "Hindu" is indeterminate—most probably a derivation from the Persian Sindhu, from which the Indus River derives its modern name. Among the ancient Greeks and Persians, Hinduism reportedly stood for "something found on the banks of the river Indus and beyond, but we know not what."[2] Likewise today, its signification often seems to depend on exclusion: what remains once Jainism, Sikhism, Islam, and a host of lesser sects are omitted.

Speculative thought within Hinduism similarly resists simple categorization. Nor do its several schools lend themselves to tidy chronological arrangement. Compounding the problem of rendering an intelligible account of Hindu mysticism *per se* is the infrequency with which traditional literature yields first-hand reports of mystical experience from Indian sages themselves. Hence, the influence of mysticism at work must be inferred for the most part, based on the ways in which certain teachings can be shown to be congenial to, or congruent with, a mystical interpretation, and, most especially by the language through which they find expression. Whether they are literally mystical artifacts, i.e., the intellectual products of mystical consciousness, remains problematic. Nonetheless, the powerful and formative impress of mysticism upon Hindu theology and philosophy is unmistakable. What can be said with confidence is

273

that mysticism is integral to the Hindu worldview, and without appreciation for the former, no adequate understanding of the latter seems possible.

Mysticism and Mystery

A further difficulty in treating Hindu mysticism arises from the "mystery-mongering" so common to more general discussions of mysticism as a whole. Even a casual perusal of the world's voluminous literature on the subject indicates how varied and incommensurable are its characterizations. Conventionally religious in tone and typical of Western writers is Dean Inge's formulation: "The attempt to realize the presence of the living God in the soul and in nature, or, more generally, the attempt to realize, in thought and in feeling, the imminence of the temporal in the eternal, and of the eternal in the temporal."[3] More rhapsodical still is a description supplied by Canon Rebeti: "A supernatural and passive attraction of the soul, towards God, coming from an internal illumination and an internal fire."[4]

Although both interpretations share the virtue of highlighting or underscoring important aspects of mystical consciousness, at best they fit only a religious, theistic viewpoint. Thereby excluded or ignored are all nontheistic manifestations, as found prominently within the Hindu, Buddhist, Taoist, and Jainist traditions. Equally egregious is the excessive clinical detachment evident among Western commentators—oftentimes to the point where mysticism's inherent spirituality and emotional coloration are lost sight of altogether.

Countless examples might be adduced. J. H. Leuba, for instance, defines "mystical" as "any experience taken by the experiencer to be a contact . . . or union of the self with a larger-than-self, be it called the World Spirit, God, the Absolute, or otherwise."[5] Elsewhere, mysticism is taken to be "the final outcome of a congenital desire for knowledge . . . which lies beyond the sphere of things and of the senses by which things are perceived."[6] According to William Clark, mysticism is "the subjective experience of a person who has what he tells others is a direct apprehension of some cosmic power or force greater than himself."[7] A peculiarly sociological perspective is offered by W. K. Wright who construes the mystical state as "the endeavor to secure consciousness of the presence of the agency through which (or through Whom) the conservation of socially recognized values is sought.[8]

But if Occidental definitions leave much to be desired (either because they tie mysticism too closely to religious theism or fix upon extraneous features), comparable efforts by non-Western apologists often fare no better. Precisely because their formulae tend to be all-inclusive, they fail to delimit or mark off anything in particular. Not atypical is a tendency to equate "mysticism" with practically any sort of spirituality. The Indian scholar Mahendranath Sircar, for example, interchangeably deploys such varied locations as "creativeness of spirit," "creative spontaneity," "inspired intuition," "communion with the center of life" and "expansive consciousness" to serve the purpose.[9]

Hardly less obscure is S. N. Dasgupta's subsumption of what he terms popular, sacrificial, devotional, meditative, and philosophical contemplation under a single ill-defined rubric. Mysticism, as he describes it, is "a belief or a view," "an active, formative, creative, elevating and enabling principle of life," "a spiritual grasp of the aims and problems of life . . . more real and ultimate than is possible by mere reason," or, finally, "a gradual ascent in the scale of spiritual values, experience and . . . ideals."[10]

The Many as One

For present purposes, it is assumed that not all forms of spirituality are necessarily mystical in nature. Further, as Hindu mysticism illustrates, the connection between mysticism and conventional religious piety may be far more adventitious than is generally acknowledged. Nor does mysticism have anything whatsoever to do with paranormal phenomena, with the occult, with miracles, visions, or the hearing of voices. Mystical consciousness bears only superficial resemblance to altered states of the mind artificially induced by means of drugs or other extraordinary expedients. Still less should mysticism be construed as something vague, misty, obscure, or "mysterious"—though, admittedly, imprecise usage of the term and its etymological derivation in English from "mystery" (Greek: *mystikos*) undoubtedly have encouraged such connotations.

On the face of it, however, the teachings of mystical contemplatives the world over (Hindus included) do seem mysterious. They defy everyday common experience, posing an affront to all reason and logic: that masked by phenomenal appearances lies a deeper noumenal reality inaccessible through ordinary sense perception or cognition; that space and time are somehow illusory; that underlying the apparent multiplicity of things in the world is a more ultimate and fundamental unity within which all distinctions and separations are dissolved; that sensible particulars derive from Infinite Being in and of itself; that individual consciousness or one's sense of self-identify might be likened to a single drop of water drawn from the vast, limitless ocean of pure consciousness, and so on.

That mystics characteristically resort to paradox and high antinomic language to capture their experience hardly helps matters. One of the most conspicuous features of mystical discourse in fact is its obscurantism, its reliance upon poetical allusion and metaphor to express what defenders insist is indescribable in nonfigurative terms. The Hindu case is particularly illustrative. Assertions to the effect that Ultimate Reality is both existent and nonexistent, for example, or that Oneness is simultaneously a "fullness" and an absolute "emptiness" are likely to strain credulity. The temptation among skeptics, understandably, is to dismiss mysticism as a psychological curiosity undeserving of serious attention, or to conclude that mystical states are aberrations most properly falling within the purview of psychopathology.

Before turning to the topic of Hindu mysticism specifically, it may prove helpful to sketch out briefly a more generous and certainly more philosophically interesting perspective. The account begins by distinguishing mystical consciousness in and of itself from whatever *ex post facto* descriptions are tendered by those who have had a mystical experience. It is significant perhaps that the language of mystics describing what they have apprehended is remarkably similar in all times and places, including India. So fundamental a uniformity would seem to lend credence to the supposition that mystical experience is basically the same, whenever and wherever it occurs.

When divergencies arise, or so the argument has it, they stem from conflicting *interpretations* of the experience's "true" meaning and significance. Each explanation draws upon beliefs, assumptions, and religious affiliations extant in a given cultural milieu, to which the interpreter (often unconsciously) gives assent. Thus, the theist is likely to report a religious theophany. The Buddhist is more apt to experience the attainment of *nirvana* resulting from the extinction of all striving and desire. The Hindu intuits Brahman; a Taoist discerns the "Way" or

"Path" undergirding existence; a Christian mystic achieves ecstatic union with the Godhead, and so forth. From the mystical experience, it has been observed, "each brings back confirmation of his own creed. Having acquired his or her own convictions through habitation or in other ways as do non-mystics, the contemplative carries theological beliefs and assumptions to the mystical experience; he or she does not derive them from that state of consciousness.[11]

It follows, accordingly, that explanations of mystical states, however interesting in their own right, could be said to be largely epiphenomenal. Variations as they surface are to be accounted for by culturally contingent interpretations imposed upon what would otherwise be recognizable as a common and universal phenomenon. Thus, in the Hindu tradition, instances of mystical experience quite likely helped shape certain doctrines and dogmas associated with Advaita and Dvaita Vedanta. In turn, these conditioned the interpretation of subsequent experiences, often in the process giving rise to elaborate intellectual structures of sufficient complexity as to overshadow and even obscure their genesis. Much the same interactive dynamic is likely to be found typical of other cultural and intellectual traditions as well.

Divested of all particularistic explanations—as afforded by the several Vedanta schools of Hinduism—the mystical state is still essentially the same, appearances to the contrary notwithstanding. What the mystic reports, apart from whatever account is offered after the fact, is an immediate, ineffable intuition. The apprehension in each case is of a unity pervading all things, a fundamental Oneness underlying the world's apparent multiplicity. Encapsulated at the core of mystical consciousness, in other words, is a single, irreducible precept—the Many are One.

How the unity behind plurality is experienced differs perhaps only as a matter of degree. Sometimes, it is said, the mystic gazes out through the senses and discerns within the ostensibly separate and distinct things of the world a luminescent and pervasive Oneness. Ordinary sense perceptions and common-sense distinctions among different objects remain. Yet paradoxically, though seen to be different, they are simultaneously grasped as being identical, as "all the same." In other cases, mystical awareness turns inward, as it were, uncovering a unity at the bottom of the self. Within the depths of the soul, consciousness finds its identity with Universal Consciousness.

Of the two "levels" or "directions" of mystical experience, introvertive or inward-looking consciousness seems the more complete. In the latter case, all perceptions are said to have disappeared. The entire content of normal waking conscious-ness—all images, sensations, feelings, emotions, and thoughts—is obliterated entirely. There is only infinite nothingness, as Hindu mystics, in common with their counterparts elsewhere, confirm. Consciousness remains, but it is not consciousness of anything. Since the subject-object distinction itself is tran-scended, strictly speaking, there cannot be a union or merging of the apprehended with Oneness. Rather, the mystical state is the One.[12]

Questions of the veracity and possible import of what mystics affirm aside, it is sufficient to note that in Hindu mysticism both "outward" and "inward" experiences tend to be bound to-gether in quite distinctive fashion. Moreover, in no other tradi-tion perhaps is the idea of the Many as One accorded so many dramatic expressions or exemplified in quite as many different ways, extending from the formative stages of Hindu thought in remote 'antiquity down to modern times. From both a literary and philosophical point of view, how the general theme is devel-oped is as illuminating as it is instructive.

Especially noteworthy is the basic continuity of Hindu mysti-cism. The concept of a supreme transcendent One was clearly prefigured in the most ancient records of the Veda. The same mystic theme was greatly expanded upon and developed in later Upanisadic literature. Thereafter, as different Vedantist schools of thought evolved over the course of centuries, the essence or core of mysticism found expression in both religious and theis-tic doctrines and in nondualistic philosophic forms. Finally, as the affirmations of more than a few modern exemplars attest, the mystical viewpoint continues to flourish in contemporary Hindu philosophy as well, advancing an intuition that is as old as recorded human thought itself. For illustrative purposes, the discussion following is confined to examples of mystical thought as expressed in the Vedas and Upanisads, including the *Bhagavad Gita;* the Advaita Vedanta of the classical thinker, Samkara; and by a modern twentieth-century philosopher, Sri Aurobindo.

Vedic Monism

The Vedas are the earliest authoritative scriptures or "revela-tions" (*sruti*, literally "what is heard") of Hinduism. Comprising three major compilations, they include the *Rigveda,* *Samaveda,* and the *Yajurveda,* to which has been added a fourth work, the *Atharvaveda.* Each consists of four parts: poetic invocations or hymns *(mantras);* ritualistic works known as the *Brahmanas;* the so-called "forest" narratives or *Aranyakas;* and the Upanisads, or philosophical-religious treatises. These last are also known as "Vedanta" or "end of the Vedas," signifying their position at the conclusion of the corpus. A still later work, the *Bhagavad Gita,* is sometimes included in the canon as well.

Lack of reliable chronological data, archaic script, indifference on the part of the ancient Aryo-Indians toward personal histories, and later textual interpolations all combine to make it impossible to fix the authorship and dates of origin of the original Vedas with much confidence. Generally, it is held they were first reduced to writing at some point prior to the fourth century B.C. or thereabouts. The Upanisads and the *Gita* almost certainly date to a later period, sometime after the middle of the third century preceding the common era.

Traditional scholarship professes to find an orderly progression in Vedic religious thought, evolving from naive animism in prehistoric times into anthropomorphic polytheism, continuing through henotheism to transcendent monotheism, and culminating finally in a full-blown immanent monism.[13] A more cautious interpretation acknowledges the possibility of concurrent lines of development, including polytheism, religious monotheism, and philosophical monism.[14] Alternatively, one might consider "levels" of thought within pre-Upanisadic literature, in a sense suggested by the difference between popular religiosity, on the one hand, and the more conceptually sophisticated if abstruse speculation of philosophers and theologians on the other.

Judging from the mantras of the *Rigveda* and the *Brahamanas* in any event, the polytheism of the earliest Indo-Aryans was thoroughly liturgical and ritualistic in character. Vedic hymns are replete with invocations to personifications of the many forces of nature and to those spirits thought to animate natural phenomena. Prominent among them were *Varuna,* the sky divinity or being, the sun-being *Mitra,* and *Agni,* the divine power of fire. Although the myriad luminous devas (*div* "to shine") of the Aryan pantheon appear to have enjoyed more or less coordinate influence, at various times certain beings were elevated to preeminence, chief among them *Varuna, Visnu, Indra, Prajapati,* and *Visavakarman.*

Even at a comparatively early point, however, there appears to have been an impetus toward consolidation and a reduction of the many spirits to a single force or power. "What is but one, wise people call by different names," affirms a passage from the Rigveda. "The worshipful divinity of the devas is one" (I.164.46). Likewise in the *Satapatha Brahmana*, an anonymous writer declares there are thirty-three deities in all, and *Prajapati* is the thirty-fourth, "including them all." Here and elsewhere is the intimation of a single divinity encompassing all others. At the same time contained in the *Atharvaveda* are numerous suggestions of a Supreme Source standing behind all the spirits and, indeed, underlying all forces of nature. The goddess *Aditi* (the "Boundless"), for example, is identified with earth, air, sky, and all the inhabitants thereof, permeating "whatever has been or whatever shall be." Clearly foreshadowed is a notion more fully laid out in the Upanisads: that immanent in nature yet inexplicably transcending it is some more ultimate, supra-sensible principle or person.

The famous "Creation Hymn" of the *Rigveda* affords the quintessential illustration of an emergent monism:

> There was then neither what is, nor what is not, there was no sky, nor the heaven which is beyond. What covered? Where is it, and in whose shelter? Was the water the deep abyss (in which it lay)?

> There was no death, hence there was nothing immortal. There was no light (distinction between night and day). That One Breathed by itself without breath, other than It there has been nothing.

> Who then knows, who has declared it here, from whence was brought this creation? The gods came later than this creation, who then knows when It arose?

> He from whom this creation arose, whether he made it or did not make it, the highest seer in the highest heaven, he ... knows, or does ... not know?[15]

The author concludes on a note of agnosticism, declaring that even the wisest sage imaginable cannot penetrate or comprehend the mystery of creation. The ultimate origin of things is at once enigmatic and unfathomable.

Anticipated in the creation hymn is a question to which later Hindu thought gave quite different answers: Is "that one" *(tad ekam)* a creator-god, separate and apart from the world? Or is it a more impersonal dynamism, a power of infinite energy and force within and behind the world? This, in turn, gave rise to further questions. If the world was born of a creator, was that being also the parent of the other spirits? Is the One a personal deity reigning over all subordinate divinities and to whom all are subservient? Or, alternatively, are the many devas simply manifestations of a Unitary Supreme, the *Purusa* (or, roughly, "Supreme Person")? And from whence came God?

On the other side, if the creative One is uncreated being, how could Brahman (that which "grows" or "bursts forth") spontaneously issue of itself ex nihilo? Further, if the First Cause of the universe unfolded of itself, then how did the world originate? What is the true nature of that unity beyond which nothing exists and within which is comprehended all that does exist? Finally, what is required of a seeker of true wisdom in securing knowledge of Brahman?

There is nothing of course to suggest that all such cosmogonic questions were explicitly formulated in quite this way, nor, certainly, were they treated in abstract philosophical terms so long as an essentially mythological world view held sway. What is significant, nevertheless, is the extent to which Indian thought had begun to explore the possibilities of a monistic explanation of reality. Already apparent are intimations of that Oneness affirmed in mystical consciousness, a conception of which would be more fully worked out in the Upanisads.

The Upanisad Brahman as Absolute

The term "Upanisad" combines a rood *sad,* meaning "to sit" with *upa,* "near" or "close" and *ni,* "devoted" or "attentive." Hence, over the course of time the word came to imply secret or esoteric teachings imparted by a master to a select, inner circle of students. Taken together, the Upanisads constitute the concluding portion of the Vedas, both chronologically and in terms of the development of ideas initially advanced in the *Brahamanas* and in *Aranyaka* literature. Differing considerably from one another in length, style, authorship, and periods of composition, the collections contain a number of disparate ideas—the interpretation, systematization, and attempted reconciliation of which were to preoccupy commentators in succeeding centuries. Doctrinal conflicts in turn gave rise to many competing schools of Vedantic thought, all sharing a common inspiration.

Some Upanisadic teachings are treated at length and emphasized through reiteration. Others are only partially realized or alluded to in a terse elliptical style. Still others are treated even more cursorily or only hinted at in various passages. Although the literature embodies no one single system of thought, its spirit is distinctly more speculative and philosophic, compared with the ritualistic discourses of earlier works. What holds the Upanisads together, conferring upon them a certain broad thematic unity, is consideration of certain recurrent issues to which their authors returned time and time again: the meaning and purpose of life, the necessary means of salvation whereby release is secured from the vicissitudes of earthly existence, and, finally, the nature of Brahman, the eternal force within which all opposites, being and nonbeing, life and death, good and evil, are ultimately reconciled.

Two correlative terms—Brahman and *Atman*—frame what rightly may be considered the single most important "great teaching" *(mahavakya)* or fundamental precept of Upanisadic thought: the oneness of the two. Brahman (variously referred to as "Absolute," "Supreme," or "Divine Power") is Ultimate Reality. *Atman* is "breath," the innermost and essential aspect of the self, the soul. The former is the origin of the outer, objective world; the latter is the locus of the internal world, of subjective consciousness. Yet both are the same—which is to say, the two are synonymous, each alike signifying the abiding source of all that is, the whole of nature, humankind included. That which represents the eternal element within the individual is identical with, and not distinguishable from, the transcendent power or sacred principle that pervades and sustains the cosmos. Herein lies the heart of mystical consciousness.

So audacious an equation, almost breath-taking in its inclusiveness, could hardly have sprung full-blown all at one. And in fact the germinal seed of the idea appears to have been forecast in much earlier Vedic literature. A classic illustration of the tendency to equate the macrocosmic with the microcosmic is found in the *Purusasukta* of the *Rigveda* where different objects in the universe are represented as aspects of a giant person, *Purusa* ("Supreme Being"). Here the deity is described as having a thousand eyes, a thousand heads, and a thousand feet. When *Purusa* was divided," the poet asks, "How many portions did they make? What do they call his mouth, his arms? What do

they call his thighs and feet?" (X.90). From his mind was gener-
ated the moon, comes the answer; the sun issued from an eye;
lesser gods were born of his mouth and breath; the sky was
fashioned from his head; the earth came from his feet, and so on.

Some take the spirit of the poem to express a precursive sort of
pantheism. More fundamentally perhaps, it reflects an attempt
(albeit in naive and literal terms) to discern an overarching correspondence between the individual and the world. A grand par-
allelism is set out, such that the attributes or features of the
individual person are mirrored by those of larger forces at work
in the natural world. Contrariwise, objects in nature are viewed
as "corresponding" to human powers. Thus, for every characteristic of human physiognomy, a counterpart is found, writ large,
as it were, in the universe—and *vice-versa.* In modern parlance,
a universal whole is comprehended within the human particular
and the particular within the universal, thereby opening up the
possibility of their merger or unification.

The Vedic habit of viewing the entire world as a cosmic person, according to one interpretation at least, was to lead eventually to the transformation of the notion of soul as a physic
principle into a world-soul or principle. *Atman,* the innermost
self of the individual, becomes the cosmic self or oversoul.
Meanwhile, a convergent line of thought had begun tracing all
of the phenomenal world back to a single source, Brahman. Ultimately, the two independent strains came together, at which
point the idea of Brahman as the primal cause of the universe
came to be identified with the internal essence of human consciousness itself, *atman.* The physical or material world, in
other words, was held to be reducible to the self; and, in turn,
the soul or self was understood to be not different from the
world. A fusion of these two themes, viz., the indistinguishabil-
ity of the noumenal self-from the phenomenal not-self or other,
and the oneness of the world's multiplicity, thereby made explicit a mystical teaching only implicit or incompletely articulated in pre-Upanisadic thought.[16]

The identification of Brahman and *Atman* as one was a subtle
idea, not easily expressible in ordinary language. Authors who
sought to explain its meaning frequently depended on simple
metaphors and concrete illustrations to convey a highly abstract
conception. The typical expedient was to represent a discourse
in which a sage or teacher is shown instructing a student. The
Chandogya Upanisad, for example, recounts the story of a
young boy by the name of Svetaketu whose father had sent him

away at the age of twelve to pursue his studies. The son remained with his teacher until the age of twenty-four, when he returned home obviously proud of his newly acquired learning. The father, Uddalaka, taking note of the young man's spiritual arrogance, questions him as to whether he has sought "that instruction by which one hears what cannot be heard, perceives what cannot be perceived, and by which one knows what cannot be known" (VI.1).[17] The son, confused, demands an explanation.

Uddalaka resorts to a series of analogies to make his point. By "understanding" a lump of clay, all that is clay can be known, since any differences are only apparent, based upon "words alone," while the reality is clay, he affirms. Knowing a nugget of gold permits one to comprehend all that is gold, since a given nugget represents only an instance or manifestation of gold itself. Likewise, a pair of scissors fashioned from iron is but a "modification" of the reality of iron. Uddalaka directs Svetaketu to break open the fruit of a *nyagrodha* (banyan) tree. The young man finds only seeds. His father has him divide one of them, whereupon Svetaketu, asked to explain what remains, confesses he sees nothing at all.

Uddalaka's response is that "from the very essence in the seed which you cannot see" issues the vast banyan tree. The son still fails to comprehend. The father then orders Svetaketu to place salt in a water container. The next day he cannot detect it, for the salt has dissolved. Told to sip the water from various sides of the container, the young man tastes the salt, acknowledging "it was there all the time though it could not be seen." So too, Uddalaka concludes, though one may not directly perceive Being *(Sat)* in and of itself, it is nonetheless present in everything.

The father's teaching is hammered home. "In the beginning," he explains, "there was existence, One only, without a second. Some say that in the beginning there was nonexistence only, and that out of that the universe was born." But how could existence proceed out of nonexistence? Uddalaka asks. "It was Being along that existed in the beginning, one only without a second" (V.2.2). Out of the One was projected the universe; Being entered into every thing. "That which is the . . . essence—in it all that exists has itself. That is truth. That is the Self. And that, Svetaketu, that thou art" (V.10.3).

Just as juice reduced by bees to honey cannot know from what flowering plant or tree it derived, or as rivers flowing into the sea lose their formerly separate identities, all things "when they are merged in that one Existence whether in dreamless sleep or in death, know nothing of their past or present state, because of the ignorance enveloping them—know not that they are merged in Pure Being and that from Pure Being they came" (VI, 9, 1–4; V1, 10, 1–3). Once again there follows the phrase: "that thou art" *(tat tvam asi).*

From Brahman derives the reality of the outer world; from *Atman,* the ground of the soul, derives the reality of the inner world, and both realities are one and the same. Throughout the Upanisads the theme is repeated. In the *Katha Upanisad,* for example, it is written: "When the soul, identified with the body and dwelling in it, is torn away from the body, is freed from it, what then remains? This, verily, is That" (II.ii.4). Later in the same work the author declares, "There is One who is the eternal Reality among non-eternal objects, the one truly conscious Entity among conscious objects, and Who though non-dual, fulfills the desires of many. Eternal peace belongs to the wise, who perceive It within themselves" (II.ii.13).

The same basic point is made in the *Tattiriya Upanisad* where the author declares, "There is a space within the heart, in it lies [Brahman] consisting of mind, immortal and luminous" (I.vi.1). From the *Brhadaranyaka Upanisad:* "That self is indeed Brahman; it is also identified with the intellect, the mind, and the vital breath, with the eyes and ears, with earth, water, air, and . . . fire and with what is other than fire, with desire and with absence of desire, with anger and with absence of anger, with righteousness and unrighteousness, with all—it is identified" (IV.iv.5).

A recurrent theme enunciated by all the worlds' great mystics reverberates throughout the Upanisadic canon. Behind all separate things and selves is one Universal Reality—unchanging, eternal, indivisible. Brahman is indescribable, limitless, timeless, beyond all matters of personality and gender, beyond good and evil, above all moral distinctions, all differences and attributes, all desires and ends, all causes and effects. And *Atman,* the Universal Soul, is Brahman.

Brahman is immanent in all things, manifest in them, expressed in and through them, yet not to be identified with them. "*Atman,*" declares the *Katha Upanisad,* "is the very soul of *dharma* (i.e., the inner foundation of all beings, without which they cannot exist)" (I.ii.13). More poetic is another declaration from the same source: "It is the sun dwelling in the right heavens. It is the air dwelling in the mid-region. It is the fire dwelling on earth. It is the guest dwelling in the house. It resides in men, in the gods, in truth, in the heavens. It is born in the water, on earth, in the sacrifice, on the mountains. It is Truth and Greatness" (II.ii.2). In the *Tattiriya Upanisad* the notion is similarly expressed that Brahman is truth, knowledge, and the infinite. From the One all else issues—air, fire, water, the earth, plants, food, humankind.

A lengthy repetitive incantation from the *Mundaka Upanisad* presses the idea that everything in the world comes from Brahman, and Brahman is immanent in all things. "As the spider sends forth and draws in its thread," declares the poet, "as plants grow on the earth, as hair grows on the head and the body of a living person—so does everything in the universe arise from the Imperishable" (I.i.7). "As from a blazing fire, sparks essentially akin to it fly forth by the thousand, so . . . do various beings come forth from the imperishable Brahman, and until It again return" (II.i.1). The self-luminous and formless, uncreated Brahman exists both within and without; it dwells radiantly in "the cave of the heart" (II.ii.2).

Strongly reminiscent of the antinomies of mystical language everywhere, a succession of passages in the *Brhadaranyaka Upanisad* once again labors to emphasize how Brahman is in the world but not of it. "He [who] is your Self, the Inner Controller, the Immortal," according to the text, "inhabits water, yet is within water, whom water does not know, whose body water is, and who controls water from within." The recitation continues, substituting fire, sky, air, heaven, sun, the moon, stars, darkness, and light and "all beings" for "water" in the same formula (III.vii.4–14).

Paradoxical descriptions of Brahman abound in the Upanisads, but they are not all unlike characterizations offered by Buddhist, Christian, or other sorts of mystics. As the *Katha Upanisad* puts it, the ultimate is "soundless, intangible, formless, undecaying, and likewise tasteless, eternal, and odorless . . . that which is, is without beginning and end" (I.iii.15). "Through never stirring," the *Isa Upanisad* observes, it "is swifter than the mind. The [senses] cannot reach It, for It moves ever in front. Though standing still, It overtakes others who are running" (4). Brahman, declares the *Aitareya Upanisad*, "is all . . . gods . . . the five great elements . . . . It is the origin of whatever breathes. All this is guided by Consciousness [which is] Brahman" (11.1.3). Again, from the *Katha Upanisad*: "It does not die. It has not sprung from anything; nothing has sprung from It. Birthless, eternal, everlasting and ancient," Brahman is "smaller than the small, greater than the great . . . hidden in the hearts of all living creatures." It is "bodiless, vast, all-pervading." Ultimate Reality, "though sitting still, travels far; though lying down, It goes everywhere" (I.ii.20–22).

Reflected also in varying degrees by the various Upanisads is what must already have become a settled conviction of the Hindu worldview, namely, that the individual human soul is subject to an indefinite succession of incarnations. Thus, according to the doctrine of *karma*, the condition of the individual in one life is determined by that soul's conduct in a previous existence. In turn, one's actions in this life inevitably affect the soul's state of being in its next incarnation, and so on. Further, it was held, release from the bondage of material existence—salvation—could be secured only by conquering—*ahamkara*—"egoism," and by transcending *samsara*, preoccupation with worldly appearances. Opinion differed as to how final deliverance might be attained. Where there was consensus, it was that the supreme goal or task was achieving immediate knowledge of Brahman.

Such a knowledge, according to the Upanisads, is neither sensory nor cognitive. It is, Uddalaka reminds his son in the *Chandogya*, that "by which one hears what cannot be heard, perceives what cannot be perceived, and by which one knows what cannot be known" (VI.1). Equally cryptic is a passage in the *Kena Upanisad* where the elusive uniqueness of mystical comprehension is contrasted with ordinary discursive knowledge: "He who says that he knows it does not really know it, and he who says that he does not know it, verily, knows it" (I.4). Yet to it, once attained, attaches an absolute certitude. If conveyed by one who does not truly understand *Atman* "It is not easily comprehended," observes the *Katha Upanisad*. "But when It is taught by him who has become one with *Atman*, there can remain no more doubt about It." This knowledge, the passage concludes emphatically, is "not to be known through argument." It "cannot be attached by reasoning" (I.ii.7–8).

The *Kena Upanisad* offers a recitation setting forth the object of mystical understanding: "That which cannot be expressed by speech, but by which speech is expressed—that alone know as Brahman" (I.5). For the word "speech" in succeeding passages other terms are substituted—mind, eye, ear, breath, and so forth—but otherwise the text repeats itself. Brahman is both apprehended and nonapprehended by the mind, perceived and not perceived, heart yet not heard, and so on. In the *Katha*

Upanisad, the narrator implies that the conscious phenomenal self cannot secure a knowledge of the absolute through volition alone. Understanding cannot be compelled. *Atman* "cannot be attained by the study of the Vedas, or by intellect, or by much study of sacred works. It is attained by him alone whom It chooses" (I.iii.9–11). True comprehension is beyond the senses, beyond mind (II.iii.7). Again, the One "is not an object of vision; no one beholds It with the eye" (II.iii.9). To those who would seek the ultimate Oneness in the material things of the world, the author advises that the effort is foredoomed to failure: "As rainwater falling on a mountain peak runs down the rocks in all directions, even so one who sees only the attributes [i.e., confuses phenomenal manifestations with their underlying reality] . . . runs after them in all directions" (II.i.14).

According to the *Mundaka Upanisad,* there are two forms of knowledge, lower and higher. The former pertains to the world and is obtained through the pursuit of such discursive subjects as grammar, astronomy, phonetics, rituals, and the like. Only the higher knowledge leads to "that by which the imperishable Brahman is attained" (I.i.5). When it is secured, "the wise behold everywhere Brahman which otherwise cannot be seen or seized, which has not root or attributes . . . which is imperishable and the source of all" (I.i.6).

Upanisadic sages differed as to what was needed for attaining knowledge of Brahman. In the *Aitareya Upanisad,* "self-knowledge" is represented as the culmination of a twofold process. The aim of the first or preliminary stage of learning is to strip away the superimposition *(adhyasa)* of "names and forms" upon Brahman. Secondly, the apparent nature of any and all attributes is revealed by their refutation *(apavada),* thereby revealing the sole reality of the One. Ultimately, by a process of negation, all that can be said of it is "not this, not this" *(Brhadaranyaka,* II.iii.6).

The *Katha Upanisad* advises "concentration on the self" as a requirement (I.ii.12). The aim or purpose, by constant meditation, is to free the intellect from all doubt and questioning. Elsewhere, in the *Kena Upanisad,* the sincere seeker after mystical truth is advised to meditate inwardly, all the while imagining that the mind has already apprehended the luminous Brahman and has become submerged in it. "The mind, as it were, goes to Brahman. The seeker . . . communes with it intimately again and again. This should be the volition of one's mind," it is suggested (IV.5). Again, in the *Mundaka,* the sage denies that *Atman* can be apprehended by study or through the intellect. Penance and renunciation, ascetic self-denial and rigorous discipline—these are useful means but are only penultimate to a larger end. They have no intrinsic importance by themselves.

So, too, in the *Brhadaranyaka*, the progression to a knowledge of the One is described in stages. Having abandoned all desire for progeny, wealth, material possessions, and earthly passions, a religious seeker after truth first becomes absorbed in spiritual studies. Then comes meditation. Only after one "is done with both meditativeness and non-meditativeness," does the contemplative seeker after the highest type of wisdom become "a knower of Brahman" (III.v.1). Calmness of mind and "meditation" *(upasana)* are cited in the *Chandogya Upanisad* as two prerequisites to *jnana*, or knowledge of the One. The aspirant must learn to discriminate between what is real and what is nonreal, to renounce the world, to concentrate upon controlling the mind and all the senses, at the same time cherishing an unwavering desire for liberation from appearances.

Whereas the *Prasna Upanisad* stresses austerity, faith, chastity, and purity as qualifications for the journey toward knowledge, in the *Svetasvatara Upanisad* a more detailed regimen is set forth. Body posture, proper breathing, concentrated meditation—all the elements of yoga are stressed. The goal—communion with "the Great Lord"—offers the aspirant salvation from "embodiment" in the world. Once "completely merged in Brahman," it is promised freedom from the ceaseless round of rebirth will be assured. All fetters fall away and "birth and death come to an end" (I.11).

The culmination of the quest for Brahman is variously characterized throughout the Upanisads as a state of utter serenity and indescribable bliss. As it is approached, the *Mandukya Upanisad* reveals, the mind enters upon something akin to a dreamless sleep *(susupti)* in which all plurality disappears. There is only pure, undifferentiated consciousness. The final state, *turiya* "is not that which is conscious of the inner [subjective] world, nor that which is conscious of the outer [objective] world, nor that which is consciousness of both, nor that which is a mass of consciousness. It is not simple consciousness nor is It unconsciousness," the author explains. "It is unperceived, unrelated, incomprehensible, uninferable, unthinkable and indescribable. The essence is . . . the cessation of all phenomena."

The passage concludes, "It is all peace, all bliss, and non-dual" (7).

There is no difficulty in discerning here a typical account of the state of unitary consciousness reported by mystics the world over. The apprehension of an ultimate oneness *(ekatva)* through "supra-consciousness," as a modern Indian writer puts its, yields a condition wherein "all ordinary experiences are submerged and dissolved in this great, infinite, limitless homogeneous experience."[18] All duality has vanished. The mind at last apprehends the whole. The experience is thus synoptic but undifferentiated, intuitive but not analytic, noetic but not discursive—it is a transcendence of all predictions, all negations and exclusions; it is the One.[19] Brahman is "foundational consciousness," as another modern interpreter phrases it, "the fundamental postulate of all knowledge. It holds the subjective and the objective world in a transcendental unity. It is the background of the empirical trinity of knowledge, knower and known. It is the indubitable ultimate . . . presupposed by all affirmations and negations, all positions and doubts and denials. It is self-luminous and self-proved."[20] One who knows Brahman becomes Brahman—this is the "ultimate teaching" of the Upanisads.

The *Bhagavad Gita*

The *Bhagavad Gita* surely ranks among the most important, best-known, and most widely read of all of India's philosophical classics. Here the theme of union with Brahman takes a distinctly different turn. Krsna, the divine being who manifests himself to the epic warrior Arjuna, is a theistic god, combining the personality of a popular folk hero with the powers of a Vedic *deva* of the sort associated with early hieratic ritualism. But the notion of an impersonal Absolute is not lacking either. "By Me," Krsna declares, "all this world is permeated, by Me whose form is unmanifest. All beings rest in Me; and I do not rest in them" (IX.4).[21] He adds, however, "And yet beings do not rest in Me . . . . Supporter of beings, and not resting in beings, is My Self, that causes beings to be" (IX.5). The implication is that God is immanent in all things, inviting a pantheistic interpretation. But there then follows a denial: God is likewise transcendent and separate from "all beings," a creator from whom everything "passes" in and out.

Subsequently, the deity promises to describe "the object of

knowledge" by which one attains freedom from death. God, the poet declares, is not "the beginningless Brahman" but the higher Divinity that rules over it (XIII.12). The Godhead is neither existent nor nonexistent. It has hands and feet on all sides, eyes, heads, and faces on all sides, hearing on all sides, and "it remains constantly enveloping all" (XIII.13). It has the semblance of the qualities of all the senses but is free from all the senses; it is unattached and yet sustains all; it is free from the "strands" of material nature, yet it experiences the material. Both "undivided in beings, and seemingly divided it remains; both as the supporter of beings it is to be known, and as their . . . originator" (XIII.16). Brahman is immovable, yet moving, afar and near, light of all light, "beyond darkness," beyond knowledge and the object of knowledge and what is to be reached by knowledge; it is "settled in the heart of all" (XIII.17). Yet the impersonal Brahman is somewhat subordinated to the personal God: God is the foundation of Brahman.

Salvation, or release from all empiric existence, the *Gita* teaches, can only be achieved through knowledge of this Supreme One. Preliminary to its acquisition are asceticism, inaction, detachment from the world, and conquest of all the desires of the flesh. More important still is *bhakti*, or "fervent devotion" and love of God, through which alone comes the soul's absorption within Him—an ecstatic extinction described variously as "perfection" or "the supreme state," *brahmanirvana*. It is the "highest station" to which having gone, one does not return, a state wherein neither the sun nor the moon nor fire illuminates (XV.6).

The famous eleventh chapter of the *Gita* is the epic poem's climax in which God reveals his supreme form to Arjuna. The divine manifestation is ordinarily invisible to the eye, unknowable to the mind—"I know all beings that have been, that are, and that shall be; but no one knows Me" (VII.26). But in a state of mystic consciousness, the whole world is revealed as united yet divided. The vision is "made up of all wonders" (XI.11). The Infinite Godhead is akin to the light of a thousand suns; his appearance is "without beginning, middle, or end, of infinite power" burning the entire universe with its radiance (XII.19). "By Me showing grace towards thee, Arjuna, this Supreme form has been manifested by My own mysterious power," God asserts. This form is "made up of splendor, universal, infinite, primal, of Mine, which has never been seen before by any other than thee" (XI.47). Thus, whereas some of the Upanisads appear to intimate that salvation comes from an intuitive apprehension of the absolute, the *Gita* on the other hand declares in unmistakable terms that release from rebirth comes not from the attainment of the impersonal Brahman (VIII.15–16), but from unswerving devotion to God (XI.54).

Advaita Vedanta

Later Hindu thought was to diverge in a number of quite different directions over the course of centuries, giving rise to the so-called "orthodox" *darsanas* or "viewpoints" of Vedanta. Principal among them were the Advaita, Visistadvaita, and Dvaita schools of thought. Others included Nyaya-Vaisesika, Purva-Mimamsa, Samkhya-Yoga, and many more. Vedanta philosophy generally first found systematic expression in the Upanisadic commentaries or "aphorisms" of Badarayana, sometimes known as Vyasa, the "Arranger" (ca. 200 B.C.). In point of fact, virtually all subsequent Vendatists took Badarayana's *sutras* as a point of departure, each of them in one way or another addressing the question of the relationship of the self or *Atman*, and Brahman.

As in the *Gita*, the impersonal Absolute or Brahman of certain of the Upanisads rather quickly underwent transformation, in the Dvaita school especially, becoming in monotheistic terms a personal Lord *(Isvara)* or God (Brahma) to whom was owed devotion and worship.[22] Advaita Vedanta, in contrast, sought to avoid the dualism implicit in the conception of a creator separate and apart from the created world. The "nondualism" or "monism" of Advaita proceeded from the effort to preserve a more rigorous and uncompromising identification of *Atman* and Brahman. More precisely, whereas "devotional" schools such as Saiva Siddhanta owed allegiance to a supreme deity, Advaita evolved a two-tiered synthesis in which it was possible at one level to conceive of a personal God, without abandoning at another level the more abstract notion of a transcendent and impersonal Oneness.

The most influential monistic interpretation of the Brahman—*Atman* equation was provided by the eighth-century Hindu theologian and philosopher Samkara (788–820), acknowledged as the fountainhead of Advaita Vedanta. For him, as for his many followers (Mandana Misra, Suresvara, Vacaspati, and others), the formula *tat tvam asi* ("that thou art") of the Upanisads meant strict numerical identity. Whatever exists is Brahman. There is only one Absolute, which is Self *(Atman)*, not to be confused with the empirical egos of individual selves in the phenomenal world. Hence, the highest spiritual task is realization of one's innermost identity with the whole of reality.

Samkara's argument opens with a frank acknowledgement of the world's existence. From the perspective of so-called "lower" knowledge *(aparavidya)*, which is logical, rational, and eminently communicable, empirical phenomena constitute a substantial and practical reality. One may speak as well, Samkara implies, of a "lower" Brahman or *Isvara* (Lord) as creator of the cosmos, through whose "potency" *(sakti)* sensible particulars manifest themselves. God puts forth his power and thereby creates the universe.

On the other hand, there is a second, "higher" knowledge *(paravidya)* which is thoroughly noncommunicable and "secret." It demands enormous powers of concentration and a habit of abstraction not easily attained by all. Whereas lower knowledge is competent only to lead to an understanding of empirical things, higher knowledge is capable of yielding insight into the inner core of things behind the divine artifice *(maya)* of the world. What the latter reveals is the sole reality of the *nirguna* Brahman or "Absolute Being" within which everything is comprehended. All else is illusory and insubstantial. From its larger perspective, Brahman is manifest as Pure Consciousness *(jnana-svarupa)* or Consciousness of the Pure Self *(svarupa-jnana)*. It is utterly devoid of all attributes *(nirguna)* and characteristics, all rational or intellectual categories *(nirvisesa)*.

At the risk of oversimplification, it remains valid to observe that for Samkara and later Advaitins, the purpose of meditative contemplation is to experience the sole reality of the One. With the realization of one's self as Brahman, the way out of bondage to the sensible world is indicated, leading to spiritual "emancipation" or release from appearances *(maya)*. The path to full mystic consciousness, or *samadhi*, is fraught with difficulty, Samkara implies. The goals must be one of stilling all actions and activity of the will. Only in a state of inward composure and quietude *(tyaga)* does the ego surrender itself, allowing the soul or spirit ultimately to find its identity with Brahman.

Of special interest is Samkara's description of the Absolute, differing only in minor particulars from descriptions supplied by other Hindu mystics. The Absolute, he claims, is neither identity nor difference, neither the one nor the many, neither unity nor diversity, but, rather, that which transcends all distinctions. Once again comes the claim that no differentiations are applicable. It is nonrelational and transphenomenal. Brahman is beyond all characterization, beyond thought *(acintya)*, nonconceptual, not an "object" in relation to a subject, nor an object possessing attributes. It is *sui generus*, not falling under any higher genus.

Pure Being, according to Samkara, possesses no qualities whatsoever. It is not related to anything else. It is without action. It cannot be sensed. It cannot be denoted by any word. The attempt to providing a positive description of Brahman, the One, only results in a connection of terms of relationships. But the Absolute has no identity in relation to differences. It is not a whole in relation to its parts, not a substance possessing attributes, not a cause in relation to effects. Hence, one can only fall back on the phrase, "It is not this, not that." It is unchanging, immutable, and absolutely abiding; it is supremely blissful, sublime, and elevating. The One is simply the "Truth of all truths" *(satyasya satyam)*.

A Modern Example

No abbreviated account of Hindu mysticism can hope to accommodate the myriad permutations of Advaita Vedantic thought in the post-Samkarite period, encompassing, for example, the so-called "qualified nondualism" or "identity-in-difference" school of the eleventh-century mystic Ramanuja and his disciples and the "dualist" Vedanta of the thirteenth-century figure Madhva. Still less is it possible to trace out the many, often convoluted paths taken by still other schools, including the Yoga of Patanjali and the theistic or atheistic strains of Samkhya, their importance to the history of Hindu mystical thought notwithstanding.

Insofar as all of the "orthodox" schools arose out of a common tradition thoroughly imbued with a mystical perspective, each in its own way responding to certain recurrent and fundamental challenges in Vedanta, any might be drawn upon to illustrate how Hindu speculative thought about mystical experience evolved over the span of time. Much the same might be said of the writing of India's leading modern thinkers: Ramakrishna, Sarvepalli Radhakrishnan, Bhagavan Das, Jiddu Krishamurti, and Rabindranath Tagore, among others. But for the most spirited restatement of the mystical outlook by a modern writer, no better illustration is afforded than that supplied by Sri Aurobindo Ghose (1872–1950) in his *magnum opus, The Life Divine.*[23]

Aurobindo begins by asserting that the earliest preoccupation of humankind, an impetus at once inevitable and ultimate, surviving all historical periods of skepticism and denial, is also the highest that thought can envisage. It manifests itself in the divination of Godhead, the impulse towards perfection, the search after pure Truth and unmixed bliss, the sense of a secret immortality. "Today," he observes, "we see a humanity satiated but not satisfied by victorious analysis of the externalities of Nature." These "persistent ideals" are "at once the contradiction of . . . normal experience and the affirmation of higher and deeper experiences" rare enough among individuals caught up in materialist preoccupations.[24]

The fulfillment of the human quest for transcendence, as Aurobindo describes it, requires extraordinary effort:

> To know, possess and be the divine being in an animal and egoistic consciousness, to convert our twilit or obscure physical mentality into the plenary supramental illumination, to build peace and a self-existent bliss where there is only a stress of transitory satisfactions besieged by physical pain and emotional suffering, to establish an infinite freedom in a world which presents itself as a group of mechanical necessities, to discover and realize the immortal mutation,—this is offered to us.[25]

In Aurobindo's view, Western materialism and Oriental idealism alike have proven themselves inadequate—the first because of narrowness and lack of spirituality, the second because of its other worldliness. Without entering upon the details of his "emergent evolutionism" as it is sometimes termed, he felt each had nevertheless paved the way for a higher synthesis. Science has served to clarify and discipline human thoughts, preparing the mind for its advance to another level of understanding. Indian metaphysics has had the role of conveying a partial truth, that reality embraces other dimensions besides that of phenomenal experience.

For Aurobindo, "the highest and most legitimate aim possible" for humankind on earth in its next stage of development is the manifestation of divine Spirit in the self and a realization of the reality of God "within and without." This constitutes the "life divine," the next and higher form of consciousness toward which humanity in its progressive self-enlargement is evolving. The eternal paradoxical truth of this vision, he writes, is "of a divine life in an animal body, an immortal aspiration of reality inhabiting a moral tenement, a single and universal consciousness representing itself in limited minds and divided egos, a transcendent, indefinable, timeless and spaceless Being who alone renders time and space and cosmos possible."[26]

In a lyrical passage anticipating the hope of today's so-called New Age visionaries in the West, Aurobindo claims all signs point to the emergence of a new spirituality out of the ashes of an age of arid intellectuality and rampant positivism. It is, he remarks, "an inner seeking and thinking, a new attempt to mystic experience, a groping after the inner self, a reawakening to some sense of the truth and power of the spirit."[27] The new consciousness in no way implies denial of the phenomenal world. Rather, as he summarizes it: "The universe is a self-creative process of a supreme Reality whose presence makes spirit the substance of things,—all things are there as the spirit's powers and means and forms of manifestation. An infinite existence, an infinite consciousness, and infinite force and will, an infinite delight of being is the Reality secret behind the appearances of the universe."[28]

In common with all mystics, Aurobindo holds that knowledge of Ultimate Reality transcends logic, reason, and empirical sensation. "The object of the mystic," he insists, "is self knowledge and God-knowledge, and that can only be arrived at by an inward and not by an outward gaze." It cannot be achieved through intellect or phenomenological analysis. Instead, "it must come by a direct vision or contact of the consciousness with the soul and body of Truth itself or through a knowledge of identity, by the self that becomes one with the self."[29] The Absolute, for Aurobindo, is "existence pure, indefinable, infinite, absolute."[30] It means "something greater than ourselves, greater than the cosmos which we live in, the supreme reality of that transcendent Being which we call God, something without which all that we see or are conscious of as existing'; . . . The Absolute is for us the Ineffable."[31]

Two successive movement of consciousness toward the One are distinguished. The first is inward. "What we discover within this secret part of ourselves is an inner being, a soul, an inner mind, an inner life, an inner subtle-physical entity" which widens itself, extending "into the consciousness of cosmic Mind." Secondly comes the "discovery of a vast static and silent self which we feel to be our real or our basic existence, the foundation of all else that we are." There may be even an "extinction" of the sense of self into "a Reality that is indefinable and inexpressible." This self, says Aurobindo, "is not only our own spiritual being but the true self of all others; it presents itself then as the underlying truth of cosmic existence."[32] Finally, "at the gates of the Transcendent stands that . . . perfect Spirit described in the Upanishads, luminous, pure, sustaining the world but inactive in it, without sinews of energy, without flaw of duality, without scar of division, unique, identical, free from all appearance of relation and of multiplicity—the pure Self of the Advaitins, the inactive Brahman, the transcendent Silence," which, he declares, is "the most powerful and convincing experience of which the human mind is capable."[33]

With Aurobindo, Hindu mysticism comes full circle, back to its roots in the distant past. Noticeably absent in his thinking is the pessimism, apathy, and resignation of which the mystic tradition stands (sometimes unjustly) accused. His is essentially an optimistic stance—too optimistic possibly—with its implicit suggestion of the inevitability of spiritual progress. Yet his faith in a new evolutionary consciousness is not altogether unappealing, given its responsiveness to both Western and Eastern spirituality. Aurobindo's vision serves admirably as an example of how robust and vigorous can be the presentation of a mystical point of view, inspired by a tradition that reaches far back to the very origins of recorded human thought.

Notes

1. See M. Hiriyanna, *Outlines of Indian Philosophy* (Bombay: George Allen and Unwin, 1973), 16.

2. Quoted in P. T. Raju, *Structural Depths of Indian Thought* (Albany: State University of New York Press, 1985), 2.

3. W. R. Inge, *Christian Mysticism* (London: Methuen & Company, 1899), 5.

4. J. Ribet, *La Mystique Divine* (Paris: Poussielgue, 1895), vol. I, 26.

5. J. H. Leuba, *The Psychology of Religious Mysticism* (New York: Harcourt, Brace & Company, 1925), 1.

6. A. B. Sharpe, *Mysticism: Its True Nature and Value* (1910), as quoted in Leuba, *Psychology of Religious Mysticism*, 2.

7. William H. Clark, *The Psychology of Religion* (New York: Macmillan, 1958), 263.

8. W. K. Wright, *A Student's Philosophy of Religion* (New York: Macmillan, 1938), 287.

9. Mahendranath Sircar, *Hindu Mysticism According to the Upanisads*

(London: Kegan Paul, Trench, Trubner & Company, 1934); reprinted New Delhi: Oriental Books Reprint Corporation, 1974, 1–5.

10. S. N. Dasgupta, *Hindu Mysticism* (New York: Frederick Ungar, 1967), viii–x.

11. G. A. Coe, "The sources of the Mystic Revelation," *Hibbert Journal* (1907–8), 360–67.1.

12. See Walter T. Stace, *Mysticism and Philosophy* (Philadelphia: J. B. Lippincott, 1960); his *Time and Eternity* (Princeton: Princeton University Press, 1952); *Religion and the Modern Mind* (Philadelphia: J. B. Lippincott, 1952); and *The Teachings of the Mystics* (New York: Mentor, 1960).

13. See Swami Prajananda, *Schools of Indian Philosophical Thought* (Calcutta: Firma K. L. Mukhopadhyay, 1973), 26–27.

14. Chandradhar Sharma, *A Critical Survey of Indian Philosophy* (New Delhi: Motilal Banarsidass, 1964), 16.

15. S. Radhakrishnan, *Indian Philosophy* (London: George Allen and Unwin, 1974), vol. I, 100–101. For commentary, consult Maurice Bloomfield, *The Religion of the Veda* (New York: B. P. Putnam and Sons, 1908), 235–39.

16. The exposition here follows Hiriyanna, Outlines, 56–57.

17. Direct quotations from the Upanisads are redactions, based on variant translations appearing in Juan Mascaro, trans., *The Upanishads* (New York: Viking Penguin, 1987); and Swami Nikhilananda, ed., *The Upanishads* (New York: Harper & Row, 1963), passim.

18. Dasgupta, *Hindu Mysticism*, 38–39.

19. G. Sundara Ramaiah, *A Philosophical Study of the Mysticism of Sankara* (Calcutta: K. P. Bagchi & Company, 1952), 2.

20. Sharma, *Critical Survey*, 28.

21. See Franklin Edgerton, trans. *The Bhagavad Gita* (New York: Harper & Row, 1964), 46. All subsequent quotations are adapted from Edgerton's translation. For commentary, consult M. N. Sircar, *Mysticism in the Bhagavad-Gita* (New Delhi: Classical Publications, 1977).

22. Consult B. N. Krishnamurti Sharma, *History of the Dvaita School of Vedanta and Its Literature* (Delhi: Motilal Banarsidass, 1981).

23. Sri Aurobindo, *The Life Divine* (New York: Greystone Press, 1949).

24. Ibid., 3.

25. Ibid., 4.

26. Ibid., 6.

27. Ibid., 772.

28. Ibid., 672.

29. Ibid., 788.

30. Ibid., 64.

31. Ibid., 339–40.

32. Ibid., 253–54.

33. Ibid., 23.

11

Islamic Mysticism

WILLIAM CHITTICK

> When you dance
> you leave the two worlds behind—
> The spiritual concert
> takes place beyond heaven and earth.
> —Rumi, *Kulliyyat-i Shams*, verse 13685

SOME time back a colleague introduced me to a student as the teacher of a course on Sufism. "Sufism?" she said, "That's dancing, isn't it?" I answered that although this is a common misperception, Sufism has little to do with dancing as such. Those Sufis who do dance, such as the famous "whirling dervishes," consider the practice a secondary and nonessential part of their spiritual way. What is more, the whole concept of "dancing" as understood by the great Sufi masters seems to have little to do with what most people understand by the term today. By way of introducing the reader to Islam's mystical dimension, let me expand on this answer in some detail.

Sufism has been found in some form or another, though perhaps not under this name, wherever a sizable community of Muslims has existed. (The word is thought to derive from Arabic *suf*, meaning "wool," from the coarse woolen garments that some of the early Muslim ascetics wore.) Within Islam, Sufism plays a role analogous to that of depth in space. The religion is not just a plane surface made up of dogma and ritual, but possesses an inner dimension that will be grasped to some degree or other by every Muslim who dedicates himself sincerely to God. The Islamic revelation, the *Koran*—which is considered to be the literal Word of God conveyed to the Prophet Muhammad by the angel Gabriel—is addressed to everyone, but not

299

everyone is expected to understand the full depth of its meaning. A religion can persuade its followers to accept certain tenets of faith and obey certain prescriptions, but it can hardly force them to understand the full significance of what they are being taught. Each individual must establish his own personal relationship with his religion and God. The profundity of the relationship will depend on his sincerity, intelligence, love, and aspiration.

Islam recognizes the existence of a vast range of human understandings, the majority of which will be satisfied by the teachings and practices that are obligatory for all Muslims. But Islam insists that "God charges no soul save to its capacity" (Koran 2:286; cf. 6:152, 7:42, etc.), which means that those who have the capacity to do so must pass beyond the surface of Islam into its depths, a region that has been mapped in detail by the saints and sages—often known as "sufis"—who have journeyed through it. Certainly you can begin this journey with only love and sincerity as your guides, but as the goal is to pass beyond your own self, and to give up your self, you need the instruction of those who are already selfless. Sufism, like other spiritual paths, insists that no real progress can be made without the guidance of a master who has reached the goal.

> Entering the Way without a guide?
> Then you'll take a hundred years to make a two-day journey![1]

Who are the Sufis? Those Muslims who, while standing with their co-religionists on the circumference of the circle of Islam—the Shari'ah or "Divine Law"—have set off on a journey within their own beings toward the circle's Center—God Himself. The model for this spiritual life was provided by the Prophet Muhammad, who said, "The Law is my words, the Way is my works, and the Truth [God] is my inward states." Muslims have followed him on this path since earliest times, often with opposition from those who lack the insight to realize that Islam is more than a plane surface, possessing as it does an inward dimension of infinite depth. The word "Sufism" itself did not come to be used until about the ninth century, three hundred years after the founding of Islam, but it has persisted as the most common designation for Islam's spiritual dimension down to the present day. In an essay—or in a book—one cannot hope to do justice to this 1,400-year-old tradition of spiritual teachings; one can only try to evoke a few characteristically Sufi—and Islamic—ways of looking at things.

The Divine Names

Neighbor, friend, companion—all are He.
In beggar's rags and sultan's satin—all are He.
Dispersed in assemblies, gathered in retreats,
By God, all are He! By God, all are He![2]

In this short Persian poem, Jami (d. 1492) employs a refrain that has echoed through Sufi writings for centuries, at least since the time of Ansari (d. 1089). At first sight, the words suggest a kind of simple-minded pantheism (the belief that the sum total of all things is God), and indeed many unsympathetic and ill-informed observers have interpreted them as such. But the Sufis were far too sophisticated to consider such formulae anything but devices to awaken forgetful and negligent human souls to a side of reality that is too often ignored. If in some sense "All things are God," it is also true that "All things are not God"; that is to say, "Nothing is God, except God Himself," a statement that paraphrases the fundamental testimony of faith *(shahadah)* in Islam: "There is no god but God." If one can say that "All are He," one must say that "Nothing is He." In short, the exact nature of the relationship between God and the world cannot easily be expressed, and hundreds of Sufi treatises have been written attempting to explain it.

It is difficult to read the *Koran* without noticing how often God is mentioned by "name." Practically every chapter begins with the words, "In the Name of God, the All-merciful, the All-compassionate"—a formula that still suffuses the lives of practicing Muslims. But God has many names besides these three, and the *Koran* makes constant reference to a large number of them. We are told that God is All-mighty, All-wise, All-gentle, All-benign, All-seeing, All-hearing, All-knowing, All-powerful, All-forgiving, All-glorious, and so forth. "To God belong the Names Most Beautiful," says the *Koran*, "so call Him by them" (7:180); traditionally, these Names are said to number ninety-nine.

The Divine Names are central to the Islamic understanding of reality. For one thing, they connect the world to God. For example, God is called by the Names Living, Knowing, Willing, and Powerful, and these are said to refer to his attributes or qualities of Life, Knowledge, Will, and Power. (The two terms—Names and Attributes—are often mentioned together and are practically synonymous; if a distinction is drawn, it is only in the sense just mentioned, e.g., God as he who is called by the *Name* Living possesses the *Attribute* of Life.) These four Names or Attributes are often viewed as the fundamental creative principles of the universe, though most of the other Names are also involved in creation. Inasmuch as God is the Living, he bestows life on living creatures; as the Powerful, he bestows power and strength. The nature of this "bestowal" is explained in many ways, which we cannot begin to enumerate here. Perhaps the simplest way to conceive of it is through the analogy of the sun and its rays: the sun corresponds to God in Himself (called the "essence" in Islamic theology), its light corresponds to God's Attributes, and the individual rays of light correspond to the "creatures," which are often referred to in theological language as God's "effects" or "acts." Just as a given ray of light that enters the window of a room is an effect of the sun, so a given creature—a tree, a bird, a river, a mountain—is an "effect" of God. If the word "act" is also employed, this is to suggest the Wisdom, Will, and Power that are involved in God's creativity.

In short, everything in the universe derives from God; all positive qualities need to be traced back to their source in the Divine. The Prophet alluded to these points when explaining the origin of the mercy and compassion found in this world: "God has one hundred mercies, of which He has sent down one mercy among jinn and men, animals and crawling things; through it they show compassion to each other, through it they have mercy upon one another, and through it the beasts are kind to their young. But God has kept back ninety-nine mercies, by which He will show mercy to His servants on the Day of Resurrection." In a similar manner, the *Koran* says as follows (note that God is speaking, employing the first person plural pronoun as is commonly the case in the text): "There is not a single thing whose treasuries are not with Us; but We only send it down in a known measure" (15:21). As explained by the great Sufi theoretician Ibn al-ʿArabi (d. 1240), these treasuries are the creative possibilities latent within the Divine Being. The famous Sufi poet Rumi (d. 1273) compares the universe to a stream of flowing water, "within which shine the Attributes of the Almighty."[3] He says: "The world is foam, God's Attributes the ocean—the foam veils you from the Ocean's purity![4] Ibn al-

ʿArabi expresses the same idea in more philosophical language when he writes: "The whole cosmos is the locus within which God's Names become manifest."[5] He concludes that, in the last analysis, "there is nothing in existence but God's Names."[6]

To express this in the words with which we started: "All are He." As Ibn al-ʿArabi writes: "There is nothing in existence but God. Though we also exist, our existence is through Him. But he who exists through something other than himself is in fact nonexistent."[7]

To say that the creatures borrow all their existence and attributes from God and that in themselves they are "nonexistent" is a little like saying that the colors we perceive all around us display nothing but the existence and attributes of light. If we look at a colored object, we seem to see an independent and self-sufficient color. Yet we know that we are only perceiving light, which has been given a particular color by the nonexistence of certain other colors, or certain wavelengths. Hence, a single light appears to us in a great variety of hues. In a similar way, the only thing we perceive in creation is God's Being—"All are He"—yet he appears to us in a tremendous variety of shapes and forms, which are called "creatures." In the words of Jami:

> The things are multi-colored windows,
>   upon which falls the rays of Being's Sun.
> Whatever tint the window takes—red, yellow, blue—
>   thus shines the Sun within it.[8]

The Sufis often quote a saying of the Prophet in which God explains why he created the universe: "I was a Hidden Treasure and I wanted (literally: I "loved") to be known, so I created the creatures." If God has not brought the world into existence, the Hidden Treasure—that is, His Names and Attributes, or more correctly, their "effects," "acts," and "properties"—would have remained hidden from sight; there would be nothing but pure light with no colors to be seen. Hence, the universe as a totality, in its full spatial and temporal extension, displays the properties of the whole array of Divine Names and Attributes in an infinite deployment.

Like the other Semitic religions, Islam maintains that man was created in God's image or, as the Prophet put it, "upon His form." Without entering into details, one can say that this was understood to mean that man is a theater within which all the Names of God are displayed in a unified whole, just as the universe manifests the properties of the Names in infinite array. The difference between a human being and any other individual creature is that he or she is made upon the form of God Himself, thus possessing at least the potentiality to display the effects and properties of all of God's Names, while other creatures manifest some of God's names, but not all of them.

It is often said that the basic divine Attributes that bring the universe into existence—attributes that are called the "Seven Leaders"—are the four mentioned above, that is, Life, Knowledge, Will, and Power, along with Speech, Generosity, and Justice. An inanimate object does not reflect any of these attributes except in a passive way; a stone certainly tells us something about the divine Will and Power, but one could hardly maintain that it possesses these attributes as its own. In contrast, a plant possesses life and exercises a certain amount of power, while animals possess the attributes of plants and add to them traces of knowledge, will, and speech. Finally, human beings manifest knowledge, will, power, and speech in a far more perfect manner than the animals, while different human individuals display these and other divine Attributes in a tremendous variety of degrees. Moreover, only at the human level can justice and generosity appear, since these demand a degree of moral and spiritual perfection. In short, only human beings have the capacity to manifest such attributes, since they alone are made upon God's form in an integral manner.

The Spoken Universe

The *Koran* refers to its own verses as "signs," since they give news of God and remind human beings of their own nature, created in the divine image. The *Koran* also refers to the things of the universe as signs, since each of them displays the properties of God's Names and Attributes; each is an effect or act of God. "And of His signs is the creation of the heavens and earth and the variety of your tongues and hues" (*Koran* 30:22). "And of His signs are the night and the day, the sun and the moon" (41:37). If everything in the outside world is a sign, so also is everything inside ourselves. "We shall show them Our signs in the universe and in their own souls" (41:53). Both inside and outside man, God's acts and effects are plain to see. "Will you not understand?" asks the *Koran* repeatedly, "Will you not remember?"

"Understanding" and "remembrance" of God's signs comes from recognizing them for what they are, whether we perceive them in the *Koran*, in nature, or in our own souls. We may "read" the signs as we read the verses of the *Koran*, and hence many Sufis spoke of the cosmic book or the book of the soul. But we may also "listen to" the signs, since the *Koran*—a term which means literally "recitation"—was recited to the Prophet by the angel Gabriel, and Muhammad in turn recited it to his followers. Indeed, recitation of the *Koran* remains the key element in most Islamic ritual. But how do we "listen" to the signs in the universe and in ourselves? Is it enough to recognize the Divine Beauty in the songs of the birds and the rustling of the leaves? Or does "listening" involve something more?

In the *Koran*, God says, "Our only word to a thing, when We desire, is to say to it 'Be!' and it is" (16:40). In other words, each thing in the universe comes into existence as a result of God's spoken word. And just as our own speech is possible only through breath, so also God's speech takes place through the divine exhalation known as the Breath of the All-merciful. According to the *Koran* (7:156), God's mercy encompasses all things. The Sufis understood this to mean that God bestows upon the creatures, through the fact that He "loves to be known," an existence that belongs only to Him. So the Mercy that encompasses all things is existence itself, which is a "mercy for everything that exists."[9] In Ibn al-ʿArabi's words, "Because of this love to be known God breathed, and the Breath became manifest."[10]

The Breath of the All merciful is existence itself, while the divine words are the particular forms and shapes within which existence becomes manifest. Though each thing is addressed by the single command "Be!" each in its own turn is a word that takes shape in the Divine Breath. Hence, "There is nothing in the cosmos—or the cosmos itself is nothing—but the words of God."[11]

> The Breath of the All-merciful bestows existence upon the forms of the possible things, just as the human breath bestows existence upon letters. So the cosmos is God's words in respect of this Breath. . . . And He has told us that His words will not be spent, so His creatures will never cease coming into existence, and He will never cease being a Creator.[12]

> It is impossible for news of God—His revelatory activity—to be cut off from the cosmos. Were it to be cut off, the cosmos would have no nourishment upon which to feed in order to stay in existence.

"Say: 'If the sea were ink for the words of my Lord, the sea would be spent before the words of my Lord are spent,' though We brought replenishment the like of it" (*Koran* 18:109).

Though all the trees in the earth were pens, and the sea [were ink]—seven seas after it to replenish it, yet would the words of God not be spent (31:27).

And God gave news that there is nothing whose creation He desires without His saying to it "Be!" So these "words of God" are not cut off; they are a nourishment that pervades every existent thing.[13]

Primordial Audition

According to the Koranic verse, "When We desire a thing, We say to it 'Be!' and it is." How can God say "Be" to a thing that does not yet exist? To avoid a complicated discussion of Islamic metaphysics, we can simply say that before the things come to exist in this world, they exist in a certain manner in the treasuries" of the unseen world, for these "things" are the potentialities of outward manifestation possessed for all eternity by the Divine Names. When God says to a thing "Be!" it enters into existence, fulfills the function for which it was created, and returns again to the unseen world. As the *Koran* insists, "Unto God all matters are returned" (2:210, 3:109, etc.).

God speaks, the things "hear" his words, and then they enter into the cosmos. How did we experience the sounds of the word "Be" that brought each and every one of us into existence? In Arabic, the term "to hear" (*sama*ʿ) is also employed to mean "listening to music" and, by extension, "music" itself. By the end of the third century of Islam (ninth Christian century), "listening to music," or "audition" as the word is often translated, became a common Sufi practice, often accompanied by dancing. Some Muslim authorities considered this a transgression of the spirit if not the letter of the Divine Law, while the Sufis defended it as a means of remembering God. There is something in music, they said, that can transport man into the invisible world, to his very origin in nonexistence. Ibn al-ʿArabi explains this as follows:

> At base the cosmos comes into existence from a single Divine Attribute, which is Speech. For the cosmos knows nothing of God but His Speech; hearing His speech, it enjoys this audition, for it cannot not come into being. Because of their audition, the creatures of the cosmos—the hearers or "auditors"—are attuned to motion,

turmoil, and transferal, for the thing that hears the word "Be" is transferred and moved from the state of non-existence into the state of existence, thus entering into the cosmos. This is the root of the movement of the People of Audition [i.e., those Sufis who listen to music and dance to it], who are the people of Ecstasy.[14]
What the people of Audition perceive in the words of the singer is God's word "Be" to a thing before it enters into existence.[15]

In trying to grasp the role of Audition in the world's creation, we must not forget that of love. It was God's love for the Hidden Treasure to be known that made Him speak the word "Be" and exhale the Breath of the All-merciful. As the source and motivating energy of the cosmos, love suffuses its existence. In Rumi's words:

> The creatures are set in motion by Love,
>   Love by God in all eternity—
> The wind dances because of the spheres,
>   the trees because of the wind.[16]

All things are moved by love, so all things are lovers.

God's wisdom in his destiny and decree made us lovers, each of
    another.
That foreordainment paired each part of the world, setting it in
    love with its mate.[17]

What then did we experience when we heard the word "Be?" We experienced love, we delighted in its melody, we danced into the created world.

The lover was at rest with existence and nonexistence. He had not
    yet seen his beloved's face when the melody of the word "Be"
    woke him from the sleep of nonexistence. The audition of that
    melody produced rapture, and that rapture *(wajd)* gave him exis-
    tence *(wujud)*. . . .
Love at times conquers the ear before the eye.
Love overwhelmed him and transformed his outward and inward
    stillness into dance and movement.[18]

Many Sufis identify the primordial music heard by man with the words of God at the "Covenant of Alast." According to the *Koran* (2:30ff), when God created Adam as His own vicegerent, he presented him to the angels and commanded them to bow down before him. At this same plane of spiritual preexistence, before Adam's entrance into the corporeal world, God made covenant with his children: "Am I not *(alast)* your Lord," He asked. They all answered, "Yea! We testify" (7:172). This Covenant of Alast has been a recurrent theme of Sufi teachings: man must remember that day and once more acknowledge his love for his true Beloved.

> The spirit has been drunk with Thee from the Day of Alast,
> though for a time it was distracted by water and clay.[19]

Just as music reminds the People of Audition of the command, "Be," intoxicating them with its beauty, so also it brings back to them the memory of the eternal covenant with their Lord.

> Junayd (d. 910) was asked, "How is it that a man can be at peace, yet when he hears the Audition he is thrown into turmoil?" He replied, "God addressed Adam's progeny at the Covenant with the words, 'Am I not your Lord?' All their spirits were overcome by the delight of these words. When they hear the Audition in this World, they enter into motion and turmoil."[20]

Imperfect Man

> Do you know what words they speak, lute and rebeck?
>   "Thou are my sufficiency, Thou art my all, Oh Loving God."
> Dry and dismal, you have no taste of Audition—
>   Listen! The world is full of song.
> Oh that Minstrel! one tune
>   and all existence began to dance.[21]

One tune—"Be"—and the creatures danced into existence, displaying the Hidden Treasure, showing those who are able to recognize the "signs" that "All are He." But the dance is not yet complete. God said, "I was a Hidden Treasure, so I loved to be *known*," that is, by the creatures that He created. No doubt all things do possess a certain knowledge of God by the very fact of their existence. According to the *Koran*, "All that is in the heavens and the earth extols God" (57:1; 59:1, etc.). Hence Ibn al-ʿArabi can write:

> Everything God created is alive and speaking, whether it be mineral, plant, or animal. This is shown by God's words, "There is nothing

that does not extol His praise, but you do not understand their extolling" (*Koran* 17:44).[22]

So each creature was created to possess a specific mode of knowledge of the Divine Reality through which it is able to praise God. But human beings, made upon God's form, were created to know God in respect of all His Names and Attributes, and this knowledge does not arise as a matter of course. Created free, man must employ his own will to actualize it. This is precisely the significance of the Covenant of Alast, when man accepted to carry God's "Trust," or the responsibility to live up to his human potentiality: "We offered the Trust to the heavens and the earth and the mountains, but they refused to carry it and were afraid of it; and man carried it" (*Koran* 33:72).

God created Adam upon His own form, so He ascribed to him all of His own Most Beautiful Names; through the power of these Names man is able to carry the Trust that was offered to him. The reality of his divine form did not allow him to reject the Trust, as did the heavens, the earth and the mountains, all of which refused to carry it.[23]

Only when man has actualized his divine form is he able to understand the true significance of "All are He." In the meantime, he remains ignorant of his own nature and the nature of the universe, continuing to imagine that "Nothing is He." Ibn al-ʿArabi explains these points by referring to the *Koran*ic verse, "He [God] is with you where you are" (57:4):

God accompanies us in our every state, but we do not accompany Him unless we stand within His limits [as prescribed by the Divine Law]. So in reality we do not accompany Him, we only accompany His statutes: He is with us, but we are not with Him.[24]

In more philosophical terms, Ibn al-ʿArabi makes the same point as follows:

God is identical with what becomes manifest [in the cosmos], but what becomes manifest is not identical with Him. For He is the Nonmanifest just as He is the Manifest (so *Koran* 57:3) in the state of His manifestation. Hence we say, "He is like the things, but the things are not like Him," since He is identical with the things, but they are not identical with Him.[25]

In short, since "Nothing is God but God Himself," we are not like him. But, one should protest, were we not created upon God's form? Does that not mean that we are like him? The answer is yes, if by "we" is meant those human beings who are "truly human," those whom the Sufis call Perfect Men, i.e., perfect human beings, whether male or female. But the vast majority of human beings have not actualized that state, so they cannot claim to possess such a likeness except in an imperfect and distorted manner.

When God created Adam as his vicegerent, he made him a Perfect Man. This means, briefly, that he made him the "locus of manifestation" for his own "all-comprehensive" Name, i.e., Allah, which is the Name that embraces and includes all ninety-nine Most Beautiful Names. For "He taught Adam the Names, all of them" (Koran 2:31). "Adam entered creation upon the form of the Name 'Allah,' since this Name embraces all the Divine Names."[26] Hence, "God's Names do not become manifest in their entirety except in the human being."[27]

In Adam, the properties of the Names were fully actualized, while in those who have not reached perfection, they are only latent. Because Adam was a Perfect Man, God made him his vicegerent and the first prophet. According to Islam, prophets are by definition sinless and inerrant, and thus Adam is not considered to have committed a sin but rather an "oversight." Ibn al-ʿArabi points out that there is a great difference between the fall of man and that of Satan:

> God did not punish Adam and Even through the fall, only Satan; for Adam was made to fall in order that God's promise could be fulfilled, since He said, "I am placing in the earth a vicegerent" (Koran 2:30). . . . So the fall of Adam and Eve was a mark of honor, while that of Satan was a mark of loss and punishment.[28]

Although Adam was a perfect Man, this is by no means true of all his children; only the prophets and saints achieve this station. That is why Ibn al-ʿArabi writes, "When a human being does not attain the rank of perfection, he is an animal whose outward form resembles the form of a man."[29]

All human beings are made upon the form of God, which means that all possess the potentiality to be Perfect Man. As Ibn al-ʿArabi points out, the Muslim authorities agree that man can assume the Names of God as his own character traits.[30] Moreover, it is an axiom of Islamic thought that there can be no fundamental plurality in the structure of reality, since that would mean two or more totally independent beings, two or more gods. "Is there a god with God?! Little indeed do you remember!" (*Koran* 27:62). Since reality is fundamentally one, all things are intimately connected. Hence the "separation" between God and His form—cannot be absolute; in some sense it must be bridgeable. The Perfect Men are those who have closed the gap between outward form and the inward reality. Outwardly they may appear to be mortals like the rest of us, but inwardly they open up to the Infinite.

Once a person traverses the spiritual path, thus bridging the gap between "Nothing is He" and "All are He," he makes actual the Names that are latent within himself. Then he can say with al-Hallaj (d. 922), "I am the Absolute Truth," or with Bayazid (d.874), "There is nothing in my robe but God."

At the station of perfection, the human being is the microcosm or "small world," containing within himself, in summary fashion, everything that is manifested in infinite detail in the outward cosmos. As the famous al-Gazzali (d. 1111) put it:

> God blessed Adam by giving him a summary form comprehending every kind of creature in the cosmos. It is as if Adam is everything in the cosmos, or a summary transcription of the whole universe.[31]

Hence Ibn al-ʿArabi refers to the world outside of man not only as the "great world" or macrocosm but also as the "great man."

> The Men of God call the cosmos the "great man," while they call its summary the "small man," since he is a being in whom God has placed all the realities of the macrocosm. So man entered into creation in the form of the cosmos, in spite of his small size; and the cosmos is upon the form of God, so man is upon the form of God, as indicated by the Prophet's words, "God created Adam upon His own form."[32]

In man is found the power of every single existent in the cosmos, since he possesses all ontological levels; for he alone was singled out for the divine form. As a result he combines the divine realities, i.e., the Names, and the realities of the cosmos.[33]

"The Perfect Man combines the form of God with the form of the cosmos. . . . He becomes a mirror in which God gazes upon His own form . . . since all the Divine names are ascribed to him."[34]

Man combines within himself the powers of the whole cosmos and of the Divine Names in their perfection. So no existent things is more perfect than the Perfect Man. That human being who does not reach perfection in this world is a rational animal, a part of the divine form, but nothing more. He does not attain to the degree of Man. On the contrary, his relation to Man is like the relation of a corpse to a human being; it is human in shape, but not in reality, for a corpse lacks all powers.[35]

The Ascent of the Soul

> For a time you were the four elements,
>   for a time an animal.
> Now you have been a spirit, so become the Beloved!
> Become the Beloved![36]

By the very fact of being made upon God's form, a human being possesses the potentiality of infinite development through the actualization of the Divine Names. The *Koran* often expresses astonishment at those who look upon God's signs in the cosmos and themselves and do not recognize that even the "natural order" is built upon transformation and change with a view toward spiritual perfection. Death and resurrection are but two further stages of the growth that begins in the womb.

> Oh men, if you are in doubt as to the Resurrection—Surely We created you of dust, then of a sperm-drop, then of a blood-clot. . . . And we establish in the wombs what We will, till a stated term. Then We deliver you as infants, then that you may come of age. (*Koran* 22:5)

The Sufis see the stages of physical life as the outward signs of an inward development, i.e., the ascent of the soul in the direction of the Divine. Rumi in particular is famous for his description of the soul's growth from a stage that is practically inanimate to one that surpasses the station of the angels. The Islamic view of the soul's ascent provides the profound reason why, though "All are God," human beings cannot be truly aware of this fact until they have attained the station of the Perfect Man. As long as we have not passed through the stages of psychic, moral, and spiritual growth and perfection, we must remain ignorant of our own true nature.

Man begins his journey to perfection at the stage of "nonexistence" with God. Once he hears the command "Be" and acknowledges God's Lordship at the Covenant of Alast, he is brought into this world, the point of creation farthest from the Origin. Then man begins his ascent to God, for all things return to Him, just as all have come from Him. These two journeys—from God to the world and from the world to God—are often referred to as the two "arcs" of the Circle of Existence.[37]

In one sense the return to God is "compulsory," since neither man nor any other creature has a choice in the matter. "To Him has surrendered whoso is in the heavens and in the earth, willingly or unwillingly, and to Him they shall be returned" (*Koran* 3:83). But there is another kind of return, known as "voluntary," that is the prerogative of human beings, since they alone, made upon God's form, have been given a sufficient share of the divine freedom to shape their own destinies. Only humans are addressed by Revelation, which provides instructions on how to return to God "willingly," before we are taken to Him through death.

In short, the soul undergoes a "natural" or "compulsory" development that leads to physical death and carries man on to the Resurrection and the meeting with God. "Oh Man! Thou are laboring unto thy Lord laboriously, and thou shalt encounter Him" (*Koran* 84:6). But the soul also undergoes a "voluntary" growth in keeping with its own free choice. If in the first case man is compelled to grow and die, in the second he is free to choose what sort of existence he will have in the next stages of his becoming. In other words, to employ a symbolism that is as current in Sufism as in Islam in general, human beings are given religious directives so that in the next life they can enter into a joyous mode of existence know as paradise, but they are free to reject the guidance that is offered and suffer the consequences, the state known as hell.

The "natural" or "compulsory" growth of the soul begins in the womb, when God "breathes of His Spirit" (*Koran* 15:29, 32:9) into the body. This spirit, coming from the realm of Alast, is a pure and living light, while the body is dark and dead clay. The conjunction of spirit and body gives rise to the soul proper, which embraces both worlds, the spiritual and the corporeal. The soul is thus the intermediary through which the pure and transcendent spirit is put in contact with the corruptible body; it is the sum total of the life and consciousness that is produced by the meeting of spirit and clay.

The human spirit—which is also God's spirit—is a ray of divine light qualified by all the Divine Names. But these Names can only manifest their properties in this world through a body, just as the Hidden Treasure can only be known by outward manifestation. Within the soul, acting as the link between the spirit and the body, the perfections latent within the Divine Names can display themselves. The image of light is helpful here: The spirit is pure light, while the body is pure darkness; the mixture of light and darkness allows the myriad colors to show their properties. Within the soul the life, knowledge, will, and power of the spirit assume specific and individual characteristics, so that each person's soul becomes distinct from everyone else's even though all men are created from the single divine spirit or divine breath.

During the soul's development, the effects of the Divine Names manifest themselves only gradually. The Sufis compare the fetus in its early stages to an inanimate object or mineral; little by little the properties of life and sensation appear within it, so that it passes to the stage of a plant. By the time the child is born, it has acquired all the attributes of an animal, though imperfectly. It is not until around the time of puberty, when the highest human faculties—intelligence and speech—begin to be perfected, that a person deserves to be called a human being, though in Ibn al-ʿArabi's terms, we all remain "animal men" until we actualize the full range of Divine Names within ourselves.

By the time of puberty, the properties of five of the Seven Leaders referred to earlier—Life, Knowledge, Will, Power, Speech—can be clearly discerned, but the other two—Generosity and Justice—may be hardly noticeable if present at all. This fact helps to show that the soul's development toward the actualization of the Divine Names does not take place as a matter of course; factors that could be called "environmental" are of importance in determining how a person's nature and character develop. If it is clear that a child's upbringing will have an effect on the extent to which knowledge and speech develop within him, it is even clearer that generosity and justice involve moral and spiritual values that are intimately connected to such considerations as the goals and ideals a person accepts for himself in life.

Islam, like other religions, discerns a normative model for human perfection and provides directives as to how to reach it. The "natural" development of the soul can never take a person to this goal. Certainly we all return to God, but will we return to his mercy or his wrath, to felicity or chastisement, to heaven or hell? Islam makes the practice of the religion incumbent upon its followers when they reach puberty, that is, when the intelligence (the divine attribute of "knowledge") has sufficiently developed to discern the difference between right and wrong. The religious prescriptions are designed to bring out those potentialities that lie hidden within man by virtue of his being made upon the divine form. Every one of the ninety-nine Most Beautiful Names must be actualized within the soul in perfect harmony with all the others.

If Sufism differs from the Islam of the masses in its vision of the soul's development, it is in the awareness of the exact nature of the goal and the intensity of the means employed to reach it. There are always certain human beings who feel compelled to return to God in the present life, those who do not have the patience to remain separated from their beloved until after death. Hence they follow the command of the Prophet, "Die before you die!" By dying to their own individual limitations, they are born into the unlimited expanse of the Divine Beauty. They have no fear of death, since they have died many times and each time been reborn to something greater. As Rumi puts it:

> I died from the mineral realm and became a plant,
> I died as a plant and became an animal.
> I died to animality and became a man.
>   Why should I fear?
> When did I ever become less through dying?
> Next time I will die to human nature,
>   so that I may spread my wings and lift up my head among the
>   angels.
> But then I will jump the stream of angelic nature, for "Everything
>   is perishing but God's Face"
>   (*Koran* 28:88).
> Once I am sacrificed as an angel,
> I will become what enters not the imagination.
> I will become nothing, for nonexistence calls to me in deafening
>   tune: "Unto Him we shall return."
>   (*Koran* 2:156)[38]

This entrance into "nonexistence," sometimes alluded to as the "annihilation" of the ego's limitations and "subsistence" in God, is the end of the path to God. Here the traveler actualizes the command of the Prophet, "Assume the character traits of

God!" "traits" which are invariably interpreted to mean the Divine Names. So central is this idea to Sufism that Ibn al-ʿArabi can write, "Assuming the traits of the Divine Names— that is Sufism."[39] His disciple al-qunawi (d. 1274) describes the ascent to God, modeled on the Prophet's ascent during the "night journey" (miʿraj), as the shucking off of creaturely limitations, stage by stage:

> The Sufi travels toward the Upper World, and from the time he separates himself from the earth he never passes by any element, ontological level, or celestial sphere without discarding within it that part of himself which corresponds to it, i.e., the part that he acquired when he first entered into this lower world. Thus he obeys God's words, "God commands you to deliver trusts back to their owners." (Koran 4:58)[40]

Every human being returns to God, whether in this world or the next. But as Ibn al-ʿArabi likes to point out, this return will be to that specific Divine Name which the person actualizes during his sojourn in the world. So one must keep in mind the different properties of the Names:

> How are the Avenger, the Terrible in Retribution, and the Severe comparable to the All-compassionate, the All-forgiving, and the Kind? . . . For each Name looks upon things in keeping with its own reality.[41]

Al-Quaniwi describes the return to the name Allah, upon the form of which man was created, as becoming established at the "Central Point of the Circle." Significant divergence from this "Point of Equilibrium," wherein are centered all the Names of Mercy and Gentleness, means falling to the periphery of existence, the domain of Wrath and Severity.

> Whoever leaves the equilibrium of the Central Point—which is the point of human perfection—will be judged in respect of his distance from or proximity to the Center. Between the total disequilibrium that pertains to satan and the perfect equilibrium manifesting all the Divine Names, are located all the habitations of the blessed and the damned.[42]

The goal of the voluntary return to God is to actualize the full range of the Divine Names, or the Name Allah, which comprehends them all. The means employed to reach the goal are varied, but they can be summarized in one word: *dhikr*, the "remembrance" of God. Remembrance is made incumbent upon Muslims in many verses of the *Koran*, a Scripture which itself was revealed as a "remembrance unto all beings" (*Koran* 12; 104, 38:87, etc.). Only through turning one's mind and indeed one's whole existence toward God can one hope to become god-like in a true sense. "God will give you what you seek. Where your aspiration lies, that you will become, for 'the bird flies with its wings, but the believer flies with his aspiration.'"[43] Constant remembrance of God through various ritual activities and the unceasing repetition of His Name fans the fire of love in the heart, "a flame that burns away everything except the Beloved."[44]

> In the outside world, wind sets the trees in motion—
> On the inside, remembrance rustles the leaves of the heart's
>   tree.[45]

For the Sufis, all creatures are signs of God, calling the soul to remembrance. Music in particular "refreshes the mind from the heaviness of human nature."[46] According to Rumi:

> We were all part of Adam,
>   we heard those melodies in paradise.
> Though water and clay have covered us with dust,
>   we still remember something of those sounds . . .
> Hence Audition is the food of lovers—
>   within it they find the image of the meeting
>   with their Beloved.[47]

Najim al-Din Razi (d. 1256) explains the attraction of music in terms of the remembrance of the primeval covenant:

> When the soul hears the singer sing words clothed in fine garment and measured rhythm, it tastes the address of "Am I not your Lord?" This sweet sound causes a movement of yearning toward God. . . . Once the soul finds the taste of this address, the bird of the spirit cannot rest but falls into turmoil. It tries to smash the cage of the bodily frame and return to its own realm.[48]

Ruzbihan (d. 1209) describes the state of the spiritual traveler who contemplates the unseen world and listens to its primordial music:

He delights in God and all but flies out of his human frame, but he remains trapped and bewildered in the cage of his own nature. As much as God's light is unveiled from him, he inclines toward the ascending stages of the spiritual realm, but he drags the tail of his physical form in this world. His delight in God makes him dance, move, and turn.[49]

Dancing, then, is the traveler's expression of his inward joy and his rejection of the limitations of his own ego. Razi explains that the soul's agitation and turmoil at being confined by the limitations of this lower world throw the body into motion. Thus, he says:

> Dancing is not to keep on jumping,
>   nor to float around without heartache like dust.
> Dancing is to jump out from the two worlds:
>   Smash your heart, transcend your soul![50]

Rumi explains that the Sufis' dance takes place within their own hearts and spirits; it is the joyful resurrection of the soul after it has been killed in the holy war against its imperfections.

> People dance and frolic in the square—
>   Sufis dance in their own blood.
> Delivered from their own hands, they clap their hands!
>   having jumped outside their own imperfection,
>   they dance.
> Within themselves their minstrels play the tambourine—
>   their uproar makes the ocean clap its waves.[51]

Dancing, then, has no necessary connection to the body, since it is a state of the soul. True music cannot be heard by the imperfect ears of animal men, and the true Sufi dance cannot be observed with the eyes, since it takes place in another world, even if, on occasion, it displays its effects in this world. If this is the case, one can understand the derision in Ruzbihan's words:

> A group of the delirious dance, recite poetry, listen to music, clap their hands, and tear their clothing, imagining that, having achieved this, they have attained to the spiritual states of the saints. What nonsense! How can you ascend in the stations of perfection through such fabrications?[52]

Jami expresses similar disgust at the excesses of certain so-called Sufis of his day:

They show no spark of remembrance's light,
    no sign of Audition's spiritual state.
Their remembrance pains their heads and necks,
    their dancing weakens their bellies and backs.[53]

The imperfect dance toward imperfection;
    the perfect move but do not "dance,"
For the bird of their spirit flaps its wings
    to gain freedom from the depths of harm.
Though a single sound causes both
    to leap up for the sake of Audition,
The perfect spread their mantel over the spheres,
    the imperfect descend into the earth. . . .
 The wretched owl sits next to the falcon,
    but once they begin to fly,
The falcon returns to the king's castle,
    the owl goes back to a corner of the ruins.
Every person inclines toward his own habitat,
    every bird flies to its own nest.[54]

Dancing with God

The Sufis follow a long and difficult path back to their Beloved; in the process they pass through numerous states of the soul—such as hope and fear, joy and sorrow, gathering and dispersion—and acquire various spiritual perfections, all of which have been described in detail in Sufi works. In *The Conference of the Birds*, one of the most famous and at the same time entertaining accounts of the spirit journey, ʿAttar (d. 1220), tells how the birds gathered together and decided to travel to their king, the Phoenix; guided by the hoopoe and undergoing many adventures on the way, they flew across the seven valleys—aspiration, love, knowledge, independence, unity, bewilderment, and annihilation—before finally reaching their goal. Other Sufis enumerate the stages of the journey as 10, 40, 100, or even 1,000. Here a single poem by Rumi, dedicated to his spiritual companion Shams-i Tabrizi, will have to suffice to suggest the trials and delights of the traveler.

Wine? I know nothing of wine—annihilated,
    without place, I know not where I am.
One minute I fall to the depths of an ocean,
    the next I rise like the sun.
one instant the world carries me in its womb,

the next I give birth to the creatures
like the world.
When the spirit's parrot nibbles sugar,
I fall down drunk and nibble the parrot.
No place in the world can hold me—
I am worthy only for that place-less Friend.
Look at me—dangerously deranged,
shouting and roaring among the profligates.
You say, "Why don't you come to yourself?"
Fine, show me myself, I'll come to it.
The shadow of the Phoenix has caressed me so often,
the bird has become shadow, I Phoenix.
I saw Beauty drunk—It said,
"I am affliction, affliction, affliction!"
A hundred souls cried out from every direction.
"I am yours . . . , yours . . . , yours . . .
"You are that burning light which said to Moses,
'I am God . . . , God . . . , God . . .'"
I said, "Shams-i Tabrizi, who are you?"
He said, "You . . . , you . . . , you. . . ."[55]

The human soul, which began its journey in the lower world
as the connecting link between the transcendent spirit and the
lifeless body, realizes the fullness of its own nature by returning
to the divine source from which it arose, yet without losing
anything actualized along the way. Having begun as a kind of
infinite potentiality, it grows by making the properties of all the
Divine Names its own. Man comes to know all creation within
his own soul, for he travels through all things and all worlds.
He keeps on ascending in the spiritual degrees until, having
reached God, he begins the never-ending journey in God and
with God. Ibn al-ʿArabi reminds us of the Koranic verse, "He is
with you wherever you are (57:4) and the fact that, though God
is with us, we are not with Him. But, once the traveler attains
to the station of the Perfect Man, "he is with God just as God
is with him."[56] The Perfect Man, descending into the unfathomable oceans of his own existence, travels with God wherever he
goes. For does not the *Koran* say that he is God "in the earth"
(43:84), and did not the Prophet report that God descends every
night to "the heaven of this lower world?" So the Perfect Man
accompanies God and each of the Divine Names as it manifests
its properties within creation. "He accompanies creation in its
journey from nonexistence to existence, and he accompanies
the prophets in their journeys, just as he accompanies Adam in
his journey from the Garden to the earth. . . ."[57] The Perfect

Man remains with God and with all things in this world and the next, free of the limitations of time and space.

The cosmos is not a static entity; it is God's never-ending revelation of the Hidden Treasure. As Ibn al-ʿArabi constantly reminds us, God is infinite, so He cannot be constrained in any manner whatsoever. As a result, his acts—the creatures—are infinitely variegated. Instant by instant all things undergo constant transformation, and no act—no "theophany" or self-manifestation of God—is ever repeated. "There is no repetition whatsoever in creation, because of the Divine Amplitude."[58]

> Because of God's theophany the existent things undergo constant transferal from state to state. . . . God reveals himself in theophany continuously. . . . His station is theophany, while the station of the existent things is change and transferal from state to state.[59]

Change, flux, and movement are intrinsic to existence. When the traveler reaches the utmost limits of the spiritual path, he enters into the oceans of divine knowledge, where all is bewilderment—not the bewilderment of being lost but the bewilderment of having found all and everything.[60] Hence, says Ibn al-ʿArabi:

> "Guidance" is to be led to bewilderment. Then you will know that the whole affair is bewilderment, that bewilderment is agitation and movement, and that movement is life. There is no rest, no death, only existence, nothing of nonexistence.[61]

So it continues for all eternity, in this world and the next. In reality the saints already taste in this world, through their bewilderment, the never-ending theophanies that the blessed find in the next.

> At every instant the people of paradise see a new creation and a new bliss . . . for if one thing were to follow another without any change, they would become bored. . . . If God did not nourish the blessed with renewal at each moment so that their bliss might continue, boredom would overcome them. Hence every time an inhabitant of paradise looks upon his own kingdom, he perceives things or forms that he has not seen before and he delights in the new appearance. Each time he eats or drinks he finds a new and delicious flavor, one he had never before tasted.[62]

In his lengthy spiritual diary, Baha Walad (d. 1230)—Rumi's father and first spiritual master—records in great detail the ex-

perience of God's continuous theophany through the phenomena and signs of the universe. Though he writes in prose, one
can see how this type of vision must be the well-spring of a
great deal of Sufi poetry.

> When I awaken from sleep I see the whole world as God's Thou-
> ness. When I begin to stir, I take God's Thou-ness in my embrace
> to see what will come to hand and enter my senses from it. . . .
> Each instant I mix with God's Thou-ness and gaze upon its inward
> wonders. I see its wonders and drink the wine of each one's taste
> such that I remain senseless until late. In the same way, the sweetest
> state of Moses was theophany and "Show me that I may behold
> Thee" (*Koran* 7:143). Each moment I take God's Thou-ness into my
> embrace: "When my servants ask about Me—I am near" (*Koran*
> 2:186). Every instant I have the ardor of Jesus, the ecstasy of Moses,
> the certainty of Muhammad, the unveilings and the ease of the
> saints, the beauty of the beloveds, and the state and sweet prosperity
> of their lovers. I have been given two feet to run to these sweet
> things of theirs. I gaze upon these wonders and say, "Oh God, give
> me of these, for Thou hast brought them into being from the Un-
> seen. Thy bounty has made them such—give also to me. Say 'Be!'
> so that it may be and also come into existence for me. . . ." The
> sweet things of the outward world take replenishment from the
> sweet things of the inward world, and the inward takes replen-
> ishment from God's Attributes. Hence the doors to the everlasting
> garden known as paradise are God's Attributes, and in each kind of
> sweet thing in the world, one door—God's Attributes—is opened,
> so that He may breathe into it and increase it. So come, let me
> throw myself before those doors of God's Attributes and enter into
> paradise, so that I may no longer remember the world but remember
> God and belong to God.[63]

The Perfect Man journeys into the Infinite, listening to the
music of God's existentiating command, repeated instant by
instant for every state and every creature. Each moment God
says "Be" and a new theophany, more glorious and perfect than
the preceding delights the eye. In the words of 'Iraqi (d. 1289):

> The song will never cease, nor the dance come to an end, in all
> eternity, for the Beloved the infinite. Here the lovers hums,

> > The moment I turn my eyes,
> >   I see Thy face,
> > The instant I lend an ear,
> >   I hear Thy voice.

So the lover continues dancing and moving, even though he may appear to be still. "You see the mountains that you suppose fixed passing by like clouds" (*Koran* 27:88). How could he remain still? Each atom of the universe prods him to motion: each atom is a word, each word gives news of a Name, each Name has a tongue, each tongue a song, and for each song the lover has an ear. Pay attention: the singer and the listener are one, for "Audition is a bird that flies from God to God."[64]

Notes

1. Rumi, *Mathnawi*, ed. R. A. Nicholson (London: Luzac, 1925–40), Book III, verse 588; cf. W. Chittick, *The Sufi Path of Love* (Albany: State University of New York Press, 1983), 123.

2. Jami, *Lawa'ih: A Treatise on Sufism*, ed. and trans. E. H. Whinfield and M. M. Kazwini (reprint; London: Theosophical Publishing House, 1978), 25 (my translation).

3. *Mathnawi*, VI 3172; cf. Chittick, *Sufi Path*, 43.

4. Rumi, *Kulliyyat-i Shams*, ed. B. Furuzanfar (Tehran: Tehran University Press, 1957–67), verse 9695.

5. *Al-Futuhat al-makkiyyah* (Beirut: Dar Sadir, n.d.), II, 34, line 3.

6. Ibid., II 303.13

7. Ibid., I 279.6.

8. *Naqd al-nusus fi sharh naqsh al-fusus*, ed. W. Chittick (Tehran: Imperial Iranian Academy of Philosophy, 1977), 72.

9. *al-Futuhat*, II 281.27.

10. Ibid., II 310.21.

11. Ibid., II 402.30.

12. Ibid., II 459.5

13. Ibid., II 90.14.

14. Ibid., II 352.14.

15. Ibid., II 366.29.

16. *Kulliyyat*, 5001; cf. Chittick, *Sufi Path*, 197.

17. Rumi, *Mathnawi*, III 4400–4401; cf. Chittick, *Sufi Path*, 198.

18. 'Iraqi, *Lama'at*, ed. J. Nurbaksh (Tehran: Khanaqah-i Ni'matallahi, 1974), 34–35; cf. W. C. Chittick and L. Wilson, *Fakhruddin 'Iraqi: Divine Flashes* (New York: Paulist Press, 1982), 108.

19. Rumi, *Kulliyyat*, 23769; cf. Chittick, *Sufi Path*, 300.

20. 'Attar, *Tadhkirat al-awliya'*, ed. M. Isti'lami (Tehran: Zuwwar, 1967), 446.

21. Jami, *Diwan*, ed. H. Radi (Tehran: Pirus, 1962), 301.

22. al-'Arabi, *al-Futuhat*, III 393.23.

23. Ibid., II 170.6.

24. Ibid., II 287.7.

25. Ibid., II 488.25.

26. Ibid., II 124.5.

27. Ibid., I 216.12.

28. Ibid., I 231.34.

29. Ibid., II 468.15.

30. *al-takhalluq bi'l-asma'*, Ibid., III 398.21.

31. *Miskat al-anwar*, ed. A. 'Afifi (Cairo: Al-Dar al-Qawmiyyah, 1964), 71; cf. W. H. T. Gairdner, *al-Ghazzali's Mishkat al-Anwar* (Lahore: Sh. Muhammad Ashraf, 1952), 134.

32. *al-Futuhat*, II 150.26.

33. Ibid., II 396.2.

34. Ibid., III 398.16.

35. Ibid., II 441.3.

36. Rumi, *Kulliyyat*, 22561; cf. Chittick, *Sufi Path*, 78.

37. Cf. Chittick, "The Circle of Spiritual Ascent According to al-Qunawi," in *Neoplatonism and Islamic Thought*, ed. P. Morewedge (Albany: State University of New York Press, 1992), 179–209.

38. *Mathnawi*, III 3901–106; cf. Chittick, *Sufi Path*, 79.

39. *al-Futuhat*, II 267.11.

40. *Miftah al-ghayb*, on the margin of al-Fanari's *Miftah al-ins* (Tehran, 1905–06), 296; cf. Chittick, "The Circle of Spiritual Ascent", 180.

41. *al-Futuhat*, II 93.19.

42. Al-Qunawi, *I'jaz al-bayan fi tafsir umm al-Qur'an* (Hyderabad-Deccan: Osmania Oriental Publications Bureau, 1949), 300; cf. Chittick, "The Circle of Spiritual Ascent", 185.

43. Rumi, *Fihi ma fihi*, ed. B. Furuzanfar (Tehran: Amir Kabir, 1969), 77; cf. A. J. Arberry, trans. *Discourses of Rumi* (London: John Murray, 1961), 89; Chittick, *Sufi Path*, 212.

44. Rumi, *Mathnawi*, V 588; cf. Chittick, *Sufi Path*, 215.

45. Rumi, *Kulliyyat*, 9778; cf. Chittick, *Sufi Path*, 159.

46. Ruzbihan, *Risalat al-quds*, ed. J. Nurbakhsh (Tehran: Khanaqah-i Ni'matallahi, 1972), 50.

47. *Mathnawi*, IV 736–37; cf. Chittick, *Sufi Path*, 326.

48. *Mirsad al-'ibad*, ed. M. A. Riyahi (Tehran: Bungah-i Tarjamah wa Nashr-i Kitab, 1973), 364–65; cf. *The Path of God's Bondsmen*, trans. H. Algar (Delmar, N.Y.: Caravan Books, 1982), 354–55.

49. *Mashrab al-arwah*, ed. N. M. Hoca (Istanbul: Edebiyat Fakültesi Matbaasi, 1974), 87.

50. *Mirsad al-'ibad*, 365, cf. *Path*, 35.

51. *Mathnawi*, III 97–98; cf. Chittick, *Sufi Path*, 327.

52. *Ghalatat al-salikin*, ed. with *Risalat al-quds* (see above, n. 48), 99.

53. Jami, *Mathnawi-yi haft awrang*, ed. M. Mudarris-i Gilani (Tehran: Sa'di, 1958), 25.

54. Ibid., 24.

55. *Kulliyyat*, ghazal no. 1526.

56. *al-Futuhat*, II 384.2; but cf. II 507.12.

57. Ibid., II 384.7.

58. Ibid., II 302.18.

59. Ibid., II 304.30.

60. Ibn Al-'Arabi, *Fusus al-hikam*, ed. A. 'Afifi (Beirut: Dar al-Kitab al-'Arabi, 1946), 73; cf. R. W. J. Austin, *Ibn Al-Arabi: The Bezels of Wisdon* (New York: Paulist Press, 1980), 79.

61. Arabi, *Fusus*, 199–200; cf. Austin, *Ibn Al-Arabi*, 254.

62. Ibn Al-'Arabi, *al-Futuhat*, II 280.27.

63. Baha' Walad, *M'arif*, ed. B. Furuzanfar (Tehran: Idara-yi Kull-i Intiba'at, 1954–59), I, 147–48; cf. Chittick, "Beatific Vision and Poetic Imagery in Baha' Walad" *Studies in Mystical Literature*, 5/2 (1985), 21–32, also *Sufi* 7 (1990), 5–9.

64. *Lama'at*, 35; cf. Chittick and Wilson, *Fakhruddin 'Iraqi*, 108–9.

12

African Mysticism

KOFI OPOKU

A basic tenet of religion is the belief that the divine communicates with humans and humans in turn can communicate with the divine. In mysticism, the divine communicates directly with humans or through intermediaries or even certain things.

This divine communication takes many diverse forms of expression and leads to the suggestion that there are many forms of mysticism. And yet, while the diversity of expression must be acknowledged, one cannot fail to see a certain vital unity of experience in mysticism, namely, the coming into immediate contact with the divine through an intuitive apprehension, rather than belief or thought. The experience that comes through intuition and feeling is inexpressible in words, and this makes complete knowledge of the content of mystical experience everywhere nearly impossible to acquire.

The divine with which direct communion is experienced also takes on many forms. It may be Ultimate Reality or Universal Principle, or the many manifestations of the spirit such as spirits or ancestors, nature spirits, and divinities. The critical factor here is that all these different manifestations represent ways in which the numinous is experienced. Evans-Pritchard wrote of the Nuer:

> The Spirits of the air are many but also one. God is manifested in, and in a sense is, each of them . . . what is distributed in a number of beings, though different, is yet the same, and though divided, yet a whole.[1]

The awareness of the multiplicity of the agents in whom the spirit lives or expresses itself, and the undivided unity of the spirit, are characteristic of the mystical experience. As Spencer wrote:

Everywhere beneath the forms of religious ceremony or observance, whether it be the cult of the ancestors, of animals, of Nature Spirits, of the Sky-God or the Earth God (or Goddess), there lies the awareness of the Transcendent, which moves men's hearts with awe. In the very nature of the religious consciousness, therefore, we have the seed of mysticism.[2]

In order to understand mysticism in African Traditional Religion, it is necessary to take African ontology[3] into consideration, noting that it is hierarchical in structure and that its most distinguishing feature is that a being in a higher category has control or power over a lower entity. Beginning from the highest to the lowest, African ontology distinguishes the Supreme Being, who goes by many African names—*Oonyame* (Akan), *Olorun* (Yoruba), *Ukulunkulu* (Zulu), *Ebangala* (Ngombe), *Ruhanga* (Uganda), *Hilolombi* (Basa), and *Namakungwe* (Illa).

The Supreme Being is essentially a spirit, and there are no visual representations of him or her. All the other beings in the ontological structure are contingent upon the first category. These are spirits, both human (ancestral) and nature, and power or energy that permeates the universe. The reality of the spirit is acknowledged in the sense that what is, is in the first place spirit, and this gives African ontology a spiritualistic character, though the reality of matter is not denied. The spiritual and natural are understood as two aspects or dimensions of one reality.[4] Human beings reflect this reality, and each person is a combination of spiritual and material factors. This does not make a person a divided entity; on the contrary, the unity of human personality is a fundamental assumption in African thought.

The spirit can wield influence over or control human beings, and the interaction between spirit and matter, spiritual beings and human beings, is therefore accepted as falling within the range of human experience. This helps human beings to derive meaning in life, enabling them to meet such problems as isolation, tragedy, and death.

Ancestors and Gods

Among the spiritual beings who interact directly with human beings are the ancestors and gods. The ancestors were once humans in society but after death they become spirits who have more power than men and women and are not subject to the limitations of time and space. In a sense, death increases one's powers, and the dead can communicate with the living through dreams and visions; and religious specialists, such as priests, priestesses, and mediums, can contact the dead and communicate with them on behalf of their relatives.

The dead also make their presence manifest by possessing the living and speaking through them. At many funerals in Ghana, it is not uncommon for the deceased to possess a relative, and those who knew the deceased could hear his or her voice speaking through the possessed person. The utterance could explain the circumstances surrounding the death of the deceased, or it may be instructions to the relatives as to what to do with some property left behind. These utterances can be taken seriously, and the possession is regarded as evidence of the power of the dead to make their wishes known. In this instance of possession by the ancestors or spirit of the dead, no training is required on the part of the possessed persons, and anybody, male or female, could become a channel for the expression or articulation of the ancestors' wishes.

The usual expression in the Akan language for such an incident is *osaman no asi ne so* (the spirit of the deceased has descended on him/her). The choice is entirely up to the spirit of the deceased and so is the initiative. The possessed person does not know and has no premonition of it. As it often happens, he or she may be attending a funeral and suddenly the spirit of the dead would come upon him or her, and the person would begin to speak. Afterward the person returns to "normal."

The ancestors may also possess people during the celebration of festivals, and an example may be taken from the *Odwira*, which is a thanksgiving, purification, and cleansing festival, celebrated once a year by the people of the Akuapem District in the Eastern Region of Ghana.

On the fourth day of the festival, a procession made up of representatives of the various houses with ancestral black stools makes its way to the original site of the town of Akropong, the capital town of the District. The purpose of the ritual is to offer the annual food offerings to the ancestors, and each household has a young maiden who carries the food and is sheltered from the sun with an umbrella carried by an attendant. The bearers of the ancestral food become possessed and are assisted from falling or stumbling by attendants who hold them and encourage them while welcoming the ancestors, whose presence is demonstrated by the state of possession.

The possessed maidens do not make any utterances that can be interpreted as messages from the ancestors, but their very demeanor, which is described as *nsamanfo no abesi* (the ancestors have descended), demonstrates the presence of the ancestors whose interest in the welfare of their descendants is unquestionable. The behavior of the possessed maidens is not regarded as abnormal in the society and is accepted as proof of the presence of spirits who interact with humans. And since a higher entity can control a lower one, the ancestral spirits can come upon a person and the experience is regarded as profoundly religious.

The Gods

The gods *Orisha* (Yoruba), *abosom* (Akan), *Vodu* (Fon), and *Alusi Ndimmuo* (Ibo) are the next category of spirits that possess people. The seizure or possession of a person by a divinity is regarded as the most profound of all religious experiences not only in Africa but also in other parts of the world. The divinities are regarded as agents or messengers of the Supreme Being. They do not have an independent existence but were brought into being to fulfill specific functions, and through them human beings relate to the Supreme Being. The divinities are therefore intermediaries and immediate objects of worship, a means to an end or "half-way houses"[5] to the Supreme Being.

The nature and function of the gods place them above human beings. They have more power than human beings, and each god has an area of competence and jurisdiction. Therefore, there are gods of fertility, epidemics, war, agriculture, nation-building, and other spheres of human endeavor, and in their areas of specialization, the gods have full powers to act. But as creatures who share the limitations of all created beings, the gods sometimes fail human beings in their expectations and so the attitude toward them is ambivalent, which contrasts with the attitude toward the Supreme Being.

African Traditional Religion makes a clear distinction between the Supreme Being and the divinities in terms of power and function. All powers in the universe are contingent on the Supreme Being. There are a number of myths that are pregnant with theological meaning which express the belief in the Supreme Being as the One who has no limits placed on Him or Her, and the One Beyond Whom There is Nothing, as the Akan name *Atoapem* shows. The Yoruba myth about *Orisha-nla*,

Olorun's agent in the creation of human beings, provides a useful illustration.

According to the story, the responsibility of giving form and shape to human bodies was assigned to *Orisha-nla,* whose instruction was to leave the bodies (dummies) in a room for *Olorun* to come and breathe life into them. *Orisha-nla* did not know what *Olorun* did to the lifeless bodies that he left in the room, and so one day he hid behind a pile of bodies he had formed in order to spy on the Creator. But since *Olorun* knows and sees everything, he entered the room, put *Orisha-nla* to sleep, and by the time he woke up, the dummies were already living people, breathing and walking about. To this day, *Orisha-nla* does not know what *Olorun* does to the bodies he forms.

The limitation of the gods is also shown by the fact that they have a generic name and there are shrines, temples, and images for them. That an image of a god can be made shows clearly that human beings know exactly what the god is like. Besides, the gods have their own servants, male or female, who serve at their respective shrines. These servants are trained to know the idiosyncrasies of the gods as well as their peculiar languages, and the servants may be said to have a private extension to the gods they serve. That the Supreme Being does not have temples, visual representations, and priests or priestesses is a reflection of the limitlessness that characterizes his or her being.

There is a highly developed tradition of the priesthood in African Traditional Religion, and it is the duty of the priest to mediate between the gods and the people. The servants of the gods receive special training before they assume office and their functions cover every facet of life and are not restricted to what may be described as "religious" concerns. It is these servants who are possessed by the gods and whose public behavior manifest the closeness of the divine to humans. Especially in West Africa, these servants are referred to as "wives of the gods," and this imagery is applied whether the servant is a male or female. The Akan refer to the *okomfo* (priest or priestess) as *Obosom yere* (wife of the god); to the Yoruba, the servant is *iyawo-orisha,* and among the Fon of Benin, the servant of the god is *Vodun-si.* The servant represents the close union between the divine and humans, and the most appropriate way to describe the nature of the relationship is to use the imagery of the intimate union between a man and his wife.

The training that the would-be priest or priestess undergoes is aimed at binding the divine and the human together in what quintessentially amounts to a sacred marriage which imposes restraints and deprives liberty. As the wife of a god, the servant passively receives messages from the divine husband while in a state of possession and performs actions with heightened intensity, which are indicative of the presence of the divine.

The priesthood is a very highly respected office in African societies, and it is open to both men and women. The choice of the candidate is entirely up to the gods, for it is they who decide who should be a servant and who should not, and the candidate and the society accept the will of the divine. A candidate for the priesthood receives an indication of the will of the divine in the form of a call; he or she becomes possessed and behaves in a manner unaccustomed to him or her. The person may become agitated and behave in an uncontrolled manner, he or she may run to and fro and stamp the ground with his or her feet, or he or she may wander in a vacant state. And on the basis of cultural insights and experiences dating from many centuries, it is known that such changed behavior may be due to either the onset of madness or the call of a god, for the call would come through possession, which indicates a call as well as a confirmation of the candidacy.

In the Akan tradition, a maxim says, *"Esono akom na esono adammo"*—there is a clear difference between possession by a god and madness. Another Akan maxim puts it this way: *"Twumasi ammo dam ante a, anka akom amma"*—literally, if Twumasi (a man) had not recovered from madness, we would not have been able to recognize possession. In other words, society would not have been able to distinguish between the state of madness, which is curable, and the state of possession, which is not subject to cure because it is not a disease. The affected person would then be taken to a shrine to see an experienced priest or priestess who would be able to tell whether it is a call by a divinity or madness. If it is the latter, treatment would begin at once, but if it is the former, the person would be sent to an appropriate shrine to begin training.

Training for the priesthood at the *Akonnedi* shrine,[6] one of the most popular shrines in Ghana and where only women are trained, will serve as an illustration of the training procedure. After a candidate has been called by the principal deity, *Akonnedi*, or any of her associate deities, the would-be priestess is taken to the shrine. It is firmly believed that no one on her own accord becomes a priestess; the initiative rests with the deities. Refusal to obey the call could result in either insanity or death. The parents or relatives could, however, plead with the chief priestess to release their child from undergoing training. If the plea is granted by the deity, the appropriate rituals would be performed; otherwise, the candidate is admitted to begin her training.

It may be pointed out that the candidate by this time will have passed the test which removes any ambiguity concerning her state of mind. The behavior that gave the initial clue and that was later confirmed does not indicate madness or any other ailment. On the contrary, the vacant state of the person in a significant way prepares her to receive what she is about to undergo, a training that will equip her to receive divine messages and instructions without the usual controls that she has in ordinary life.

The trainee is first given a haircut, and her fingernails are clipped, which is a symbolic way of shedding her old life in order to acquire a new one. After this haircut, her hair will not be cut again until the end of the training period, usually after three years. She is then given a ritual bath with an herbal decoction by a senior priestess for the next seven days. This cleanses her and makes her ritually pure while, at the same time, it gives her strength and power from the divinity she is about to serve.

A set of ten rules is then given to her to abide strictly by, and it includes not leaving the precincts of the shrine; abstaining from sex during the period of training; leaving the shrine during her menstrual period; never returning to her home until the end of her training; not talking to or shaking hands with her relatives for the duration of her training; not taking any alcohol; and not being disobedient to her elders. For, as a priestess, she will also be a servant both of the deity to whom she has dedicated herself and to the elders of the shrine, as well as the general public. A haughty priestess does great disservice to the deity she serves, as well as to her profession, and obedience, therefore, is a cardinal virtue for the priesthood.

After familiarizing herself with all the rules, the trainee settles in to the daily household chores of the shrine, goes on errands, and learns to live and cooperate with other priestesses-in-training, for quarreling is strictly forbidden. She then begins to learn the texts of the songs and dances of the particular deity she is preparing to serve, as well as songs of other divinities associated with the *Akonnedi* shrine. Right from the beginning she is also taught traditional medicine.

The art of divination is then taught to the trainee, and she begins to use her divining pot, *korow*. To enable her to "see" and "hear" her deity when she looks into the divining pot, medicines are rubbed into her eyes and ears. She practices at the divining pot throughout her training period in order to acquire this particularly important skill, for it is by looking into the divining pot that a priestess diagnoses diseases and prescribes cures, all of which are imparted to her by the deity. She also learns to identify other spirits that may appear in the divining pot and to interpret their messages correctly.

If, at the end of the first year, the priestess-in-training has acquitted herself credibly and has given ample evidence of her qualification and aptitude for the job, she is tattooed on her right shoulder, back, and joints. The tattooing ceremony is evidence that she has been confirmed and stabilized. Thereafter, the trainee continues her training for two more years and takes a final examination at the end of the training period. A graduation ceremony, *akomyi*, is held for priestesses who pass the final examination. This has been described as follows:

> The *Akomyi* marks the emergence of the priestess into her new life, and all the ceremonies performed at the various states during the day are meant to emphasize the idea of newness and emergence into the new life. The whole range of ceremonies also symbolizes death and resurrection. The casting away of old clothes and the putting on of new ones and the reunion with relatives, the cutting of hair and the shaving of armpits, the clipping of the nails as well as the ritual bath in the well, all make the same point—that the old has passed, and the new has emerged to take its place. After this day the priestess is reunited with her family, and all the prohibitions relating her dealing with them are lifted. . . . The jubilation and felicitations and the warm embraces by members of her family are reminiscent of a welcome accorded to someone who has returned from a long journey.[7]

The new priestess is on her own after the *akomyi* ceremony, but she continues her association with the chief priestess at the shrine and visits at least once a year to receive blessings and consult the chief priestess and also to participate in some of the major festivals of the shrine. Her manner of dressing and the beads she wears single her out as a priestess of a particular deity. She is an important figure in society and begins to perform her daily and weekly duties of ministering to the needs of the community and all others—pouring libations, healing the sick and afflicted, treating the barren, offering prayers for the community, and being possessed by her deity to bring messages to the devotees of the divinity as well as other clients, and explaining the causes of events in human life which lie beyond common-sense explanations—explanations that people look for when misfortunes occur.

Mediums

Linking human beings with the living-dead and the spirits are the mediums, who are channels of communication from the other world. Through these channels knowledge of things which would otherwise be impossible or extremely difficult to know reaches human beings. The distinctive fact about mediums and what gives them the important place they occupy in African societies is that they serve as mouthpieces of the spirits and are said to be "in touch." They thus constitute living proof of the communication that exists between human beings and the spirits, which is a normal feature of religious experience, and the people who demonstrate this experience are also normal people in the communities.

It is usually through possession that the medium becomes the channel through which the spirits communicate with humans. During the state of possession in which the medium is said to have been descended upon by a spirit, the medium loses his or her own being and becomes a pliable tool or instrument in the hands of the particular spirit that is manifesting itself. All through the time the medium is possessed, he or she is not aware of what he or she says or does.

While the medium is in a state of possession, people with particular problems may address questions to her and receive answers from the spirits or gods. The communication that takes place at this time is a one-way: gods and spirits to humans. Rarely do people send messages to the spirits through a possessed medium.

The initiative in communication during possession rests with the spirits or gods and Mbiti[8] has suggested that the communication could be likened to a radio set between two termini. The source of the communication is the spirits or gods, and the recipients are diviners, priests and priestesses, or medicine men and women. The spirit communicators are not harmful but friendly, and they may come as individual spirits, or they may come in their numbers. In either case, the departure of the spirit or spirits leaves the medium exhausted, and he or she collapses into the arms of attendants.

The role and function of mediums in African societies are quite similar, and what David Lan says about mediums in Zimbabwe is equally true of West African mediums:

> When possessed, the medium is thought to lose all control of body and mind. He may be referred to as *homwe*, which means pocket or little bag. The medium is simply the receptacle, the vessel of the spirit. He has no specialized knowledge or unusual qualities of his own. But this attitude to the mediums contains a paradox. Although the medium is thought of as an ordinary person, when a particular woman or man is selected from all others, they are marked out as extraordinary, as unique. The medium combines in one body two contradictory aspects: he has no special qualities, and he is as close an anyone can come to divinity. He has no influence on the will of the ancestor, yet the ancestor cannot act without him. He is a person of no special powers and he is a source of the most significant powers on earth.[9]

Diviners

Diviners engage in a form of religious communication in which supernatural powers give direct information to humans. These answers are more immediate, and the diviners, unlike in other forms of religious communication, make no attempt to change the will of the supernatural agents. They merely try to discover the will of the supernatural powers and thereby to prognosticate coming events unknown to humans. Thus, the diviners foretell the future but they are also capable of explaining past events. Having ascertained the unknown, diviners may then resort to prayers or sacrifices as a practical response to the supernatural directive.

Divinatory practices become necessary in human situations where answers or decisions, which are not to be taken lightly, are sought. People may resort to divination to find out the cause of an illness or the person responsible for a particular conjunction of events that causes an unhappy change of fortune. The need to confirm such important social decisions as the choice of a marriage partner or the most suitable candidate in a royal succession would be met by divination. Also when the guilt or innocence of a person needs to be detected or a new settlement is to be built, recourse would be had to divination.

Divination may thus be seen as an expression of human finiteness, since humans cannot penetrate the future with any degree of certainty; neither is human knowledge absolute, hence, the search for the knowledge or will of the supernatural which does not suffer from the limitations characteristic of humans. The supernatural thus initiates the communication process, or humans may approach the supernatural with specific questions and receive answers. The supernatural can also communicate through dreams and trances.

Diviners employ specific methods of finding the unknown, using kola nuts, cowrie shells, pebbles, water, entrails of animals, palm nuts, etc. One of the highly developed forms of divination in Africa is *Ifa*, found among the Yoruba in Nigeria and the Benin Republic, with traces among other West African Peoples. It is an extremely complicated arrangement of numbers and their interpretation, and its importance has been underscored by Abimbola, who wrote:

> The Yoruba regard Ifa as a repository of their beliefs and moral values. The Ifa divination system and the extensive poetic chants associated with it are used by the Yoruba to validate important aspects of their culture. Ifa divination is therefore performed by the Yoruba during all their important rites of passage, such as naming and marriage ceremonies, funeral rites and the installation of kings. In traditional Yoruba society, the authority of Ifa permeates every aspect of life because the Yoruba regard Ifa as the voice of the divinity and the wisdom of the ancestors.[10]

The importance of *Ifa* is also brought out in the following lines of *Ifa* poetry: "Ifa is a master of today, / Ifa is the master of the day after tomorrow; / To Ifa belongs all the four days created by the divinities on earth."[11]

Seers

Seers are also religious and cultic functionaires who play an important role in divine-human communication. Seers are able to "see" what other persons cannot ordinarily see or know what is unknown to others. Seers can foresee events before they take place as a result of their ability to get in touch with the supernatural. They also receive revelations through visions and dreams, but unlike priests and priestesses, there is no special training for seers.

The priests, priestesses, mediums, and seers as well as medicine men and women, all participate in and experience divine-human communication. But this experience is not restricted to religious and cultural functionaries alone; ordinary people also experience it, and both the functionaries' experience and that of the ordinary people reinforce each other. It is a normal cultural experience that the supernatural and humans do not live in isolated worlds, but that there is communication between the two worlds.

Divine-human communication does not manifest itself only in an outward manner; there is also an inward side to which scant attention has been paid in the literature. This is not due to the fact that evidence for an inward side of the experience of divine-human communication was lacking in Africa, but because researchers were simply so swayed by the prevalence of the outward display of the presence of the supernatural that they did not bother to look for it elsewhere. Moreover, problems of language made it impossible for researchers to communicate with individuals with such experiences. And part of the problem was also due to the Western assumption, which was erroneous, that Africans externalized or acted out their religion rather than thought it, and this led to concentration of attention on the outward display of the presence of the divine.

The external manifestation of divine-human communication takes the form of possession which, in the African context as well as in others, is a culturally accepted way of showing the presence of the supernatural. Those who are possessed by the supernatural and who therefore behave in an "unusual" manner to the observer, are not necessarily abnormal, hysterical, or badly adjusted people seeking to escape from responsibility by fleeing into a world of fantasy. On the contrary, such people are perfectly normal human beings, who are respected in their communities, and are regarded as performing an important function in society by being the mouthpiece of the gods or spirits, to bring messages and help people in need, and to the community at large. Their going into possession is a measure of the responsibility they carry, for they do not go into possession or state of trance for themselves, but rather for the sake of the community and the individuals who require answers from the supernatural, which are needed to cope with daily life in the world.

The mediums are able to bring messages or answers that are helpful because, in the opinion and cultural experience of the societies in which they function, they are a socially accepted group of religious functionaries who are normal and do not therefore suffer from what observers may call "hysterical dissociation." The state of possession enables the mediums not only to participate in the nature but also in the wisdom of the divinity whose messages through the mediums are regarded as helpful by those who receive them.

The mediums go into trance only to return from it and not to remain in a permanent state of change which would drastically alter their lives as human beings. As Zahan wrote:

> Indeed, if the African neglects nothing in resolutely undertaking the path to celestial metamorphoses, he still insists on retaining his status as a man and living his life on earth. His mysticism thus does not correspond to a definitive and total change but rather to an indefinitely repeated experience of the divine.[12]

The state of trance does not always occur amidst drumming, dancing, and singing, for mediums also become possessed without any "fanfare." Because the initiative resides with the supernatural, which has superhuman powers, the gods decide at will when and where to descend on the mediums, although there are culturally established occasions during which the gods descend to possess their mediums. This only goes to suggest that there is not one way alone in which the supernatural makes its descent to give messages, direction, advice, or even a cure, all of which are helpful to the clients.

The identity of the spirits that possess mediums is known in each society, for usually these spirits are worshipped or are recognized to be part of the pantheon with specific functions. The possessed person takes on the idiosyncrasies of the spirit that makes its presence felt in the medium, and people immediately recognize the spirit in question. As Noel King wrote:

> If it is Shango, the thunderer, the possessed will be hot tempered, jerky in movement, flaring out in anger. If it is Yemoja, the female spirit of the river, the possessed will take on the great calm sweeping characteristics of that mighty one. People may ask questions of the possessed and receive answers in the name of the divine.[13]

Western writers tend to make a differentiation between African mysticism and other forms of mysticism, based on what they suppose to be the role of God or the Supreme Being in African Traditional Religion. And the fact that God does not possess individual mediums and that there is no worship or temples or shrines dedicated to him or her has been pointed out as evidence of the minor role God plays in African Traditional Religion. Paraphrasing Roger Bastide, Parrinder wrote:

> He distinguished the possessing powers of the mediums, their controls, as either ancestors or natural forces and concluded that this gave them a mystical participation with spirits of each, water, fire, minerals and the like. This, thought Bastide, produced an immanental mysticism, of the earth, but it was different from Christian mysticism, which is of the heavens and ascensional. There seems to be no African mysticism of God because although a Supreme Being is widely believed in, he is thought to be far away and he has no general worship or places dedicated to him.[14]

The role of God in African Traditional Religion has been consistently misinterpreted by Western writers who wrote, and are still writing, from the assumption of a permanent disjuncture between the mind of Africans and that of Westerners to the extent that both people could not think about the same thing at the same time. Whatever exists in Africa must of necessity be different from what is in Europe. Besides, Westerners found an absence of their own image of God in Africa. God in the Western tradition is an essentially male reality, a human figure of Caucasian origin that excludes women and significantly added to the Western feeling of superiority over others. The view of the male generic character of the *imago dei*, which is found in Augustine[15] and Aquinas,[16] gave strength to the Western image of God. This image has recently been assailed with refreshing clarity of thought by feminist writers, such as Mary Daly in her book, *Beyond God the Father*.[17]

It may be pointed out that the Western image of God that was held out as a model had so many human weaknesses in it as to make God nothing but a limited and incomplete (male) and partial human who dwells in temples made by human hands (in the many cathedrals), and is a prop for human oppression. This God was no greater than the human (Western) understanding of him.

And because there was no such counterpart in Africa, Western writers concluded that God was absent in the African tradition, or was too far removed from human beings in Africa. But the African image of God is that of an essentially spiritual reality with nothing human in it. Hence, the Supreme Being is neither male nor female and as a spirit there are no visual representations of it. Visual representations reflect limitation and since the Supreme Being has no limitations he or she is never given physical features. The Zulu name *Ukulunkulu*, Great Spirit, aptly describes the nature of the Supreme Being.

The absence of temples or shrines is also a measure of the lack of limitations on the Supreme Being. For the Supreme Being cannot be confined to a temple, as the Yoruba say, "Since *Olurun* is everywhere it is foolish to try to confine him (her) to a temple." The Akan of Ghana also say, "If you want to speak to God, speak to the winds." Like the winds, God is everywhere. The whole universe is the temple of the Supreme Being rather than temples raised by human hands, which are a monument to human architectural skill.

In the African religious tradition, no one speaks for the Supreme Being, and this accounts for the reason why there are no priests or priestesses for God. There is no human being who has a private extension to the Supreme Being to the extent that he or she understands the peculiar language of the Supreme Being. Rather, the Supreme Being is accessible to all, as the Akan say: "*Obi Kwan nsi obi kwan mu*" ("No person's path crosses the other person's path"). In other words, each person has a direct access or channel to the Supreme Being without having to pass through someone else. The absence of priests or priestesses or spokespersons of the Supreme Being goes to show the revered position rather than an absence of knowledge of him or her, whereas in the traditions in which human beings speak for God, God becomes human and changes his mind from generation to generation. God was said to support slavery which was his explicit will at one time, but in another generation the same God was said to abhor it. This raises the question: Did God say slavery was his will, or did human beings put words into God's mouth and get him to say what they (humans) wanted him to say?[18]

The Supreme Being has agents who are spirits with limitations, and they are the ones with shrines, temples, and priests or priestesses. In the African scheme of things, it makes sense for the Supreme Being to have agents or intermediaries with whom human beings interact. These agents do not have an independent existence, and they derive their existence and power from the Supreme Being, who is the ground of being.

These gods or spirits are those which possess mediums and other people, for it is unthinkable for the Ground of Being to possess an individual. There are agents or lesser powers who do that without any disastrous consequences to the persons concerned. That the Supreme Being does not possess people in the African tradition does not show his or her lack of involvement in the lives of African people. The Supreme Being is involved in the life of people since the spirits who are divine agents are involved in the lives of people.

The distinction between immanental and ascensional mysticism therefore comes from a blurred and truncated understanding of the meaning of reality and the relationship between the spirits and the Supreme Being. Furthermore, it overlooks the fact that the mystical experience, the correct and most sublime of which is not limited to one religious tradition (the ascensional or heavenly versus the immanental mysticism of Bastide), brings human beings into instantaneous contact with Ultimate Reality. This reality is one, but it is human language of description which is expressed in the categories of human thought that brings about different apprehensions of it.

The mystical experience in the African tradition has not received a great deal of articulation which may enable others to appreciate the depth and meaning of African mystical experience. But words, however, eloquent and explicit, are still inadequate to express the mystical experience; and however widely different African mystics may appear to be from others, they nevertheless by their experiences, which indicate immediate contact with the supernatural, give an indication of the same vital apprehension of truth.[19]

In his assessment of African spirituality, Dominique Zahan said, "African spirituality does not cede anything to that of the great religions. In both cases, the human being is in search of a sort of deliverance capable of transfiguring his terrestrial condition."[20] African concepts[21] of the human person, which are essentially mystical, make it possible for humans to have contact with the supernatural. It is because there is something in humans, which is the deepest self of a person (the *okra* of the Akan or the *emi* of the Yoruba) and which links each person directly with God or the Ground of Being, that human beings can have a mystical experience in which they came into immediate contact with the supernatural. The contact is not made with an entity that is totally alien to humans, but rather with something in the human person that links each person with the Supreme Being. There is a symbol in the Akan tradition called "*Onyame bewu an mawu*"—(lit.) "I shall only die if *Onyame* (God) dies," which is a reference to the *okra*, the undying part of each person that is a part of *Onyame* in humans and helps to distinguish human beings from animals. The notion of the *okra* shows that what is clearly eternal in us humans is linked with God, and while *Onyame* is clearly not human, he or she lives in each person's life.

Mysticism in Traditional African Religion shows clearly that human individuality is not final, and that it is within the range of human experience for humans to go beyond the limitations of their distinct selves to make contact with the supernatural, thus making mysticism, in J. N. Findlay's words, "the fullest extension of the common way of humanity."[22] Contact with the supernatural enables African mystics to heal, predict, and receive illumination or insight, to give guidance to those who search for it, and contribute profoundly to the search for meaning in human life.

Notes

1. E. E. Evans-Pritchard, *Nuer Religion* (London: Oxford University Press, 1956), 51, 52.

2. Sidney Spencer, *Mysticism in World Religion* (South Brunswick, N.J.: A. S. Barnes and Co., 1963), 17.

3. For an excellent discussion of African ontology, see Kwame Gyekye, *An Essay on African Philosophical Thought: The Akan Conceptual Scheme* (Cambridge and New York: Cambridge University Press, 1987).

4. Ibid., 57–79.

5. E. B. Idowu, *Olodumare, God in Yoruba Belief* (London: Longmans, 1962).

6. For further details, see Kofi Asare Opoku, *West African Traditional Religion* (Singapore: Far Eastern Publishers, 1978).

7. Ibid., 88–89.

8. John S. Mbiti, *African Religions and Philosophy* (New York: Praeger, 1969).

9. David Lan, *Guns and Rain: Guerrillas and Spirit Mediums in Zimbabwe* (London and Berkeley: University of California Press, 1985), 49.

10. Wande Abimbola, *Ifa Divination Poetry* (New York: Nok Publishers Ltd., 1977), v.

11. Ibid., 15.

12. Dominique Zahan, *The Religion, Spirituality and Thought of Traditional Africa* (Chicago and London: University of Chicago Press, 1979), 127.

13. Noel King, *African Cosmos: An Introduction to Religion in Africa* (Belmont, Calif.: Wadsworth Publishing Company, 1986), 60.

14. Geoffrey Parrinder, *Mysticism in the World's Religions* (New York: Oxford University Press, 1976), 84.

15. Whitney J. Oates, ed., *Basic Writings of Saint Augustine* (New York: Random House, 1948).

16. Father Humbert Everest, *The Summa Theologica of St. Thomas Aqui-*

nas (London: Burns, Oates & Washbourne, 1937), Part 1, Q 92, 1 and 2; Q 99, 2; Part 3, Supplement, Q 39, 1.

17. Mary Daly, *Beyond God the Father* (Boston: Beacon Press, 1973).

18. For a fuller discussion of the role of God in Africa, see Kofi Asare Opoku, *West African*, 14–34.

19. See Spencer, *Mysticism*, 17.

20. Ibid., 126.

21. For a discussion of African concepts of the human person, see Kofi Asare Opoku, *West African*, 91–139.

22. J. N. Findlay, *Ascent to the Absolute* (London: Allen and Unwin, 1970), 164.

Contributors

PAULA ALLEN is Professor of English at the University of California, Los Angeles. Her publications include *Grandmothers of the Light: A Medicine Women's Sourcebook* (1991), *Spider Woman's Granddaughters* (1989 and 1990), *Skins and Bones* (1988); *The Sacred Hoop* (1986), *The Woman Who Owned the Shadows* (1983); and *Studies in American Indian Literature* (1982). She was awarded the Native American Prize for Literature in 1990.

DONALD H. BISHOP is Emeritus Professor of Philosophy at Washington State University where he taught from 1959 to 1991. He taught previously at Hampton College and Iowa Wesleyan College and at Tunghai University, Taiwan. He received a Fulbright award for study in Taiwan in 1964 and travel and research grants from the Society for Religion in Higher Education; the American Council of Learned Societies; the Indian Council for Cultural Relations; the Pacific Cultural Foundation, Taiwan; the Chinese Philosophical Association; and the Institute of Global Conflict and Cooperation. In addition to numerous articles published in Western and Eastern journals, he edited and contributed to *Indian Thought: An Introduction* (1975), *Thinkers of the Indian Renaissance* (1982; second edition, 1993), *Chinese Thought: An Introduction* (1985). He initiated and directed the Peace Studies program at Washington State University from 1986 to 1991.

WILLIAM CHITTICK is Associate Professor of Religious Studies in the Department of Comparative Studies, State University of New York, Stony Brook. Among his publications are *The Sufi Path of Love: The Spiritual Teachings of Rumi* (1983), *The Psalms of Islam* (1988), *The Sufi Path of Knowledge: Ibn al-Arabi's Metaphysics of Imagination* (1989), and *Faith and Practice of Islam: Three Thirteenth Century Sufi Texts* (1992).

BINA GUPTA is Professor of Philosophy and Director of South Asia Language and Area Center at the University of Missouri-

Columbia. She is the author of *Vedanta: Epistemological Analysis and Interpretation* (1991), editor of *Sexual Archetypes: East and West,* and co-editor of *Issues and Problems in Philosophy: A Cross-Cultural Perspective.* She is Philosophy Editor for *South Asia in Review,* a trustee of the American Institute of Indian Studies, and a member of the Executive Committee of the Society for Asian and Comparative Philosophy.

LESLIE KAWAMURA is Head of the Department of Religious Studies, University of Calgary, Calgary, Alberta, Canada.

KUANG-MING WU is Head of the Institute of Philosophy, National Chung Cheng University, Taiwan. He was previously Professor of Philosophy at the University of Wisconsin, Oshkosh. His book *Chuang Tzu: World Philosopher at Play* was published in 1982.

CHRISTOPHER LUCAS was Professor in the Department of Higher and Adult Education, University of Missouri-Columbia. He is currently Chair of the Department of Education at Kent State University. He is author of the book, *What Is Philosophy of Education?*

RUTH MAJERCIK is a Lecturer in the Department of Religious Studies at the University of California, Santa Barbara. She is the author of *The Chaldean Oracles: Text, Translation, Commentary* (1989), and is currently engaged in research on the relation between Platonism and Gnosticism. Her most recent publication is an article entitled, "The Existence-Life-Intellect Triad in Gnosticism and NeoPlatonism," which appeared in the *Classical Quarterly* 42 (1992). She currently chairs the Seminar on Gnosticism and Later Platonism of the Society of Biblical Literature.

KOFI OPOKU is a Professor at the Institute of African Studies, the University of Ghana. He taught at the University of Northern Iowa in 1989–90 and Lafayette College in 1990–91.

WARREN STEINKRAUS was Professor of Philosophy at the State University of New York, Oswego, from 1964 to 1987. He was chairman of the Philosophy Department at Iowa Wesleyan College from 1956 to 1959 and Union College from 1959 to 1964. He was honorable Professor of Philosophy at Benaras Hindu

University in 1977–78. He joined the editorial board of the *Journal of Social Philosophy* in 1981 and the *Personalist Forum* in 1985. His book *Philosophy of Art* was published in 1974 and he has edited or co-edited *Art and Logic in Hegel's Philosophy* (1980), the anthology *New Studies in Berkley's Philosophy* (1981), and *Studies in Personalism* (1984). For many years he was book review editor for the journal *Idealistic Studies*.

SANDRA A. WAWRYTKO is in the Department of Religion and the Asian Studies Program at San Diego State University. She is editor of *Buddhist Ethics and Modern Society* (1992), editor of *Buddhist Behavioural Codes (sila/vinaya)* (1993), and author of *Crystal: Spectrums of Chinese Culture through Poetry* (1994). She is executive director of the International Society for Philosophy and Psychotherapy and a member of the executive committee of the International Society for Chinese Philosophy.

ELLIOTT WOLFSON is Associate Professor in the Skirball Department of Hebrew and Judaic Studies, New York University. His major area of expertise is Medieval Jewish Mysticism. He is author of *The Book of the Pomegranate: Moses de Leon's Sefer ha-Rimmon* (1988), *Through a Speculum That Shines: Visionary Experience in Medieval Jewish Mysticism* (1992), and *Hekhalot Mysticism* (1993), as well as numerous articles in scholarly journals and books on the history of Jewish mysticism.

Index

(Continued from front flap)

ticism is not a special or unique kind of experience but a part of our common or everyday experience and existence. Considering Hindu mysticism, writers Bina Gupta and Christopher Lucas argue that despite differences among Hindu schools of thought, the mystical state they refer to is the same, with differences being one of degree or relation to appearances. William Chittick then shows that Islamic mysticism goes far beyond the popular conceptions of Sufism and whirling dervishes. The book concludes with a discussion of native African religions and their concept of how the Divine and humans communicate with one another.

Written in an accessible yet comprehensible style, this is a valuable book for both the layman and the scholar.

About the Editor

Donald H. Bishop received a B.S. degree from Cornell University in 1947, a M.Div. degree from Yale Divinity School in 1950, and a Ph.D. from the University of Edinburgh, Scotland, in 1953. He taught at Hampton College, Iowa Wesleyan College, Tunghai University in Taiwan, the University of Idaho, and the University of Colorado at Boulder, and spent thirty-two years in the Philosophy Department at Washington State University at Pullman before retiring in 1991. While at Washington State, he initiated and led the Peace Studies Program and served as chairperson of the Religious Studies Program from 1984 to 1991. He has edited and contributed to three books dealing with the philosophies and religions of China and India.